Praise for *Data Wrangling with Python*

"This should be required reading for any new data scientist, data engineer or other technical data professional. This hands-on, step-by-step guide is exactly what the field needs and what I wish I had when I first starting manipulating data in Python. If you are a data geek that likes to get their hands dirty and that needs a good definitive source, this is your book."

—*Dr. Tyrone Grandison, CEO, Proficiency Labs Intl.*

"There's a lot more to data wrangling than just writing code, and this well-written book tells you everything you need to know. This will be an invaluable step-by-step resource at a time when journalism needs more data experts."

—*Randy Picht, Executive Director of the Donald W. Reynolds Journalism Institute at the Missouri School of Journalism*

"Few resources are as comprehensive and as approachable as this book. It not only explains what you need to know, but why and how. Whether you are new to data journalism, or looking to expand your capabilities, Katharine and Jacqueline's book is a must-have resource."

—*Joshua Hatch, Senior Editor, Data and Interactives,*
The Chronicle of Higher Education *and* The Chronicle of Philanthropy

"A great survey course on everything—literally everything—that we do to tell stories with data, covering the basics and the state of the art. Highly recommended."

—*Brian Boyer, Visuals Editor, NPR*

"*Data Wrangling with Python* is a practical, approachable guide to learning some of the most common tasks you'll ever have to do with code: find, extract, tidy and examine data."

—Chrys Wu, technologist

"This book is a useful response to a question I often get from journalists: 'I'm pretty good using spreadsheets, but what should I learn next?' Although not aimed solely at a journalism readership, *Data Wrangling with Python* provides a clear path for anyone who is using spreadsheets and wondering how to improve her skills to obtain, clean, and analyze data. It covers everything from how to load and examine text files to automated screen-scraping to new command-line tools for performing data analysis and visualizing the results.

"I followed a well-worn path to analyzing data and finding meaning in it: I started with spreadsheets, followed by relational databases and mapping programs. They are still useful tools, but they don't take full advantage of automation, which enables users to process more data and to replicate their work. Nor do they connect seamlessly to the wide range of data available on the Internet. Next to these pillars we need to add another: a programming language. While I've been working with Python and other languages for a while now, that use has been haphazard rather than methodical.

"Both the case for working with data and the sophistication of tools has advanced during the past 20 years, which makes it more important to think about a common set of techniques. The increased availability of data (both structured and unstructured) and the sheer volume of it that can be stored and analyzed has changed the possibilities for data analysis: many difficult questions are now easier to answer, and some previously impossible ones are within reach. We need a glue that helps to tie together the various parts of the data ecosystem, from JSON APIs to filtering and cleaning data to creating charts to help tell a story.

"In this book, that glue is Python and its robust suite of tools and libraries for working with data. If you've been feeling like spreadsheets (and even relational databases) aren't up to answering the kinds of questions you'd like to ask, or if you're ready to grow beyond these tools, this is a book for you. I know I've been waiting for it."

—Derek Willis, News Applications Developer at ProPublica and Cofounder of OpenElections

Data Wrangling with Python

Jacqueline Kazil and Katharine Jarmul

Beijing · Boston · Farnham · Sebastopol · Tokyo

Data Wrangling with Python

by Jacqueline Kazil and Katharine Jarmul

Published by O'Reilly Media, Inc., 1005 Gravenstein Highway North, Sebastopol, CA 95472.

O'Reilly books may be purchased for educational, business, or sales promotional use. Online editions are also available for most titles (*http://oreilly.com/safari*). For more information, contact our corporate/institutional sales department: 800-998-9938 or *corporate@oreilly.com*.

Acquisitions Editor: Meghan Blanchette	**Indexer:** WordCo Indexing Services, Inc.
Editor: Dawn Schanafelt	**Interior Designer:** David Futato
Production Editor: Matthew Hacker	**Cover Designer:** Randy Comer
Copyeditor: Rachel Head	**Illustrator:** Rebecca Demarest
Proofreader: Jasmine Kwityn	

February 2016:   First Edition

Revision History for the First Edition
2016-02-02   First Release
2017-01-27   Second Release

See *http://oreilly.com/catalog/errata.csp?isbn=9781491948811* for release details.

978-1-4919-4881-1

[LSI]

Table of Contents

Preface

Welcome to *Data Wrangling with Python*! In this book, we will help you take your data skills from a spreadsheet to the next level: leveraging the Python programming language to easily and quickly turn noisy data into usable reports. The easy syntax and quick startup for Python make programming accessible to everyone.

Imagine a manual process you execute weekly, such as copying and pasting data from multiple sources into one spreadsheet for processing. This might take you an hour or two every week. But after you've automated and scripted this task, it may take only 30 seconds to process! This frees up your time to do other things or automate more processes. Or imagine you are able to transform your data in such a way that you can execute tasks you never could before because you simply did not have the ability to process the information in its current form. But after working through Python exercises with this book, you should be able to more effectively gather information from data you previously deemed inaccessible, too messy, or too vast.

We will guide you through the process of data acquisition, cleaning, presentation, scaling, and automation. Our goal is to teach you how to easily wrangle your data, so you can spend more time focused on the content and analysis. We will overcome the limitations of your current tools and replace manual processing with clean, easy-to-read Python code. By the time you finish working through this book, you will have automated your data processing, scheduled file editing and cleanup tasks, acquired and parsed data from locations you may not have been able to access before, and processed larger datasets.

Using a project-based approach, each chapter will grow in complexity. We encourage you to follow along and apply the methods using your own datasets. If you don't have a particular project or investigation in mind, sample datasets will be available online for your use.

Who Should Read This Book

This book is for folks who want to explore data wrangling beyond desktop tools. If you are great at Excel and want to take your data analysis to the next level, this book will help! Additionally, if you are coming from another language and want to get started with Python for the purpose of data wrangling, you will find this book useful.

If you come across something you do not understand, we encourage you to reach out so that we can improve the content of the book, but you should also be prepared to supplement your learning by searching the Internet or inquiring online (*http://bit.ly/ ask_programming_qs*). We've included a few tips on debugging in Appendix E, so you can take a look there as well!

Who Should Not Read This Book

This book is definitely not meant for experienced Python programmers who already know which libraries and techniques to use for their data wrangling needs (for those folks, we recommend Wes McKinney's *Python for Data Analysis*, also from O'Reilly). If you are an experienced Python developer or a developer in another language with data analysis capabilities (Scala, R), this book is probably not for you. However, if you are an experienced developer in a web language that lacks data analysis capabilities (PHP, JavaScript), this book can teach you about Python via data wrangling.

How This Book Is Organized

The structure of the book follows the life span of an average data analysis project or story. It starts with formulating a question, then moves on to acquiring the data, cleaning the data, exploring the data, communicating the data findings, scaling with larger datasets, and finally automating the process. This approach allows you to move from simple questions to more complex problems and investigations. We will cover basic means of communicating your findings before we get into advanced data-gathering techniques.

If the material in some of these chapters is not new to you, it is possible to use the book as a reference or skip sections with which you are already familiar. However, we recommend you take a cursory view of each section's contents, to ensure you don't miss possible new resources and techniques.

What Is Data Wrangling?

Data wrangling is about taking a messy or unrefined source of data and turning it into something useful. You begin by seeking out raw data sources and determining their value: How good are they as datasets? How relevant are they to your goal? Is there a better source? Once you've parsed and cleaned the data so that the datasets are usable, you can utilize tools and methods (like Python scripts) to help you analyze them and present your findings in a report. This allows you to take data no one would bother looking at and make it both clear and actionable.

What to Do If You Get Stuck

Don't fret—it happens to everyone! Consider the process of programming a series of events where you get stuck over and over again. When you are stuck and you work through the problem, you gain knowledge that allows you to grow and learn as a developer and data analyst. Most people do not master programming; instead, they master the process of getting unstuck.

What are some "unsticking" techniques? First, you can use a search engine to try to find the answer. Often, you will find many people have already run into the same problem. If you don't find a helpful solution, you can ask your question online. We cover a few great online and real-life resources in Appendix B.

Asking questions is hard. But no matter where you are in your learning, do not feel intimidated about asking the greater coding community for help. One of the earliest questions (*http://bit.ly/git_ops_question*) one of this book's authors (Jackie) asked about programming in a public forum ended up being one that was referenced by many people afterward. It is a great feeling to know that a new programmer like yourself can help those that come after you because you took a chance and asked a question you thought might be stupid.

We also recommend you read "How to Ask Questions" (*http://bit.ly/ask_program ming_qs*), before posting your questions online. It covers ways to help frame your questions so others can best help you.

Lastly, there are times when you will need an extra helping hand in real life. Maybe the question you have is multifaceted and not easily asked or answered on a website or mailing list. Maybe your question is philosophical or requires a debate or rehashing of different approaches. Whatever it may be, you can find folks who can likely answer your question at local Python groups. To find a local meetup, try Meetup (*http://www.meetup.com/*). In Chapter 1, you will find more detailed information on how to find helpful and supportive communities.

Conventions Used in This Book

The following typographical conventions are used in this book:

Italic

    Indicates new terms, URLs, email addresses, filenames, directory names and paths, and file extensions.

`Constant width`

    Used for program listings, as well as within paragraphs to refer to program elements such as variable or function names, databases, data types, environment variables, statements, and keywords.

`Constant width italic`

    Shows text that should be replaced with user-supplied values or by values determined by context.

    This element signifies a tip or suggestion.

    This element signifies a general note.

    This element indicates a warning or caution.

Using Code Examples

We've set up a data repository on GitHub at *https://github.com/jackiekazil/data-wrangling*. In this repository, you will find the data we used along with some code samples to help you follow along. If you find any issues in the repository or have any questions, please file an issue (*https://github.com/jackiekazil/data-wrangling/issues*).

This book is here to help you get your job done. In general, if example code is offered with this book, you may use it in your programs and documentation. You do not need to contact us for permission unless you're reproducing a significant portion of the code. For example, writing a program that uses several chunks of code from this book does not require permission. Selling or distributing a CD-ROM of examples from O'Reilly books does require permission. Answering a question by citing this book and quoting example code does not require permission. Incorporating a significant amount of example code from this book into your product's documentation does require permission.

We appreciate, but do not require, attribution. An attribution usually includes the title, author, publisher, and ISBN. For example: "*Data Wrangling with Python* by Jacqueline Kazil and Katharine Jarmul (O'Reilly). Copyright 2016 Jacqueline Kazil and Kjamistan, Inc., 978-1-4919-4881-1."

If you feel your use of code examples falls outside fair use or the permission given above, feel free to contact us at *permissions@oreilly.com*.

O'Reilly Safari

 *Safari* (formerly Safari Books Online) is a membership-based training and reference platform for enterprise, government, educators, and individuals.

Members have access to thousands of books, training videos, Learning Paths, interactive tutorials, and curated playlists from over 250 publishers, including O'Reilly Media, Harvard Business Review, Prentice Hall Professional, Addison-Wesley Professional, Microsoft Press, Sams, Que, Peachpit Press, Adobe, Focal Press, Cisco Press, John Wiley & Sons, Syngress, Morgan Kaufmann, IBM Redbooks, Packt, Adobe Press, FT Press, Apress, Manning, New Riders, McGraw-Hill, Jones & Bartlett, and Course Technology, among others.

For more information, please visit *http://oreilly.com/safari*.

How to Contact Us

Please address comments and questions concerning this book to the publisher:

O'Reilly Media, Inc.
1005 Gravenstein Highway North
Sebastopol, CA 95472
800-998-9938 (in the United States or Canada)
707-829-0515 (international or local)
707-829-0104 (fax)

We have a web page for this book, where we list errata, examples, and any additional information. You can access this page at *http://bit.ly/data_wrangling_w_python*.

To comment or ask technical questions about this book, send email to *bookquestions@oreilly.com*.

For more information about our books, courses, conferences, and news, see our website at *http://www.oreilly.com*.

Find us on Facebook: *http://facebook.com/oreilly*

Follow us on Twitter: *http://twitter.com/oreillymedia*

Watch us on YouTube: *http://www.youtube.com/oreillymedia*

Acknowledgments

The authors would like to thank their editors, Dawn Schanafelt and Meghan Blanchette, for their tremendous help, work, and effort—this wouldn't have been possible without you. They would also like to thank their tech editors, Ryan Balfanz, Sarah Boslaugh, Kat Calvin, and Ruchi Parekh, for their help in working through code examples and thinking about the book's audience.

Jackie Kazil would like to thank Josh, her husband, for the support on this adventure—everything from encouragement to cupcakes. The house would have fallen apart at times if he hadn't been there to hold it up. She would also like to thank Katharine (Kjam) for partnering. This book would not exist without Kjam, and she's delighted to have had a chance to work together again after years of being separated. Lastly, she would also like to thank her mom, Lydie, who provided her with so many of the skills, except for English, that were needed to finish this book.

Katharine Jarmul would like to send a beary special thanks to her partner, Aaron Glenn, for countless hours of thinking out loud, rereading, debating whether Unix should be capitalized, and making delicious pasta while she wrote. She would like to thank all four of her parents for their patience with endless book updates and dong bells. Sie möchte auch Frau Hoffmann für ihre endlose Geduld bei zahllosen Gesprächen auf Deutsch über dieses Buch bedanken.

## CHAPTER 1

Introduction to Python

Whether you are a journalist, an analyst, or a budding data scientist, you likely picked up this book because you want to learn how to analyze data programmatically, summarize your findings, and clearly communicate those findings to others. You might show your findings in a report, a graphic, or summarized statistics. Essentially, you are trying to tell a story.

Traditional storytelling or journalism often uses an individual story to paint a relatable face on overall findings or trends. In that type of storytelling, the data becomes a secondary feature. However, other storytellers, such as Christian Rudde, author of *Datacylsm* (*http://dataclysm.org/*) (Broadway Books) and one of the founders of OkCupid, argue the data itself is and should be the primary subject.

To begin, you need to identify the topic you want to explore. Perhaps you are interested in exploring communication habits of different people or societies, in which case you might start with a specific question (e.g., what are the qualities of successful information sharing among people on the Web?). Or you might be interested in historical baseball statistics and question whether they show changes in the game over time.

After you have identified your area of interest, you need to find data you can examine to explore your topic further. In the case of human behavior, you could investigate what people share on Twitter, drawing data from the Twitter API (*https://dev.twit ter.com/overview/api*). If you want to delve into baseball history, you could use Sean Lahman's Baseball Database (*http://bit.ly/lahman_baseball_stats*).

The Twitter and baseball datasets are examples of large, general datasets which should be filtered and analyzed in manageable chunks to answer your specific questions. Sometimes smaller datasets are just as interesting and meaningful, especially if your topic touches on a local or regional issue. Let's consider an example.

While writing this book, one of the authors read an article (*http://bit.ly/grad_seat ing_charge*) about her public high school,[1] which had reportedly begun charging a $20 fee to graduating seniors and $200 a row for prime seating at the graduation ceremony.

According to the local news report, "the new fees are a part of an effort to cover an estimated $12,000 in graduation costs for Manatee High School after the financially strapped school district pulled its $3,400 contribution this year."

The article explains the reason why the graduation costs are so high in comparison to the school district's budget. However, it does not explain why the school district was unable to make its usual contribution. The question remained: Why is the Manatee County School District so financially strapped that it cannot make its regular contribution to the graduating class?

The initial questions you have in your investigation will often lead to deeper questions that define a problem. For example: What has the district been spending money on? How have the district's spending patterns changed over time?

Identifying our specific topic area and the questions we want to anwer allows us to identify the data we will need to find. After formulating these questions, the first dataset we need to look for is the spending and budget data for the Manatee County School District.

Before we continue, let's look at a brief overview of the entire process, from initial identification of a problem all the way to the final story (see Figure 1-1).

Once you have identified your questions, you can begin to ask questions about your data, such as: Which datasets best tell the story I want to communicate? Which datasets explore the subject in depth? What is the overall theme? What are some datasets associated with those themes? Who might be tracking or keeping this data? Are these datasets publicly available?

 When you begin the storytelling process, you should focus on researching the questions you want to answer. Then you can figure out which datasets are most valuable to you. In this initial stage, don't get too caught up in the tools you'll use to analyze the data or the data wrangling process.

---

1 Public high schools in the United States are government-run schools funded largely by taxes from the local community, meaning children can attend and be educated at little to no cost to their parents.

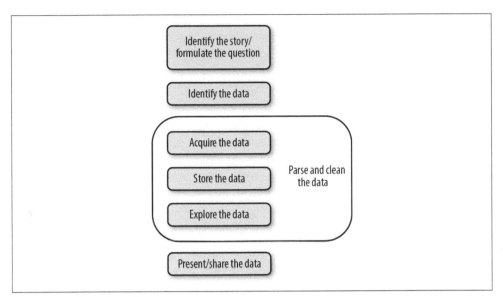

Figure 1-1. Data handling process

Finding Your Datasets

If you use a search engine to find a dataset, you won't always find the best fit. Sometimes you need to dig through a website for the data. Do not give up if the data proves hard to find or difficult to acquire!

If your topic is exposed in a survey or report or it seems likely a particular agency or organization might collect the data, find a contact number and reach out to the researchers or organization. Ask them politely and directly how you might access the data. If the dataset is part of a government entity (federal, state, or local), then you may have legal standing under the Freedom of Information Act (*http://bit.ly/wikipedia_foia*) to obtain direct access to the data. We'll cover data acquisition more fully in Chapter 6.

Once you have identified the datasets you want and acquired them, you'll need to get them into a usable format. In Chapters 3, 4, and 5, you will learn various techniques for programmatically acquiring data and transforming data from one form to another. Chapter 6 will look at some of the logistics behind human-to-human interaction with regard to data acquisition and lightly touch on legalities. In the same Chapters 3 through 5, we will present how to extract data from CSV, Excel, XML, JSON, and PDF files, and in Chapters 11, 12, and 13 you will learn how to extract data from websites and APIs.

If you don't recognize some of these acronyms, don't worry! They will be explained thoroughly as we encounter them, as will other technical terms with which you may not be familiar.

After you have acquired and transformed the data, you will begin your initial data exploration. Here, you will seek stories the data might expose—all while determining what is useful and what can be thrown away. You will play with the data by manipulating it into groups and looking at trends among the fields. Then you'll combine datasets to connect the dots and expose larger trends and uncover underlying inconsistencies. Through this process you will learn how to clean the data and identify and resolve issues hidden in your datasets.

While learning how to parse and clean data in Chapters 7 and 8, you will not only use Python but also explore other open source tools. As we cover data issues you may encounter, you will learn how to determine whether to write a cleanup script or use a ready-made approach. In Chapter 7, we'll cover how to fix common errors such as duplicate records, outliers, and formatting problems.

After you have identified the story you want to tell, cleaned the data, and processed it, we will explore how to present the data using Python. You will learn to tell the story in multiple formats and compare different publication options. In Chapter 10, you will find basic means of presenting and organizing data on a website.

Chapter 14 will help you scale your data-analysis processes to cover more data in less time. We will analyze methods to store and access your data, and review scaling your data in the cloud.

Chapter 14 will also cover how to take a one-off project and automate it so the project can drive itself. By automating the processes, you can take what would be a one-time special report and make it an annual one. This automation lets you focus on refining your storytelling process, move on to another story, or at least refill your coffee. Throughout this book the main tool used is the Python programming language. It will help us work through each part of the storytelling process, from initial exploration to standardization and automation.

Why Python

There are many programming languages, so why does this book use Python? Depending on what your background is, you may have heard of one or more of the following alternatives: R, MATLAB, Java, C/C++, HTML, JavaScript, and Ruby. Each of these has one or more primary uses, and some of them can be used for data wrangling. You can also execute a data wrangling process in a program like Excel. You can often program Excel and Python to give you the same output, but one will likely be more efficient. In some cases, though, a program like Excel can't handle the task. We chose Python over the other options because Python is easy to get started with and handles data wrangling tasks in a simple and straightforward way.

If you would like to learn the more technical labeling and classification of Python and other languages, check out Appendix A. Those explanations will enable you to converse with other analysts or developers about why you're using Python. As a new developer, we believe you will benefit from Python's accessibility, and we hope this book will be one of many useful references in your data wrangling toolbox.

Aside from the benefits of Python as a language, it also has one of the most open and helpful communities. No community is perfect, but the Python community works to create a supportive environment for newcomers: sometimes this is with locally hosted tutorials, free classes, and meetups, and at other times it is with larger conferences that bring people together to solve problems and share knowledge.

Having a larger community has obvious benefits—there are people who can answer your questions, people who can help brainstorm your code's or module's structure, people you can learn from, shared code you can build upon. To learn more, check out Appendix B.

The community exists because people support it. When you are first starting out with Python, you will take from the community more than you contribute. However, there is quite a lot the greater community can learn from individuals who are not experts. We encourage you to share your problems and solutions. This will help the next person who has the same problems, and you may uncover a bug that needs to be addressed in an open source tool.

Many members of the Python community no longer have the *fresh eyes* you currently possess. As you begin typing Python, you should consider yourself part of the programming community. Your contributions are as valuable as those of the individuals who have been programming for 20 years.

Without further ado, let's get started with Python!

Getting Started with Python

Your initial steps with programming are the most difficult (not dissimilar to the first steps you take as a human!). Think about times you started a new hobby or sport. Getting started with Python (or any other programming language) will share some similar angst and hiccups. Perhaps you are lucky and have an amazing mentor to help you through the first stages. If not, maybe you have experience taking on similar challenges. Regardless of how you get through the initial steps, if you do encounter difficulties, remember this is often the hardest part.

 We hope this book can be a guide for you, but it's no substitute for good mentorship or broader experiences with Python. Along the way, we'll provide tips on some resources and places to look if a problem you encounter isn't addressed.

To avoid getting bogged down in an extensive or advanced setup, we will use a very minimal initial setup for our Python environment. In the following sections, we will select a Python version, install Python and a tool to help us with external code and libraries, and install a code editor so we can write and run our code.

Which Python Version

You will need to choose which version of Python to use. Python versions are actually versions of something called the *Python interpreter*. The interpreter allows you to read, write, and run Python on your computer. Wikipedia (*http://bit.ly/wikipe dia_interpreter*) describes it as follows:

> In computer science, an interpreter is a computer program that directly executes, i.e. performs, instructions written in a programming or scripting language, without previously compiling them into a machine language program.

No one is going to ask you to memorize this definition, so don't worry if you do not completely understand this. When Jackie first got started in programming, this was the part in introductory books where she felt that she would never get anywhere, because she didn't understand what "batch compiling" meant. If she didn't understand that, how could she program? We will talk about compiling later, but for now let's summarize the definition like so:

> An interpreter is the computer program that reads and executes your Python code.

There are two *major* Python versions (or interpreters), Python 2.X and Python 3.X. The most recent version of Python 2.X is 2.7, which is the Python version used in this book. The most recent version of Python 3.X is Python 3.5, which is also the newest Python version available. For now, assume code you write for 2.7 will not work in 3.4. The term used to describe this is to say that 3.4 breaks *backward compatibility*.

You can write code to work with both 2.7 and 3.4; however, this is not a requirement nor the focus of this book. Getting preoccupied with doing this at the beginning is like living in Florida and worrying about how to drive in snow. One day, you might need this skill, but it's not a concern at this point in time.

Some people reading this book are probably asking themselves why we decided to use Python 2.7 and not Python 3.4. This is a highly debated topic within the Python community. Python 2.7 is a well-utilized release, while 3.X is currently being adopted. We want to make sure you can find easy-to-read and easy-to-access resources and that your operating system and services support the Python version you use.

Quite a lot of the code written in this book will work with Python 3. If you'd like to try out some of the examples with Python 3, feel free; however, we'd rather you focus on learning Python 2.7 and move on to Python 3 after completing this book. For more information on the changes required to make code Python 3–compliant, take a look at the change documentation (*https://docs.python.org/3.0/whatsnew/3.0.html*).

As you move through this book, you will use both self-written code and code written by other (awesome) people. Most of these external pieces of code will work for Python 2.7, but might not yet work for 3.4. If you were using Python 3, you would have to rewrite them—and if you spend a lot of time rewriting and editing every piece of code you touch, it will be very difficult to finish your first project.

Think of your first pieces of code like a rough draft. Later, you can go back and improve them with further revisions. For now, let's begin by installing Python.

Setting Up Python on Your Machine

The good news is Python can run on any operating system. The bad news is not all operating systems have the same setup. There are two major operating systems we will discuss, in order of popularity with respect to programming Python: Mac OS X and Windows. If you are running Mac OS X or Linux, you likely already have Python installed. For a more complete installation, we recommend searching the Web for your flavor of Linux along with "advanced Python setup" for more advice.

OS X and Linux are a bit easier to install and run Python code on than Windows. For a deeper understanding of why these differences exist, we recommend reading the history of Windows versus Unix-based operating systems. Compare the Unix-favoring view presented in Hadeel Tariq Al-Rayes's "Studying Main Differences Between Linux & Windows Operating Systems" (*http://bit.ly/linux_v_windows*) to Microsoft's "Functional Comparison of UNIX and Windows" (*http://bit.ly/unix_v_windows*).

If you use Windows, you should be able to execute all the code; however, Windows setups may need additional installation for code compilers, additional system libraries, and environment variables.

To set up your computer to use Python, follow the instructions for your operating system. We will run through a series of tests to make sure things are working for you the way they should before moving on to the next chapter.

Mac OS X

Start by opening up Terminal (*http://en.wikipedia.org/wiki/Terminal_(OS_X)*), which is a command-line interface that allows you to interact with your computer. When PCs were first introduced, command-line interfaces were the only way to interact with computers. Now most people use graphical interface operating systems, as they are more easily accessible and widely distributed.

There are two ways to find Terminal on your machine. The first is through OS X's Spotlight. Click on the Spotlight icon—the magnifying glass in the upper-right corner of your screen—and type "Terminal." Then select the option that comes up next to the Applications classification.

After you select it, a little window will pop up that looks like Figure 1-2 (note that your version of Mac OS X might look different).

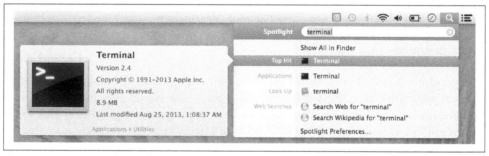

Figure 1-2. Terminal search using Spotlight

You can also launch Terminal through the Finder. Terminal is located in your *Utilities* folder: Applications → Utilities → Terminal.

After you select and launch Terminal, you should see something like Figure 1-3.

At this time it is a good idea to create an easily accessible shortcut to Terminal in a place that works well for you, like in the Dock. To do so, simply right-click on the Terminal icon in your Dock and choose Options and then "Keep in Dock." Each time you execute an exercise in this book, you will need to access Terminal.

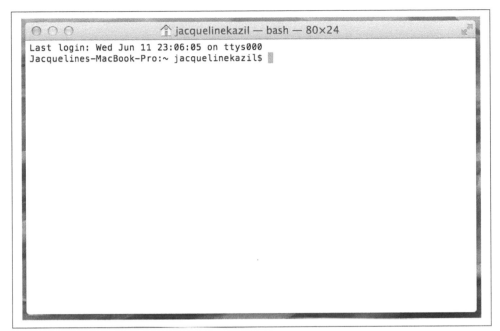

Figure 1-3. A newly opened Terminal window

And you're done. Macs come with Python preinstalled, which means you do not need to do anything else. If you'd like to get your computer set up for future advanced library usage, take a look at Appendix D.

Windows 8 and 10

Windows does not come with Python installed, but Python has a special Windows installer (*https://www.python.org/downloads/windows/*). You'll need to determine if you are running 32- or 64-bit Windows (*http://bit.ly/32-_or_64-bit*). If you are running 64-bit Windows, you will need to download the x86-64 MSI Installer from the downloads page. If not, you can use the x86 MSI Installer.

Once you have downloaded the installer, simply double-click on it and step through the prompts to install. We recommend installing for all users. Click on the boxes next to the options to select them all, and also choose to install the feature on your hard drive (see Figure 1-4).

After you've successfully installed Python, you'll want to add Python to your environment settings. This allows you to interact with Python in your *cmd* utility (the Windows command-line interface). To do so, simply search your computer (*http://bit.ly/how_2_search*) for "environment variable." Select the option "Edit the system environment variables," then click the Environment Variables...button (see Figure 1-5).

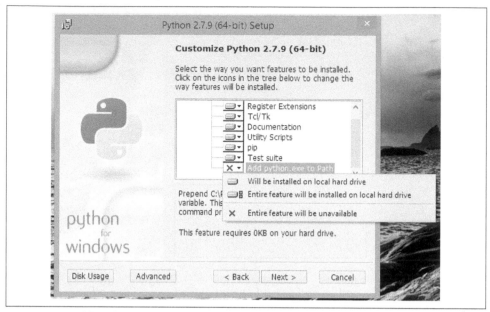

Figure 1-4. Adding features using the installer

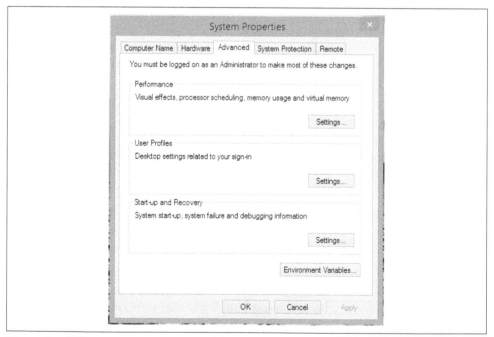

Figure 1-5. Editing environment variables

Scroll down in the "System variables" list and select the `Path` variable, then click "Edit." (If you don't have a `Path` variable listed, click "New" to create a new one.)

Add this to the end of your `Path` value, ensuring you have a semicolon separating each of the paths (including at the end of the existing value, if there was one):

```
C:\Python27;C:\Python27\Lib\site-packages\;C:\Python27\Scripts\;
```

The end of your `Path` variable should look similar to Figure 1-6. Once you are done editing, click "OK" to save your settings.

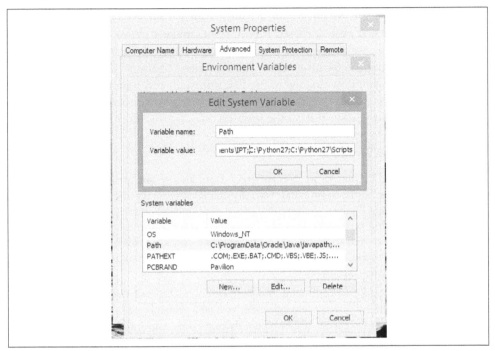

Figure 1-6. Adding Python to Path

Test Driving Python

At this point, you should be on the command line (Terminal or *cmd*[2]) and ready to launch Python. You should see a line ending with a $ on a Mac or a > on Windows. After that prompt, type `python`, and press the Return (or Enter) key:

```
$ python
```

---

2 To open the *cmd* utility in Windows, simply search for Command Prompt or open All Programs and select Accessories and then Command Prompt.

If everything is working correctly, you should receive a Python prompt (>>>), as seen in Figure 1-7.

```
Jacquelines-MacBook-Pro:~ jacquelinekazil$ python
Python 2.7.5 (default, Mar  9 2014, 22:15:05)
[GCC 4.2.1 Compatible Apple LLVM 5.0 (clang-500.0.68)] on darwin
Type "help", "copyright", "credits" or "license" for more information.
>>> ▐
```

Figure 1-7. Python prompt

For Windows users, if you don't see this prompt, make sure your `Path` variable is properly set up (as described in the preceding section) and everything installed correctly. If you're using the 64-bit version, you may need to uninstall Python (you can use the install MSI you downloaded to modify, uninstall, and repair your installation) and try installing the 32-bit version. If that doesn't work, we recommend searching for the specific error you see during the installation.

>>> Versus $ or >

The Python prompt is different from the system prompt ($ on Mac/Linux, > on Windows). Beginners often make the mistake of typing Python commands into the default terminal prompt and typing terminal commands into the Python interpreter. This will *always* return errors. If you receive an error, keep this in mind and check to make sure you are entering Python commands *only* in the Python interpreter.

If you type a command into your Python interpreter that should be typed in your system terminal, you will probably get a `NameError` or `SyntaxError`. If you type a Python command into your system terminal, you will probably get a bash error, `command not found`.

When the Python interpreter starts, we're given a few helpful lines of information. One of those helpful hints shows the Python version we are using (Figure 1-7 shows Python 2.7.5). This is important in the troubleshooting process, as sometimes there are commands or tools you can use with one Python version that don't work in another.

Now, let's test our Python installation by using a quick `import` statement. Type the following into your Python interpreter:

```
import sys
import pprint
pprint.pprint(sys.path)
```

The output you should recieve is a list of a bunch of directories or locations on your computer. This list shows where Python is looking for Python files. This set of commands can be a useful tool when you are trying to troubleshoot Python import errors.

Here is one example output (your list will be a little different from this; also, note also that some lines have been wrapped to fit this book's page constraints):

```
['',
 '/usr/local/lib/python2.7/site-packages/setuptools-4.0.1-py2.7.egg',
 '/usr/local/lib/python2.7/site-packages/pip-1.5.6-py2.7.egg',
 '/usr/local/Cellar/python/2.7.7_1/Frameworks/Python.framework/Versions/2.7/
   lib/python27.zip',
 '/usr/local/Cellar/python/2.7.7_1/Frameworks/Python.framework/Versions/2.7/
   lib/python2.7',
 '/usr/local/Cellar/python/2.7.7_1/Frameworks/Python.framework/Versions/2.7/
   lib/python2.7/lib-tk',
 '/Library/Python/2.7/site-packages',
 '/usr/local/lib/python2.7/site-packages']
```

If your code was unsuccessful, you will have received an error. The easiest way to debug Python errors is to read them. For example, if you type in `import sus` instead of `import sys`, you will get the following output:

```
>>> import sus
Traceback (most recent call last):
  File "<stdin>", line 1, in <module>
ImportError: No module named sus
```

Read the last line: `ImportError: No module named sus`. This line tells you there is an import error, because there is no `sus` module in Python. Python has searched through the files on your computer and cannot find an importable Python file or folder of files called *sus*.

If you make a typo in the code you transfer from this book, you will likely get a syntax error. In the following example, we purposely mistyped `pprint.pprint` and instead entered `pprint.print(sys.path())`:

```
>>> pprint.print(sys.path())
  File "<stdin>", line 1
    pprint.print(sys.path())
              ^
SyntaxError: invalid syntax
```

We purposely mistyped it, but during the writing of this book, one of the authors *did* mistype it. You need to get comfortable troubleshooting errors as they arise. You should acknowledge that errors will be a part of the learning process as a developer. We want to make sure you are comfortable seeing errors; you should treat them as opportunities to learn something new about Python and programming.

Import errors and syntax errors are some of the most common you will see while developing code, and they are the easiest to troubleshoot. When you come across an error, web search engines will be useful to help you fix it.

Before you continue, make sure to exit from the Python interpreter. This takes you back to the Terminal or *cmd* prompt. To exit, type the following:

```
exit()
```

Now your prompt should return to $ (Mac/Linux) or > (Windows). We will play more with the Python interpreter in the next chapter. For now, let's move on to installing a tool called *pip*.

Install pip

pip (*http://pip.readthedocs.org/en/latest/*) is a command-line tool used to manage shared Python code and libraries. Programmers often solve the same problems, so folks end up sharing their code to help others. That is one key part of the open source software culture.

Mac users can install pip (*http://bit.ly/install_pip*) by running a simple downloadable Python script in Terminal. You will need to be in the same folder you downloaded the script into. For example, if you downloaded the script into your *Downloads* folder, you will need to change into that folder from your Terminal. One easy shortcut on a Mac is to press the Command key (Cmd) and then drag your *Downloads* folder onto your Terminal. Another is to type some simple bash commands (for a more comprehensive introduction to bash, check out Appendix C). Begin by typing this into your Terminal:

```
cd ~/Downloads
```

This tells your computer to *change directory* into the *Downloads* subfolder in your home folder. To make sure you are in your *Downloads* folder, type the following into your Terminal:

```
pwd
```

This asks the Terminal to show your *present working directory*, the folder you are currently in. It should output something like the following:

```
/Users/your_name/Downloads
```

If your output looks similar, you can run the file by simply using this command:

```
sudo python get-pip.py
```

Because you are running a sudo command (meaning you are using special permissions to run the command so it can install packages in restricted places), you will be prompted to type in your password. You should then see a series of messages installing the package.

On Windows, you likely already have pip installed (it comes with the Windows installation package). To check, you can type `pip install ipython` into your *cmd* utility. If you receive an error, download the pip installation script and use `chdir C:\Users \YOUR_NAME\`Downloads to change into your *Downloads* folder (substituting your computer's home directory name for `YOUR_NAME`). Then, you should be able to execute the downloaded file by typing `python get-pip.py`. You will need to be an administrator on your computer to properly install everything.

When you use pip, your computer searches PyPI (*http://pypi.python.org*) for the specified code package or library, downloads it to your machine, and installs it. This means you do not have to use a browser to download libraries, which can be cumbersome.

We're almost done with the setup. The final step is installing our code editor.

Install a Code Editor

When writing Python, you'll need a code editor, as Python requires special spacing, indentation, and character encoding to run properly. There are many code editors to choose from. One of the authors of this book uses Sublime (*http://www.sublime text.com/*). It is free, but suggests a nominal fee after a certain time period to help support current and future development. You can download Sublime here (*http:// www.sublimetext.com/*). Another completely free and cross-platform text editor is Atom (*https://atom.io/*).

Some people are particular about their code editors. While you do not have to use the editors we recommend, we suggest avoiding Vim, Vi, or Emacs unless you are already using these tools. Some programming purists use these tools exclusively for their code (one of the authors among them), because they can navigate the editor completely by keyboard. However, if you choose one of these editors without having any experience with it, you'll likely have trouble making it through this book as you'll be learning two things at once.

 Learn one thing at a time, and feel free to try several editors until you find one that lets you code easily and freely. For Python development, the most important thing is having an editor you feel comfortable with that supports many file types (look for Unicode and UTF-8 support).

After you have downloaded and installed your editor of choice, launch the program to make sure the installation was successful.

Optional: Install IPython

If you'd like to install a slightly more advanced Python interpreter, we recommend installing a library called IPython (*http://ipython.org/install.html*). We review some benefits and use cases as well as how to install IPython in Appendix F. Again, this is not required, but it can be a useful tool in getting started with Python.

Summary

In this chapter, we learned about the two popular Python versions. We also completed some initial setup so we can move forward with data wrangling:

1. We installed and tested Python.

2. We installed pip.

3. We installed a code editor.

This is the most basic setup required to get started. As you learn more about Python and programming, you will discover more complex setups. Our aim here was to get you started as quickly as possible without getting too overwhelmed by the setup process. If you'd like to take a look at a more advanced Python setup, check out Appendix D.

As you work through this book, you might encounter tools you need that require a more advanced setup; in that event we will show you how to create a more complex setup from your current basic one. For now, your first steps in Python require only what we've shown here.

Congratulations—you have completed your initial setup and run your first few lines of Python code! In the next chapter, we will start learning basic Python concepts.

## CHAPTER 2

Python Basics

Now that you are all set up to run Python on your computer, let's go over some basics. We will build on these initial concepts as we move through the book, but we need to learn a few things before we are able to continue.

In the previous chapter, you tested your installation with a couple of lines of code:

```
import sys
import pprint
pprint.pprint(sys.path)
```

By the end of this chapter, you will understand what is happening in each of those lines and will have the vocabulary to describe what the code is doing. You will also learn about different Python data types and have a basic understanding of introductory Python concepts.

We will move quickly through this material, focusing on what you need to know to move on to the next chapters. New concepts will come up in future chapters as we need them. We hope this approach allows you to learn by applying these new concepts to datasets and problems that interest you.

Before we continue, let's launch our Python interpreter. We will be using it to run our Python code throughout this chapter. It is easy to skim over an introductory chapter like this one, but we cannot emphasize enough the importance of physically typing what you see in the book. Similar to learning a spoken language, it is most useful to learn by doing. As you type the exercises in this book and run the code, you will encounter numerous errors, and debugging (working through these errors) will help you gain knowledge.

Basic Data Types

In this section, we will go over simple data types in Python. These are some of the essential building blocks for handling information in Python. The data types we will learn are strings, integers, floats, and other non–whole number types.

Strings

The first data type we will learn about is the string. You may not have heard the word *string* used in this context before, but a string is basically text and it is denoted by using quotes. Strings can contain numbers, letters, and symbols.

These are all strings:

```
'cat'
'This is a string.'
'5'
'walking'
'$GOObarBaz340    '
```

If you enter each of those values into your Python interpreter, the interpreter will return them back to you. The program is saying, "Hey, I heard you. You said, 'cat' (or whatever you entered)."

The content of a string doesn't matter as long as it is between matching quotes, which can be either single or double quotes. You must begin and end the string with the same quote (either single or double):

```
'cat'
"cat"
```

Both of these examples mean the same thing to Python. In both cases, Python will return `'cat'`, with single quotes. Some folks use single quotes by convention in their code, and others prefer double quotes. Whichever you use, the main thing is to be consistent in your style. Personally, we prefer single quotes because double quotes require us to hold down the Shift key. Single quotes let us be lazy.

Integers and Floats

The second and third data types we are going to learn about are integers and floats, which are how you handle numbers in Python. Let's begin with integers.

Integers

You may remember integers from math class, but just in case you don't, an integer is a whole number. Here are some examples:

```
10
1
0
-1
-10
```

If you enter those into your Python interpreter, the interpreter will return them back to you.

Notice in the string example in the previous section, we had a `'5'`. If a number is entered within quotes, Python will process the value as a string. In the following example, the first value and second value are not equal:

```
5
'5'
```

To test this, enter the following into your interpreter:

```
5 == '5'
```

The == tests to see if the two values are equal. The return from this test will be true or false. The return value is another Python data type, called a Boolean. We will work with Booleans later, but let's briefly review them. A Boolean tells us whether a statement is *True* or *False*. In the previous statement, we asked Python whether 5 the integer was the same as `'5'` the string. What did Python return? How could you make the statement return True? (Hint: try testing with both as integers or both as strings!)

You might be asking yourself why anyone would store a number as a string. Sometimes this is an example of improper use—for example, the code is storing `'5'` when the number should have been stored as 5, without quotes. Another case is when fields are manually populated, and may contain either strings or numbers (e.g., a survey where people can type *five* or *5* or *V*). These are all numbers, but they are different representations of numbers. In this case, you might store them as strings until you process them.

One of the most common reasons for storing numbers as strings is a purposeful action, such as storing US postal codes. Postal codes in the United States consist of five numbers. In New England and other parts of the northeast, the zip codes begin with a zero. Try entering one of Boston's zip codes into your Python interpreter as a string and as an integer. What happens?

```
'02108'
02108
```

Python will throw a `SyntaxError` in the second example (with the message `invalid token` and a pointer at the leading zero). In Python, and in numerous other languages, "tokens" are special words, symbols, and identifiers. In this case, Python does not know how to process a normal (non-octal) number beginning with zero, meaning it is an invalid token.

Floats, decimals, and other non–whole number types

There are multiple ways to tell Python to handle non–whole number math. This can be very confusing and appear to cause rounding errors if you are not aware how each non–whole number data type behaves.

When a non–whole number is used in Python, Python defaults to turning the value into a float. A float uses the built-in floating-point data type for your Python version. This means Python stores an approximation of the numeric value—an approximation that reflects only a certain level of precision.

Notice the difference between the following two numbers when you enter them into your Python interpreter:

```
2
2.0
```

The first one is an integer. The second one is a float. Let's do some math to learn a little more about how these numbers work and how Python evaluates them. Enter the following into your Python interpreter:

```
2/3
```

What happened? You got a `zero` value returned, but you were likely expecting `0.6666666666666666` or `0.6666666666666667` or something along those lines. The problem was that those numbers are both integers and integers do not handle fractions. Let's try turning one of those numbers into a float:

```
2.0/3
```

Now we get a more accurate answer of `0.6666666666666666`. When one of the numbers entered is a float, the answer is also a float.

As mentioned previously, Python floats can cause accuracy issues (*https://docs.python.org/2/tutorial/floatingpoint.html*). Floats allow for quick processing, but, for this reason, they are more imprecise.

Computationally, Python does not see numbers the way you or your calculator would. Try the following two examples in your Python interpreter:

```
0.3
0.1 + 0.2
```

With the first line, Python returns `0.3`. On the second line, you would expect to see `0.3` returned, but instead you get `0.30000000000000004`. The two values `0.3` and `0.30000000000000004` are not equal. If you are interested in the nuances of this, you can read more in the Python docs (*http://bit.ly/floating_point_math*).

Throughout this book, we will use the `decimal` module (or library) (*https://docs.python.org/2/library/decimal.html*) when accuracy matters. A module is a section or library of code you import for your use. The `decimal` module makes your numbers (integers or floats) act in predictable ways (following the concepts you learned in math class).

In the next example, the first line imports `getcontext` and `Decimal` from the `decimal` module, so we have them in our environment. The following two lines use `getcontext` and `Decimal` to perform the math we already tested using floats:

```
from decimal import getcontext, Decimal
getcontext().prec = 1
Decimal(0.1) + Decimal(0.2)
```

When you run this code, Python returns `Decimal('0.3')`. Now when you enter `print Decimal('0.3')`, Python will return `0.3`, which is the response we originally expected (as opposed to `0.30000000000000004`).

Let's step through each of those lines of code:

```
from decimal import getcontext, Decimal    ❶
getcontext().prec = 1                       ❷
Decimal(0.1) + Decimal(0.2)                 ❸
```

❶ Imports `getcontext` and `Decimal` from the `decimal` module.

❷ Sets the rounding precision to one decimal point. The `decimal` module stores most rounding and precision settings in a default *context*. This line changes that context to use only one-decimal-point precision.

❸ Sums two decimals (one with value `0.1` and one with value `0.2`) together.

What happens if you change the value of `getcontext().prec`? Try it and rerun the final line. You should see a different answer depending on how many decimal points you told the library to use.

As stated earlier, there are many mathematical specifics you will encounter as you wrangle your data. There are many different approaches to the math you might need to perform, but the decimal type allows us greater accuracy when using nonwhole numbers.

Numbers in Python

The different levels of accuracy available in Python's number types are one example of the nuisances of the Python language. We will learn more about numeric and math libraries in Python as we learn more about data wrangling in this book. If you are curious now, here are some Python libraries you will become familiar with if you are going to do math beyond the basics:

- `decimal` (*https://docs.python.org/2/library/decimal.html*), for fixed-point and floating-point arithmetic
- `math` (*https://docs.python.org/2/library/math.html*), for access to the mathematical functions defined by the C standard
- `numpy` (*http://bit.ly/numpy_math*), a fundamental package for scientific computing in Python
- `sympy` (*http://docs.sympy.org/latest/index.html*), a Python library for symbolic mathematics
- `mpmath` (*http://mpmath.org/*), a Python library for real and complex floating-point arithmetic with arbitrary precision

---

We've learned about strings, integers, and floats/decimals. Let's use these basic data types as building blocks for some more complex ones.

Data Containers

In this section, we'll explain data containers, which hold multiple data points. It should be noted, however, that these containers are data types as well. Python has a few common containers: variables, lists, and dictionaries.

Variables

Variables give us a way to store values, such as strings or numbers or other data containers. A variable is made of a string of characters, which is often a lowercase word (or words connected with underscores) that describes what is contained.

Let's try creating a simple variable. In your Python interpreter, try the following:

```
filename = 'budget.csv'
```

If you entered this correctly, your interpreter should return nothing. This is different from when we entered a string into the Python interpreter. If you simply entered `'budget.csv'` into your Python interpreter, it would output `'budget.csv'`.

When you create a variable, you are assigning what the program would normally output to the variable as its value. That is why nothing is returned when you create a new variable. In our example, our variable is called `filename` and it holds the string we typed (`'budget.csv'`) as its value.

Object-Oriented Programming

You may have heard of *object-oriented programming*, or *OOP* for short. Python is an object-oriented programming language. The "object" in OOP can be any of the data types we learned about in this chapter such as strings, variables, numbers or floats.

In the example given in the text, our object is a string and it is stored now in `filename`. Every variable we define is a Python object. In Python, we use objects to store data we need later. These objects often have different qualities and actions they can perform, but they are all objects.

For example, each integer object can be added to another integer using a + symbol (the addition operator). As you continue learning Python, you will learn more of the qualities and actions of these objects and their underlying types—and come to appreciate object-oriented programming as a result!

When we created a string of letters and assigned it to the variable called `filename`, we followed some general variable naming principles. Don't worry about memorizing these rules, but do keep them in mind if you receive an error in your code after defining a new variable:

- Underscores are OK, hyphens are not.
- Numbers are OK, but variable names cannot start with a number.
- For reading ease, use lowercase letters with words separated by underscores.

Try the following code:

```
1example = 'This is going to break.'
```

What happened? What kind of error did you get? You should have gotten a syntax error, because you violated the second rule.

As long as you do not break Python's rules around naming variables, you can name the variable almost anything. To illustrate:

```
horriblevariablenamesarenotdescriptiveandtoolong = 'budget.csv'
```

As you can tell, this variable name is too long and not descriptive. Also, the lack of underscores makes it hard to read. What makes a good variable name? Ask yourself: What is something that will make sense to me six months from now and help me understand the code when I have forgotten everything?

Let's move on to a more reasonable variable name—cats. The value doesn't have to be a filename, as in our previous example. Your variables can have a variety of values and names. Let's pretend we are counting our cats, so we want to assign an integer to the variable cats:

```
cats = 42
```

If our Python script keeps track of how many cats we have, we don't need to know the exact value at any one point in time. All we need to know is that the value is stored in the variable cats, so if we call cats in our interpreter or use it in another part of our code, it will always return the current number of cats.

To *call* a variable is to ask Python for its value. Let's call cats. Type cats into your interpreter. You should get 42 in return. When you type filename, you should get the string 'budget.csv' in return. Try this on your machine:

```
>>> cats
42
>>> filename
'budget.csv'
>>>
```

If you type in a variable name that does not exist (or if you misspelled either of those) you will see the following error:

```
>>> dogs
Traceback (most recent call last):
  File "<stdin>", line 1, in <module>
NameError: name 'dogs' is not defined
```

As stated earlier, it is important to learn how to read errors, so you can understand what you did wrong and how to fix it. In this example, the error says, *dogs* is not defined which means we did not define a variable named dogs. Python doesn't know what we are asking it to call because we have not defined that variable.

You would get the same error if your forgot to include the quotes in 'budget.csv' in our first example. Try this in your Python interpreter:

```
filename = budget.csv
```

The error returned is NameError: *name budget* is not defined. This is because Python does not know budget.csv is supposed to be a string. Remember, a string is always denoted using quotes. Without those quotes, Python tries to interpret it as another variable. The main takeaway from this exercise is to note which line the error is on and ask yourself, what might be incorrect? In our dogs example, the error message tells us it's on *line 1*. If we had many lines of code, the error might show *line 87*.

All of the examples presented so far have been short strings or integers. Variables can also hold long strings—even ones spanning multiple lines. We chose to use short strings in our examples because long strings are not fun for you (or us) to type.

Try out a variable that holds a long string. Note that our string also has a single quote, meaning we must use double quotes to store it:

```
recipe = "A recipe isn't just a list of ingredients."
```

Now if you type recipe, you will get the long string that was stored:

```
>>>recipe
"A recipe isn't just a list of ingredients."
```

Strings or integers are not required data types for variables. Variables can hold all sorts of different Python data types, which we will learn more about in the following sections.

Lists

A list is a group of values that have some relationship in common. You use a list in Python similarly to how you would use it in normal language. In Python, you can create a list of items by placing them within square brackets([ ]) and separating them with commas.

Let's make a list of groceries in Python:

```
['milk', 'lettuce', 'eggs']
```

This list is made of strings, not variables. This is recognizable, because the words are enclosed in quotes. If these were variables, they would not have the quotes around them.

If you press Return, Python will return the following:

```
['milk', 'lettuce', 'eggs']
```

You have made your first Python list: a list of strings. You can make lists of any Python data type, or any mixture of data types (i.e., floats and strings). Let's make a list of integers and floats:

```
[0, 1.0, 5, 10.0]
```

Now, let's store our list in a variable, so we can use it later in our code. Variables are helpful because they prevent us from having to type out our data time and time again. Typing out data by hand is error-prone and isn't very efficient if your list is, say, 5,000 items long. Just as we mentioned earlier, variables are a way to store values in an aptly named container.

Try the following in your Python interpreter:

```
shopping_list = ['milk', 'lettuce', 'eggs']
```

When you press Return, you should see a new line. It will appear as if nothing happened. Remember earlier when we had the list echoed back to us? Now, Python is storing the list in the shopping_list variable. If you call your variable by typing shopping_list into your Python prompt, you should get the following returned:

```
shopping_list
['milk', 'lettuce', 'eggs']
```

Lists can also store variables. Let's say we have variables representing counts of animals we are tracking in an animal shelter:

```
cats = 2
dogs = 5
horses = 1
```

Now, we can take the counts of those animals and put them in a list:

```
animal_counts = [cats, dogs, horses]
```

If you enter animal_counts into your Python interpreter, Python will return the following value:

```
[2, 5, 1]
```

The variables hold the information for us. When we type the variables, Python returns the underlying values stored in our variables.

You can also create lists of lists. Let's say we have a list of names for our animals:

```
cat_names = ['Walter', 'Ra']
dog_names = ['Joker', 'Simon', 'Ellie', 'Lishka', 'Fido']
horse_names = ['Mr. Ed']
animal_names = [cat_names, dog_names, horse_names]
```

If you enter animal_names into your Python interpreter, Python will return the following value:

```
[['Walter', 'Ra'], ['Joker', 'Simon', 'Ellie', 'Lishka', 'Fido'], ['Mr. Ed']]
```

You didn't have to type out all those names to create a list of lists. The original variables (cat_names, dog_names, horse_names), which are lists, are still accessible. For example, if you type cat_names, you will get ['Walter', 'Ra'] in return.

Now that we've explored lists, we'll move on to a slightly more complex data container, called a dictionary.

Dictionaries

A dictionary is more complex than a variable or list, and it is aptly named. Think of a Python dictionary like a dictionary in the traditional sense of the word—as a resource you can use to look up words to get their definitions. In a Python dictionary, the words you look up are called the *keys* and the definitions of these words are called the *values*. In Python, the key is something that points to a value.

Let's go back to our animals. animal_numbers holds a list of the different numbers of animals we have, but we don't know which number belongs to which animal type. A dictionary is a great way to store that information.

In the following example, we are using the animal types as the keys, and the counts of each animal type as the values:

```
animal_counts = {'cats': 2, 'dogs': 5, 'horses': 1}
```

If we want to access one of the values using a key, we can do so by accessing the key from the dictionary (like looking up a word in a normal dictionary). To perform this lookup in Python—say, for the number of dogs we have—we can type the following:

```
animal_counts['dogs']
```

You should see 5 returned, because we set the key 'dogs' equal to the value 5 in our dictionary ('dogs': 5). As you can see, a dictionary is very useful when you have matching keys and values you want to store. Dictionaries can be very powerful depending on what your needs are, so let's take a longer look at using lists with dictionaries.

With our earlier list of animal names, it was hard to tell which list of names belonged to which type of animal. It was not clear which list contained the names of the cats, which one had the names of the dogs, and which held the names of the horses. With a dictionary, however, we can make this distinction clearer:

```python
animal_names = {
    'cats': ['Walter', 'Ra'],
    'dogs': ['Joker', 'Simon', 'Ellie', 'Lishka', 'Fido'],
    'horses': ['Mr. Ed']
    }
```

Here is another way to write the same underlying values using more variables:

```python
cat_names = ['Walter', 'Ra']                                        ❶
dog_names = ['Joker', 'Simon', 'Ellie', 'Lishka', 'Fido']
horse_names = ['Mr. Ed']

animal_names = {
    'cats': cat_names,                                              ❷
    'dogs': dog_names,
    'horses': horse_names
    }
```

❶ This line defines the variable cat_names as a list of cat names (a list of strings).

❷ This line uses the variable cat_names to pass that list of names as the value for the key 'cats' in the dictionary.

Both versions give us the same dictionary, although in slightly different ways.[1] As you learn more Python, you will be better able to determine when defining more variables makes sense and when it is not useful. For now, you can see it is easy to use many different defined variables (like cat_names and dog_names) to create new variables (like animal_names).

 While Python does have spacing and formatting rules, you do not have to format a dictionary as we have done here. However, your code should be as easy to read as possible. Making sure your code is readable is something for which you and other developers you work with will be thankful.

What Can the Various Data Types Do?

Each of the basic data types can do a variety of things. Here is a list of the data types we've learned about so far, followed by examples of the kinds of actions you can tell them to do:

---

1 They are not exactly the same dictionary, since the second example uses objects that could be modified. For more reading on the differences, check out Appendix E.

- Strings
  - — Change case
  - — Strip space off the end of a string
  - — Split a string
- Integers and decimals
  - — Add and subtract
  - — Simple math
- Lists
  - — Add to or subtract from the list
  - — Remove the last item of the list
  - — Reorder the list
  - — Sort the list
- Dictionaries
  - — Add a key/value pair
  - — Set a new value to the corresponding key
  - — Look up a value by the key

 We've purposely not mentioned variables in this list. The things a variable can do depend on the item it contains. For example, if a variable is a string, then it can do everything a string can do. If a variable is a list, then it can do different things only lists can do.

Think of the data types as nouns and the things they can do as verbs. For the most part, the things data types can do are called *methods*. To access a data type's method, or make the data type do something, you use dot notation (`.`). For example, if you have a string assigned to a variable you named `foo`, you can call the `strip` method of that string by typing `foo.strip()`. Let's look at few of these methods in action.

When we call a string's methods, these actions are part of the default Python libraries every Python installation shares (similar to the default applications that come preinstalled on your phone). These methods will be there on every computer running Python, so every Python string can share the same methods (just like every phone can make a phone call and every Apple phone can send an iMessage). A vast assortment of built-in methods and basic data types are included in the Python standard library (*https://docs.python.org/2/library/*) (also known as *stdlib*), including the Python data types you are now using.

String Methods: Things Strings Can Do

Let's use our initial variable, `filename`. Originally, we defined the variable using `filename = 'budget.csv'`. That was pretty convenient. Sometimes, though, things are not so convenient. Let's go through a few examples:

```
filename = 'budget.csv          '
```

You'll notice our `filename` string now has a lot of extra spaces we probably need to strip off. We can use the Python string's `strip` method, a built-in function that removes unnecessary whitespace from the beginning and end of a string:

```
filename = 'budget.csv          '
filename = filename.strip()
```

If you do not reassign the variable (set `filename` equal to the output of `filename.strip()`), then the modifications you made to `filename` will not be stored.

If you enter `filename` in your Python interpreter, you should now see the spaces have been stripped off.

Let's say our filename needs to be in all capital letters. We can transform all the letters to uppercase using the Python string's built-in `upper` method:

```
filename = 'budget.csv'
filename.upper()
```

Your output should now show that we have properly uppercased the filename:

```
'BUDGET.CSV'
```

In this case, we did *not* reassign the uppercase string to the variable `filename`. What happens when you call `filename` in your interpreter again? The output should still read `'budget.csv'`. If you don't want to modify your variable but want to transform it for one-time use, you can call methods like `upper`, as they will return the modified string *without* changing the underlying variable.

What if we wanted to reassign the variable by storing the return value using the same variable name? In the following, we are changing the value of the `filename` variable to be uppercase:

```
filename = 'budget.csv'          ❶
filename = filename.upper()      ❷
```

❶ If you call `filename` after this line, the output will be `'budget.csv'`.

❷ If you call `filename` after this line, the output will be `'BUDGET.CSV'`.

We could condense this code to run on one line:

```
filename = 'budget.csv'.upper()
```

The number of lines you use for your code is sometimes a matter of personal style or preference. Make choices that make sense to you but keep your code clear, easy to read, and obvious.

We only covered two string methods in these examples, `strip` and `upper`, but there are many other built-in string methods. We will learn more about these methods as we work with strings in our data wrangling.

Numerical Methods: Things Numbers Can Do

Integers and floats/decimals are mathematical objects. If you enter `40 + 2`, Python returns 42. If you want to store the answer in a variable, you assign it to a variable just as we did in the string examples:

```
answer = 40 + 2
```

Now, if you type `answer`, you will get 42 in return. Most of the things you can do with integers are pretty predictable, but there may be some special formatting you need to use so your Python interpreter understands the math you want to perform. For example, if you wanted to square 42, then you would enter `42**2`.

Integers, floats, and decimals also have many other methods, some of which we will encounter as we learn about data wrangling.

List Methods: Things Lists Can Do

There are a few must-know methods for lists. Let's start with an empty list and use a method to add values to it.

First, define an empty list like so:

```
dog_names = []
```

If you enter `dog_names` into your interpreter, it will return [], Python's way of showing an empty list. Earlier in the chapter, we had a bunch of names stored in that variable, but we *redefined* it in the last line so now it is an empty list. The built-in `append` method adds items to the list. Let's use it now and add "Joker" to the list:

```
dog_names.append('Joker')
```

Now, if you enter `dog_names`, your list will return one item: `['Joker']`.

On your own, build out the list using the `append` method until you have a list that looks like this:

```
['Joker', 'Simon', 'Ellie', 'Lishka', 'Turtle']
```

Let's say you accidentally added `'Walter'`, one of the cat names:

```
dog_names.append('Walter')
```

You can remove it with the Python list's built-in `remove` method:

```
dog_names.remove('Walter')
```

While there are many more built-in methods for lists, append and remove are among the most commonly used.

Dictionary Methods: Things Dictionaries Can Do

To learn some useful dictionary methods, let's build our dictionary of animal counts from scratch.

In the next example, we create an empty dictionary. Then, we add a key and define the value of that key:

```
animal_counts = {}
animal_counts['horses'] = 1
```

Adding an object to a dictionary (animal_counts['horses']) is a little different from adding an object to a list. This is because a dictionary has both a key and a value. The key in this case is 'horses' and the value is 1.

Let's define the rest of the dictionary with our animal counts:

```
antmal_counts['cats'] = 2
animal_counts['dogs'] = 5
antmal_counts['snakes'] = 0
```

Now when you type animal_counts in your Python interpreter, you should get the following dictionary: {'horses': 1, 'cats': 2, 'dogs': 5, 'snakes': 0}. (Since Python dictionaries don't store order, your output might look different but should contain the same keys and values.)

We are working with a very small example, but programming is not always so convenient. Imagine a dictionary of animal counts for all domesticated animals in the world. As the programmer, we might not know all of the different types of animal this animal_counts dictionary holds. When handling a large and unknown dictionary, we can use dictionary methods to tell us more about it. The following command returns all the keys the dictionary holds:

```
animal_counts.keys()
```

If you have been following along with the exercises, if you type this in your interpreter will return a list of keys that looks like this:

```
['horses', 'cats', 'dogs', 'snakes']
```

You can take any of those keys and retrieve the value associated with it from the dictionary. The following lookup will return the number of dogs:

```
animal_counts['dogs']
```

The output for this line is 5.

If you wanted to, you could save that value in a new variable so you don't have to look it up again:

```
dogs = animal_counts['dogs']
```

Now, if you enter the variable dogs directly, Python will return 5.

Those are some of the basic things you can do with a dictionary. Just like with strings and lists, we will learn more about dictionaries as we apply more complex problems to our code.

Helpful Tools: type, dir, and help

There are a couple of built-in tools in the Python standard library that can help you identify what data types or objects you have and what things you can do with them (i.e., what their methods are). In this section, we will learn about three tools that come as part of the Python standard library.

type

type will help you identify what kind of data type your object is. To do this in your Python code, wrap the variable in type()—for example, if the variable name is dogs, then you would enter type(dogs) into the Python prompt. This is extremely helpful when you are using a variable to hold data and need to know what type of data is in the variable. Consider the zip code example from earlier in the chapter.

Here, we have two different uses for the value 20011. In the first case, it is a zip code stored as a string. In the second case, it is an integer:

```
'20011'
20011
```

If those values were stored in variables, they would be further obscured and we might not know or remember whether we used a string or an integer.

If we *pass* the value to the built-in method type, then Python will tell us what kind of data type the object is. Try it:

```
type('20011')
type(20011)
```

The first line returns str. The second line returns int. What happens when you pass a list to type? And a variable?

Identifying the type of an object can be very helpful when you are trying to troubleshoot an error or work with someone else's code. Remember when we tried to subtract a list from another list (in "Addition and Subtraction" on page 32)? Well, you cannot subtract a string from a string either. So, the string `'20011'` has very different possible methods and use cases than the integer `20011`.

dir

dir will help you identify all the things a particular data type can do, by returning a list of built-in methods and properties. Let's try it out with the string `'cat,dog,horse'`:

```
dir('cat,dog,horse')
```

For now, ignore everything at the beginning of the returned list (the strings starting with double underscores). These are internal or *private* methods Python uses.

The methods that are most useful are contained in the second part of the returned list output. Many of these methods are obvious, or self-documenting. You should see some of the methods we used on strings earlier in this chapter:

```
[...,
 '__sizeof__',
 '__str__',
 '__subclasshook__',
 '_formatter_field_name_split',
 '_formatter_parser',
 'capitalize',
 'center',
 'count',
 'decode',
 'encode',
 'endswith',
 'expandtabs',
 'find',
 'format',
 'index',
 'isalnum',
 'isalpha',
 'isdigit',
 'islower',
 'isspace',
 'istitle',
 'isupper',
 'join',
 'ljust',
 'lower',
 'lstrip',
 'partition',
 'replace',
 'rfind',
 'rindex',
 'rjust',
 'rpartition',
```

```
'rsplit',
'rstrip',
'split',
'splitlines',
'startswith',
'strip',
'swapcase',
'title',
'translate',
'upper',
'zfill']
```

If you look at the string `'cat,dog,horse'`, it looks like it is a list saved in a string. It's actually a single value, but with the Python string's built-in `split` method we can divide the string into smaller pieces by splitting it on the comma character, like so:

```
'cat,dog,horse'.split(',')
```

Python will return a list:

```
['cat', 'dog', 'horse']
```

Now let's call the `dir` method on our list:

```
dir(['cat', 'dog', 'horse'])
```

There are not as many options as for strings, but let's try a few. First, let's turn the list into a variable. You should know how to assign the list to a variable by now, but here's an example:

```
animals = ['cat', 'dog', 'horse']
```

Now, let's try some new methods we found using `dir` on a list with our variable `animals`:

```
animals.reverse()
animals.sort()
```

After you run each of those lines, print out the value of animals so you can see how the the method has modified the list. What output did you expect? Was it the same that you saw? Try using the `dir` method on integers and floats. (Hint: `dir` expects you to pass only one object, so try `dir(1)` or `dir(3.0)`). Are there methods you didn't expect?

As you can see, `dir` gives you insight into the built-in methods for each Python data type; these methods can prove valuable when wrangling data using Python. We recommend taking time to experiment with the listed methods that interest you and testing more methods with different data types.

help

The third helpful built-in Python method we will review in this chapter is the `help` method. This method will return the documentation for an object, method, or module—although it is often written in a very technical (sometimes cryptic) manner. Let's review the help for the `split` method we used in the previous section. If you didn't know you needed to put the character you wanted to split the string on inside the parentheses, how would you know what the Python string's `split` method expected? Let's pretend we didn't know how to use `split` and called it without passing ',':

```
animals = 'cat,dog,horse'
animals.split()
```

This code returns the following:

```
['cat,dog,horse']
```

Looks good, right? Not upon closer inspection. As we can see, Python took our string and put it into a list, but didn't split the words into pieces using the commas. This is because the built-in `split` method defaults to splitting the string on spaces, not commas. We have to tell Python to split on the commas by passing a comma string (',') into the method.

To help us understand how the method works, let's pass it to `help`. First, we have to redefine our `animals` variable, because we turned it into a list. Let's turn it back into a string, then look up how `split` works:

```
animals = 'cat,dog,horse'
help(animals.split) ❶
```

❶ This line passes `animals.split`—without the `()`—to the `help` method. You can pass any object, method, or module to the `help` method, but as seen here, you should not include the end parentheses when passing methods.

Python returns the following:

```
split(...)
    S.split([sep [,maxsplit]]) -> list of strings

    Return a list of the words in the string S, using sep as the
    delimiter string.  If maxsplit is given, at most maxsplit
    splits are done. If sep is not specified or is None, any
    whitespace string is a separator and empty strings are removed
    from the result.
```

The first line of the description reads: `S.split([sep [,maxsplit]])` → `list of strings`. In English, this tells us that for a string (`S`) we have a method (`split`) with a first possible argument (a.k.a. thing we can pass), `sep`, and a second possible argument, `maxsplit`. The square brackets (`[]`) around the argument names indicate that they are optional, not mandatory. This method returns (`->`) a list of strings.

The following line reads: `"Return a list of the words in the string S, using sep as the delimiter string."` `sep` is an argument passed to the `split` method that is used as a *separator*. A *delimiter* is a character or series of characters used to separate fields. For example, in a comma-delimited file, the comma is the delimiter. The comma is also the delimiter in the string we created, as it separates the words we want in our list.

 Once you have finished reading documentation (using arrows to scroll up and down), you can exit `help` by typing `q`.

The `help` description also tells us that spaces, or *whitespace*, are the default delimiter if no other delimiter is specified. This tells us that if we had a string `'cat dog horse'` the `split` method would not require us to pass a delimiter inside the (). As you can see, the built-in `help` method can teach you a lot about what a method expects you to use and whether it's a good fit for the problem you are solving.

Putting It All Together

Let's test our new skills. Try the following:

1. Create a string, a list, and a dictionary.
2. Look up the possible methods of each of these data types using the `dir` method.
3. Try applying some of the built-in methods you discovered, until one throws an error.
4. Look up the method documentation using `help`. Try to figure out what the method does and what you might need to do differently to make it work.

Congrats! You just learned how to program. Programming is not about memorizing everything; rather, it is about troubleshooting when things go awry.

What Does It All Mean?

At the beginning of the chapter, we promised that by the end you would understand these three lines:

```
import sys
import pprint
pprint.pprint(sys.path)
```

Knowing what we now know, let's break it down. In "Floats, decimals, and other non–whole number types" on page 20, we imported the decimal library. It looks like we are importing some modules from the Python standard library here—sys and pprint.

Let's get some help on these. (Make sure you import them, or help will throw an error!) Because pprint is an easier read, let's look at that one first:

```
>>>import pprint
>>>help(pprint.pprint)

Help on function pprint in module pprint:

pprint(object, stream=None, indent=1, width=80, depth=None)
    Pretty-print a Python object to a stream [default is sys.stdout].
```

Excellent. According to the pprint.pprint() documentation, the method outputs an easy-to-read display of whatever was passed to it.

As we learned in the previous chapter, sys.path shows where Python looks to find modules. What kind of type is sys.path?

```
import sys
type(sys.path)
```

A list. We know how to use lists! We now also know if we pass a list to pprint.pprint, it makes it look really nice. Let's try to apply this to our list of lists holding animal names. First, let's add a few more names to make it really messy:

```
animal_names = [
    ['Walter', 'Ra', 'Fluffy', 'Killer'],
    ['Joker', 'Simon', 'Ellie', 'Lishka', 'Fido'],
    ['Mr. Ed', 'Peter', 'Rocket','Star']
    ]
```

Now, let's pprint the variable animal_names:

```
pprint.pprint(animal_names)
```

What we get in return is the following:

```
[['Walter', 'Ra', 'Fluffy', 'Killer'],
 ['Joker', 'Simon', 'Ellie', 'Lishka', 'Fido'],
 ['Mr. Ed', 'Peter', 'Rocket', 'Star']]
```

To summarize, here is what each of those original lines of code does:

```
import sys          ❶
import pprint       ❷
pprint.pprint(sys.path)  ❸
```

❶ Imports Python's sys module

❷ Imports Python's `pprint` module

❸ Passes `sys.path`, a list, to `pprint.pprint` so the list is displayed in a way that's clear and easy to read

If you pass a dictionary to `pprint.pprint`, what happens? You should see a well-formatted dictionary output.

Summary

Data types and containers are how Python understands and stores data. There are more types than the few core ones we learned about in this chapter, which are shown in Table 2-1.

Table 2-1. Data types

Name	Example
String	`'Joker'`
Integer	`2`
Float	`2.0`
Variable	`animal_names`
List	`['Joker', 'Simon', 'Ellie', 'Lishka', 'Fido']`
Dictionary	`{'cats': 2, 'dogs': 5, 'horses': 1, 'snakes': 0}`

As you know, some data types can be contained within others. A list can be a bunch of strings or integers or a mixture of the two. A variable can be a list or a dictionary or a string or a decimal. As we saw with our variable `animal_names`, a list can also be a list of lists. As we gain more Python knowledge, we will learn more about these data types, how they work and how we can utilize them for our data wrangling needs.

In this chapter, we also learned about built-in methods and things we can do with objects in Python. Additionally, we learned some simple Python methods and tools we can use to help figure out what kind of data type an object is and what we can do with it. Table 2-2 summarizes these tools.

Table 2-2. Helper tools

Example	What it does
`type('Joker')`	Returns what kind of object 'Joker' is.
`dir('Joker')`	Returns a list of all the things the object 'Joker' can do (methods and properties).
`help('Joker'.strip)`	Returns a description of a specific method (in this case, `strip`) so we can better understand how to use it.

In the next chapter, we will learn how to open various file types and store data in the Python data types we learned in this chapter. By converting our data from files into Python objects, we can unleash the power of Python and data wrangling can soon become an easy task.

## CHAPTER 3

Data Meant to Be Read by Machines

Data can be stored in many different formats and file types. Some formats store data in a way easily handled by machines, while others store data in a way meant to be easily readable by a human. Microsoft Word documents are an example of the latter, while CSV, JSON, and XML are examples of the former. In this chapter, we will cover how to read files easily handled by machines, and in Chapters 4 and Chapter 5 we will cover files made for human consumption.

File formats that store data in a way easily understood by machines are commonly referred to as *machine readable*. Common machine-readable formats include the following:

- Comma-Separated Values (CSV)
- JavaScript Object Notation (JSON)
- Extensible Markup Language (XML)

In spoken and written language, these data formats are typically referred to by their shorter names (e.g., CSV). We will be using these acronyms.

When looking for data or requesting data from an organization or agency, the formats described in this chapter are your best available resource. They are more easily used and ingested by your Python scripts than human-readable formats, and are usually easy to find on data websites.

CSV Data

The first machine-readable file type we will learn about is CSV. CSV files, or CSVs for short, are files that separate data columns with commas. The files themselves have a *.csv* extension.

Another type of data, called tab-separated values (TSV) data, sometimes gets classified with CSVs. TSVs differ only in that they separate data columns with tabs and not commas. The files themselves usually have a *.tsv* extension, but sometimes have a *.csv* extension. Essentially, *.tsv* and *.csv* files will act the same in Python.

If the file has a *.tsv* file extension, then it's likely TSV data. If the file has a *.csv* file extension, it's probably CSV data, but it could be TSV data. Make sure to open and view your file so you know what you're dealing with before you begin importing your data.

For our CSV sample in this chapter, we will look at data from the World Health Organization (WHO). The WHO has a lot of great datasets (*http://apps.who.int/gho/data/node.main*) in different formats. The one selected for this example contains life expectancy rates worldwide by country. If you visit the web page (*http://bit.ly/ life_expectancy_data*) for life expectany rates data, you will find a couple of different versions of this dataset. For this example, we are using CSV (text only) (*http://bit.ly/ life_expectancy_csv*).

If you open the file in your text editor,[1] you will see data holding rows containing the values in Table 3-1.

Table 3-1. Two sample data records[a]

CSV headers	Sampler rec 1	Sampler rec 2
Indicator	Life expectancy at age 60 (years)	Life expectancy at birth (years)
PUBLISH STATES	Published	Published
Year	1990	1990
WHO region	Europe	Americas
World Bank income group	High-income	Lower-middle-income
Country	Czech Republic	Belize
Sex	Female	Both sexes
Display Value	19	71
Numeric	19.00000	71.00000
Low	*no value*	*no value*
High	*no value*	*no value*
Comments	*no value*	*no value*

[a] Bold items are included in the sample data.

To make the data easier to read, a sample of the data with trimmed-down fields is shown here. You should see something similar to this when you open the CSV file in your text editor:

---

1 To complete the exercises in this chapter, you will need a good text editor. If you haven't already installed one, follow the instructions in "Install a Code Editor" on page 15.

```
"Year",  "Country","Sex","Display Value","Numeric"
"1990","Andorra","Both sexes","77","77.00000"
"2000","Andorra","Both sexes","80","80.00000"
"2012","Andorra","Female","28","28.00000"
"2000","Andorra","Both sexes","23","23.00000"
"2012","United Arab Emirates","Female","78","78.00000"
"2000","Antigua and Barbuda","Male","72","72.00000"
"1990","Antigua and Barbuda","Male","17","17.00000"
"2012","Antigua and Barbuda","Both sexes","22","22.00000"
"2012","Australia","Male","81","81.00000"
```

Another way to preview the file is to open it in a spreadsheet program such as Excel or Google Spreadsheets. Those programs will display each entry of data as a separate row.

How to Import CSV Data

Now that we have learned a little bit about the data, let's open the file in Python and convert the data into a form Python can understand. This only takes a couple of lines of code:

```
import csv

csvfile = open('data-text.csv', 'rb')
reader = csv.reader(csvfile)

for row in reader:
    print row
```

Let's go through each line. In the previous chapter, we did all of our coding in the Python interpreter, but as the code gets longer and more complicated, it is easier to write and run code from a file. After we walk through this bit of code, we will save the code to a *.py* file, which is a Python file, and run the file from the command line.

The first line of the script imports a library called csv (*https://docs.python.org/3/library/csv.html*):

```
import csv
```

A Python *library* is a package of code that provides functionality you can use in your Python programs. The csv library we are importing comes with your Python installation as part of the standard library (or *stdlib*). Once we import a library into our file, we can use it. If we did not have this library, this script would be a lot longer—the csv library gives us helper functions so we don't have to write as much code to perform a more complex task.

The second line of code takes our *data-text.csv* file, which should be located in the same folder as the script, and passes it to the open function:

```
csvfile = open('data-text.csv', 'rb')
```

A *function* is a piece of code that performs a task when it is invoked. It is very similar to the Python data type *methods* we learned about in Chapter 2. Sometimes functions will take an input (or inputs). These inputs are called *arguments*. The function performs an action based on the arguments. Sometimes functions also return an output, which can then be stored or used.

open is a built-in function in Python (*https://docs.python.org/2/library/func tions.html*), meaning the act of opening a file is so common that the core Python contributors felt it should be added to every Python installation. When we use the open function, we pass a filename as the first argument (here we used `'data-text.csv'`) and then we optionally specify which mode this file should be opened in (we used `'rb'`). If you visit the docs for the open (*https://docs.python.org/2/library/func tions.html#open*) function, you will find that the argument `'rb'` means that we open the file as *read-only* and in *binary* mode. Opening the file in binary mode allows our code to run on both Windows and Unix-based operating systems. The other common mode is *write* (`'w'`, or `'wb'` for *write* in *binary* mode).

If you want to read, open in read mode. If you intend to write, open the file in write mode.

We store the output of this function in the variable csvfile. csvfile now holds an open file as its value.

In the next line, we pass csvfile to the reader function in the csv module. This function tells the csv module to read the open file as a CSV:

```
reader = csv.reader(csvfile)
```

The output of the function csv.reader(csvfile) is stored in the reader variable. The reader variable now holds a Python CSV reader with the opened file. This CSV reader allows us to easily view data from our file using simple Python commands. In the last piece of code, we have something called a for loop.

A for loop is a way of iterating over Python objects, commonly used with lists. A for loop tells Python code, "For each thing in this list of things, do something." The first word used after for in a for loop is the variable that will hold each object in the list (or other iterable object). The code below the for loop uses that variable to perform more functions or calculations on the item. For that reason, it is best to use a word which conveys meaning, so you and others can easily read and understand the code.

Remember our invalid token error from Chapter 2? In Python, for is another special token, and it can only be used for creating for loops. Tokens help translate what we type in our interpreters or scripts into something our computers can run and execute.

Try running the following example in your Python interpreter:

```python
dogs = ['Joker', 'Simon', 'Ellie', 'Lishka', 'Fido']
for dog in dogs:
    print dog
```

With this for loop, we store each dog name in the for loop variable dog. For each of the iterations of our for loop, we print out the dog's name (held in the variable dog). When the for loop has gone through each dog's name (or item in the list), the code is finished running.

Closing Indented Code Blocks in IPython

When writing for loops or other indented blocks in an IPython terminal, make sure your prompt has returned from an indented block style . . . to a new In prompt. The easiest way to do this is to simply hit Return after you are finished entering your final indented lines. You should see your prompt ask for another In before entering code outside of your loop:

```python
In [1]: dogs = ['Joker', 'Simon', 'Ellie', 'Lishka', 'Fido']

In [2]: for dog in dogs:
   ...:     print dog      ❶
   ...:                    ❷
Joker
Simon
Ellie
Lishka
Fido

In [3]:                    ❸
```

❶ IPython begins an auto-indented prompt (. . . : followed by four spaces).

❷ Press Return on the blank line to close the indented block and execute the code.

❸ A new prompt appears when IPython is done with the code.

In the case of the code we are using to read our CSV, our reader object is a Python container holding the data rows. In our reader for loop, we hold each row of data in the variable row. The next line states that for each row, we want Python to print the row:

```
for row in reader:
    print row
```

Now that we can import and loop through our data, we can really begin to explore it.

Saving the Code to a File; Running from Command Line

As you are working on code as a developer, you will want to save even partial bits of in-progress code to review and use later. If you are interrupted, being organized and saving your code means you can seamlessly pick up where you left off.

Let's save the file that has our code up to this point, and run it. The code should look like this (if you haven't already, open up your text editor, create a new file, and type this code into it):

```
import csv

csvfile = open('data-text.csv', 'rb')
reader = csv.reader(csvfile)

for row in reader:
    print row
```

 Pay attention to capitalization, spacing, and new lines. Your code will not work if each line has different spacing or there are odd capitals. Write the code *exactly* as we have done, using four spaces to indent lines. This is important because Python is case-sensitive and uses indentation to indicate structure.

Save the code using your text editor as a *.py* (Python) file. The full filename should be something like *import_csv_data.py*.

Put the data file *data-text.csv* in the same folder where you just saved your Python file. If you want to put the file in another location, you will need to update the code appropriately for your new file location.

Opening Files from Different Locations

In the current code, we pass the path of the file to the open function like this:

```
open('data-text.csv', 'rb')
```

However, if our code was in a subfolder called *code*, we would need to modify the script to look there. That is, we would instead need to use:

```
open('data/data-text.csv', 'rb')
```

In the preceding example, we would have a file structure that looks like this:

```
data_wrangling/
`-- code/
    |-- import_csv_data.py
    `-- data/
        `-- data-text.csv
```

If you have trouble locating your file, open up your command line and use the following commands on your Mac or Linux machine to navigate through your folders:

- ls returns a list of files.
- pwd shows your current location.
- cd ../ moves to the parent folder.
- cd ../../ moves two levels up.
- cd data moves into a folder called *data* that is inside the folder you are currently in (use ls to check!).

For more on navigating on the command line, including an entire section for Windows users, check out Appendix C.

After you save the file, you can run it using the command line. If you don't already have it open, open your command line (Terminal or *cmd*), and navigate to where the file is located. Let's assume that you put the file in *~/Projects/data_wrangling/code*. To navigate there using the Mac command line, you would use the change directory or folder command (cd):

```
cd ~/Projects/data_wrangling/code
```

After you get to the right location, you can run the Python file. Up until this point, we were running our code in the Python interpreter. We saved the file as *import_csv_data.py*. To run a Python file from the command line, you simply type python, a space, and then the name of the file. Let's try running our import file:

```
python import_csv_data.py
```

Your output should look like a bunch of lists—something like the data shown here, but with many more records:

```
['Healthy life expectancy (HALE) at birth (years)', 'Published', '2012',
 'Western Pacific', 'Lower-middle-income', 'Samoa', 'Female', '66',
 '66.00000', '', '', '']
['Healthy life expectancy (HALE) at birth (years)', 'Published', '2012',
 'Eastern Mediterranean', 'Low-income', 'Yemen', 'Both sexes', '54',
 '54.00000', '', '', '']
['Healthy life expectancy (HALE) at birth (years)', 'Published', '2000',
 'Africa', 'Upper-middle-income', 'South Africa', 'Male', '49', '49.00000',
 '', '', '']
```

```
['Healthy life expectancy (HALE) at birth (years)', 'Published', '2000',
 'Africa', 'Low-income', 'Zambia', 'Both sexes', '36', '36.00000', '', '', '']
['Healthy life expectancy (HALE) at birth (years)', 'Published', '2012',
 'Africa', 'Low-income', 'Zimbabwe', 'Female', '51', '51.00000', '', '', '']
```

Did you get this output? If not, stop for a minute to read the error you received. What does it tell you about where you might have gone wrong? Take time to search for the error and read a few ways people have fixed the same error. If you need extra help on troubleshooting how to get past the error, take a look at Appendix E.

 For a lot of our code from this point onward, we will do the work in a code editor, save the file, and run it from the command line. Your Python interpreter will still be a helpful tool to try out pieces of code, but as code gets longer and more complex it becomes harder to maintain in a code prompt.

With the current code we are writing, along with many other solutions we'll write, there are often many ways to solve a problem. csv.reader() returns each new line of your file as a list of data and is an easy-to-understand solution when you begin. We are going to modify our script slightly to make our list rows into dictionary rows. This will make our data a little easier to read, compare, and understand as we explore our dataset.

In your text editor, take line 4, reader = csv.reader(csvfile), and update it to read reader = csv.DictReader(csvfile). Your code should now look like this:

```
import csv

csvfile = open('data-text.csv', 'rb')
reader = csv.DictReader(csvfile)

for row in reader:
    print row
```

When you run the file again after saving it, each record will be a dictionary. The keys in the dictionary come from the first row of the CSV file. All the subsequent rows are values. Here is an example row of output:

```
{
    'Indicator': 'Healthy life expectancy (HALE) at birth (years)',
    'Country': 'Zimbabwe',
    'Comments': '',
    'Display Value': '49',
    'World Bank income group': 'Low-income',
    'Numeric': '49.00000',
    'Sex': 'Female',
    'High': '',
    'Low': '',
    'Year': '2012',
```

```
        'WHO region': 'Africa',
        'PUBLISH STATES': 'Published'
    }
```

At this point, we have successfully imported the CSV data into Python, meaning we were able to get the data from the file into a usable format Python can understand (dictionaries). Using a `for` loop helped us see the data so we could visually review it. We were able to use two different readers from the `csv` library to see the data in both a list and a dictionary form. We will be using this library again as we start exploring and analyzing datasets. For now, let's move on to importing JSON.

JSON Data

JSON data is one of the most commonly used formats for data transfers. It is preferred, because it is clean, easy to read, and easy to parse. It is also one of the most popular data formats that websites use when transmitting data to the JavaScript on the page. Many sites have JSON-enabled APIs, which we will review in Chapter 13. For this section, we will continue using the worldwide life expectancy rates data. This data is not in available in JSON form from the WHO, but we have created a JSON version for the purposes of this book; it's available in the code repository (*https://github.com/jackiekazil/data-wrangling*).

 If a file has a *.json* file extension, then it's probably JSON data. If it has a *.js* file extension, it is probably JavaScript, but in some rare cases it might be a poorly named JSON file.

If you open the JSON file in your code editor, you will see that each data record looks a lot like a Python dictionary. There is a key and value for each row, separated by a :, with each entry separated by a ,. There are also opening and closing curly braces ({}). Here is a sample record from the JSON file:

```
[
  {
    "Indicator":"Life expectancy at birth (years)",
    "PUBLISH STATES":"Published",
    "Year":1990,
    "WHO region":"Europe",
    "World Bank income group":"High-income",
    "Country":"Andorra",
    "Sex":"Both sexes",
    "Display Value":77,
    "Numeric":77.00000,
    "Low":"",
    "High":"",
    "Comments":""
```

```
        },
    ]
```

Depending on the formatting, sometimes a JSON file can look exactly like a dictionary. In this sample, each entry is a Python dictionary (defined by the { and }) and those dictionaries are all held in a list, which is defined by the [and].

How to Import JSON Data

Importing a JSON file is even easier than importing a CSV file in Python. The following code will open, load, import, and print a JSON data file:

```
import json                                    ❶

json_data = open('data-text.json').read()      ❷

data = json.loads(json_data)                    ❸

for item in data:                               ❹
    print item
```

❶ Imports the json (*https://docs.python.org/2/library/json.html*) Python library, which we will use to process the JSON.

❷ Uses the built-in Python function open to open the file. The filename is *data-text.json* (and this is the first argument for our open function). This line of code calls the open file's read method, which will read the file and store it in the json_data variable.

❸ Uses json.loads() to load JSON data into Python. The data variable catches the output.

❹ Iterates over the data using a for loop and prints each item, which will be the output in this example.

If you run python import_json_data.py from the command line, the output will show a dictionary for each record in the JSON file. It should look almost exactly like the final CSV output. Remember to copy the data file into the folder or to change the file path to reflect it's location.

At the end of the CSV section, we learned how to save a file and run it from the command line. With this example, let's start with a blank file and build up to that.

For a quick overview:

1. Create a new file in your code editor.

2. Save it as *import_json_data.py* in the folder holding your code.

3. Move (or save) the data file to the folder where you are storing your code. (Make sure to rename the file so it matches the name you use in the code. The book uses *data-text.json*.)

4. Go back to your code editor, which should still have the *import_json_data.py* file open.

Let's read through the code and compare it to the CSV import file. First, we import Python's built-in `json` library:

```
import json
```

Then we use the `open` function we are already familiar with to open the file *data-text.json* and call the `read` method on the open file:

```
json_data = open('data-text.json').read()
```

In the CSV file, we did not call `read`. What is the difference? In the CSV example, we opened the file in read-only mode, but in the JSON example, we are reading the contents of the file into our `json_data` variable. In the CSV example, the `open` function returns an object that is a *file*, but in the JSON example, we first open and then read the file, so we have a `str` (string). This difference is based on the fact that the Python `json` and `csv` libraries handle input in different ways. If you tried to pass a string into the CSV reader, it would throw an error, and the JSON `loads` function would throw an error if you passed it a file.

The good news is that Python makes it easy to write a string to a file (e.g., if you needed to use the CSV reader but only had a string), and it's also easy to read a file into a string. To Python, a closed file is just a filename string waiting to be opened and read. Getting data from a file, reading it into a string, and passing that string to a function requires just a few lines of Python code.

 From the folder where you have the JSON file stored, you can type the following into your Python interpreter and see what kind of object type each version outputs:

```
filename = 'data-text.json'
type(open(filename, 'rb'))      # similar to csv code
type(open(filename).read())     # similar to json code
```

The Python `json` library's `loads` function expects a string, not a file. The Python `csv` library's `reader` function expects an open file. In the next line of our script, we will use the `loads` function, which loads a JSON string into Python. The output of this function is assigned to a variable called `data`:

```
data = json.loads(json_data)
```

To preview our data, we iterate over each item and print it out. This isn't necessary for our code, but it helps us preview the data and make sure it's in the proper form:

```
for item in data:
    print item
```

Once you are done writing your file you can save and run it. As you can see, opening and converting a JSON file to a list of dictionaries in Python is quite easy. In the next section, we will explore more customized file handling.

XML Data

XML is often formatted to be both human and machine readable. However, the CSV and JSON examples were a lot easier to preview and understand than the XML file for this dataset. Luckily for us, the data is the same, so we are familiar with it. Download and save the XML version (*http://bit.ly/life_expectancy_xml*) of the life expectancy rates data (*http://bit.ly/life_expectancy_data*) in the folder where you are saving content associated with this chapter.

If a file has an *.xml* file extension, then it's XML data. If it has an *.html* or *.xhtml* file extension, it can sometimes be parsed using XML parsers.

As we do with all of our data, let's open the file in a code editor to preview it. If you scroll through the file, you will see the familiar data we covered in the CSV example. The data looks different, though, because it's presented in XML format, using things called *tags*.

XML is a markup language, which means it has a document structure that contains formatted data. XML documents are essentially just specially formatted data files.

The following snippet is a sampling of the XML data we are working with. In this example, <Observation />, <Dim />, and <Display /> are all examples of tags. Tags (or nodes) store data in a hierarchical and structured way:

```
<GHO ...>
    <Data>
        <Observation FactID="4543040" Published="true"
        Dataset="CYCU" EffectiveDate="2014-03-27" EndDate="2900-12-31">
            <Dim Category="COUNTRY" Code="SOM"/>
            <Dim Category="REGION" Code="EMR"/>
            <Dim Category="WORLDBANKINCOMEGROUP" Code="WB_LI"/>
```

```
        <Dim Category="GHO" Code="WHOSIS_000002"/>
        <Dim Category="YEAR" Code="2012"/>
        <Dim Category="SEX" Code="FMLE"/>
        <Dim Category="PUBLISHSTATE" Code="PUBLISHED"/>
        <Value Numeric="46.00000">
            <Display>46</Display>
        </Value>
    </Observation>
    <Observation FactID="4209598" Published="true"
    Dataset="CYCU" EffectiveDate="2014-03-25" EndDate="2900-12-31">
        <Dim Category="WORLDBANKINCOMEGROUP" Code="WB_HI"/>
        <Dim Category="YEAR" Code="2000"/>
        <Dim Category="SEX" Code="BTSX"/>
        <Dim Category="COUNTRY" Code="AND"/>
        <Dim Category="REGION" Code="EUR"/>
        <Dim Category="GHO" Code="WHOSIS_000001"/>
        <Dim Category="PUBLISHSTATE" Code="PUBLISHED"/>
        <Value Numeric="80.00000">
            <Display>80</Display>
        </Value>
    </Observation>
  </Data>
</GHO>
```

Data values can be stored in two places in an XML file: either in between two tags, as in `<Display>46</Display>`, where the value for the `<Display>` tag is 46; or as an *attribute* of a tag, as in `<Dim Category="COUNTRY" Code="SOM"/>`, where the value of the `Category` attribute is `"COUNTRY"` and the value of the `Code` attribute is `"SOM"`. XML attributes store extra information for a particular tag, nested inside a single tag.

Whereas in JSON you might store data in key/value pairs, in XML you can store data in pairs or groups of threes or fours. The XML tags and attributes hold data, similar to the JSON keys. So when we look again at the `Display` tag, the value for that tag is held within the opening and closing portions of the tag. When we view the `Dim` node, we see it has two different attributes with values (`Category` and `Code`). XML formatting allows us to store more than one attribute in each node. For those of you familiar with HTML, this should look familiar. That's because HTML is closely related to XML; they both carry attributes inside nodes (or tags), and they are both Markup languages (*https://en.wikipedia.org/wiki/Markup_language*).

Although there are some well-known standards for forming XML tags and naming attributes, much of the structure is dictated by the person (or machine) who designs or creates the XML. You can never assume consistency if you're using datasets from different sources. For more reading on XML best practices, IBM has provided some great talking points. (*http://bit.ly/elements_v_attributes*)

How to Import XML Data

Because we have an understanding of the data, let's import the file into a usable form for Python. To get the data out of XML form and into Python, we will write the following code:

```
from xml.etree import ElementTree as ET

tree = ET.parse('data-text.xml')
root = tree.getroot()

data = root.find('Data')

all_data = []

for observation in data:
    record = {}
    for item in observation:

        lookup_key = item.attrib.keys()[0]

        if lookup_key == 'Numeric':
            rec_key = 'NUMERIC'
            rec_value = item.attrib['Numeric']
        else:
            rec_key = item.attrib[lookup_key]
            rec_value = item.attrib['Code']

        record[rec_key] = rec_value

    all_data.append(record)

print all_data
```

As you can see, this is a little more complicated than the CSV and JSON examples.

Let's take a closer look. Create a new file in your code editor and save it to the folder where you have been putting your code. Name it *import_xml_data.py*. Also, if you downloaded the data directly from the WHO site and not the book's repository, rename the saved XML file *data-text.xml* and put it in the same folder as your new code.

First, let's import `ElementTree` (*http://bit.ly/elementtree_api*), part of the built-in library we are going to use to parse the XML:

```
from xml.etree import ElementTree as ET
```

As mentioned earlier, there are often multiple solutions to a problem. While we use ElementTree in this example, there is another library you could use called lxml (*http://lxml.de/*), and yet another called minidom (*http://bit.ly/minimal_dom*).

Because all three of these solutions can be used to solve the same problem, if you find a good example using one of the libraries, we encourage you to explore the data using another library as well. As you learn Python, choose libraries that seem easiest for you to understand (it just so happens that in many cases these are the best choices).

This import statement has an extra component we did not have last time: as ET. We are importing ElementTree, but will refer to it as ET. Why? Because we are lazy and do not want to type out ElementTree every time we want to use the library. This is a common practice when importing classes or functions with long names, but it is not mandatory. The as tells Python we want to use ET to represent ElementTree.

Next, we call the parse method on the ET class, which will parse data from the filename we pass. Because we are parsing a file located in the same folder, the filename needs no file path:

```
tree = ET.parse('data-text.xml')
```

The parse method returns a Python object people normally store in a variable tree. When talking about XML, the *tree* is the whole XML object stored in a way Python can understand and parse.

To understand how to traverse the tree (and data contained therein), we begin at the root of the tree. The root is the first XML tag. To start at the root of the tree, we call the getroot function:

```
root = tree.getroot()
```

If you were to take a moment to print out root by adding print root after the previous statement, you would find it prints out the Python representation of the root element in the XML tree (it should look like <Element 'GHO' at 0x1079e79d0>[2]). From this representation, we can quickly tell ElementTree identified the root or outermost tag of the XML document as an XML node with a tag name GHO.

Now that we've identified the root, we need to figure out how to access the data we want. After analyzing the data in this chapter's CSV and JSON sections, we know

---

[2] When using Python objects with a longer numeric and hex string, this is Python's way of showing memory address information. It's not necessary for our data wrangling needs so please ignore it if your memory addresses don't look like ours.

what data we'd like to review. We need to traverse the XML tree and extract that same data. In order to understand what we're looking for, we need to understand the overall structure and format of the XML tree. Here, we've slimmed down the XML file we are using and removed the data, so we can view *just* the core structure:

```
<GHO>
    <Data>
        <Observation>
            <Dim />
            <Dim />
            <Dim />
            <Dim />
            <Dim />
            <Dim />
            <Value>
                <Display>
                </Display>
            </Value>
        </Observation>
        <Observation>
            <Dim />
            <Dim />
            <Dim />
            <Dim />
            <Dim />
            <Dim />
            <Value>
                <Display>
                </Display>
            </Value>
        </Observation>
    </Data>
</GHO>
```

In reviewing this structure, we can see each "row" of data is held in an `Observation` tag. The data for each of these rows is then held in the `Dim`, `Value`, and `Display` nodes within each `Observation` node.

So far we have three lines of code. To investigate how we can use Python to extract these nodes, let's add `print dir(root)` to the end of our current code, then save the file and run it on the command line:

```
python import_xml_data.py
```

You will see all the methods and properties of the `root` variable. Your code should look like this:

```
from xml.etree import ElementTree as ET

tree = ET.parse('data-text.xml')
root = tree.getroot()
```

```
print dir(root)
```

When you run the file, you should see this output:

```
['__class__', '__delattr__', '__delitem__', '__dict__', '__doc__',
 '__format__', '__getattribute__', '__getitem__', '__hash__', '__init__',
 '__len__', '__module__', '__new__', '__nonzero__', '__reduce__',
 '__reduce_ex__', '__repr__', '__setattr__', '__setitem__', '__sizeof__',
 '__str__', '__subclasshook__', '__weakref__', '_children', 'append', 'attrib',
 'clear', 'copy', 'extend', 'find', 'findall', 'findtext', 'get',
 'getchildren', 'getiterator', 'insert', 'items', 'iter', 'iterfind',
 'itertext', 'keys', 'makeelement', 'remove', 'set', 'tag', 'tail', 'text']
```

Let's assume our file is too large for us to open, and that we don't know the structure of the file. This is often the case with larger XML datasets. What can we do? Let's start by calling dir(root) to review the root object's methods. We notice the getchildren method as a potential solution for seeing children in the Observation nodes. After reading the latest documentation (*http://bit.ly/getchildren*) and a question on Stack Overflow (*http://bit.ly/get_subelements*), we find the getchildren method will return the subelements, but the method has been deprecated. When a method you want to use is or will soon become deprecated, you should attempt to use what the authors of the library suggest as a replacement.

 When a method, class, or function is *deprecated*, it means this functionality will likely be removed from future releases of the library or module. For this reason, you should *always* avoid using deprecated methods or classes and make sure you read through the documentation, as the authors have likely recommended what to use going forward.

Based on what the documentation is recommending, if we want to view subelements for the root tree, we should use list(root). If we have a very large file, returning direct subelements will give us a view of the data and its structure, without overwhelming us with too many lines of output. Let's try that.

Replace this line:

```
print dir(root)
```

with this line:

```
print list(root)
```

Run the file again from your command line. You should end up with the following output, which is a list of Element objects (for our purposes, *elements* are XML nodes):

```
[<Element 'QueryParameter' at 0x101bfd290>,
 <Element 'QueryParameter' at 0x101bfd350>,
 <Element 'QueryParameter' at 0x101bfd410>,
```

```
<Element 'QueryParameter' at 0x101bfd590>,
<Element 'QueryParameter' at 0x101bfd610>,
<Element 'QueryParameter' at 0x101bfd650>,
<Element 'Copyright' at 0x101bfd690>,
<Element 'Disclaimer' at 0x101bfd710>,
<Element 'Metadata' at 0x101bfd790>,
<Element 'Data' at 0x102540250>]
```

The list contains Element objects called QueryParameter, Copyright, Disclaimer, Metadata, and Data. We can traverse these elements and explore the contents so we better understand how to extract the data we are after.

When searching for data stored in an XML tree, the Data element is likely a good place to start. Now we have found the Data element, and we can focus on that subelement. There are a couple of ways to get the Data element, but we will use the find method. The root element's find method allows us to search for a subelement using the tag name. Then, we will get the Element's children and see what we should do next.

Replace this line:

```
print list(root)
```

with this:

```
data = root.find('Data')

print list(data)
```

 There is also a findall method we could use. The difference between find and findall is that find will return the first matching element, while findall will return all of the matching elements. We know there is only one Data Element, so we can use find instead of findall. If there was more than one Element, we would want to use the findall method to get the whole list of matching elements and iterate over them.

When you rerun your file with the new lines of code, you will see a dizzying output of a list of Observation elements. These are our data points. Although there is a lot of information output, you can tell it is a list because the last character is a], which symbolizes the end of a list.

Let's iterate over the list of data. Each Observation represents a row of data, so they should have more information contained inside. We can iterate over those elements individually to see what subelements exist. With a Python Element objects, we can iterate over all of the subelements similar to how we would a list. Therefore, we can iterate over each Observation and iterate over each subelement in the Observation elements. This is our first time using a loop within a loop, and it should show us whether there are more subelements we can use to extract data.

 Because XML stores data in nodes, subnodes, and attributes, you'll often want to take the approach of exploring each node and subnode (or element and subelement) until you get a good idea of not only how the data is structured but also how Python *sees* the data.

Replace this line:

```
print list(data)
```

with these lines:

```
for observation in data:
    for item in observation:
        print item
```

and rerun the file.

The output is a bunch of `Dim` and `Value` objects. Let's try a couple of different ways to explore what might be contained in these elements. There are a few ways you can view data within Python's `Element` object. One of the attributes of every `Element` node is `text`, which displays the text contained inside the node.

Replace this line:

```
print item
```

with this line:

```
print item.text
```

and rerun the file.

What happened? You should have gotten a lot of `None` values back. This is because `item.text` does not exist for those elements because there is no text between the elements' tags. Look at how `<Dim />` is structured in the data samples. For example:

```
<Dim Category="YEAR" Code="2000"/>
```

In Python, `item.text` is only useful if your elements are structured with text in the nodes, like the following:

```
<Dim Category="YEAR">2000</Dim>
```

For the second example, `item.text` returns `2000`.

XML data can be structured in many different ways. The information we need is located in the XML; it just wasn't in the first place we looked. Let's continue to explore.

Another place to look is in child elements. Child elements are subelements of a parent element. Let's check if we have any child elements. Replace this line:

```
print item.text
```

with this line:

```
print list(item)
```

When you rerun the code with that change, the output shows that some (but not all) elements have children. That's interesting! These are actually `Value` elements. Look at how these are structured in the data sample:

```
<Value>
    <Display>
    </Display>
</Value>
```

If we want to explore those child elements, we'll need another loop similar to the loop we wrote to go through the items in each `Observation`.

There is another method we can call for each `Element` object in Python, called `attrib`, which returns the attributes for each node. As we know from reviewing XML structure, if nodes don't have values between the tags, they usually have attributes within the tags.

To see what attributes we have in our nodes, replace:

```
print list(item)
```

with this line:

```
print item.attrib
```

When we rerun the code, we see the data contained in the attributes output as a bunch of dictionaries. Rather than storing each element and the attributes in separate dictionaries, we want each full row of data in a dictionary together. Here is one record from our `attrib` output:

```
{'Category': 'PUBLISHSTATE', 'Code': 'PUBLISHED'}
{'Category': 'COUNTRY', 'Code': 'ZWE'}
{'Category': 'WORLDBANKINCOMEGROUP', 'Code': 'WB_LI'}
{'Category': 'YEAR', 'Code': '2012'}
{'Category': 'SEX', 'Code': 'BTSX'}
{'Category': 'GHO', 'Code': 'WHOSIS_000002'}
{'Category': 'REGION', 'Code': 'AFR'}
{'Numeric': '49.00000'}
```

Because we ended up with a dictionary for every record in our CSV example, let's try to put this output in a similar form. The keys in our XML data dictionary will be slightly different, because the WHO does not provide the same data in the XML dataset as in the CSV dataset. We will work to get our data in the following form, but ignore the difference in key names. Ultimately, this will not affect how we use the data.

Just to remind you, here is a sample record from the CSV reader:

```
{
    'Indicator': 'Healthy life expectancy (HALE) at birth (years)',
    'Country': 'Zimbabwe',
    'Comments': '',
    'Display Value': '51',
    'World Bank income group': 'Low-income',
    'Numeric': '51.00000',
    'Sex': 'Female',
    'High': '',
    'Low': '',
    'Year': '2012',
    'WHO region': 'Africa',
    'PUBLISH STATES': 'Published'
}
```

Here is the goal for a sample record using our XML data. We aim to have it in this format by the time we are done parsing our XML tree:

```
{
    'COUNTRY': 'ZWE',
    'GHO': 'WHOSIS_000002',
    'Numeric': '49.00000',
    'PUBLISHSTATE': 'PUBLISHED',
    'REGION': 'AFR',
    'SEX': 'BTSX',
    'WORLDBANKINCOMEGROUP': 'WB_LI',
    'YEAR': '2012'
}
```

Notice the High and Low fields are missing. If they existed in our XML dataset, we would add them to the keys of our new dictionary. The Display Value is also missing. We decided not to include it, as it's the same as the Numeric value.

Currently, your code should look like this:

```
from xml.etree import ElementTree as ET

tree = ET.parse('data-text.xml')
root = tree.getroot()

data = root.find('Data')

for observation in data:
    for item in observation:
        print item.attrib
```

To create the data structure, we need to first create an empty dictionary for each record. We will use this dictionary to add keys and values, then we will append each record to a list, so we have a final list of all of our records (similar to our CSV data).

Let's add our empty dictionary and an empty list to hold our data in. Add `all_data = []` on a new line above the outer `for` loop and `record = {}` as the first line in the `for` loop, like so:

```
all_data = []

for observation in data:
    record = {}
    for item in observation:
        print item.attrib
```

Now we need to figure out what our key and values are for each line and add them to our record's dictionary. For each `attrib` call, we get a dictionary with one or more value and key combinations returned, like this:

```
{'Category': 'YEAR', 'Code': '2012'}
```

It looks like the value of the `Category` key (here, `YEAR`) should be the key for our dictionary, and the value of `Code` (here, `2012`) should be set as the value for that key. As you'll recall from Chapter 2, a dictionary key should be easily used for lookup (like `YEAR`) and dictionary value should contain the value associated with that key (like `2012`). With that knowledge, the preceding line would become:

```
'YEAR': '2012'
```

Update `print item.attrib` to `print item.attrib.keys()` in your code, then rerun it:

```
for item in observation:
    print item.attrib.keys()
```

It will output the keys of each attribute dictionary. We want to check the keys so we can form the keys and values of the new item dictionary. We end up with two different outputs: `['Category', 'Code']` and `['Numeric']`. Let's tackle one at a time. Based on our initial investigation, for the elements with both `Category` and `Code`, we know we need to use the `Category` values as keys and the `Code` values as values.

To do this, add `[0]` to the end of `item.attrib.keys()`:

```
for item in observation:
    lookup_key = item.attrib.keys()[0]
    print lookup_key
```

This is called *indexing*. It will return the first item in the list.

If we rerun the code and look at the output, we now have the following:

```
Category
Category
Category
Category
Category
Category
Category
Numeric
```

Now that we have the key names, we can look up the values. We need the values of the Category key to use as the keys in our new dictionary. Update the inner for loop by creating a new variable, rec_key, which stores the value returned from item.attrib[lookup_key]:

```
for item in observation:
    lookup_key = item.attrib.keys()[0]
    rec_key = item.attrib[lookup_key]
    print rec_key
```

With these updates, rerun the code from your command line. For each record, we get the following values:

```
PUBLISHSTATE
COUNTRY
WORLDBANKINCOMEGROUP
YEAR
SEX
GHO
```

```
REGION
49.00000
```

These all look like great keys for our new dictionary, except for the last one. This is because the last element is a Numeric dictionary instead of the Category ones we have been working with. If we want to retain that data for our use, we need to set up a special case for those numeric elements using an if statement.

Python's if Statement

In its most basic form, the if statement is a way to control the flow of your code. When you use an if statement, you are telling the code: if this condition is met, then do something particular.

Another way to use if is followed with an else. An if-else statement says: if the first condition is met, then do something, but if it is not, then do what is in the else statement.

Besides if and if-else, you will see == as a comparison operator. While = sets a variable equal to a value, == tests to see if two values are equal. In addition, != tests to see if they are not equal. Both of these operators return Boolean values: True or False.

Try the following examples in your Python interpreter:

```
x = 5

if x == 5:
    print 'x is equal to 5.'
```

What did you see? x == 5 will return True, and so the text will have printed. Now try:

```
x = 3

if x == 5:
    print 'x is equal to 5.'
else:
    print 'x is not equal to 5.'
```

Because x equals 3 and not 5 in this example, you should have received the print statement in the else block of code. You can use if and if-else statements in Python to help guide the logic and flow of your code.

We want to see when lookup_key is equal to Numeric, and use Numeric as the key instead of the value (like we did with the Category keys). Update your code with the following:

```
for item in observation:

    lookup_key = item.attrib.keys()[0]
```

```
    if lookup_key == 'Numeric':
        rec_key = 'NUMERIC'
    else:
        rec_key = item.attrib[lookup_key]

    print rec_key
```

If you run your updated code, all of your keys should now look like keys. Now, let's pull out the values we want to store in our new dictionary and associate them with those keys. In the case of Numeric, it's simple, because we just want the Numeric key's value. Make the following changes to your code:

```
    if lookup_key == 'Numeric':
        rec_key = 'NUMERIC'
        rec_value = item.attrib['Numeric']
    else:
        rec_key = item.attrib[lookup_key]
        rec_value = None

    print rec_key, rec_value
```

If you run the updated code, you will see the rec_value for Numeric is properly matched. For example:

```
    NUMERIC 49.00000
```

For all other values, we set the rec_value to None. In Python, None is used to represent a null value. Let's populate those with real values. Remember each record has a Category and a Code key, like so: {'Category': 'YEAR', 'Code': '2012'}. For these elements, we want to store the Code value as the rec_value. Update the line rec_value = None, so your if-else statement looks like the one shown here:

```
    if lookup_key == 'Numeric':
        rec_key = 'NUMERIC'
        rec_value = item.attrib['Numeric']
    else:
        rec_key = item.attrib[lookup_key]
        rec_value = item.attrib['Code']

    print rec_key, rec_value
```

Rerun the code, and you should now see that we have values for our rec_key and our rec_value. Let's build the dictionary:

```
    if lookup_key == 'Numeric':
        rec_key = 'NUMERIC'
        rec_value = item.attrib['Numeric']
    else:
        rec_key = item.attrib[lookup_key]
        rec_value = item.attrib['Code']
```

```
        record[rec_key] = rec_value ❶
```

❶ Adds each key and value to the record dictionary.

We also need to add each record to our all_data list. As we saw in "List Methods:
Things Lists Can Do" on page 32, we can use the list's append method to add values to
our list. We need to append each record at the end of the outer for loop, as that is
when it will have all of the keys for each of the subelements. Finally, we will add a
print at the end of the file, to show our data.

Your full code to transform the XML tree to a dictionary should look like this:

```python
from xml.etree import ElementTree as ET

tree = ET.parse('data-text.xml')
root = tree.getroot()

data = root.find('Data')

all_data = []

for observation in data:
    record = {}
    for item in observation:

        lookup_key = item.attrib.keys()[0]

        if lookup_key == 'Numeric':
            rec_key = 'NUMERIC'
            rec_value = item.attrib['Numeric']
        else:
            rec_key = item.attrib[lookup_key]
            rec_value = item.attrib['Code']

        record[rec_key] = rec_value

    all_data.append(record)

print all_data
```

Once you run the code, you will see a long list with a dictionary for each record, just
like in the CSV example:

```
{'COUNTRY': 'ZWE', 'REGION': 'AFR', 'WORLDBANKINCOMEGROUP': 'WB_LI',
 'NUMERIC': '49.00000', 'SEX': 'BTSX', 'YEAR': '2012',
 'PUBLISHSTATE': 'PUBLISHED', 'GHO': 'WHOSIS_000002'}
```

As you can see, extracting data from the XML was a little more complicated. Sometimes CSV and JSON files won't be as easy to process as they were in this chapter, but
they are usually more easily processed than XML files. However, looking at the XML

data allowed you to explore and grow as a Python developer, giving you a chance to create empty lists and dictionaries and populate them with data. You also honed your debugging skills as you explored how to extract data from the XML tree structure. These are valuable lessons in your quest to become a better data wrangler.

Summary

Being able to handle machine-readable data formats with Python is one of the must-have skills for a data wrangler. In this chapter, we covered the CSV, JSON, and XML file types. Table 3-2 provides a reminder of the libraries we used to import and manipulate the different files containing the WHO data.

Table 3-2. File types and file extensions

File type	File extensions	Python library
CSV, TSV	.csv, .tsv	csv (*https://docs.python.org/2/library/csv.html*)
JSON	.json, .js	json (*https://docs.python.org/2/library/json.html*)

We also covered a few new Python concepts. At this point, you should know how to run Python code from the Python interpreter and how to save the code to a new file and run it from the command line. We also learned about importing files using import, and how to read and open files with Python on your local filesystem.

Other new programming concepts we covered include using for loops to iterate over files, lists, or trees and using if-else statements to determine whether a certain condition has been met and to do something depending on that evaluation. Table 3-3 summarizes those new functions and code logic you learned about here.

Table 3-3. New Python programming concepts

Concept	Purpose
import (*http://bit.ly/python_import*)	Imports a module into the Python space
open (*http://bit.ly/python_open*)	Built-in function that opens a file in Python on your system
for loop (*http://bit.ly/basic_for_loops*)	A piece of code that runs *n* times
if-else statement (*http://bit.ly/simple_if_statements*)	Runs a piece of code if a certain condition is met
== (*http://bit.ly/python_comparisons*) (equal to operator)	Tests to see if one value is equal to another
Indexing a sequence (*http://bit.ly/python_sequence_types*)	Pulls out the *n*th object in the sequence (string, list, etc.)

Lastly, in this chapter we started to create and save a lot of code files and data files. Assuming you did all the exercises in this chapter, you should have three code files and three data files. Earlier in the chapter, there was a recommendation for how to organize your code. If you have not done this already, do it now. Here is one example of how to organize your data so far:

```
data_wrangling/
    code/
        ch3_easy_data/
            import_csv_data.py
            import_xml_data.py
            import_json_data.py
            data-text.csv
            data-text.xml
            data-json.json
        ch4_hard_data/
            ...
```

Now, on to harder data formats!

## CHAPTER 4

Working with Excel Files

Unlike the previous chapter's data, not all the data in this and the following chapter will easily import into Python without a little work. This is because some data formats were made to be machine readable, while others, such as the ones we'll look at next, were meant to be interacted with through desktop tools. In this chapter and the next, we will look at two example file types—Excel files and PDFs—and provide some generic instructions to follow if you encounter a different file type.

So far in this book, the solutions you've learned about for importing data have been pretty standard. In this chapter, we will begin to learn about processes which will vary greatly each time you perform them. Although the processes are more difficult, the end goal is the same: to extract the useful information and put it into a usable format in Python.

The examples we use in this chapter and the next contain data from UNICEF's 2014 report on The State of the World's Children (*http://www.unicef.org/sowc2014/ numbers/*). The data is available in PDF and Excel format.

When you have to extract data from files in these more difficult formats, you might think there is someone out there who hates you, because it can be painful. We assure you in most cases, the person who generated the file with the data inside simply did not identify the importance of also releasing it in a machine-readable format.

Installing Python Packages

Before we can continue, we need to learn how to install external Python packages (or libraries). Up until this point, we were using Python libraries that came standard with Python when you installed it. Do you remember importing the csv and json packages in Chapter 3? Those were packages in the standard library—they came with your Python installation.

Python comes with a set of frequently used libraries. Because many libraries serve a niche purpose, you have to explicitly install them. This is so your computer doesn't get bloated with every Python library available.

Python packages are collected in an online directory called PyPI (*https://pypi.python.org/pypi*), which stores the packages along with their metadata and any documentation.

In this chapter, we are looking at Excel files. If you visit PyPI in your browser, you can search for libraries relating to Excel (*http://bit.ly/excel_packages*) and see lists of matching package results you can download. This is one way to explore which package you should use.

We will be using pip from this point forward to install packages. There are multiple ways to install pip (*http://bit.ly/install_pip*), and you should have already done so in Chapter 1 of this book.

First, we will be evaluating Excel data. Let's install the package to do that— xlrd (*https://pypi.python.org/pypi/xlrd/0.9.3*). To install the package, we use pip in the following way:

```
pip install xlrd
```

To remove the package, we would run the `uninstall` command:

```
pip uninstall xlrd
```

Try installing, uninstalling, and then reinstalling xlrd. It's good to get a handle on the `pip` commands, as you'll be using them throughout this book and your data wrangling career.

Why did we choose xlrd when there are many possible packages? Choosing a Python library is an imperfect process. There are different ways to go about your selection. Don't worry about trying to figure out what is the *right* library. When you are perfecting your skills and you find a couple of options, use the library that makes sense to you.

The first thing we recommend is searching the Web to see which libraries other people recommend. If you search for "parse excel using python" (*http://bit.ly/parse_excel_using_python*), you will find the xlrd library surfaces at the top of the search results.

However, the answer is not always obvious. In Chapter 13, we will learn more about the selection process when looking into Twitter libraries.

Parsing Excel Files

Sometimes the easiest way to extract data from an Excel sheet is finding a better way to get the data. There are times when parsing is not the answer. Before you start parsing, ask yourself the following questions:

- Have you tried to find the data in another form? Sometimes other forms might be available from the same source.
- Have you tried to use a phone to figure out if the data is available in another form? Check out Chapter 6 for more tips.
- Have you tried to export the tab or tabs into CSV form from Excel (or your document reader)? This is a good solution if you only have a couple of tabs of data or isolated data in one tab on the Excel sheet.

If you have exhausted these options and you still don't have the data you need, you'll need to use Python to parse your Excel file.

Getting Started with Parsing

The library we identified for parsing Excel files is xlrd. This library is part of a series of libraries for working with Excel files in Python (*http://www.python-excel.org/*).

There are three main libraries for handling Excel files:

xlrd
    Reads Excel files

xlwt
    Writes and formats Excel files

xlutils
    A set of tools for more advanced operations in Excel (requires xlrd and xlwt)

You'll need to install each separately if you want to use them; however, in this chapter we will only use xlrd. Because we want to read Excel files into Python, you'll need to make sure you have xlrd installed before continuing:

```
pip install xlrd
```

If you get the following error, that means you don't have pip installed:

```
-bash: pip: command not found
```

For installation instructions, refer to "Install pip" on page 14 or *https://pip.pypa.io/en/latest/installing/*.

Set up your work environment for this Excel file by doing the following (or something like it, depending on your organizational system):

1. Create a folder for your Excel work.
2. Create a new Python file called *parse_excel.py* and put it in the folder you created.
3. Place the Excel file from the book's repository (*https://github.com/jackiekazil/data-wrangling*) called *SOWC 2014 Stat Tables_Table 9.xlsx* in the same folder.

From this folder, type the following command in your terminal to run the script from the command line:

```
python parse_excel.py
```

By the end of this chapter, we will write a script to parse child labor and marriage data stored in this Excel file.

To start our script, we need to import xlrd and open our Excel workbook in Python. We store the opened file in the book variable:

```
import xlrd

book = xlrd.open_workbook('SOWC 2014 Stat Tables_Table 9.xlsx')
```

Unlike CSVs, Excel books can have multiple tabs or sheets. To get at our data, we are going to pull out only the sheet with the data we want.

If you have a couple of sheets, you could just guess at the index, but that won't work if you have lots of sheets. So, you should know about the command book.sheet_by_name(*somename*), where *somename* is the name of the sheet you want to access.

Let's check out the names of the sheets we have:

```
import xlrd

book = xlrd.open_workbook('SOWC 2014 Stat Tables_Table 9.xlsx')

for sheet in book.sheets():
    print sheet.name
```

The sheet that we are looking for is Table 9. So, let's put that into our script:

```
import xlrd

book = xlrd.open_workbook('SOWC 2014 Stat Tables_Table 9.xlsx')
sheet = book.sheet_by_name('Table 9')

print sheet
```

If you run that code, it exits with an error that provides you with the following information:

```
xlrd.biffh.XLRDError: No sheet named <'Table 9'>
```

At this point, you might be really confused. The problem lies in the difference between what we see and what actually exists.

If you open up your Excel workbook and select the name of the sheet by double-clicking it, you will find that there is an extra space at the end. This space is not visible to users in the browser. In Chapter 7, we will learn how to troubleshoot this in Python. For now, update your code to reflect the space.

Change this line:

```
sheet = book.sheet_by_name('Table 9')
```

to this:

```
sheet = book.sheet_by_name('Table 9 ')
```

Now, if we run our script it should work. You will see output similar to this:

```
<xlrd.sheet.Sheet object at 0x102a575d0>
```

Let's explore what we can do with a sheet. Add the following after you assign the sheet variable and rerun your script:

```
print dir(sheet)
```

In the returned list, you'll see a method called nrows. We will use this method to iterate over all rows. If we write print sheet.nrows, the total number of rows will be returned.

Try this now:

```
print sheet.nrows
```

You should have gotten back 303. We need to iterate over each row, which means we need a for loop. As we learned in "How to Import CSV Data" on page 46, for loops iterate over items in a list, so we need to turn 303 into a list we can iterate over 303 times. To do this, we will use the range function.

What Is range()?

Remember how we mentioned that Python has some helpful built-in functions? Well, range is one of those. The range (*http://bit.ly/python_range*) function will take the number as an argument and output a list of that many items.

To see how it works, open up your Python interpreter and try the following:

```
range(3)
```

The output should be:

```
[0, 1, 2]
```

Three items were returned. Now, we can create a for loop to loop three times by iterating over that list.

Some things to note about range:

- The list returned starts with 0. This is because Python starts list counts with 0. If you need your list to start at 1, you can set the start and end of the range. For example, range(1, 4) would return [1, 2, 3]. Notice the last number is not included in the list, so to get [1, 2, 3] we had to set the end number to 4.

- There is another function called xrange in Python 2.7. There are slight differences, but not anything you would notice unless you are processing very large datasets—xrange is faster.

With the addition of the range function we can transform 303 into a list our for loop can iterate over, our script should look like the following:

```
import xlrd

book = xlrd.open_workbook('SOWC 2014 Stat Tables_Table 9.xlsx')
sheet = book.sheet_by_name('Table 9 ')

for i in range(sheet.nrows):          ❶
    print i                           ❷
```

❶ Loops over the index i in range(303), which will be a list of 303 integers incrementing by one.

❷ Outputs i, which will be the numbers from 0 to 302.

From here, we need to do a lookup on each of the rows to pull out the contents of each row instead of just printing the number. To do a lookup, we will use i as an index reference to take the nth row.

To get each row's values we will use `row_values`, which was another method returned by `dir(sheet)` earlier. We can see from the `row_values` documentation (*http://bit.ly/ xlrd_row_values*) that the method expects an index number and returns the corresponding row's values. Update your `for` loop to reflect this and rerun your script:

```
for i in range(sheet.nrows):
    print sheet.row_values(i)          ❶
```

❶ Uses `i` as the index to look up the row's values. Because it is in a `for` loop that spans the length of the sheet, we call this method for each row in our sheet.

When you run this code, you will see a list for each row. The following is a subset of the data you'll see:

```
['', u'TABLE 9. CHILD PROTECTION', '', '', '', '', '', '', '', '', '', '',
'', '', '', '', '', '', '', '', '', '', '', '', '', '', '', '', '', '',
'', '', '', '', '', '', '', '', '', '', '', '', '', '']
['', '', u'TABLEAU 9. PROTECTION DE L\u2019ENFANT', '', '', '', '', '',
'', '', '', '', '', '', '', '', '', '', '', '', '', '', '', '', '', '',
'', '', '', '', '', '', '', '', '', '', '', '', '', '', '', '']
['', '', '', u'TABLA 9. PROTECCI\xd3N INFANTIL', '', '', '', '', '', '',
'', '', '', '', '', '', '', '', '', '', '', '', '', '', '', '', '', '',
'', '', '', '', '', '', '', '', '', '', '', '', '', '']
['', '', '', '', '', '', '', '', '', '', '', '', '', '', '', '', '', '',
'', '', '', '', '', '', '', '', '', '', '', '', '', '', '', '', '', '',
'', '', '', '', '', '']
['', u'Countries and areas', '', '', u'Child labour (%)+\n2005\u20132012*',
'', '', '', '', '', u'Child marriage (%)\n2005\u20132012*', '', '', '',
u'Birth registration (%)+\n2005\u20132012*', '', u'Female genital mutilation/
cutting (%)+\n2002\u20132012*', '', '', '', '', '', u'Justification of wife
beating (%)\n 2005\u20132012*', '', '', '', u'Violent discipline
(%)+\n2005\u20132012*', '', '', '', '', '', '', '', '', '', '', '', '', '',
'', '', '', '']
```

Now that we can see each row, we need to pull out the information we want. To help us determine what information we need and how to get it, it's much easier to open up the file in a program for displaying Excel files, such as Microsoft Excel on Windows or Numbers on Mac. If you visit the second tab on the spreadsheet, you will notice quite a few header rows.

In our code, we will aim to grab the English text. However, if you want an extra challenge, try to pull out the French or Spanish headings and countries.

On the second tab, look at the information you can extract and think about how to best organize it. We provide one possible way to do this here, but there are many different ways using different data structures.

For this exercise, we will pull out child labor and child marriage statistics. The following is one way to organize the data—we'll use this as an example to work toward:

```
{
    u'Afghanistan': {
        'child_labor': {
            'female': [9.6, ''],  ❶
            'male': [11.0, ''],
            'total': [10.3, '']},
        'child_marriage': {
            'married_by_15': [15.0, ''],
            'married_by_18': [40.4, '']
        }
    },
    u'Albania': {
        'child_labor': {
            'female': [9.4, u'  '],
            'male': [14.4, u'  '],
            'total': [12.0, u'  ']},
        'child_marriage': {
            'married_by_15': [0.2, ''],
            'married_by_18': [9.6, '']
        }
    },
    ...
}
```

❶ If you are viewing the data in Excel, some of these numbers might appear off. This is because Excel will often round numbers. We are showing the numbers you will find when you use Python to parse the cells.

 Planning what you want the outcome to look like and writing an example of your data will save you time as you begin coding. Once you have identified how you'd like to format your data, you can ask yourself, "What do I need to do next to get there?" This is especially helpful when you feel blocked on your next step.

There are two Python constructs we are going to use to pull the data out. The first method we will use is a *nested* for loop, which is a for loop inside another for loop. This is often used when you have x rows that contain y objects. To access each object you need a for loop for each row, then another for loop for each object. We also used a nested for loop in an example in Chapter 3.

We are going to use a nested for loop to output each cell from each row. This will output the items we saw earlier, where each row was listed.

```
for i in xrange(sheet.nrows):
    row = sheet.row_values(i)          ❶
```

```
    for cell in row:            ❷
        print cell               ❸
```

❶ Takes the list that is each row and saves it to the row variable. This makes our code more readable.

❷ Loops over each item in the list, which represents each cell for the current row.

❸ Outputs the cell value.

If you run your complete code with the nested for loop, you will notice your output is not so helpful anymore. That brings us to the second mechanism to explore our Excel file—*a counter*.

What Is a Counter?

A counter is a way to control the flow of your program. By using a counter, you can control your for loop by adding an if statement and increasing the count with each iteration of the loop. If the count ends up greater than a value of your choosing, the for loop will no longer process the code controlled by it. Try the following example in your interpreter:

```
count = 0                      ❶

for i in range(1000):          ❷
    if count < 10:             ❸
        print i
    count += 1                 ❹

print 'Count: ', count         ❺
```

❶ Sets the count variable equal to 0

❷ Creates a loop with items in the range of 0 to 999

❸ Tests if the count is less than 10; if so, prints 1

❹ Increases the count, so the count grows with each loop

❺ Outputs the final count

Let's add a counter to our code so we can step through the cells and rows to find what we want to pull out. Be careful where you place the counter—you will have very different results if you place it on the cell level versus the row level.

Reset your `for` loop to look like the code shown here:

```
count = 0
for i in xrange(sheet.nrows):
    if count < 10:
        row = sheet.row_values(i)
        print i, row          ❶

    count += 1
```

❶ Outputs `i` and the row so we can actually see which row number has which information

Now, if we go back to what we want our final output to look like, what we really need to figure out is where the country names begin. Remember, the country names are the first keys of our output dictionary:

```
{
    u'Afghanistan': {...},
    u'Albania': {...},
    ...
}
```

If you run your script with the counter in it where `count < 10`, you will see from the output that we have not yet reached the row where the country names start.

Because we are skipping a few lines to get to the data we are interested in, we are looking to identify which row number we will need to start our data collection. From our previous attempt, we know the country names start past row 10. But how can we tell where to start?

The answer is in the next code example, but before you look, try updating the counter to start at the row where the country names start. (There are multiple ways to do this, so if your answer is slightly different than what we have in the following code example, that's OK.)

After you identify the proper row number, you will need to add an `if` statement to begin pulling out values after that row. This is so we only work with the data below that line.

If you were able to get that working, your code should like something like this:

```
count = 0

for i in xrange(sheet.nrows):
    if count < 20:               ❶
        if i >= 14:              ❷
            row = sheet.row_values(i)
            print i, row
        count += 1
```

❶ This line will iterate through the first 20 rows to identify which row the country names begin on.

❷ This `if` statement starts the output at the point where the country rows appear.

At this point, you should have output that looks like this:

```
14 ['', u'Afghanistan', u'Afghanistan', u'Afganist\xe1n', 10.3, '', 11.0, '',
9.6, '', 15.0, '', 40.4, '', 37.4, '', u'\u2013', '', u'\u2013', '',
u'\u2013', '', u'\u2013', '', 90.2, '', 74.4, '', 74.8, '', 74.1, '', '', '',
'', '', '', '', '', '', '', '', '', '']
15 ['', u'Albania', u'Albanie', u'Albania', 12.0, u' ', 14.4, u' ', 9.4,
u' ', 0.2, '', 9.6, '', 98.6, '', u'\u2013', '', u'\u2013', '', u'\u2013',
'', 36.4, '', 29.8, '', 75.1, '', 78.3, '', 71.4, '', '', '', '', '', '', '',
'', '', '', '', '', '']
16 ['', u'Algeria', u'Alg\xe9rie', u'Argelia', 4.7, u'y', 5.5, u'y', 3.9,
u'y', 0.1, '', 1.8, '', 99.3, '', u'\u2013', '', u'\u2013', '', u'\u2013', '',
u'\u2013', '', 67.9, '', 87.7, '', 88.8, '', 86.5, '', '', '', '', '', '', '', '',
'', '', '', '', '', '']
.... more
```

Now, we need to turn each row into our dictionary format. This will make the data more meaningful to us when we try to do other things with it in future chapters.

Looking back at our earlier example of how we want our output to be organized, we are going to need a dictionary and we are going to use countries as keys. To pull out the country names, we will need to do some indexing.

What Is Indexing?

As you'll recall from Chapter 3, indexing is a way a to pull an item out of a set of objects, such as a list. In the case of the Excel file we are parsing, when we pass `i` to `sheet.row_values()`, the method `row_values` uses `i` as an index. Let's practice indexing in the Python interpreter.

Create a sample list:

```
x = ['cat', 'dog', 'fish', 'monkey', 'snake']
```

To pull out the second item, you can refer to the item by adding an index, as shown here:

```
>>>x[2]
'fish'
```

If this isn't the result you expected, remember that Python starts counting at 0. So, to get the second item as humans would identify it, we have to use the number 1:

```
>>>x[1]
'dog'
```

You can also take a negative index:

```
>>>x[-2]
'monkey'
```

What is the difference in behavior between positive and negative indexes? You can see that one counts from the beginning (positive) while the other counts from the end (negative).

Slicing is another useful practice related to indexing. Slicing allows you to take a "slice" out of another list or iterable object. For example:

```
>>>x[1:4]
['dog', 'fish', 'monkey']
```

Notice that, as with ranges, the slice starts at the first number, but the second number is read as "up to, but not including."

If you don't include the first or last number, the slice will go to the end. Here are a few examples:

```
x[2:]
['fish', 'monkey', 'snake']

x[-2:]
['monkey', 'snake']

x[:2]
['cat', 'dog']

x[:-2]
['cat', 'dog', 'fish']
```

Slicing on other iterable objects works the same way as with lists.

Let's add a dictionary to our code, and then pull out the country name from each row and add it as a key to our dictionary.

Update your for loop to reflect this:

```
count = 0
data = {}                               ❶

for i in xrange(sheet.nrows):
    if count < 10:
        if i >= 14:
            row = sheet.row_values(i)
            country = row[1]            ❷
            data[country] = {}          ❸
    count += 1

print data                              ❹
```

❶ This creates an empty dictionary to store our data.

❷ `row[1]` pulls out the country from each row we iterate over.

❸ `data[country]` adds the country as a key to the `data` dictionary. We set the value to another dictionary, because that is where we are going to store our data in the following steps.

❹ This outputs the data, so we can see what it looks like.

At this point, your output should look something like this:

```
{u'Afghanistan': {}, u'Albania': {}, u'Angola': {}, u'Algeria': {},
u'Andorra': {}, u'Austria': {}, u'Australia': {}, u'Antigua and Barbuda': {},
u'Armenia': {}, u'Argentina': {}}
```

Now, we need to match up each of the values in the rest of the row with the proper values in the spreadsheet, then store them in our dictionary.

 As you try to pull out all the values and check them against your Excel sheet, you will make lots of errors. That is fine and expected. This process should be embraced—it means you're working your way through the problem.

First, let's create an empty version of our data structure where we can store our data. Let's also remove our counter, as we know that the rows of data start at line 14. Because we know `xrange` can accept a start and end point, we can begin our counting at 14 and end at the end of the file. Let's take a look at our updated code:

```
data = {}

for i in xrange(14, sheet.nrows):          ❶
    row = sheet.row_values(i)
    country = row[1]

    data[country] = {                       ❷
        'child_labor': {                    ❸
            'total': [],                    ❹
            'male': [],
            'female': [],
        },
        'child_marriage': {
            'married_by_15': [],
            'married_by_18': [],
        }
    }

print data['Afghanistan']                   ❺
```

❶ We can remove all of our references to the counter and just begin our for loop starting at the 14th row of our sheet. This line begins the loop with a value of 14, so we automatically skip the lines we don't need for our dataset.

❷ This line expands the dictionary to multiple lines to fill out the other data points.

❸ This creates the key child_labor and sets it equal to another dictionary.

❹ The dictionary has strings to explain each part of the data it holds. For each of these keys, the values are lists.

❺ This outputs the values associated with the key Afghanistan.

Our output data for Afghanistan looks like this:

```
{
    'child_labor': {'total': [], 'male': [], 'female': []},
    'child_marriage': {'married_by_18': [], 'married_by_15': []}
}
```

Let's now populate the data. Because we have access to each column of each row using the index, we can populate these lists with the values from the sheet. By looking at our sheet and lining up which columns relate to which parts of the data, we can update the data dictionary to reflect the following:

```
data[country] = {
    'child_labor': {
        'total': [row[4], row[5]],                    ❶
        'male': [row[6], row[7]],
        'female': [row[8], row[9]],
    },
    'child_marriage': {
        'married_by_15': [row[10], row[11]],
        'married_by_18': [row[12], row[13]],
    }
}
```

❶ Because there are two cells for each of the columns, our code stores both values. Because in this line our child labor totals are the fifth and sixth columns and we know Python is zero-indexed, we want the fourth and fifth indexes.

When we run our code again, we get output like this:

```
{
  'child_labor': {'female': [9.6, ''], 'male': [11.0, ''], 'total': [10.3, '']},
  'child_marriage': {'married_by_15': [15.0, ''], 'married_by_18': [40.4, '']}}
}
```

Before you continue, output a couple of records and check the number in the dictionary. It is easy to end up one index off and ruin the rest of your data.

Finally, to preview our data, we can use pprint instead of a print statement. In complicated data structures (like dictionaries), this makes it a lot easier to review the output. Add the following to the end of your file to preview the data in a formatted fashion:

```
import pprint          ❶
pprint.pprint(data)     ❷
```

❶ Imports the pprint library. Normally, import statements come at the beginning of the file, but we are putting it here for simplicity. After you are done, you will want to delete these lines, because they are not critical to your script.

❷ Passes data to the pprint.pprint() function.

If you scroll through your output, you will notice the majority of it looks good. But there are a couple of records that seem out of place.

If you look at the spreadsheet, you should note the last row for countries is Zimbabwe. So, we want to look for when the country is equal to 'Zimbabwe', and exit there. To exit, we add a break to our code, which is how we prematurely break the for loop to continue with the rest of script. Let's add that as our stopping point. At the end of the for loop, add the following and rerun your code:

```
if country == 'Zimbabwe':    ❶
    break                    ❷
```

❶ If the country is equal to Zimbabwe…

❷ Exits out of the for loop.

After adding the break, did you end up with a NameError: name 'country' is not defined error? If so, check your indentation. The if statement should be indented four spaces to be in the for loop.

Stepping through code can be helpful in identifying an issue. If you need to troubleshoot to figure out what a variable, such as country, is equal to in a for loop, try adding print statements inside the for loop and watching the values before your script exits with an error. They will likely give you a hint as to what is happening.

At this point, our script's output matches our end goal. The last thing we want to do to our script is to make sure we document it with some comments.

Comments

Use comments in your code as a way to help the future you (and others) understand why you did something. To comment in your code, put a # before the comment:

```
# This is a comment in Python. Python will ignore this line.
```

For a multiline comment, use the following format:

```
"""
    This is the formatting for a multiline comment.
    If your comment is really long or you want to
    insert a longer description, you should use
    this type of comment.
"""
```

Your script should now look something like this:

```
"""
    This is a script to parse child labor and child marriage data.      ❶
    The Excel file used in this script can be found here:
        http://www.unicef.org/sowc2014/numbers/
"""

import xlrd
book = xlrd.open_workbook('SOWC 2014 Stat Tables_Table 9.xlsx')

sheet = book.sheet_by_name('Table 9 ')

data = {}
for i in xrange(14, sheet.nrows):
    # Start at 14th row, because that is where the country data begins   ❷

    row = sheet.row_values(i)

    country = row[1]

    data[country] = {
        'child_labor': {
            'total': [row[4], row[5]],
            'male': [row[6], row[7]],
            'female': [row[8], row[9]],
        },
        'child_marriage': {
            'married_by_15': [row[10], row[11]],
            'married_by_18': [row[12], row[13]],
        }
    }
```

```
if country == 'Zimbabwe':
    break

import pprint
pprint.pprint(data)                                          ❸
```

❶   This is a multiline comment used to generally describe what is going on in this script.

❷   This is a single-line comment to document why we start on line 14 and not earlier.

❸   We can and should remove these lines as we move beyond simple parsing of data into data analysis.

At this point, we have a similar output to the previous chapter's data. In the next chapter, we will take this a step further and parse the same data from a PDF.

Summary

The Excel format is an odd in-between category that is *kind of* machine readable. Excel files were not meant to be read by programs, but they are parsable.

To handle this nonstandard format, we had to install external libraries. There are two ways to find libraries: by looking on PyPI (*https://pypi.python.org/pypi*), the Python package index, or by searching for tutorials and how-tos to see what other people have done.

Once you have identified the library you want to install, use the `pip install` command to do it; to uninstall a library, use `pip uninstall`.

Besides learning how to parse Excel using the `xlrd` library, we also learned a few new Python programming concepts, which are summarized in Table 4-1.

Table 4-1. New Python programming concepts

Concept	Purpose
range and xrange (*http://bit.ly/python_range*)	This turns a number into a consecutive list of numbers. Example: `range(3)` will output `[0, 1, 2]`.
Counting starts at 0, not 1	This is a computer construct to be aware of; it occurs throughout programming. It is important to note when using `range`, indexing, or slicing.
Indexing and slicing (*http://bit.ly/cutting_slicing_strings*)	Use this to pull out a specific subset of a string or list.

Concept	Purpose
Counters	Use this as a tool to control `for` loops.
Nested `for` loops	Use when iterating over a data structure within a data structure, such as a list of lists, a list of dictionaries, or a dictionary of dictionaries.
`pprint`	`pprint` is a way to output data into the terminal in a nice format. This is good to use when programming with complicated data structures.
`break`	You can exit from a `for` loop early by using `break`. This will stop executing the loop and continue on to the next part of the script.
Commenting	It is important to keep all your code commented, so you know what is happening for future reference.

As you read on and dig into PDFs, you will learn the importance of exploring alternatives to the data you have or finding alternate ways to locate and find data you need to answer your research questions.

## CHAPTER 5

PDFs and Problem Solving in Python

Publishing data only in PDFs is criminal, but sometimes you don't have other options. In this chapter, you are going to learn how to parse PDFs, and in doing so you will learn how to troubleshoot your code.

We will also cover how to write a script, starting with some basic concepts like imports, and introduce some more complexity. Throughout this chapter, you will learn a variety of ways to think about and tackle problems in your code.

Avoid Using PDFs!

The data used in this section is the same data as in the previous chapter, but in PDF form. Normally, one does not seek data in difficult-to-parse formats, but we did for this book because the data you need to work with may not always be in the ideal format. You can find the PDF we use in this chapter in the book's GitHub repository (*https://github.com/jackiekazil/data-wrangling*).

There are a few things you need to consider before you start parsing PDF data:

- Have you tried to find the data in another form? If you can't find it online, try using a phone or email.
- Have you tried to copy and paste the data from the document? Sometimes, you can easily select, copy, and paste data from a PDF into a spreadsheet. This doesn't always work, though, and it is not scalable (meaning you can't do it for many files or pages quickly).

If you can't avoid dealing with PDFs, you'll need to learn how to parse your data with Python. Let's get started.

Programmatic Approaches to PDF Parsing

PDFs are more difficult to work with than Excel files because each one can be in an unpredictable format. (When you have a series of PDF files, parsing comes in handy, because hopefully they will be a consistent set of documents.)

PDF tools handle documents in various ways, including by converting the PDFs to text. As we were writing this book, Danielle Cervantes started a conversation about PDF tools on a listserv for journalists called NICAR. The conversation led to the compilation of the following list of PDF parsing tools:

- ABBYY's Transformer
- Able2ExtractPro
- Acrobat Professional
- Adobe Reader
- Apache Tika
- Cogniview's PDF to Excel
- CometDocs
- Docsplit
- Nitro Pro
- PDF XChange Viewer
- pdfminer
- pdftk
- pdftotext
- Poppler
- Tabula
- Tesseract
- xPDF
- Zamzar

Besides these tools, you can also parse PDFs with many programming languages—including Python.

 Just because you know a tool like Python doesn't mean it's always the best tool for the job. Given the variety of tools available, you may find another tool is easier for part of your task (such as data extraction). Keep an open mind and investigate many options before proceeding.

As mentioned in "Installing Python Packages" on page 73, PyPI is a convenient place for us to look for Python packages. If you search for "PDF" (*http://bit.ly/pdf_pack ages*), you'll get a bunch of results, similar to those shown in Figure 5-1.

Package	Weight*	Description
PDF 1.0	11	PDF toolkit
PDFTron-PDFNet-SDK-for-Python 5.7	11	A top notch PDF library for PDF rendering, conversion, content extraction, etc
agenda2pdf 1.0	9	Simple script which generates a book agenda file in PDF format, ready to be printed or to be loaded on a ebook reader
aws.pdfbook 1.1	9	Download Plone content views as PDF
buzzweb2pdf 0.1	9	An Open Source tool to convert HTML documentation with an index page into a single PDF.
ckanext-pdfview 0.0.1	9	View plugin for rendering PDFs on the browser
cmsplugin-pdf 0.5.1	9	A reusable Django app to add PDFs to Django-CMS.
collective.pdfjs 0.4.3	9	pdf.js integration for Plone
collective.pdfLeadImage 0.2	9	Automatically creates contentleadimage from pdf cover
collective.pdfpeek 2.0.0	9	A Plone 4 product that generates image thumbnail previews of PDF files stored on ATFile based objects.
collective.sendaspdf 2.10	9	An open source product for Plone to download or email a page seen by the user as a PDF file.
django-easy-pdf 0.1.0	9	Django PDF views, the easy way

Figure 5-1. PDF packages on PyPI

If you start looking through these options to get more information on each of the libraries, none of them will look like an obvious choice for parsing PDFs. If you try a couple more searches, such as "parse pdf," (*http://bit.ly/parse_pdf_packages*) more options will surface, but there is no obvious leader. So, we went back to search engines to look for what people are using.

Watch the publication dates on the materials you find when you are looking for libraries or solutions. The older a post or question is, the greater the probability it might be out of date and no longer usable. Try searching within the past two years, then extend further only if needed.

After looking at various tutorials, documentation, blog posts, and a couple of helpful articles (*http://bit.ly/manipulating_pdfs_python*) such as this one, we decided to try the slate library (*https://pypi.python.org/pypi/slate*).

slate worked well for what we needed, but this won't always be the case. It's OK to abandon something and start over. If there are multiple options, use what makes sense to you, even if someone tells you that it is not the "best" tool. Which tool is best is a matter of opinion. When you're learning how to program, the *best* tool is the most intuitive one.

Opening and Reading Using slate

We decided to use the `slate` library for this problem, so let's go ahead and install it. On your command line, run the following:

```
pip install slate
```

Now you have `slate` installed, so you can create a script with the following code and save it as *parse_pdf.py*. Make sure it is in the same folder as the PDF file, or correct the file path. This code prints the first two pages of the file:

```
import slate                    ❶

pdf = 'EN-FINAL Table 9.pdf'    ❷

with open(pdf, 'rb') as f:      ❸
    doc = slate.PDF(f)          ❹

for page in doc[:2]:            ❺
    print page
```

❶   Imports the `slate` library.

❷   Creates a string variable to hold the file path—make sure your spaces and cases match exactly.

❸   Passes the filename string to Python's `open` function, so Python can open the file. Python will open the file as the variable `f`.

❹   Passes the opened file known as `f` to `slate.PDF(f)`, so `slate` can parse the PDF into a usable format.

❺   Loops over the first couple of pages in the doc and outputs them, so we know everything is working.

Usually pip will install all necessary dependencies; however, it depends on the package managers to list them properly. If you see an `ImportError`, using this library or otherwise, you should carefully read the next line and see what packages are not installed. If you received the message `ImportError: No module named pdfminer.pdfparser` when running this code, it means installing `slate` did not properly install `pdfminer`, even though it's a requirement. To do so, you need to run `pip install --upgrade --ignore-installed slate==0.3 pdfminer==20110515` (as documented in the slate issue tracker (*https://github.com/timClicks/slate/issues/5*)).

Run the script, and then compare the output to what is in the PDF.

Here is the first page:

```
TABLE 9Afghanistan 10  11  10  15  40  37  -  -  -  -  90  74  75  74Albania
12  14  9  0  10  99  -  -  -  36  30  75  78  71Algeria 5 y 6 y 4 y 0  2  99
-  -  -  -  68  88  89  87Andorra -  -  -  -  -  100 v -  -  -  -  -  -  -
-Angola 24 x 22 x 25 x -  -  36 x -  -  -  -  -  -  -  -Antigua and Barbuda
-  -  -  -  -  -  -  -  -  -  -  -  -  -  -Argentina 7 y 8 y 5 y -  -  99 y
-  -  -  -  -  -  -  -Armenia 4  5  3  0  7  100  -  -  -  20  9  70  72
67Australia -  -  -  -  -  100 v -  -  -  -  -  -  -  -Austria -  -
-  -  -  100 v -  -  -  -  -  -  -  -Azerbaijan 7 y 8 y 5 y 1  12  94  -  -
-  58  49  75  79  71Bahamas -  -  -  -  -  -  -  -  -  -  -  -  -
-Bahrain 5 x 6 x 3 x -  -  -  -  -  -  -  -  -  -Bangladesh 13    18
8    29  65  31  -  -  -  -  33 y -  -  -Barbados -  -  -  -  -  -  -  -
-  -  -  -  -  -Belarus 1    1    2    0 3  100 y -  -  -  4  4  65 y 67 y 62
yBelgium -  -  -  -  -  100 v -  -  -  -  -  -  -  -Belize 6    7    5
3  26  95  -  -  -  -  9  71  71  70Benin 46    47    45    8  34  80  13  2 y
1  14  47  -  -  -Bhutan 3  3  3  6  26  100  -  -  -  -  68  -  -  -Bolivia (
Plurinational    State of) 26 y 28 y 24 y 3  22  76 y -  -  -  -  16  -  -
-Bosnia and Herzegovina 5    7    4    0 4  100  -  -  -  6  5  55  60
50Botswana 9 y 11 y 7 y -  -  72  -  -  -  -  -  -  -  -Brazil 9 y 11 y 6 y
11  36  93 y -  -  -  -  -  -  -Brunei Darussalam -  -  -  -  -  -  -
-  -  -  -  -  -  -Bulgaria  -  -  -  -  -  100 v -  -  -  -  -  -  -
-Burkina Faso 39  42  36  10  52  77  76  13  9  34  44  83  84  82Burundi
26    26    27    3  20  75  -  -  -  44  73  -  -  -Cabo Verde 3 x,y 4 x,y 3
x,y 3  18  91  -  -  -  16 y 17  -  -  -Cambodia 36 y 36 y 36 y 2  18  62  -
-  -  22 y 46 y -  -  -Cameroon 42    43    40    13  38  61  1  1 y 7  39
47  93  93  93Canada -  -  -  -  -  -  100 v -  -  -  -  -  -  -Central
African Republic 29    27    30    29  68  61  24  1  11  80 y 80  92  92
92Chad 26    25    28    29  68  16  44  18 y 38  -  62  84  85  84Chile 3 x 3
x 2 x -  -  100 y -  -  -  -  -  -  -China -  -  -  -  -  -  -  -  -  -
-  -  -  -Colombia 13 y 17 y 9 y 6  23  97  -  -  -  -  -  -  -  -Comoros
27 x 26 x 28 x -  -  88 x -  -  -  -  -  -  -  -Congo 25    24    25    7  33
91  -  -  -  -  76  -  -  -TABLE 9    CHILD PROTECTIONCountries  and
areasChild labour (%)+ 2005-2012*Child marriage (%) 2005-2012*Birth
registration (%)+ 2005-2012*totalFemale genital mutilation/cutting (%)+
2002-2012*Justification of  wife beating (%) 2005-2012*Violent discipline (%)+
2005-2012*prevalenceattitudestotalmalefemalemarried by 15married by
18womenagirlsbsupport for the practicecmalefemaletotalmalefemale78    THE
STATE OF THE WORLD'S CHILDREN 2014 IN NUMBERS
```

If you look at your PDF, it's easy to see the pattern of rows in the page. Let's check what data type the page is:

```
for page in doc[:2]:
    print type(page)        ❶
```

❶ Updates from print page to print type(page) in your code.

Running that generates the following output:

```
<type 'str'>
<type 'str'>
```

So, we know a `page` in `slate` is a long string. This is helpful because we now understand we can use string methods (for a refresher on these, refer back to Chapter 2).

Overall, this file was not difficult to read. Because it contains only tables and barely any text, `slate` could parse it pretty well. In some cases, the tables are buried inside the text, so you might have to skip lines to get to the data you need. If you do have to skip lines, you can follow the pattern in the Excel example in the previous chapter, where we created a counter incremented by one for each row, used it to find the region, and then used the technique described in "What Is Indexing?" on page 83 to select only the data we needed.

Our end goal is to get the data from the PDF into the same format as the Excel file output. To do so, we need to break the strings apart to pull out each row. The thought process behind this is to look for patterns to identify where a new row begins. That might sound easy, but it can get pretty complicated.

When dealing with large strings, people often use regular expressions (RegEx). If you aren't familiar with regex and writing regex searches, this could be a difficult approach. If you are up for the challenge and want to learn more about regex with Python, check out the section "RegEx Matching" on page 183. For our purposes, we'll try a simpler approach to extract our data.

Converting PDF to Text

First we want to convert the PDF to text; then we will parse it. This approach is better if you have a very large file or files. (In the `slate` library, our script will parse the PDF every time it runs. This can be very time- and memory-consuming with large or numerous files).

To convert our PDF to text, we will need to use `pdfminer`. Start by installing that:

```
pip install pdfminer
```

Once you install `pdfminer`, a command called `pdf2txt.py` is available, which will convert your PDF to file to text. Let's do that now. We can run the following command to convert the PDF to text in the same folder so all of our materials are together:

```
pdf2txt.py -o en-final-table9.txt EN-FINAL\ Table\ 9.pdf
```

The first argument (`-o en-final-table9.txt`) is the text file we want to create. The second argument (`EN-FINAL\ TABLE\ 9.pdf`) is our PDF. Make sure to use the correct capitalization and capture any spaces in the filename. Spaces will need to be preceded with a backslash (\). This is referred to as *escaping*. Escaping tells the computer the space is part of whatever is being typed out.

Autocompletion Using Tab

The Tab key in the terminal is your new best friend. For the second argument in the command you just ran, you could have typed EN, then pressed the Tab key twice. If there is only one possibility, your computer will fill in the rest of the filename. If there are multiple possibilities, it will give you a warning sound and return a list of possible options. This is a great technique for entering long folder/filenames with funky characters.

Try this. Change to your home directory (cd ~/ on Unix-based systems or cd %cd% on Windows). Now, let's say you want to cd into your *Documents* directory. Try typing cd D + Tab + Tab. What happened? What were the other files or folders in your home directory that started with D? (Perhaps *Downloads*?)

Now try cd Doc + Tab + Tab. You should be able to autocomplete to your *Documents* folder.

After running this command, we have a text version of our PDF in a file called *en-final-table9.txt*.

Let's read our new file into Python. Create a new script with the following code in the same folder as your previous script. Call it *parse_pdf_text.py*, or something similar that makes sense to you:

```
pdf_txt = 'en-final-table9.txt'
openfile = open(pdf_txt, 'r')

for line in openfile:
    print line
```

We can read in the text line by line and print each line, showing we have the table in text form.

Parsing PDFs Using pdfminer

Because PDFs are notoriously difficult to work with, we'll be learning how to work through problems in our code and do some basic troubleshooting.

We want to start collecting the country names, because the country names are going to be the keys in our final dataset. If you open up your text file, you will find that the eighth line is the last line before the countries start. That line has the text *and areas*:

```
 5    TABLE 9      CHILD PROTECTION
 6
 7    Countries
 8    and areas
 9    Afghanistan
10    Albania
11    Algeria
12    Andorra
```

If you look through the text document, you will see that this is a consistent pattern. So, we want to create a variable which acts as an on/off switch to start and stop the collection process when it hits the line *and areas*.

To accomplish this we will update the for loop to include a *Boolean* variable, which is a True/False variable. We want to set our Boolean to True when we hit the *and areas* lines:

```
country_line = False                        ❶
for line in openfile:

    if line.startswith('and areas'):        ❷
        country_line = True                 ❸
```

❶ Sets country_line to False, because by default the line is not a country line.

❷ Searches for a line that starts with *and areas*.

❸ Sets country_line to True.

The next thing we need to find is when to set the Boolean back to False. Take a moment to look at the text file to identify the pattern. How do you know when the list of countries ends?

If you look at the follow excerpt, you will notice there is a blank line:

```
45    China
46    Colombia
47    Comoros
48    Congo
49
50    total
51    10
52    12
```

But how does Python recognize a blank line? Add a line to your script to print out the Python representation of the line (see "Formatting Data" on page 164 for more on string formatting):

```
country_line = False
for line in openfile:
    if country_line:                          ❶
        print '%r' % line                     ❷

    if line.startswith('and areas'):
        country_line = True
```

❶ If country_line is True, which it will be after the previous iteration of the for loop...

❷ ... then print out the Python representation of the line.

If you look at the output, you will notice that all the lines now have extra characters at the end:

```
45    'China \n'
46    'Colombia \n'
47    'Comoros \n'
48    'Congo \n'
49    '\n'
50    'total\n'
51    '10   \n'
52    '12   \n'
```

The \n is the symbol of the end of a line, or a *newline* character. This is what we will now use as the marker to turn off the country_line variable. If country_line is set to True but the line is equal to \n, our code should set country_line to False, because this line marks the end of the country names:

```
country_line = False
for line in openfile:

    if country_line:                          ❶
        print line

    if line.startswith('and areas'):
        country_line = True
    elif country_line:
        if line == '\n':                      ❷
            country_line = False
```

❶ If country_line is True, print out the line so we can see the country name. This comes first because we don't want it after our *and areas* test; we only want to print the actual country names, not the *and areas* line.

❷ If country_line is True and the line is equal to a newline character, set country_line to False, because the list of countries has ended.

Now, when we run our code, we get what looks like all the lines with countries returned. This will eventually turn into our country list. Now, let's look for the markers for the data we want to collect and do the same thing. The data we are looking for is the child labor and child marriage figures. We will begin with child labor data—we need total, male, and female numbers. Let's start with the total.

We will follow the same pattern to find total child labor:

1. Create an on/off switch using `True`/`False`.

2. Look for the starter marker to turn it on.

3. Look for the ending marker to turn it off.

If you look at the text, you will see the starting marker for data is *total*. Look at line 50 in the text file you created to see the first instance:[1]

```
45    China
46    Colombia
47    Comoros
48    Congo
49
50    total
51    10
52    12
```

The ending marker is once again a newline or \n, which you can see on line 71:

```
68    6
69    46
70    3
71
72    26  y
73    5
```

Let's add this logic to our code and check the results using `print`:

```
country_line = total_line = False          ❶
for line in openfile:

    if country_line or total_line:          ❷
        print line

    if line.startswith('and areas'):
        country_line = True
    elif country_line:
        if line == '\n':
            country_line = False
```

---

1 Your text editor likely has an option to turn on line numbers, and might even have a shortcut to "hop" to a particular line number. Try a Google search if it's not obvious how to use these features.

```
    if line.startswith('total'):                    ❸
        total_line = True
    elif total_line:
        if line == '\n':
            total_line = False
```

❶ Sets total_line to False.

❷ If country_line or total_line is set to True, outputs the line so we can see what data we have.

❸ Checks where total_line starts and set total_line to True. The code following this line follows the same construction we used for the country_line logic.

At this point, we have some code redundancy. We are repeating some of the same code, just with different variables or on and off switches. This opens up a conversation about how to create non-redundant code. In Python, we can use *functions* to perform repetitive actions. That is, instead of manually performing those sets of actions line by line in our code, we can put them in a function and *call* the function to do it for us. If we need to test each line of a PDF, we can use functions instead.

 When first writing functions, figuring out where to place them can be confusing. You need to write the code for the function *before* you want to call the function. This way Python knows what the function is supposed to do.

We will name the function we are writing turn_on_off, and we will set it up to receive up to four arguments:

- line is the line we are evaluating.
- status is a Boolean (True or False) representing whether it is *on* or *off*.
- start is what we are looking for as the start of the section—this will trigger the *on* or True status.
- end is what we are looking for as the end of the section—this will trigger the *off* or False status.

Update your code and add the shell for the function above your for loop. Do not forget to add a description of what the function does—this is so when you refer back to the function later, you don't have to try to decipher it. These descriptions are called *docstrings*:

```
def turn_on_off(line, status, start, end='\n'):                    ❶
    """
        This function checks to see if a line starts/ends with a certain   ❷
        value. If the line starts/ends with that value, the status is
        set to on/off (True/False).
    """
    return status                                                  ❸

country_line = total_line = False
for line in openfile:
    .....
```

❶ This line begins the function and will take up to four arguments. The first three, line, status, and start, are *required* arguments—that is, they must be provided because they have no default values. The last one, end, has a default value of a newline character, as that appears to be a pattern with our file. We can override the default value by passing a different value when we call our function.

❷ Always write a description (or docstring) for your function, so you know what it does. It doesn't have to be perfect. Just make sure you have something. You can always update it later.

❸ The return statement is the proper way to exit a function. In this case, we are going to return status, which will be True or False.

Arguments with Default Values Always Come Last

When writing a function, arguments without a default value always have to be listed before arguments with a default value. This is why end='\n' is the last argument in our example. We can see an argument has a default value, as it will be listed like a keyword and value pair (i.e., *value_name=value*), with the default value given after the = sign (\n in our example).

Python evaluates function arguments when the function is called. If we called the function for countries, it would look like this:

```
turn_on_off(line, country_line, 'and areas')
```

This takes advantage of the default end value. If you wanted to override the default with two newline characters we would do the following:

```
turn_on_off(line, country_line, 'and areas', end='\n\n')
```

Let's pretend we set status to have a default value of False. What would we need to change?

Here is the original first line of the function:

```
def turn_on_off(line, status, start, end='\n'):
```

Here are two possible ways to update it:

```
def turn_on_off(line, start, end='\n', status=False):
def turn_on_off(line, start, status=False, end='\n'):
```

The status argument will have to be moved after the required arguments. When calling the new function, we can use defaults for end and status, or we can override them:

```
turn_on_off(line, 'and areas')
turn_on_off(line, 'and areas', end='\n\n', status=country_line)
```

If you accidentally list arguments with defaults before required arguments, Python will throw an error: SyntaxError: non-default argument follows default argument. You don't need to memorize this, but be aware so if you see the error, you recognize what it's referencing.

Now, let's move the code from our for loop into the function. We want to replicate the logic we had with country_line in our new turn_on_off function:

```
def turn_on_off(line, status, start, end='\n'):
    """
        This function checks to see if a line starts/ends with a certain
        value. If the line starts/ends with that value, the status is
        set to on/off (True/False).
    """

    if line.startswith(start):            ❶
        status = True
    elif status:
        if line == end:                   ❷
            status = False
    return status                         ❸
```

❶ Replaces what we are searching for on the starting line with the start variable.

❷ Replaces the end text we used with the end variable.

❸ Returns the status based on the same logic (end means False, start means True).

Let's now call the function in our for loop, and check out what our script looks like all together thus far:

```
pdf_txt = 'en-final-table9.txt'
openfile = open(pdf_txt, "r")


def turn_on_off(line, status, start, end='\n'):
    """
```

```
    This function checks to see if a line starts/ends with a certain
    value. If the line starts/ends with that value, the status is
    set to on/off (True/False).
    """
    if line.startswith(start):
        status = True
    elif status:
        if line == end:
            status = False
    return status


country_line = total_line = False                                    ❶

for line in openfile:
    if country_line or total_line:                                   ❷
        print '%r' % line

    country_line = turn_on_off(line, country_line, 'and areas')      ❸
    total_line = turn_on_off(line, total_line, 'total')              ❹
```

❶ In Python syntax, a series of = symbols means we are assigning each of the variables listed to the final value. This line assigns both `country_line` and `total_line` to `False`.

❷ We want to still keep track of our lines and the data they hold when we are *on*. For this, we are employing or. A Python or says if one or the other is true, do the following. This line says if either `country_line` or `total_line` is `True`, print the line.

❸ This calls the function for countries. The `country_line` variable catches the returned status that the function outputs and updates it for the next `for` loop.

❹ This calls the function for totals. It works the same as the previous line for country names.

Let's start to store our countries and totals in lists. Then we will take those lists and turn them into a dictionary, where the country will be the key and the total will be the value. This will help us troubleshoot to see if we need to clean up our data.

Here's the code to create the two lists:

```
countries = []                                                      ❶
totals = []                                                         ❷
country_line = total_line = False
for line in openfile:
                                                                    ❸
    if country_line:
        countries.append(line)                                     ❹
```

```
    elif total_line:
        totals.append(line)                                    ❺

    country_line = turn_on_off(line, country_line, 'and areas')
    total_line = turn_on_off(line, total_line, 'total')
```

❶ Creates empty countries list.

❷ Creates empty totals list.

❸ Note that we've removed the `if country_line or total_line` statement. We will break this out separately below.

❹ If it's a country line, this line adds the country to the country list.

❺ This line collects totals, the same as we did with countries.

We are going to combine the totals and countries by "zipping" the two datasets. The `zip` function takes an item from each list and pairs them together until all items are paired. We can then convert the zipped list to a dictionary by passing it to the `dict` function.

Add the following to the end of the script:

```
import pprint                                                  ❶
test_data = dict(zip(countries, totals))                       ❷
pprint.pprint(test_data)                                       ❸
```

❶ Imports the `pprint` library. This prints complex data structures in a way that makes them easy to read.

❷ Creates a variable called `test_data`, which will be the countries and totals zipped together and then turned into a dictionary.

❸ Passes `test_data` to the `pprint.pprint()` function to pretty print our data.

If you run the script now, you will get a dictionary that looks like this:

```
{'\n': '49    \n',
 ' \n': '\xe2\x80\x93  \n',
 '    Republic of Korea \n': '70   \n',
 '    Republic of) \n': '\xe2\x80\x93  \n',
 '    State of) \n': '37  \n',
 '    of the Congo \n': '\xe2\x80\x93  \n',
 '    the Grenadines \n': '60  \n',
 'Afghanistan \n': '10   \n',
 'Albania \n': '12   \n',
 'Algeria \n': '5  y \n',
```

```
'Andorra \n': '\xe2\x80\x93     \n',
'Angola \n': '24  x \n',
'Antigua and Barbuda \n': '\xe2\x80\x93     \n',
'Argentina \n': '7  y \n',
'Armenia \n': '4   \n',
'Australia \n': '\xe2\x80\x93     \n',
......
```

At this point, we are going to do some cleaning. This will be explained in greater detail in Chapter 7. For now, we need to clean up our strings, as they are very hard to read. We are going to do this by creating a function to clean up each line. Place this function above the for loop, near your other function:

```
def clean(line):
    """
        Cleans line breaks, spaces, and special characters from our line.
    """
    line = line.strip('\n').strip()                               ❶
    line = line.replace('\xe2\x80\x93', '-')                      ❷
    line = line.replace('\xe2\x80\x99', '\'')

    return line                                                   ❸
```

❶ Strips \n off of the line and reassigns the output to line so now line holds the cleaned version

❷ Replaces special character encodings

❸ Returns our newly cleaned string

In the cleaning we just did, we could combine method calls like this:

```
line = line.strip('\n').strip().replace(
    '\xe2\x80\x93', '-').replace('\xe2\x80\x99s', '\'')
```

However, well-formatted Python code lines should be no greater than 80 characters in length. This is a recommendation, not a rule, but keeping your lines restricted in length allows your code to be more readable.

Let's apply the clean_line function in our for loop:

```
for line in openfile:
    if country_line:
        countries.append(clean(line))
    elif total_line:
        totals.append(clean(line))
```

Now if we run our script, we get something that looks closer to what we are aiming for:

```
{'Afghanistan': '10',
 'Albania': '12',
 'Algeria': '5  y',
 'Andorra': '-',
 'Angola': '24  x',
 'Antigua and Barbuda': '-',
 'Argentina': '7  y',
 'Armenia': '4',
 'Australia': '-',
 'Austria': '-',
 'Azerbaijan': '7  y',
 ...
```

If you skim the list, you will see our approach is not adequately parsing all of the data. We need to figure out why this is happening.

It looks like countries with names spread over more than one line are separated into two records. You can see with this Bolivia: we have records reading `'Bolivia (Pluri national': ''`, and `'State of)': '26 y'`,.

The PDF itself can be used as a visual reference to show you how the data should be organized. You can see these lines in the PDF, as shown in Figure 5-2.

Bhutan	3	3	3
Bolivia (Plurinational State of)	26 y	28 y	24 y
Bosnia and Herzegovina	5	7	4
Botswana	9 y	11 y	7 y
Brazil	9 y	11 y	6 y

Figure 5-2. Bolivia in the PDF

 PDFs can be rabbit holes. Each PDF you process will require its own finesse. Because we are only parsing this PDF once, we are doing a lot of hand-checking. If this was a PDF we needed to parse on a regular basis, we would want to closely identify patterns over time and programmatically account for those, along with building checks and testing our code to ensure our import is accurate.

There are a couple of ways to approach this problem. We could try to create a placeholder to check for blank total lines and combine those with the following data lines. Another solution is to keep track of which countries have records spanning more than one line. We will try the second approach, as our dataset isn't too large.

We will create a list of the first lines for each multiline country record and use this list to check each line in our script. You will want to put this list before your for loop. Often, reference items are put near the top of the script so they are easy to find and change as needed.

Let's add Bolivia (Plurinational to a list of double-lined countries:

```
double_lined_countries = [
    'Bolivia (Plurinational',
]
```

Now we need to update our for loop to check if the previous line is in the double_lined_countries list, and, if so, combine that line with the current line. To do so, we will create a previous_line variable. Then, we will populate the previous_line variable at the end of the for loop. Only then will we be able to combine the rows when the code hits the next iteration of the loop:

```
countries = []
totals = []
country_line = total_line = False
previous_line = ''                                              ❶

for line in openfile:
    if country_line:
        countries.append(clean(line))
    elif total_line:
        totals.append(clean(line))

    country_line = turn_on_off(line, country_line, 'and areas')
    total_line = turn_on_off(line, total_line, 'total')

    previous_line = line                                        ❷
```

❶ Creates the previous_line variable and sets it to an empty string.

❷ Populates the previous_line variable with the current line at the end of the for loop.

Now we have a previous_line variable and we can check to see if the previous_line is in double_lined_countries so we know when to combine the previous line with the current line. Furthermore, we will want to add the new combined line to the countries list. We also want to make sure we do not add the line to the countries list if the first part of the name is in the double_lined_countries list.

Let's update our code to reflect these changes:

```
if country_line:                                                ❶
    if previous_line in double_lined_countries:
        line = ' '.join([clean(previous_line), clean(line)])    ❷
        countries.append(line)
```

```
    elif line not in double_lined_countries:
        countries.append(clean(line))
```
❸

❶ We want the logic in the `if country_line` section because it is only relevant to country names.

❷ If the `previous_line` is in the `double_lined_countries` list, this line joins the `previous_line` with the current line and assigns the combined lines to the `line` variable. `join`, as you can see, binds a list of strings together with the preceding string. This line uses a space as the joining character.

❸ If the line is not in the `double_lined_countries` list, then the following line adds it to the countries list. Here, we utilize `elif`, which is Python's way of saying `else if`. This is a nice tool to use if you want to include a different logic flow than `if - else`.

If we run our script again, we see `'Bolivia (Plurinational State of)'` is now combined. Now we need to make sure we have all the countries. We will do this manually because our dataset is small, but if you had a larger dataset, you would automate this.

Automating Your Data Checking

How do you know when to manually check the data and when to automate it with Python? Here are a few tips:

- If you are parsing the data over and over again on a regular basis, automate it.
- If you have a large dataset, you should probably automate it.
- If you have a manageable dataset and you are only parsing the data once, then you have a choice. In our example, the dataset is pretty small, so we won't automate it.

Look at the PDF in a PDF viewer to identify all the double-lined country names:

```
Bolivia (Plurinational State of)
Democratic People's Republic of Korea
Democratic Republic of the Congo
Lao People's Democratic Republic
Micronesia (Federated States of)
Saint Vincent and the Grenadines
The former Yugoslav Republic of Macedonia
United Republic of Tanzania
Venezuela (Bolivarian Republic of)
```

We know this is likely not how Python sees it, so we need to print out the countries as Python sees them and add those to the list:

```
if country_line:
    print '%r' % line                                    ❶
    if previous_line in double_lined_countries:
```

❶ Adds a `print '%r'` statement to output the Python representation

Run your script to populate the `double_lined_countries` list with the Python representation:

```
double_lined_countries = [
    'Bolivia (Plurinational \n',
    'Democratic People\xe2\x80\x99s \n',
    'Democratic Republic \n',
    'Micronesia (Federated \n',
    #... uh oh.
]
```

We are missing `Lao People's Democratic Republic` from our output, but it's on two lines in the PDF. Let's go back to the text version of the PDF and see what happened.

After looking at the text, can you identify the issue? Look at the `turn_on_off` function. How does that work in relation to how this text is written?

The problem turns out to be a blank line or \n right after the *and areas* we were looking for as a marker. If you look at the text file that we created, you will see the stray blank line on line number 1343:

```
...
1341 Countries
1342 and areas
1343
1344 Iceland
1345 India
1346 Indonesia
1347 Iran (Islamic Republic of)
...
```

That means our function didn't work. There are multiple ways we could approach this problem. For this example, we could try adding in more logic to make sure our *on/off* code works as intended. When we start to collect countries, there should be at least one country collected before we turn off the country collection. If no countries have been collected, then we should not turn off the collecting action. We can also use the previous line as a way to solve this problem. We can test the previous line in our *on/off* function and ensure it's not in a list of special lines.

In case we come across any other anomalies, let's set up this special line:

```
def turn_on_off(line, status, start, prev_line, end='\n'):
    """
        This function checks to see if a line starts/ends with a certain
        value. If the line starts/ends with that value, the status is
        set to on/off (True/False) as long as the previous line isn't special.
    """
    if line.startswith(start):
        status = True
    elif status:
        if line == end and prev_line != 'and areas': ❶
            status = False
    return status
```

❶ If the line is equal to end and the previous line is not equal to *and areas*, then we can turn data collection off. Here, we are using != which is Python's way of testing "not equal." Similar to ==, != returns a Boolean value.

You will also need to update your code to pass the previous line:

```
country_line = turn_on_off(line, country_line, previous_line, 'and areas')
total_line = turn_on_off(line, total_line, previous_line, 'total')
```

Let's go back to the original task we were working on—creating our list of double-lined countries so that we can make sure to collect both lines. We left off here:

```
double_lined_countries = [
    'Bolivia (Plurinational \n',
    'Democratic People\xe2\x80\x99s \n',
    'Democratic Republic \n',
]
```

Looking at the PDF, we see the next one is Lao People's Democratic Republic. Let's start adding from there by looking back at our script output:

```
double_lined_countries = [
    'Bolivia (Plurinational \n',
    'Democratic People\xe2\x80\x99s \n',
    'Democratic Republic \n',
    'Lao People\xe2\x80\x99s Democratic \n',
    'Micronesia (Federated \n',
    'Saint Vincent and \n',
    'The former Yugoslav \n',
    'United Republic \n',
    'Venezuela (Bolivarian \n',
]
```

If your list looks like the preceding list, when you run the script, you should have an output that pulls in the country names split over two lines. Make sure to add a print statement to the end of your script to view the country list:

```
import pprint
pprint.pprint(countries)
```

Now that you have spent a bit of time with the country list, can you think of another approach to solve this issue? Take a look at a few of the second lines:

```
'    Republic of Korea \n'
'    Republic \n'
'    of the Congo \n'
```

What do they have in common? They start with spaces. Writing code to check whether a line begins with three spaces would be more efficient. However, taking the approach we did allowed us to discover we were losing part of our dataset as it was being collected. As your coding skills develop, you will learn to find different ways to approach the same problem and determine which works best.

Let's check to see how our total numbers line up with our countries. Update the pprint statement to match the following:

```
import pprint
data = dict(zip(countries, totals))        ❶
pprint.pprint(data)                        ❷
```

❶ Zips the countries and totals lists together by calling `zip(countries, totals)`. This turns them into a tuple. We then change the tuple into a dictionary, or dict (for easier reading), by passing it to the `dict` function.

❷ Prints out the data variable we just created.

What you will see returned is a dictionary where the country names are the keys and the totals are the values. This is not our final data format; we are just doing this to see our data so far. The result should look like this:

```
{'': '-',
'Afghanistan': '10',
 'Albania': '12',
 'Algeria': '5  y',
 'Andorra': '-',
 'Angola': '24  x',
 ...
}
```

If you check this again alongside the PDF, you will notice it falls apart right at the point of the first country on a double line. The numbers pulled in are the ones from the *Birth registration* column:

```
{
...
'Bolivia (Plurinational State of)': '',
'Bosnia and Herzegovina': '37',
'Botswana': '99',
'Brazil': '99',
...
}
```

If you look at the text version of the PDF, you will notice there is a gap between the numbers when the country is on a double line:

```
6
46
3

26   y
5
9   y
```

In the same way we accounted for this in the country name collection, we need to account for this in data collection. If we have a blank space in our data lines, we need to make sure we don't collect it—that way, we only collect the data that matches the countries we've been collecting. Update your code to the following:

```
for line in openfile:
    if country_line:
        print '%r' % line
        if previous_line in double_lined_countries:
            line = ' '.join([clean(previous_line), clean(line)])
            countries.append(line)
        elif line not in double_lined_countries:
            countries.append(clean(line))

    elif total_line:
        if len(line.replace('\n', '').strip()) > 0:            ❶
            totals.append(clean(line))

    country_line = turn_on_off(line, country_line, previous_line,
                               'and areas')

    total_line = turn_on_off(line, total_line, previous_line,
                             'total')
    previous_line = line
```

❶ We know from experience the PDF uses newlines as blank lines. On this line, the code replaces newlines with nothing and strips whitespace to clean it. Then this code tests whether the string still has a length greater than zero. If so, we know there is data and we can add it to our data (totals) list.

After running our updated code, things fall apart again at our first double line. This time we are pulling in those *Birth registration* numbers again, aligned with our first double-lined country. All the following values are also incorrect. Let's go back to the text file and figure out what is happening. If you look at the numbers in that column in the PDF, you can find the pattern in the text version of the PDF starting on line number 1251:

```
1250
1251    total
1252    -
```

```
1253    5   x
1254    26
1255    -
1266    -
```

If you look closely, you will notice the title of the *Birth registration* column ends in *total*:

```
266     Birth
267     registration
268     (%)+
269     2005-2012*
270     total
271     37
272     99
```

Right now the function collecting totals is looking for *total*, so this column is getting picked up before we even get to the next line of countries. We also see that the *Violent discipline (%)* column has a label for *total* with a blank line above it. This follows the same pattern as the *total* we want to collect.

Encountering back-to-back bugs likely means the problem exists in the larger logic you've constructed. Because we started our script using these *on/off* switches, to fix the underlying problem we would need to rework the logic there. We'd need to figure out how to best determine the right column, maybe by collecting column names and sorting them. We might need to determine a way to see if the "page" has changed. If we keep quick-fixing the solution, we will likely run into more errors.

 Only spend as much time on a script as you think you need to invest. If you are trying to build a sustainable process you can run on a large dataset multiple times over a long period, you are going to want to take the time to carefully consider all of the steps.

This is the process of programming—write code, debug, write code, debug. No matter how experienced a computer programmer you are, there will be moments when you introduce errors in your code. When learning to code, these moments can be demoralizing. You might think, "Why isn't this working for me? I must not be good at this." But that's not true; programming takes practice, like anything else.

At this point, it's clear our current process isn't working. Based on what we now know about the text file, we can tell we began with a false notion that the file defines the beginning and end of each section using text. We could begin again with this file, starting at a new point; however, we want to explore some other ways of problem solving to fix the errors and get the data we want.

Learning How to Solve Problems

There are a variety of exercises you can try to parse the PDF script while also challenging your ability to write Python. First, let's review our code so far:

```python
pdf_txt = 'en-final-table9.txt'
openfile = open(pdf_txt, "r")

double_lined_countries = [
    'Bolivia (Plurinational \n',
    'Democratic People\xe2\x80\x99s \n',
    'Democratic Republic \n',
    'Lao People\xe2\x80\x99s Democratic \n',
    'Micronesia (Federated \n',
    'Saint Vincent and \n',
    'The former Yugoslav \n',
    'United Republic \n',
    'Venezuela (Bolivarian \n',
]


def turn_on_off(line, status, prev_line, start, end='\n', count=0):
    """
        This function checks to see if a line starts/ends with a certain
        value. If the line starts/ends with that value, the status is
        set to on/off (True/False) as long as the previous line isn't special.
    """
    if line.startswith(start):
        status = True
    elif status:
        if line == end and prev_line != 'and areas':
            status = False
    return status


def clean(line):
    """
        Clean line breaks, spaces, and special characters from our line.
    """
    line = line.strip('\n').strip()
    line = line.replace('\xe2\x80\x93', '-')
    line = line.replace('\xe2\x80\x99', '\'')

    return line


countries = []
totals = []
country_line = total_line = False
previous_line = ''
```

```
    for line in openfile:
        if country_line:
            if previous_line in double_lined_countries:
                line = ' '.join([clean(previous_line), clean(line)])
                countries.append(line)
            elif line not in double_lined_countries:
                countries.append(clean(line))

        elif total_line:
            if len(line.replace('\n', '').strip()) > 0:
                totals.append(clean(line))

        country_line = turn_on_off(line, country_line, previous_line,
                                   'and areas')
        total_line = turn_on_off(line, total_line, previous_line,
                                 'total')
        previous_line = line


import pprint
data = dict(zip(countries, totals))
pprint.pprint(data)
```

There are multiple solutions to the problems we are facing; we'll walk through some of them in the following sections.

Exercise: Use Table Extraction, Try a Different Library

After scratching our heads at the perplexities illustrated by this PDF-to-text conversion, we went searching for alternatives to using pdfminer for table extraction. We came across pdftables (*http://pdftables.readthedocs.org/*), which is a presumed-defunct library (the last update from the original maintainers was more than two years ago).

We installed the necessary libraries (*http://bit.ly/pdftables_install*), which can be done simply by running pip install pdftables and pip install requests. The maintainers didn't keep all the documentation up to date, so certain examples in the documentation and *README.md* were blatantly broken. Despite that, we did find one "all in one" function we were able to use to get at our data:

```
from pdftables import get_tables

all_tables = get_tables(open('EN-FINAL Table 9.pdf', 'rb'))

print all_tables
```

Let's start a new file for our code and run it (pdf_table_data.py). You should see a whirlwind of data that looks like the data we want to extract. You will notice not all of the headers convert perfectly, but it seems every line is contained in the all_tables variable. Let's take a closer look to extract our headers, data columns, and notes.

You might have noticed `all_tables` is a list of lists (or a *matrix*). It has every row, and it also has rows of rows. This probably is a good idea in table extraction, because that's essentially what a table is—columns and rows. The `get_tables` function returns each page as its own table, and the each of those tables has a list of rows with a contained list of columns.

Our first step is to find the titles we can use for our columns. Let's try viewing the first few rows to see if we can identify the one containing our column headers:

```
print all_tables[0][:6]
```

Here we are just looking at the first page's first six rows:

```
... [u'',
 u'',
 u'',
 u'',
 u'',
 u'',
 u'Birth',
 u'Female',
 u'genital mutila',
 u'tion/cutting (%)+',
 u'Jus',
 u'tification of',
 u'',
 u'',
 u'E'],
[u'',
 u'',
 u'Child labour (%',
 u')+',
 u'Child m',
 u'arriage (%)',
 u'registration',
 u'',
 u'2002\u201320',
 u'12*',
 u'wife',
 u'beating (%)',
 u'',
 u'Violent disciplin',
 u'e (%)+ 9'],
[u'Countries  and areas',
 u'total',
 u'2005\u20132012*male',
 u'female',
 u'2005married by 15',
 u'\u20132012*married by 18',
 u'(%)+ 2005\u20132012*total',
 u'prwomena',
 u'evalencegirlsb',
```

```
u'attitudessupport for thepracticec',
u'2male',
u'005\u20132012*female',
u'total',
u'2005\u20132012*male',
u'female'],...
```

We can see the titles are included in the first three lists, and they are *messy*. However, we can also see from our `print` statement that the rows are actually fairly clean. If we manually set up our titles by comparing them to the PDF, as shown here, we might have a clean dataset:

```
headers = ['Country', 'Child Labor 2005-2012 (%) total',
           'Child Labor 2005-2012 (%) male',
           'Child Labor 2005-2012 (%) female',
           'Child Marriage 2005-2012 (%) married by 15',
           'Child Marriage 2005-2012 (%) married by 18',
           'Birth registration 2005-2012 (%)',
           'Female Genital mutilation 2002-2012 (prevalence), women',
           'Female Genital mutilation 2002-2012 (prevalence), girls',
           'Female Genital mutilation 2002-2012 (support)',
           'Justification of wife beating 2005-2012 (%) male',
           'Justification of wife beating 2005-2012 (%) female',
           'Violent discipline 2005-2012 (%) total',
           'Violent discipline 2005-2012 (%) male',
           'Violent discipline 2005-2012 (%) female'] ❶


for table in all_tables:
    for row in table:
        print zip(headers, row) ❷
```

❶ Adds all of our headers, including the country names, to one list. We can now zip this list with rows to have our data aligned.

❷ Uses the `zip` method to zip together the headers with each row.

We can see from the output of our code that we have matches for some of the rows, but there are also many rows that are not country rows (similar to what we saw earlier when we found extra spaces and newlines in our table).

We want to programmatically solve this problem with some tests based on what we've learned so far. We know some of the countries span more than one row. We also know the file uses dashes (-) to show missing data, so completely empty rows are not actual data rows. We know from our previous print output that the data starts for each page on the fifth row. We also know the last row we care about is Zimbabwe. Let's combine our knowledge and see what we get:

```
for table in all_tables:
    for row in table[5:]: ❶
```

```
        if row[2] == '': ❷
            print row
```

❶ Isolates only the rows for each page we want, meaning only the slice from the fifth index onward

❷ If there is data that looks null, prints out the row to see what's in that row

When you run the code, you'll see there are some random blank rows scattered throughout the list that aren't part of the country names. Maybe this is the cause of our problems in the last script. Let's try to just get the country names put together and skip other blank rows. Let's also add in the test for Zimbabwe:

```
first_name = ''

for table in all_tables:
    for row in table[5:]:
        if row[0] == '': ❶
            continue
        if row[2] == '':
            first_name = row[0] ❷
            continue
        if row[0].startswith('    '): ❸
            row[0] = '{} {}'.format(first_name, row[0])
        print zip(headers, row) ❹
        if row[0] == 'Zimbabwe':
            break ❺
```

❶ If the data row is missing index 0, it has no country name and is a blank row. The next line skips it using `continue`, which is a Python keyword that tells the for loop to go to the next iteration.

❷ If the data row is missing index 2, we know this is probably the first part of a country name. This line saves the first part of the name in a variable `first_name`. The next line moves on to the next row of data.

❸ If the data row starts with spaces, we know it's the second part of a country name. We want to put the name back together again.

❹ If we are right in our hypothesis, we can match these things by printing out the results for human review. This line prints out each iteration so we can see them.

❺ When we reach Zimbabwe, this line breaks out of our for loop.

Most of the data looks good, but we are still seeing some anomalies. Take a look here:

```
[('Country', u'80      THE STATE OF T'),
('Child Labor 2005-2012 (%) total', u'HE WOR'),
('Child Labor 2005-2012 (%) male', u'LD\u2019S CHILDRE'),
```

```
('Child Labor 2005-2012 (%) female', u'N 2014'),
('Child Marriage 2005-2012 (%) married by 15', u'IN NUMBER'),
('Child Marriage 2005-2012 (%) married by 18', u'S'),
('Birth registration 2005-2012 (%)', u''),
.....
```

We see the line number is at the beginning of the section we thought was the country name. Do you know any countries that have numbers in their name? We sure don't! Let's put in a test for numbers and see if we can lose the bad data. We also noticed our two-line countries are not properly mapping. From the looks of it, the `pdftables` import autocorrected for spaces at the beginning of lines. How kind! Now we should add in a test and see if the very last line has a `first_name` or not:

```
from pdftables import get_tables
import pprint

headers = ['Country', 'Child Labor 2005-2012 (%) total',
            'Child Labor 2005-2012 (%) male',
            'Child Labor 2005-2012 (%) female',
            'Child Marriage 2005-2012 (%) married by 15',
            'Child Marriage 2005-2012 (%) married by 18',
            'Birth registration 2005-2012 (%)',
            'Female Genital mutilation 2002-2012 (prevalence), women',
            'Female Genital mutilation 2002-2012 (prevalence), girls',
            'Female Genital mutilation 2002-2012 (support)',
            'Justification of wife beating 2005-2012 (%) male',
            'Justification of wife beating 2005-2012 (%) female',
            'Violent discipline 2005-2012 (%) total',
            'Violent discipline 2005-2012 (%) male',
            'Violent discipline 2005-2012 (%) female']

all_tables = get_tables(open('EN-FINAL Table 9.pdf', 'rb'))

first_name = False
final_data = []

for table in all_tables:
    for row in table[5:]:
        if row[0] == '' or row[0][0].isdigit():
            continue
        elif row[2] == '':
            first_name = row[0]
            continue
        if first_name: ❶
            row[0] = u'{} {}'.format(first_name, row[0])
            first_name = False ❷
        final_data.append(dict(zip(headers, row)))
        if row[0] == 'Zimbabwe':
            break

pprint.pprint(final_data)
```

❶ Manipulates the country name entry in the row if it has a `first_name`

❷ Sets `first_name` back to `False`, so our next iteration operates properly

We now have our completed import. You'll need to further manipulate the data if you want to match the exact structure we had with our Excel import, but we were able to preserve the data in our rows from the PDF.

 `pdftables` is not actively supported, and the people who developed it now only offer a new product to replace it as a paid service (*https://pdftables.com/*). It's dangerous to rely on unsupported code, and we can't depend on `pdftables` to be around and functional forever.[2] Part of belonging to the open source community, however, is giving back; so we encourage you to find good projects and help out by contributing and publicizing them in the hopes that projects like `pdftables` stay open source and continue to grow and thrive.

Next, we'll take a look at some other options for parsing PDF data, including cleaning it by hand.

Exercise: Clean the Data Manually

Let's talk about the elephant in the room. Throughout this chapter, you might have wondered why we haven't simply edited the text version of the PDF for easier processing. You could do that—it's one of many ways to solve these problems. However, we challenge you to process this file using Python's many tools. You won't always be able to edit PDFs manually.

If you have a difficult PDF or other file type presenting issues, it's possible extraction to a text file and some hand–data wrangling are in order. In those cases, it's a good idea to estimate how much time you're willing to spend on manual manipulation and hold yourself to that estimate.

For more on data cleanup automation, check out Chapter 8.

Exercise: Try Another Tool

When we first started to look for a Python library to use for parsing PDFs, we found `slate`—which looked easy to use but required some custom code—by searching the Web to see what other people were using for the task.

---

2 It does seem there are some active GitHub forks (*https://github.com/drj11/pdftables/network*) that may be maintained and supported. We encourage you to keep an eye on them for your PDF table parsing needs.

To see what else was out there, instead of searching for "parsing pdfs python," we tried searching for "extracting tables from pdf," which gave us more distinct solutions for the table problem (including a blog post reviewing several tools (*http://bit.ly/ extract_data_from_pdf*)).

With a small PDF like the one we are using, we could try Tabula (*http://tabula.technol ogy/*). Tabula isn't always going to be the solution, but it has some good capabilities.

To get started with Tabula:

1. Download Tabula (*http://bit.ly/extract_data_from_pdf*).
2. Launch the application by double-clicking on it; this will launch the tool in your browser.
3. Upload the child labor PDF.

From here, you need to adjust the selection of the content Tabula tries to grab. Getting rid of the header rows enables Tabula to identify the data on every page and automatically highlight it for extraction. First, select the tables you are interested in (see Figure 5-3).

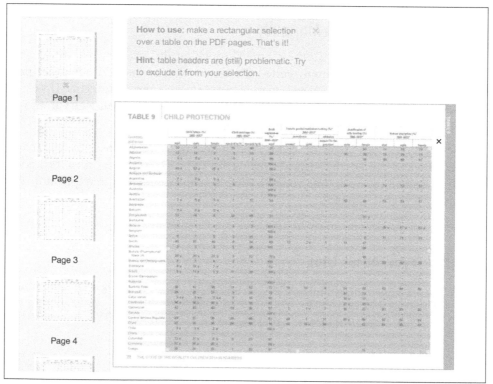

Figure 5-3. Select tables in Tabula

Next, download the data (see Figure 5-4).

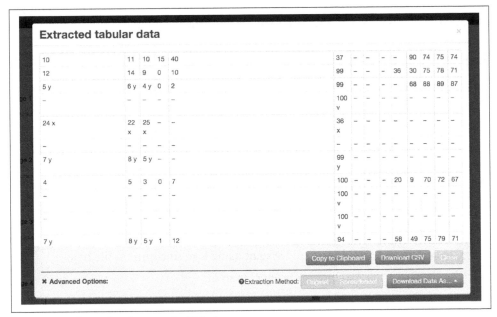

Figure 5-4. Download screen in Tabula

Click "Download CSV" and you will get something that looks like Figure 5-5.

10	11	10	15	40	37	–	–	–	–		90	74	75	74
12	14	9	0	10	99	–	–	–	–	36	30	75	78	71
5 y	6 y	4 y	0	2	99	–	–	–	–		68	88	89	87
–	–	–	–	–	100 v	–	–	–	–	–	–	–	–	–
24 x	22 x	25 x	–	–	36 x	–	–	–	–	–	–	–	–	–
–	–	–	–	–	–	–	–	–	–	–	–	–	–	–
7 y	8 y	5 y	–	–	99 y	–	–	–	–	–	–	–	–	–
4	5	3	0	7	100	–	–	–	–	20	9	70	72	67
–	–	–	–	–	100 v	–	–	–	–	–	–	–	–	–
–	–	–	–	–	100 v	–	–	–	–	–	–	–	–	–
7 y	8 y	5 y	1	12	94	–	–	–	–	58	49	75	79	71
–	–	–	–	–	–	–	–	–	–	–	–	–	–	–
5 x	6 x	3 x	–	–	–	–	–	–	–	–	–	–	–	–
13	18	8	29	65	31	–	–	–	–	33 y	–	–	–	–
–	–	–	–	–	–	–	–	–	–	–	–	–	–	–
1	1	2	0	3	100 y	–	–	–	–	4	4	65 y	67 y	62 y
–	–	–	–	–	100 v	–	–	–	–	–	–	–	–	–
6	7	5	3	26	95	–	–	–	–		9	71	71	70
46	47	45	8	34	80	13	2 y		1	14	47	–	–	–

Figure 5-5. Exacted data in CSV form

It's not perfect, but the data is cleaner than we received from pdfminer.

The challenge will be to take the CSV you created with Tabula and parse it. It is different from the other CSVs we parsed (in Chapter 3) and a little messier. If you get stumped, put it aside and come back to it after reading Chapter 7.

Uncommon File Types

So far in this book, we have covered CSV, JSON, XML, Excel, and PDF files. Data in PDFs can be difficult to parse, and you may think the world of data wrangling can't get any worse—sadly, it can.

The good news is, there's probably no problem you will face that someone hasn't solved before. Remember, asking the Python or greater open source communities for help and tips is *always* a great solution, even if you come away learning you should keep looking for more accessible datasets.

You may encounter problems if the data has the following attributes:

- The file was generated on an old system using a an uncommon file type.
- The file was generated by a proprietary system.
- The file isn't launchable in a program you have.

Solving problems related to uncommon file types is simply a matter of building on what you have already learned:

1. Identify the file type. If this is not easily done through the file extension, then use the `python-magic` (*https://pypi.python.org/pypi/python-magic/0.4.6*) library.
2. Search the Internet for "how to parse <file extension> in Python," replacing "<file extension>" with the actual file extension.
3. If there is no obvious solution, try opening the file in a text editor or reading the file with Python's `open` function.
4. If the characters look funky, read up on Python encoding. If you are just getting started with Python character encoding, then watch the PyCon 2014 talk "Character encoding and Unicode in Python" (*http://bit.ly/fischer_nam_pycon2014*).

Summary

PDF and other hard-to-parse formats are the worst formats you will encounter. When you find data in one of these formats, the first thing you should do is see if you can acquire the data in another format. With our example, the data we received in the CSV format was more precise because the numbers were rounded for the PDF charts. The more raw the format, the more likely it is to be accurate and easy to parse with code.

If it is not possible to get the data in another format, then you should try the following process:

1. Identify the data type.
2. Search the Internet to see how other folks have approached the problem. Is there a tool to help import the data?
3. Select the tool that is most intuitive to you. If it's Python, then select the library that makes the most sense to you.
4. Try to convert the data to a an easier to use format.

In this chapter, we learned about the libraries and tools in Table 5-1.

Table 5-1. New Python libraries and tools

Library or tool	Purpose
slate	Parses the PDF into a string in memory every time the script is run
pdfminer	Converts the PDF into text, so you can parse the text file
pdftables	Uses pdfminer to first parse into text and then attempt to match rows and find tables
Tabula	Offers an interface to extract PDF data into CSV format

Besides learning about new tools, we also learned a few new Python programming concepts, which are summarized in Table 5-2.

Table 5-2. New Python programming concepts

Concept	Purpose
Escaping characters (*http://learnpythonthehardway.org/book/ex10.html*)	Escaping tells the computer there is a space or special character in the file path or name by preceding it with a backslach (\). One usage is to put a \ in front of spaces to escape them.
\n	The \n is the symbol of the end of a line, or a *new line* in a file.
elif (*https://docs.python.org/2/tutorial/controlflow.html*)	In the process of writing if-else statements, we can add extra conditions to test again—if something, if else something different, if else another thing, else (finally) the last something.
Functions (*http://bit.ly/python_functions*)	Functions in Python are used to execute a piece of code. By making reusable code into functions, we can avoid repeating ourselves.
zip (*http://bit.ly/python_zip*)	zip is a built-in Python function that takes two iterable objects and outputs them into a list of tuples.

Concept	Purpose
Tuples (*http://bit.ly/ python_tuple*)	A tuple is like a list, but immutable, meaning it cannot be updated. To update a tuple, it would have to be stored as a new object.
`dict` conversion (*http:// bit.ly/python_dict*)	`dict` is a built-in Python function that attempts to convert the input into a dictionary. To be used properly, the data should look like key-value pairs.

In the next chapter, we'll talk about data acquisition and storage. This will provide more insight on how to acquire alternative data formats. In Chapters 7 and 8, we cover data cleaning, which will also help in the complexity of processing PDFs.

## CHAPTER 6

Acquiring and Storing Data

Finding your first dataset(s) to investigate might be the most important step toward acheiving your goal of answering your questions. As we mentioned in Chapter 1, you should first spend some time refining your question until you have one specific enough to identify good data about but broad enough to be interesting to you and others.

Alternatively, you might have a dataset you already find interesting, but no compelling question. If you don't already know and trust the data source, you should spend some time investigating. Ask yourself: is the data valid? Is it updated? Can I rely on future or current updates and publications?

In this chapter, we will review where you can save and store data for later use. If databases are new to you, we will review when and how to use them and demonstrate how to set up a simple database to store your data. For those of you who are already familiar with databases or if your source is a database, we will cover some basic database connection structures in Python.

Don't worry if you haven't yet decided on a dataset; we will use several examples you can access in this book's repository (*https://github.com/jackiekazil/data-wrangling*).

 We strongly encourage you to come up with some applicable questions to use throughout this book so you can better learn by doing. These could be questions you've been meaning to research or questions related to the data explored in the book. Even if the questions you pick are simple, it's best to learn by writing some of your own code.

Not All Data Is Created Equal

Although we'd like to believe in the veracity and quality of every dataset we see, not all datasets will measure up to our expectations. Even datasets you currently use could prove to be ineffective and inefficient sources after further research. As you explore automated solutions to the data wrangling problems you face, you will find the tools Python can help determine good versus bad data and help suss out the viability of your data. We will cover more about those tools as we unravel data cleaning and data exploration with Python in Chapters 7 and 8, and automation in Chapter 14.

When first getting hold of new data, we recommend performing a data *smell test* to decide whether you trust the data and if it is a reliable source of information. You can ask yourself:

- Is the author a veritable source I can contact if I have questions or concerns?
- Does the data appear to be regularly updated and checked for errors?
- Does the data come with information as to how it was acquired and what types of samples were used in its acquisition?
- Is there another source of data that can verify and validate this dataset?
- Given my overall knowledge of the topic, does this data seem plausible?

If you answered "yes" to at least three of those questions, you are on the right track! If you answered "no" to two or more of them, you might need to do some more searching to find data you can reliably defend.

 You might need to reach out to the author and/or organization who initially published and collected the data to request more information. Often, a quick call or email to the right person can help you answer one or more of those questions and prove how reliable and informed your data source is.

Fact Checking

Fact checking your data, although sometimes annoying and exhausting, is paramount to the validity of your reporting. Depending on your dataset, fact checking may involve:

- Contacting the source(s) and verifying their latest methods and releases
- Determining other good sources for comparison
- Calling an expert and talking with them about good sources and veritable information

- Researching your topic further to determine whether your sources and/or datasets are credible

Libraries and universities with access to subscriber-only publishing and educational archives are great resources for fact checking. If you can access tools like LexisNexis (*http://lexisnexis.com*), the Congressional Quarterly Press Library (*http://library.cqpress.com*), JSTOR (*http://jstor.org*), Cornell University's arXiv project (*http://arxiv.org*), and Google's Scholar search (*http://scholar.google.com/*), you can determine what others have studied and said about the topic.

Google Search can also help in fact checking. If someone says the data comes from a published source, chances are there are other folks who have either fact checked that claim or have proof of that claim. Again, you need to use your own discretion when reviewing things published online. Is the source veritable? Does the argument seem cogent and make sense? Does the proof appear valid? Evaluate your results with these questions in mind.

 Government bureaus have vast datasets. If you'd like to study a phenomenon in your local city, state, or country, you can usually find someone via phone or email who has a useful dataset. Census bureaus worldwide regularly release census data and are a good first place to start if you're stumped on what questions you'd like to answer.

Once you have verified and fact checked your initial dataset, it will be easier to both script it and determine the data's validity in the future. You can even use some of the tips you learn throughout this book (particularly in Chapter 14) to create scripts and auto-update your data.

Readability, Cleanliness, and Longevity

If your dataset appears completely illegible, there is still hope: you can use the lessons in Chapter 7 to clean it with code. Luckily, if it was created by a computer, it can likely be read by a computer. More difficulty exists in attempting to get data from "real life" onto our computers. As we saw in Chapter 5, PDFs and uncommon data file types can be difficult, but not impossible to work with.

We can use Python to help us read illegible data, but the illegibility may mean the data doesn't come from a good source. If it is massive and generated by a computer, that is one thing—database dumps are never pretty. However, if the data you have is illegible and from a human source, it may point to an issue of data cleanliness and veritability.

Another issue you face is whether your data has *already* been cleaned. You can determine this by asking more about how the data is collected, reported, and updated. You should be able to determine:

- How clean is the data?
- Has someone taken the time to show statistical error rates or update erroneous entries or misreported data?
- Will further updates be published or sent to you?
- What methods were used in the collection of the data, and how were those methods verified?

 If your source uses standardized and rigorous research and collection methods, you can likely reuse your cleaning and reporting scripts with little modification for years to come. Those systems don't normally change regularly (as change is both costly and time-intensive). Once you've scripted your cleanup, you can easily process next year's data and skip directly to data analysis.

In addition to cleanliness and readability, you care about the longevity of your data. Are you dealing with regularly collected and updated data? On what schedule is the data released and updated? Knowing how often an organization updates its data will help you determine your ability to use the data for years to come.

Where to Find Data

Just as there is more than one way to verify a source or script a PDF parser, there are many ways to find data. In this section, we'll review the methods you can use both on and offline.

Using a Telephone

Look at the data file and ask yourself, how did the data get there? File types like Excel, PDF, or even Word usually involve a human in the process, and that person got the data from a source.

If you identify the person who collected the data, you might be able to get ahold of the raw data. This raw data may be in an easy-to-parse file format, like a CSV or database. The person you speak with can also answer questions about methods of collection and update timelines.

Here are some tips for finding a human from a data file:

- Search the file for contact information.
- Look for a byline—if there is no name, look for the organization.
- Search for the filename and the title of the document on the Web.
- Look at the file metadata by right-clicking and selecting "Properties" on Windows or "Get Info" on a Mac.

Reach out to any person you find. If that is not the person who created the file, then simply ask them if they know who did. Don't be shy—your interest in their topic of study and work can be refreshing and flattering.

Dealing with a Communications Official

If you run into a situation where the file was generated by an organization that wants you to talk to their communications representative, this can mean delays. Remember the game Telephone, where one person says something to another person and that person repeats what they heard to the next person and by the end of the chain the phrase is unrecognizable?

You can do two things to move this communication along efficiently. First, work to build trust. If there are no competing interests, share the work you are interested in doing and how you will attribute the organization as your data source. This indicates you are an indirect advocate for their work and the organization will gain good press for sharing information. Second, ask the communications representative for a conference call or supervised discussion. By communicating via telephone rather than an email thread, you can get accurate answers to your questions in a timely fashion.

After you find someone to reach out to, try to reach them by phone or in person. Emails are easy to misread and usually end in extended messaging. Here are some example questions to help you think about what to ask:

- Where did you get the data on pages 6 through 200?
- Does it come in other formats, such as JSON, CSV, XML, or a database?
- How was the data gathered?
- Can you describe the data collection methods?
- What do the abbreviations mean?
- Will this data be updated? How and when?
- Is there anyone else who can add more information?

Depending on your time constraints and the goal of your project, you may want to get started with data exploration while you wait for your questions to be answered.

US Government Data

For those interested in studying phenomena in the United States, recent pushes by the Obama administration to release readily accessible data online have provided easy access to regular govenment agency reporting. A quick browse on Data.gov (*http://data.gov*) reveals storm data (*http://bit.ly/storm_events*), graduation and dropout rates (*http://bit.ly/grad_dropout_rates_2011-12*), endangered species data (*http://bit.ly/endandered_density*), crime statistics (*http://bit.ly/total_crime_index*), and many other interesting datasets.

Beyond federal data, states and local agencies have their own sites to release data—we've highlighted a few here:

- Education data (*http://datainventory.ed.gov/InventoryList*)
- Election results (*http://www.fec.gov/pubrec/electionresults.shtml*)
- Census data (*http://census.ire.org/*)
- Environmental data (*http://www.epa.gov/enviro/about-data*)
- Labor statistics (*http://bls.gov*)

If you can't find the information you need publicly listed, do not hesitate to give the agency or bureau a call and request data over the phone. Many government offices have interns and staffers who handle public requests for information.

FOIA How-To

You can submit a Freedom of Information Act (or FOIA) request to any local, state, or federal government agency in the United States. This request should be simple and straightforward. Depending on what information you are looking for and how specifically you can describe it, your mileage may vary.

The US Goverment has a FOIA website (*http://bit.ly/foia_online*) you can use to submit and track your requests for certain agencies; however, most agencies have instructions on how to submit FOIA requests on their own sites. In your request, you should include contact information, a description of what records you seek, and what you are willing to pay if there are reproduction fees.

It's good practice to try to be fairly specific about what records you are looking for, without unnecessarily limiting your search. As you can imagine, being too broad might mean the agency returns millions of records (which you now have to sort through and potentially pay for). Alternatively, if you are overly specific, it could mean you miss a relevant record that would shed more light on the topic. Of course, you can always submit more FOIA requests based on the information you find with your first request. That's half the fun, right?

If you would like to request government and agency information outside of the United States, Wikipedia has a great list of Freedom of Information laws across the globe (*http://bit.ly/foi_laws*). For more on FOIA in the United States, see the Electronic Frontier Foundation's tips (*https://www.eff.org/issues/transparency/foia-how-to*).

Government and Civic Open Data Worldwide

Depending on what country you want to research and whether you live there, there are many ways to acquire government data. Because we are more familiar with US policies, we do not claim this is an extensive listing of possibilities. If you come across other useful open data not covered in this book that you'd like to share, feel free to reach out to us!

We still recommend fact checking government datasets, particularly if the government has a history of human rights violations. Use your best judgment when approaching all data and do not hesitate to pick up the phone or email the listed contact to further inquire about data collection methods.

EU and UK

If you are interested in data from the European Union or the United Kingdom, there are many data portals available. Several of the following sites are put together by organizations and open data enthusiasts, so feel free to reach out directly to the site owner if you are looking for a particular dataset:

- Public Data EU (*http://publicdata.eu/*)
- Open Data Europa (*http://open-data.europa.eu*)
- Linked Open Data Around-The-Clock (*http://latc-project.eu/*)
- UK Government Data (*http://data.gov.uk/*)

Africa

If you are interested in data from African nations, there are many projects working to amass data and build APIs for developer use. Many African nations also use their own open data portals (a quick Google search can usually identify these). We've singled out some useful regional projects:

- Africa Open Data (*http://africaopendata.org/*)
- Code for South Africa (*http://code4sa.org/*)
- Code for Africa (*http://www.codeforafrica.org/*)

- Open Data for Africa (*http://opendataforafrica.org/*)

Asia

If you are interested in data from Asian nations, most run their own open data sites. We've identified a few with impressive datasets and some regional data from organizations:

- Open Cities Project (*http://www.opencitiesproject.org/*)
- Open Nepal (*http://data.opennepal.net/*)
- National Bureau of Statistics of China (*http://www.stats.gov.cn/english/*)
- Open Data Hong Kong (*https://opendatahk.com/*)
- Indonesian Government Open Data (*http://data.go.id/*)

Non-EU Europe, Central Asia, India, the Middle East, and Russia

Many Central Asian, Central European, and Middle Eastern countries outside of the EU have their own government open data sites. We have highlighted a few, but your linguistic skills will be paramount if you know what regions and countries you'd like to target and want to access data in the native tongue (although Google Chrome will attempt to translate web pages automatically, so you may still be able to find useful data even if you don't speak the language):

- Russian Government Data Website (*http://data.gov.ru/*)
- PakReport—Pakistan Open Data and Maps (*http://pakreport.org/*)
- Open Data India (*http://www.data.gov.in/*)
- Turkey Open Statistics (*http://www.turkstat.gov.tr/*)

South America and Canada

Many South American nations have their own open data sites, found easily by search. Canada also has an open data portal for statistics. We have highlighted a few sites but encourage you to seek out particular sectors or governments you are interested in by searching online:

- Canada Statistics (*http://www.rdc-cdr.ca/datasets-and-surveys*)
- Open Canada (*http://open.canada.ca/en*)
- Open Data Brasil (*http://dados.gov.br/*)
- Open Data Mexico (*http://datos.gob.mx/*)

- Open Data Latin America (*http://www.opendatalatinoamerica.org/*)
- Developing in the Caribbean (*http://developingcaribbean.com/*)

Organization and Non-Government Organization (NGO) Data

Organizations—both the locally run and international—are great sources for datasets that cross state or national borders, such as data on climate change, international business and trade, and global transportation. If your topic is something the government might not collect (data on religious details, drug use, community-based support networks, etc.) or if the government in question is an unreliable source or lacks an open data portal, you might be able to find the data via an NGO or open data organization. We've listed some here, but there are many more fighting for open exchange and access to data:

- United Nations Open Data (*http://data.un.org/*)
- United Nations Development Program Data (*http://open.undp.org/*)
- Open Knowledge Foundation (*https://okfn.org/*)
- World Bank Data (*http://data.worldbank.org/*)
- WikiLeaks (*https://wikileaks.org/*)
- International Aid and Transparency Datasets (*http://www.iatiregistry.org/*)
- DataHub (*http://datahub.io/*)
- Population Reference Bureau (*http://www.prb.org/DataFinder.aspx*)

Education and University Data

Universities and graduate departments around the world are constantly researching and releasing datasets, covering everything from advances in biological science to the interrelatedness of native cultures with neighboring ecological habitats. It's hard to imagine a subject not broached within the educational sphere, so universities are a great place to get the latest topical data. Most researchers are happy to hear someone is interested in their topic, so we encourage you to reach out to the appropriate departments and authors directly for more information. If you're not sure where to start, here are a few good options:

- Lexis Nexis (*http://lexisnexis.com*)
- Google Scholar search (*http://scholar.google.com*)
- Cornell University's arXiv project (*http://arxiv.org*)
- UCI Machine Learning Datasets (*http://archive.ics.uci.edu/ml/*)

- Common Data Set Initiative (*http://www.commondataset.org/*)

Medical and Scientific Data

Similar to universities, scientific and medical research departments and organizations are an excellent resource for a broad array of data. Navigating scientific research can prove daunting, but don't fret—if you can find the datasets used for the research, they usually come without the same research paper jargon. If you have a specific researcher or study in mind, we recommend reaching out directly; we've collected a few of the aggregators into the following list:

- Open Science Data Cloud (*https://www.opensciencedatacloud.org/publicdata/*)
- Open Science Directory (*http://www.opensciencedirectory.net/*)
- World Health Organization Data (*http://www.who.int/gho/database/en/*)
- Broad Institute Open Data (*http://www.broadinstitute.org/scientific-community/data*)
- Human Connectome Project (neuro pathway mapping) (*http://www.humanconnectomeproject.org/*)
- UNC's Psychiatric Genomics Consortium (*http://www.med.unc.edu/pgc/*)
- Social Science Datasets (*http://3stages.org/idata/*)
- CDC Medical Data (*http://www.cdc.gov/nchs/fastats/*)

Crowdsourced Data and APIs

If your idea or question is better answered by crowdsourcing, the Internet and its many forums, services, and social media outlets allow you to create your own questions and answer them with the help of some data mining. Services like Twitter and Instragram boast billions of users and easy-to-use application programming interfaces (or APIs). APIs are protocols or tools that allow software or code to interact with another system. In our case, we are usually dealing with web-based APIs where we can send web requests and ask for data from the service. With normally less than an hour of set-up time, API access will put millions of records at your fingertips.

We will take a more in-depth look at APIs in Chapter 13, but for now some of the basic challenges and benefits of using an API are reviewed in Table 6-1.

Table 6-1. Using an API

Pros	Cons
Immediate access to data you can use	Unreliability of mass API system (selection bias)
Vast quantities of data	Data overload
You don't have to worry about storage; you can just access the data from the service's storage	Reliability and dependence on access—API limitations or downtime

As you can see, there are benefits and compromises. If you find an API you want to use, create a few rules around how you will use it and what to do if it is not accessible (you may want to store responses locally to avoid downtime issues). Collecting enough responses over time can also help eliminate some selection bias in your research.

Outside of social web services, there are a variety of sites where you can post your own questions and ideas and ask for a crowdsourced reply. Whether you want to go to an expert forum related to the topic or post a survey and circulate it though your own channels is up to you, but be aware when using your own research questions and methods that you must account for whatever size and sampling errors arise. For a more detailed introduction to writing your own survey along with citations for more information, the University of Wisconsin's survey guide (*http://bit.ly/survey_guide*) can be a good starting point.

For other crowdsourced data, take a look at:

- Gallup Polls (*http://www.gallup.com/home.aspx*)
- European Social Survey (*http://www.europeansocialsurvey.org/data/*)
- Reuters Polls (*http://polling.reuters.com/*)

The amount of data available is enormous, and it's no small task sorting through all of the noise to get a good idea of what questions you can answer and how you should go about answering them. Let's walk through a few case studies to give you a better idea of how to go about pursuing the data that helps answer your questions.

Case Studies: Example Data Investigation

We will outline a few different areas of interest and questions so you have a good idea of how you can begin.

Ebola Crisis

Let's say you are interested in investigating the Ebola crisis in West Africa. How might you begin? To start with, you might quickly Google "Ebola crisis data." You will find there are many international organizations working to track the spread of the virus, and those organizations put numerous tools at your disposal. First, you may find the World Health Organization's situation report (*http://bit.ly/who_ebola_reports*). The WHO site has information on the latest cases and deaths, interactive maps showing affected regions, and key performance indicators for response measures, and it appears to be updated on a weekly basis. The data is available in CSV and JSON format, and it's a veritable, reliable, and regularly updated source of information.

Rather than stopping at the first result you turn up, you keep digging to see what other sources are available. Upon further searching, we find a GitHub repository run by user cmrivers (*https://github.com/cmrivers/ebola*), which is a raw data collection of data sources from a variety of governmental and media sources. Because we know the user and can contact them via their contact information, we can also verify when was the last time these sources were updated and ask any questions about the collection methods. The formats are ones we know how to handle (CSV, PDF files), so they shouldn't present a problem.

As you dig further, you might focus on one particular question, like "What precautions are being taken for safe burial?" You find a report on safe and dignified burials (*http://bit.ly/burial_teams*) maintained by Sam Libby (*https://data.hdx.rwlabs.org/user/libbys*). Perfect! If and when you have any questions, you can contact Sam directly.

You've found a good initial list of sources, verified they are from organizations you can trust, and identified someone you can ask for more information as your research progresses. Now, let's take a look at another example.

Train Safety

Let's say you're interested in train safety in the United States. Maybe your question is: What are the negative factors affecting train safety? To begin, you might look at some previous research around train safety. You come across the Federal Railroad Administration (FRA), whose core duty is to ensure railroad safety and usability. As you read some of the reports and fact sheets on the FRA website (*https://www.fra.dot.gov*), you determine most reports indicate train accidents occur due to poor track maintenance or human error.

You're interested in the human side of things, so you start digging a little more. You find that the FRA has numerous reports on railroad employees and safety. You find a report on sleep patterns of railroad workers (*http://bit.ly/work_sleep_sched_data*), which could shed some light on how human errors occur. You also find some information about federal regulations for drug and alcohol testing of railroad employees (*http://bit.ly/fra_drug_alcohol_testing*).

Now you might have more questions you can specify to narrow down what you *really* want to know. Maybe your question is now, "How often are railroad accidents caused by alcohol?" Or "How often are train engineers overworked or working while exhausted?" You have some initial trusted datasets and the ability to call the FRA and request more information as your research progresses.

Football Salaries

Now let's say you're interested in football (the kind with the feet, not the pigskin one) salaries. How much are these players making, and how significant is each player's impact on his team?

As you first start searching, you determine you should focus on one league, given the disparate data. Let's say you choose the English Premier League. You find a listing of Premier League club salaries (*http://bit.ly/epl_salaries_by_club*) on a site you may never have heard of before. It seems the author has also compiled lists of each team and how much each player is getting paid (*http://bit.ly/2014_man_city_salaries*). To better understand where the data is coming from and to make sure you can trust the source, you should reach out to the author listed on the page and get more information.

If you're also searching for endorsements, you may come across the Statistica charts (*http://bit.ly/2014_soccer_player_earnings*) outlining endorsement and salary data for the top-paid football players. You'll probably want to reach out and see if there is updated data on endorsements so you can compare the most recent season.

Now that you have some salary data, you'll want to look at statistics on how good the top-paid players are. You find some player statistics on the Premier League's website (*http://bit.ly/epl_players_index*). This is data you can likely only get by web scraping (more on this in Chapter 11), but you know you can trust the source. Another search for statistics on players turns up some more data on top assists (*http://bit.ly/espn_epl_top_assists*). You can also analyze penalty try statistics (*http://bit.ly/epl_2015-16_penalties*). Again, you should investigate the validity of any source you use that's not easily verified.

Now you can begin your your analysis to see how much each football player's goals, red cards, and penalty kicks are worth!

Child Labor

Finally, let's take a dive into the questions we will be answering with further chapters in this book. We'll focus on the international crisis of child labor. When we think about international topics, we immediately turn to international organizations.

We find UNICEF's open data site dedicated to reporting on child labor (*http://data.unicef.org/child-protection/child-labour.html*). In fact, UNICEF has entire datasets on women and children's well-being and status (*http://www.childinfo.org/mics.html*) across the globe. These might prove fruitful for answering questions such as "Does early marriage affect child labor rates?"

When looking for government data, we identify the US Department of Labor's annual reports (*http://www.dol.gov/ilab/reports/child-labor/*) on child labor across the globe. These will be a great cross reference for our UNICEF datasets.

Additionally, we find the International Labor Organization's (ILO) trend report on child labor (*http://bit.ly/child_labour_trends08-12*). The ILO report seems to have links to many different datasets and should be a good reference for historical data on child labor.

We've amassed several datasets to use throughout the next chapters. We've included them all in the data repository (*https://github.com/jackiekazil/data-wrangling*) so you can use them and follow along.

Now that we've explored how to identify questions and find resources, let's look at storing our data.

Storing Your Data: When, Why, and How?

Once you've located your data, you need a place to store it! Sometimes, you'll have received data in a clean, easy-to-access, and machine-readable format. Other times, you might want to find a different way to store it. We'll review some data storage tools to use when you first extract your data from a CSV or PDF, or you can wait and store your data once it's fully processed and cleaned (which we will cover in Chapter 7).

Where Should I Store My Data?

Your initial question will be whether to store your data someplace other than in the files from which you extracted it. Here's a great set of questions to help you figure this out:

- Can you open your dataset in a simple document viewer (like Microsoft Word), without crashing your computer?

- Does the data appear to be properly labeled and organized, so you can easily pluck out each piece of information?

- Is the data easily stored and moved if you need to use more than one laptop or computer while working on it?

- Is the data real-time and accessible via an API, meaning you can get the data you need by requesting it live?

If you answered "yes" to all of these questions, chances are you do *not* need to worry about storing your data another way. If you had mixed answers, you *might* want to store your data in a database or flat files. If your answer was "no" to all of these questions, read on, my friend; we have solutions for you!

So, let's say your dataset is disparate: a file from here, a report from there; some of it easy to download and access, but other bits you might need to copy or scrape from the Web. We will review how to clean and combine datasets in Chapters 7 and 9, but now let's talk about how we can store data in a shared place.

 If you are going to be using datasets from multiple computers, it's always a good idea to store them on a network or the Internet (hello cloud computing!), or have them on an external hard drive or USB stick. Keep this in mind when you are working with a team who may need data access from different locations or computers. If you're working on a single computer, make sure you have a data backup strategy. The worst thing about losing your laptop will be losing the data you spent months acquiring and cleaning.

Databases: A Brief Introduction

Databases—learn to love them, love to hate them. As a developer, you'll likely find yourself using many different types of databases throughout your education and work. This section is by no means intended as a comprehensive overview of databases, but we aim to provide a brief introduction to basic database concepts. If you already know and use databases actively, give this section a quick review and move on to the other storage solutions and when to use them.

Have you ever looked up a number on your phone using Siri? Have you ever searched Google? Have you ever clicked on a hashtag on Twitter or Instagram? Each of these actions involves a simple search and a response from a database (or a series of databases, or a database cache). You have a question (What funny new Maru videos are on YouTube?), you ask a particular database (YouTube Search), and get a fun(ny) response—a listing of search results to enjoy.

In the following sections, we outline two major database types, highlighting the pros and cons of each as well as their different strengths and weaknesses. For the purposes of data wrangling, you absolutely *do not* need to use a database; however, as you become more advanced at data wrangling and analysis, database use and knowledge will become more important and help advance your ability to store and analyze data.

If you're interested in databasing, we will give a few tips on how to use Python with databases; but we clearly don't have enough time here to fully cover the topic. We highly recommend you search out more information, videos, and tutorials based on your interest in this section.

Relational Databases: MySQL and PostgreSQL

Relational databases are great for data coming from a variety of sources with varying levels of interconnectedness. Relational data exemplifies its name: if your data has connections similar to a family tree, a relational database like MySQL will likely work well for you.

Relational data usually uses a series of unique identifiers to actively match datasets. In SQL, we normally call them *IDs*. These IDs can be used by other sets of data to find and match connections. From these connected datasets, we can make what we call *joins*, which allow us to access connected data from many different datasets at once. Let's look at an example.

I have a really awesome friend. Her name is Meghan. She has black hair and works at *The New York Times*. In her spare time, she likes to go dancing, cook food, and teach people how to code. If I had a database of my friends and used SQL to represent their attributes, I might break it down like so:

```
**friend_table: ❶
friend_id        ❷
friend_name
friend_date_of_birth
friend_current_location
friend_birthplace
friend_occupation_id


**friend_occupation_table:
friend_occupation_id
friend_occupation_name
friend_occupation_location

**friends_and_hobbies_table:
friend_id
hobby_id

**hobby_details_table:
hobby_id
hobby_name
hobby_level_of_awesome
```

❶ In my database of friends, each of these sections (marked with **) would be *tables*. In relational databasing, tables usually hold information about a specific topic or object.

❷ Each of the pieces of information a table holds are called *fields*. In this case, the `friend_id` field holds a unique ID for each friend in my `friend_table`.

With my database, I can ask: What are Meghan's hobbies? To access the information, I would say to the database, "Hey, I'm looking for my friend Meghan. She lives in New York and here is her birthday; can you tell me her ID?" My SQL database will respond to this query with her `friend_id`. I can then ask my `friend_and_hobbies_table` (which properly matches hobby IDs with the friend IDs) what hobbies match up with this friend ID and it will respond with a list of three new hobby IDs.

Because these IDs are numbers, I want to learn more about what they mean. I ask the `hobby_details_table`, "Can you tell me more about these hobby IDs?" and it says, "Sure! One is dancing, one is cooking food, and one is teaching people how to code." Aha! I have solved the riddle, using just an initial friend description.

Setting up and getting data into a relational database can involve many steps, but if your datasets are complex with many different relationships, it shouldn't take more than a few steps to figure out how to join them and get the information you desire. When building relational databases, spend time mapping out the relations and their attributes, similar to what we did with the friend database. What are the different types of data, and how can they be mapped to one another?

In relational database *schema,* we figure out how we want to match data by thinking about how we will most often use the data. You want the queries you ask the database to be easy to answer. Because we thought we might use occupation to help identify a friend, we put the `occupation_id` in the `friend-table`.

Another thing to note is there are several different kinds of relationships. For example, I can have many friends with cooking as a hobby. This is what we call a *many-to-many* relationship. If we were to add a table such as `pets`, that would add a different kind of relationship—a *many-to-one*. This is because a few of my friends have more than one pet, but each pet belongs to only one friend. I could look up all the pets of a friend by using their `friend_id`.

If learning more about SQL and relational databases interests you, we recommend taking a longer look at SQL. Learn SQL The Hard Way (*http://sql.learncodethehard way.org/*) and SQLZOO (*http://sqlzoo.net*) are great first places to start. There are some slight differences in syntax between PostgreSQL and MySQL, but they both follow the same basics, and learning one over the other is a matter of personal choice.

MySQL and Python

If you are familiar with (or learning) MySQL and you'd like to use a MySQL database, there are Python bindings to easily connect. You will need to perform two steps. First, you must install a MySQL driver. Then, you should use Python to send authentication information (user, password, host, database name). There is a great Stack Overflow write-up (*http://bit.ly/mysql_python*) covering both.

PostgreSQL and Python

If you are familiar with (or learning) PostgreSQL and you'd like to use a PostgreSQL database, there are Python bindings for PostgreSQL, too. You will also need to perform two steps: installing a driver and then connecting with Python.

There are many PostgreSQL drivers for Python (*https://wiki.postgresql.org/wiki/Python*), but the most popular one is Psycopg (*http://initd.org/psycopg/*). Psycopg's installation page (*http://initd.org/psycopg/docs/install.html*) has details about getting it running on your machine and there is a lengthy introduction on how to use it with Python (*https://wiki.postgresql.org/wiki/Psycopg2_Tutorial*) on the PostgreSQL site.

Non-Relational Databases: NoSQL

Let's say you like the idea of using a database, but mapping out all those relations gives you the heebie-jeebies. Maybe it's just that you don't really understand how the data connects right now. Maybe it's that you have flat data (i.e., nonrelational data that doesn't necessarily map well). Or maybe you don't have a deeper interest in learning SQL. Luckily, there is a database out there for you.

NoSQL and other nonrelational databases store data in a flat format, usually JSON. As we discussed in Chapter 3, JSON uses a simple lookup for information. Going back to the data shared in the previous section about my friend, what if I just had the data stored in nodes that allow me to look up more information about that friend? It might look like so:

```
{
    'name': 'Meghan',
    'occupation': { 'employer': 'NYT',
                    'role': 'design editor',
                },
    'birthplace': 'Ohio',
    'hobbies': ['cooking', 'dancing', 'teaching'],
}
```

As you can see, I can have a simple list of all of my friend's attributes, without having to create tables.

What, you may ask, is the benefit of relational data? Depending on who you ask, you might get very different responses—within computer science and among developers this is a hotly debated topic. Our opinion is there are many advances SQL has made to allow for quick lookups when your data is structured with a vast network of relations. There are also plenty of advances nonrelational databases have made in speed, availability, and duplication.

In the end, if you have a stronger interest in learning one over the other, let that guide your decision rather than determining now what your dataset looks like. If you need to migrate it one way or another, there are tools that will help you migrate in either direction.[1]

MongoDB with Python

If you already have data in a nonrelational database structure or you are hoping to learn by doing, it's very easy to connect NoSQL databases using Python. Although there are plenty to choose from, one of the most popular NoSQL database frameworks is MongoDB (*http://mongodb.org/*). To use MongoDB, you need to first install the drivers (*http://docs.mongodb.org/ecosystem/drivers/python/*) and then use Python to connect. There was a great "Getting Started with MongoDB" (*http://bit.ly/pycon2012_presentations*) presentation at PyCon 2012; this is a useful place to get started learning about MongoDB and how to connect using Python.

Setting Up Your Local Database with Python

One of the easiest ways to get started with databases and Python is to use a simple library to help you ramp up quickly. For the purpose of this book, we recommend starting with Dataset (*http://dataset.readthedocs.org/en/latest/*). Dataset is a *wrapper library*, which means it helps speed development by translating our readable Python code into the database code we want to work with.

If you already have a SQLite, PostgreSQL, or MySQL database, you can plug it right in by following the quickstart guide (*http://bit.ly/dataset_quickstart*). If you *don't* yet have one of those, it will create one for you as you use the tool. Let's take a look at getting it running on your computer.

The first thing you will need to do is install Dataset (*http://bit.ly/dataset_install*). If you are already using pip, then simply type `pip install dataset`.

You then need to decide on the backend you will use. If you are already using PostgreSQL or MySQL, simply set up a new database following the proper syntax for your chosen database. If you are new to databases, we will use SQLite. First, download

---

1 For more reading on database migration between SQL and NoSQL databases, check out Matt Asay's writeup on migrating Foursquare to a NoSQL database from a relational database (*http://bit.ly/migrate_rdb_nosql*). Additionally, there are some Quora writeups (*http://bit.ly/migrate_mongodb_mysql*) covering migration in the opposite direction.

your operating system's SQLite binary (*http://www.sqlite.org/download.html*). Open the downloaded file and follow the installation instructions.

Open your terminal and change (cd) to your project folder holding your Python data wrangling scripts. To create your new SQLite database, type:

```
sqlite3 data_wrangling.db
```

You should see a prompt beginning with sqlite> asking you to enter SQL. Now that you've confirmed you have *sqlite3* running on your computer, you can exit the SQLite terminal by typing .q. Upon exit, list the files in your current folder. You should now have a file called *data_wrangling.db*—that's your database!

Once you have SQLite installed and your first database running, it's time to get it working with Dataset. Let's try the following code in a Python shell:

```
import dataset

db = dataset.connect('sqlite:///data_wrangling.db')

my_data_source = {
    'url':
    'http://www.tsmplug.com/football/premier-league-player-salaries-club-by-club/',
    'description': 'Premier League Club Salaries',
    'topic': 'football',
    'verified': False,
} ❶

table = db['data_sources'] ❷
table.insert(my_data_source) ❸

another_data_source = {
    'url':
    'http://www.premierleague.com/content/premierleague/en-gb/players/index.html',
    'description': 'Premier League Stats',
    'topic': 'football',
    'verified': True,
}

table.insert(another_data_source)

sources = db['data_sources'].all() ❹

print sources
```

❶ Creates a Python dictionary of the data we are looking to save. We are saving the sources for our football research. We added information about the topic, description, URL, and whether we have verified the data yet.

❷ Creates a new table called data_sources.

❸ Inserts our first data source into our new table.

❹ Shows all of the data sources we have stored in our `data_sources` table.

You have now set up your first relational table using SQLite, and done your first Python database interactions. As the book progresses, you will be able to add more data and tables to your database. Having all of your data stored in one place helps keep your data organized and your research focused.

When to Use a Simple File

If your dataset is small, most likely a simple file, rather than a database, will do. You might want to take a look at Chapter 7 and start with some sanitizing techniques before saving it, but keeping it in a CSV or some other simple file format is perfectly fine. The same `csv` module we worked with to import CSVs (see "How to Import CSV Data" on page 46) also has some easy-to-use writer classes (*http://bit.ly/writer_objects*).

Your main consideration when using simple files is making sure you have easy access and backup. To manage these needs, you can store your data on a shared network drive or in a cloud-based service (Dropbox, Box, Amazon, Google Drive). Using one of these services usually means you will also have backup options, management capabilities, and the ability to share files. This is extremely helpful for those "oops, I overwrote the data file" moments.

Cloud-Storage and Python

Depending on your cloud storage solution, you should research the best way to get Python connected to your data. Dropbox has great Python support, and their Getting Started with Python (*http://bit.ly/python_core_api*) guide provides a good introduction. Google Drive is a bit more complex, but the Python Quick start (*https://github.com/googledrive/python-quickstart*) guide will help you through the first steps. There are also some Google Drive Python API wrappers, like PyDrive (*https://github.com/googledrive/PyDrive*), that allow you to use Google Drive without knowing much Python. We highly recommend GSpread (*https://github.com/burnash/gspread*) for managing spreadsheets on Google Drive.

If you have your own cloud servers, you might need to research the best way to connect to them. Python has built in URL request, FTP (File Transfer Protocol), and SSH/SCP (Secure Sell/Secure Copy) methods, all documented in the Python stdlib. We will also cover some useful libraries for managing cloud services in Chapter 14.

Local Storage and Python

The simplest and most straightforward way to store your data is locally. You can open documents on your filesystem with one line of Python (the open command (*https://docs.python.org/2/library/functions.html#open*)). You can also update and save new files as you work with the data using the built-in `file.write` method (*http://bit.ly/file_write_method*).

Alternative Data Storage

There are many new and interesting ways to store data which don't involve the afore-mentioned paths. Depending on your use case, there may be a better way to store the data you are looking to use. Here are a few interesting ones:

Hierarchical Data Format (HDF)
> HDF is a file-based scalable data solution allowing you to quickly store large datasets to a filesystem (local or otherwise). If you are already familiar with HDF, Python has an HDF5 driver, h5py (*http://www.h5py.org/*), which connects Python to HDF5.

Hadoop
> Hadoop is a big data distributed storage system, allowing you to store and process data across clusters. If you are already working with Hadoop or are familiar with Hadoop, Cloudera has a Guide to Python Frameworks for Hadoop (*http://bit.ly/py-hadoop*) with some great getting-started code samples.

Summary

Congratulations! You've gotten through some of the largest questions facing your project: How can I find useful data? How can I access and store the data? We hope you feel confident with the sources you have acquired and the veritability of your first dataset(s). We also hope you have a solid plan for backup and data storage.

You can use the skills you've honed in this chapter on future datasets, even if it's just spending a few hours on data sites exploring questions that pop into your mind.

You should now feel confident:

- Determining the value and use of a dataset you find
- Picking up the phone to reach out for more information
- Deciding where you might first look for data to answer a question
- Implementing a safe and hassle-free way to store your data
- Validating the data you have found

- Building relational models of the data

You've also been introduced to the concepts in Table 6-2.

Table 6-2. New Python and programming concepts and libraries

Concept/library	Purpose
Relational databases (e.g., MySQL and PostgreSQL)	Storing relational data in an easy way
Non-relational databases (e.g., MongoDB)	Storing data in a flat way
SQLite (*https://www.sqlite.org/*) setup and usage	Easy-to-use SQL-based storage that works well for simple projects
Dataset (*https://dataset.readthedocs.org/en/latest/*) installation and usage	Easy-to-use Python database wrapper

You'll be using all of these skills and more as you move forward in future chapters. In the next chapter, you'll be learning all about cleaning your data, finding inconsistencies with the code, and getting it closer to a fully running script or program so you can analyze your data and output results to share with the world.

## CHAPTER 7

Data Cleanup: Investigation, Matching, and Formatting

Cleaning up your data is not the most glamourous of tasks, but it's an essential part of data wrangling. Becoming a data cleaning expert requires precision and a healthy knowledge of your area of research or study. Knowing how to properly clean and assemble your data will set you miles apart from others in your field.

Python is well designed for data cleanup; it helps you build functions around patterns, eliminating repetitive work. As we've already seen in our code so far, learning to fix repetitive problems with scripts and code can turn hours of manual work into a script you run once.

In this chapter, we will take a look at how Python can help you clean and format your data. We'll also use Python to locate duplicates and errors in our datasets. We will continue learning about cleanup, especially automating our cleanup and saving our cleaned data, in the next chapter.

Why Clean Data?

Some data may come to you properly formatted and ready to use. If this is the case, consider yourself lucky! Most data, even if it is cleaned, has some formatting inconsistencies or readability issues (e.g., acronyms or mismatched description headers). This is especially true if you are using data from more than one dataset. It's unlikely your data will properly join and be useful unless you spend time formatting and standardizing it.

Cleaning your data makes for easier storage, search, and reuse. As we explored in Chapter 6, it's much easier to store your data in proper models if it's cleaned first. Imagine if you had columns or fields in your dataset which should be saved as a particular data type (such as dates or numbers or email addresses). If you can standardize what you expect to see and clean or remove records that don't fit, then you ensure your data's consistency and eliminate hard work later when you need to query assets living in your dataset.

If you'd like to present your findings and publish your data, you'll want to publish the cleaned version. This gives other data wranglers the opportunity to easily import and analyze the data. You can also publish the raw data alongside your finished dataset with notations on what steps you took to clean and normalize it.

As we work on cleaning our data, for our benefit and the benefit of others, we want to document the steps we have taken so we can accurately defend our dataset and its use in our studies. By documenting our process, we ensure we can reproduce it when new data comes out.

One powerful tool if you are using IPython to interact with your data is to use the IPython magic commands, such as `%logstart` (*http://bit.ly/logstart*) or to start logging and `%save` (*http://bit.ly/ ipython_save*) to save your session for later use. This way you can begin building scripts, not just hacking in a Python terminal. As your Python knowledge increases, you can refine the scripts to share with others. For more reading on IPython, check out Appendix F.

Let's start by investigating data cleaning basics, learning how to format our data and properly match datasets together.

Data Cleanup Basics

If you have been working through the code in the preceding chapters, you have already used some data cleanup concepts. In Chapter 4, we worked on importing data from Excel sheets and creating a dictionary to represent that data. Modifying and standardizing the data into a new data format is data cleanup.

Because we've already investigated some UNICEF datasets related to child labor (see "Child Labor" on page 139), let's dive into the raw UNICEF data. The initial datasets most UNICEF reports accumulate are the Multiple Indicator Cluster Surveys (MICS) (*http://mics.unicef.org/surveys*). These surveys are household-level surveys performed by UNICEF workers and volunteers to help research the living conditions of women and children throughout the world. In looking through the latest surveys, we pulled some data from Zimbabwe's latest MICS to analyze.

To begin our analysis, we downloaded the latest surveys after first requesting access for educational and research purposes from UNICEF. After getting access (which took approximately a day), we were able to download the raw datasets. Most MICS raw data is in SPSS format, or *.sav* files. SPSS is a program used by social scientists to store and analyze data. It's a great tool for some social science statistics, but it's not very useful for our Python needs.

In order to convert the SPSS files to something we can use, we used the open source project PSPP (*https://www.gnu.org/software/pspp/*) to view the data, and then a few simple R commands to convert the SPSS data into *.csv* files (*http://bit.ly/spss_to_csv*) for easy use with Python. There are some good projects using Python to interact with SPSS files (*https://pypi.python.org/pypi/savReaderWriter*) as well, but they required more work and setup than the R commands. You'll find the updated CSV in this book's repository (*https://github.com/jackiekazil/data-wrangling*).

Let's get started with our data cleanup by diving into the files and taking a look at the data. Often your first cleanup steps come from a simple visual analysis. Let's dig into our files and see what we find!

Identifying Values for Data Cleanup

We begin our data cleanup with a simple review of the fields we find and any visual inconsistencies we can see. If you start your data cleanup by making your data *look* cleaner, you will have a good idea of the initial problems you must conquer as you normalize your data.

Let's take a look at our *mn.csv* file. The file contains raw data and uses codes (acronyms) as headers which likely contain some easily translatable meaning. Let's take a look at the column headers in our *mn.csv* file:

```
"","HH1","HH2","LN","MWM1","MWM2", ...
```

Each of these represents a question or data in the survey, and we'd like the more human-readable versions. Searching via Google, we locate the human-readable values for those headings on the World Bank site for sharing MICS data (*http://bit.ly/selected_papua_mics2011*).

 Take time to first investigate whether data like the abbreviation listing on the World Bank site exists to help with your cleanup needs. You can also pick up the phone and give the organization a call to ask if they have an easy-to-use abbreviation list.

Using some web scraping skills you'll become acquainted with in Chapter 11, we were able to get a CSV of these headers with their English variants and the questions used to calculate their values from the World Bank site for MICS data. We've included the new headers from our web scraper in the book's repository (*mn-headers.csv*). We want to match up this data with our survey data so we have readable questions and answers. Let's look at a few ways we can do that.

Replacing headers

The most straightforward and obvious way to make the headers more readable is to merely replace the short headers with longer English ones we can understand. How might we go about header substitution using Python? First, we'll need to import both the *mn.csv* and *mn-headers.csv* files using the `csv` module we learned about in Chapter 3 (see the following code for importing). Throughout this chapter and the following chapters, feel free to write code in either scripts or in your terminal (such as IPython). This will allow you to interact with the data before saving it to a file:

```
from csv import DictReader

data_rdr = DictReader(open('data/unicef/mn.csv', 'rb'))
header_rdr = DictReader(open('data/unicef/mn_headers.csv', 'rb'))

data_rows = [d for d in data_rdr]       ❶
header_rows = [h for h in header_rdr]

print data_rows[:5]      ❷
print header_rows[:5]
```

❶ This code writes the iterable `DictReader` object into a new list so we can preserve the data and reuse it. We're using the list generator format so we can do it in one simple line of code that's readable and clear.

❷ This prints just a slice of the data, by using the Python list's `slice` method to show the first five elements of our new lists and get an idea of the content.

In the fourth line of code, we used a *list generator* function for Python. Python list generators have the following format:

```
[func(x) for x in iter_x]
```

A list generator starts and ends with list brackets. Then it takes an iterable object (`iter_x`) and passes each row or value from `iter_x` into `func(x)` to create new values for the new list. Here, we are not doing anything with the function part of the list generator; we only want the row as it currently stands. In future chapters, we'll use the ability to pass each row or value from the iterable into a function to clean or change the data before we put it into the list. List generators are a great example of the easy-to-read and easy-to-use syntax Python is well known for. You could achieve the same functionality using a `for` loop, but that would require more code:

```
new_list = []
for x in iter_x:
    new_list.append(func(x))
```

As you can see, using a list generator saves us a few lines of code, and offers superior performance and memory efficiency.

We want to replace the `data_row` dictionary headers with the readable headers from our file. As we can see from our output, the `header_rows` dictionaries hold both the short and longer values. The current short headers are contained under the `Name` field, and the longer, more readable headers are saved under the `Label` field. Let's see how easily we can match them up using some Python string methods:

```
for data_dict in data_rows:  ❶
    for dkey, dval in data_dict.items():  ❷
        for header_dict in header_rows:  ❸
            for hkey, hval in header_dict.items():
                if dkey == hval:  ❹
                    print 'match!'
```

❶ Iterates over each of our data records. We will try to use the keys in each of these dictionaries to match our headers.

❷ Iterates over each key and value in each data row so we can replace all of the keys with the more readable header labels (to view each key-value pair in the data dictionary, we use the Python dictionary's `items` method).

❸ Iterates over all header rows of data, so we can get the readable labels. It's not the fastest way to do this, but it makes sure we don't miss any.

❹ Prints found matches between the data list keys (MWB3, MWB7, MWB4, MWB5...) and the header dictionary data.

By running the code, we see we have many matches. Let's see if we can use similar logic to replace the titles with better ones. We know we can match them really easily. However, we only found the row we wanted to match. Let's see if we can figure out how to match the keys from the data list with the values from the row in the header row we found:

```
new_rows = []  ❶

for data_dict in data_rows:
    new_row = {}  ❷
    for dkey, dval in data_dict.items():
        for header_dict in header_rows:
            if dkey in header_dict.values():  ❸
                new_row[header_dict.get('Label')] = dval  ❹
    new_rows.append(new_row)  ❺
```

❶ Creates a new list to populate with cleaned rows.

❷ Creates a new dictionary for each row.

❸ Here, we use the dictionary's `values` method instead of iterating over every key and value of the header rows. This method returns a list of only the values in that dictionary. We are also using Python's `in` method, which tests whether an object is a member of a list. For this line of code, the object is our key, or the abbreviated string, and the list is the values of the header dictionary (which contains the abbreviated headers). When this line is true, we know we have found the matching row.

❹ Adds to our `new_row` dictionary every time we find a match. This sets the dictionary key equal to the `Label` value in the header row, replacing those short `Name` values with the longer, more readable `Label` values, and keeps the values set to the data row values.

❺ Appends the new cleaned dictionary we created to our new array. This is indented to ensure we have all the matches before going to the next row.

You can see from a simple print of the first record of our new values that we have successfully made the data readable:

```
In [8]: new_rows[0]
Out[8]: {
    'AIDS virus from mother to child during delivery': 'Yes',
    'AIDS virus from mother to child during pregnancy': 'DK',
    'AIDS virus from mother to child through breastfeeding': 'DK',
    'Age': '25-29',
    'Age at first marriage/union': '29',...
```

One easy way to determine whether you have the proper indentation for your function is to look at other lines with the same indentation. Always ask yourself: What other code logically goes with this step? When should I move on to the next step in the process?

There isn't always only one good solution to data cleanup problems, so let's see if we can solve our unreadable header problem another way using a different technique.

Zipping questions and answers

Another way to fix the label problem is to use Python's `zip` method:

```
from csv import reader ❶

data_rdr = reader(open('data/unicef/mn.csv', 'rb'))
header_rdr = reader(open('data/unicef/mn_headers.csv', 'rb'))

data_rows = [d for d in data_rdr]
header_rows = [h for h in header_rdr]

print len(data_rows[0]) ❷
print len(header_rows)
```

❶ This time, instead of using `DictReader`, we use the simple `reader` class. The simple `reader` creates a list for each row, rather than a dictionary. Because we want to use `zip`, we need lists instead of dictionaries, so we can zip the list of header values with the list of data values.

❷ These lines create lists for our header and data readers and print them to see if they are the same length.

Oops—our printed length output shows we have a mismatch in the length of our data and headers! Our data shows only 159 rows while our header list shows we have 210 possible headers. This likely means MICS uses more questions for other countries or provides more questions to choose from than we have in our Zimbabwe dataset.

We need to further investigate which headers are used in the dataset and which ones we can leave behind. Let's take a closer look to find which ones don't align properly:

```
In [22]: data_rows[0]
Out[22]: ['',
 'HH1',
 'HH2',
 'LN',
 'MWM1',
 'MWM2',
 'MWM4',
 'MWM5',
 'MWM6D',
 'MWM6M',
 'MWM6Y',
 ... ]

In [23]: header_rows[:2]
Out[23]: [
```

```
        ['Name', 'Label', 'Question'],
        ['HH1', 'Cluster number', '']]
```

OK, so we can clearly see here we need to match the `data_rows` second row with the first index of the `header_rows`. Once we identify which ones don't match, we want to toss them out of the `header_rows` so we can zip the data properly:

```
bad_rows = []

for h in header_rows:
    if h[0] not in data_rows[0]:  ❶
        bad_rows.append(h)  ❷

for h in bad_rows:
    header_rows.remove(h)  ❸

print len(header_rows)
```

❶ Tests if the first element of the header row (the shorthand version of the header) is in the first row of the data (all shortened headers).

❷ Appends the rows identified as having mismatched headers to our new list, `bad_rows`. We use this in the next step to identify rows to remove.

❸ Uses the list's `remove` method to remove a particular row of data from a list. This method is often useful in situations where you can identify one specific row (or set of rows) you want to remove from a list.

Aha! So now we can see we are *nearly* matching. We have 159 values in our data rows and 150 values in our header list. Now let's see if we can figure out why we don't have those nine matching headers in our header list:

```
all_short_headers = [h[0] for h in header_rows]  ❶

for header in data_rows[0]:  ❷
    if header not in all_short_headers:  ❸
        print 'mismatch!', header  ❹
```

❶ Uses Python list comprehension to make a list of all the short headers by collecting only the first element of each header row.

❷ Iterates over the headers in our dataset to see which ones don't align with our cleaned header list.

❸ Singles out the headers that don't match from our abbreviated list.

❹ Uses `print` to display the mismatches. If you need a quick way to print two strings on the same line, you can simply use a `,` in between them to concatenate the strings with a space.

When you run this code, your output should look something like:

```
mismatch!
mismatch! MDV1F
mismatch! MTA8E
mismatch! mwelevel
mismatch! mnweight
mismatch! wscoreu
mismatch! windex5u
mismatch! wscorer
mismatch! windex5r
```

From the output and our current knowledge of the data, we can see that only a few of the mismatched headers (those with capitals) are ones we might want to fix. The lowercase titles are used for UNICEF internal methodology and don't line up with questions we have for our own investigation.

Because the `MDV1F` and `MTA8E` variables were not found with the web scraper we built to collect headers from the World Bank site, we need to investigate what they mean using our SPSS viewer. (The other option is to drop these rows and move on.)

 When you are dealing with raw data, sometimes you'll find that getting it into a usable form means dropping data you don't need or data that's difficult to clean. In the end, the determining factor should not be sloth, but instead whether the data is essential to your questions.

After opening the SPSS viewer, we can see `MDV1F` matches the label "If she commits infidelity: wife beating justified" and matches up with another longer set of questions regarding domestic abuse. We have other questions related to relationship abuse, so it's probably a good idea to include this. Investigating the `MTA8E` header shows it matches up with a different series of questions, about which type of tobacco is smoked by the person. We have added both to a new file, *mn_headers_updated.csv*.

Now we can retry the original code, this time using our updated headers file:

Let's look at it all together and make a few changes so we can try zipping our headers and data together. The following script requires a lot of memory, so if you have less than 4GB RAM, we recommend running it in an IPython terminal or notebook to help mitigate segmentation faults:

```
from csv import reader

data_rdr = reader(open('data/unicef/mn.csv', 'rb'))
```

```
header_rdr = reader(open('data/unicef/mn_headers_updated.csv', 'rb'))

data_rows = [d for d in data_rdr]
header_rows = [h for h in header_rdr if h[0] in data_rows[0]]  ❶

print len(header_rows)

all_short_headers = [h[0] for h in header_rows]

skip_index = []  ❷

for header in data_rows[0]:
    if header not in all_short_headers:
        index = data_rows[0].index(header)  ❸
        skip_index.append(index)

new_data = []

for row in data_rows[1:]:  ❹
    new_row = []
    for i, d in enumerate(row):  ❺
        if i not in skip_index:  ❻
            new_row.append(d)
    new_data.append(new_row)  ❼

zipped_data = []

for drow in new_data:
    zipped_data.append(zip(header_rows, drow))  ❽
```

❶ Uses list comprehension to quickly remove mismatched headers. As you can see, we can also use an if statement inside a list comprehension. Here, the code makes a list of rows from the header rows list, as long as the first header row element (abbreviated header) is in the headers from the data rows.

❷ Creates a list to hold the indexes of data rows whose data we aren't interested in keeping.

❸ Utilizes the Python list's index method to return the indexes we should skip because the headers aren't in the abbreviated list. The next line will save the indexes of the data rows that don't match our headers, so we can skip collecting that data.

❹ Slices the list holding the survey data to include only data rows (all rows except the first row) and then iterates through them.

❺ Uses the enumerate function to isolate the indexes of the data rows to skip. This function takes an iterable object (here, the data row list) and returns the numeric index and value for each item. It assigns the first value (index) to i and assigns the data value to d.

❻ Tests to make sure the index is not in the list we want to skip.

❼ After going through each item (or "column") in the data row, adds the new entry to the new_data list.

❽ Zips each row (now exactly matched with header and data) and adds it to a new array, zipped_data.

We can now print out a row of our new dataset and see if we have what we expected:

```
In [40]: zipped_data[0]
Out[40]: [(['HH1', 'Cluster number', ''], '1'),
(['HH2', 'Household number', ''], '17'),
(['LN', 'Line number', ''], '1'),
(['MWM1', 'Cluster number', ''], '1'),
(['MWM2', 'Household number', ''], '17'),
(['MWM4', "Man's line number", ''], '1'),
(['MWM5', 'Interviewer number', ''], '14'),
(['MWM6D', 'Day of interview', ''], '7'),
(['MWM6M', 'Month of interview', ''], '4'),
(['MWM6Y', 'Year of interview', ''], '2014'),
(['MWM7', "Result of man's interview", ''], 'Completed'),
(['MWM8', 'Field editor', ''], '2'),
(['MWM9', 'Data entry clerk', ''], '20'),
(['MWM10H', 'Start of interview - Hour', ''], '17'),
....
```

We have all of the questions and answers together in tuples, and every row has all of the matching data with headers. To be certain we have everything correct, let's take a look at the end of that row:

```
(['TN11', 'Persons slept under mosquito net last night',
'Did anyone sleep under this mosquito net last night?'], 'NA'),
(['TN12_1', 'Person 1 who slept under net',
'Who slept under this mosquito net last night?'], 'Currently married/in union'),
(['TN12_2', 'Person 2 who slept under net',
'Who slept under this mosquito net last night?'], '0'),
```

This looks strange. It seems like we might have some mismatches. Let's do a reality check and use our newly learned zip method to see if our headers match up properly:

```
data_headers = []

for i, header in enumerate(data_rows[0]): ❶
    if i not in skip_index: ❷
        data_headers.append(header)

header_match = zip(data_headers, all_short_headers) ❸
```

```
print header_match
```

❶ Iterates over the headers in the data list.

❷ By using if...not in..., returns True only for indexes *not* included in skip_index.

❸ Zips the new lists of headers together so we can visually check for the mismatch.

Aha! Did you see the error?

```
....
('MHA26', 'MHA26'),
('MHA27', 'MHA27'),
('MMC1', 'MTA1'),
('MMC2', 'MTA2'),
....
```

Everything is matching until this point, when it appears our header file and data file diverge in regards to question order. Because the zip method expects everything to appear in the same order, we must reorder our headers to match the dataset before we can use it. Here's our new try at matching our data:

```
from csv import reader

data_rdr = reader(open('data/unicef/mn.csv', 'rb'))
header_rdr = reader(open('data/unicef/mn_headers_updated.csv', 'rb'))

data_rows = [d for d in data_rdr]
header_rows = [h for h in header_rdr if h[0] in data_rows[0]]

all_short_headers = [h[0] for h in header_rows]

skip_index = []
final_header_rows = []        ❶

for header in data_rows[0]:
    if header not in all_short_headers:
        index = data_rows[0].index(header)
        skip_index.append(index)
    else:                       ❷
        for head in header_rows:    ❸
            if head[0] == header:     ❹
                final_header_rows.append(head)
                break ❺

new_data = []

for row in data_rows[1:]:
    new_row = []
```

```
        for i, d in enumerate(row):
            if i not in skip_index:
                new_row.append(d)
        new_data.append(new_row)

    zipped_data = []

    for drow in new_data:
        zipped_data.append(zip(final_header_rows, drow))  ❻
```

❶ Makes a new list to contain the final properly ordered header rows.

❷ Uses an `else` statement to include only columns where we have a match.

❸ Iterates over our `header_rows` until there's a match.

❹ Tests the short header to see if the question lines up. We use == to test for a match.

❺ Uses `break` to exit the `for head in header_rows` loop once a match is found. This makes it faster and doesn't hurt the outcome.

❻ Zips our new `final_header_rows` list with the header rows in the proper order.

After running our new code, we want to take a look at the end of our first entry:

```
(['TN12_3', 'Person 3 who slept under net',
'Who slept under this mosquito net last night?'], 'NA'),
(['TN12_4', 'Person 4 who slept under net',
'Who slept under this mosquito net last night?'], 'NA'),
(['HH6', 'Area', ''], 'Urban'),
(['HH7', 'Region', ''], 'Bulawayo'),
(['MWDOI', 'Date of interview women (CMC)', ''], '1372'),
(['MWDOB', 'Date of birth of woman (CMC)', ''], '1013'),
(['MWAGE', 'Age', ''], '25-29'),
```

This looks like a good match. We can likely improve the clarity of our code; however, we have found a good way to preserve most of the data and zip our data together, and it works relatively fast.

> You will always need to evaluate how complete you need the data to be and what level of effort fits your project's cleanup needs. If you are only using one part of the data, it's likely you don't need to retain it all. If the dataset is your primary research source, it's worth more time and effort to keep it complete.

In this section, we've learned some new tools and methods to identify what's wrong or needs cleaning and implemented fixes by combining the Python we know with our own problem-solving techniques. Our first data cleanup effort (replacing the header text) preserved fewer columns and didn't show us we had some missing headers. However, as long as the resulting dataset had the columns we needed, this would be sufficient, and it was faster and required less code.

Think about these types of issues as you clean your data. Is it essential that you have all the data? If so, how many hours is it worth? Is there an easy way to preserve everything you need and still clean it up properly? Is there a repeatable way? These questions will help guide you in cleaning up your datasets.

Now that we have a good list of data to work with, we'll move on to other types of cleanup.

Formatting Data

One of the most common forms of data cleanup is getting your unreadable or hard-to-read data and data types to fit a proper readable format. Especially if you need to create reports with the data or downloadable files, you'll want to make sure it goes from being machine readable to human readable. And if your data needs to be used alongside APIs, you might need specially formatted data types.

Python gives us a ton of ways to format strings and numbers. We used %r, which shows the Python representation of the object in a string or Unicode, in Chapter 5 to debug and show our results. Python also has string formatters %s and %d, which represent strings and digits, respectively. We often use these in conjuction with the print command.

A more advanced way to turn objects into strings or Python representations is to utilize the format method. As clarified in the Python documentation (*https://docs.python.org/2/library/stdtypes.html#str.format*), this method lets us define a string and pass the data as arguments or keyword arguments into the string. Let's take a closer look at format:

```
for x in zipped_data[0]:
    print 'Question: {}\nAnswer: {}'.format( ❶
        x[0], x[1]) ❷
```

❶ format uses {} to represent where to put the data and the \n newline character to create breaks between the lines.

❷ Here, we pass the first and second values of the question and answer tuple.

You should see something like this:

```
Question: ['MMT9', 'Ever used Internet', 'Have you ever used the Internet?']
Answer: Yes
Question: ['MMT10', 'Internet usage in the last 12 months',
```

```
'In the last 12 months, have you used the Internet?']
Answer: Yes
```

This is fairly difficult to read. Let's try cleaning it up a bit more. From our output, we can see the question tuple has an abbreviation as the 0-index value and a description of the question as the 1-index value. We'd like to just use the second part of the array, which gives us a nice title. Let's try again:

```
for x in zipped_data[0]:
    print 'Question: {[1]}\nAnswer: {}'.format(
        x[0], x[1]) ❶
```

❶ This time we use the ability to single out the index in the format syntax 1, making the output more readable.

Let's see what output we get:

```
Question: Frequency of reading newspaper or magazine
Answer: Almost every day
Question: Frequency of listening to the radio
Answer: At least once a week
Question: Frequency of watching TV
Answer: Less than once a week
```

Now our output is readable. Hooray! Let's take a look at a few of the other options available with the `format` method. Our current dataset doesn't have a large amount of numeric data, so we'll just use some example numbers to show more formatting options for different numerical types:

```
example_dict = {
    'float_number': 1324.321325493,
    'very_large_integer': 43890923148390284,
    'percentage': .324,
}

string_to_print = "float: {float_number:.4f}\n" ❶
string_to_print += "integer: {very_large_integer:,}\n" ❷
string_to_print += "percentage: {percentage:.2%}" ❸

print string_to_print.format(**example_dict) ❹
```

❶ Uses a dictionary and accesses the values of the dictionary using the keys. We use a `:` to separate the key name and the pattern. Passing `.4f` tells Python to make the number a float (`f`) and show the first four decimal digits (`.4`).

❷ Uses the same format (with the key name and colon) and inserts commas (`,`) to separate thousands.

❸ Uses the same format (with the key name and colon) but inserts a percentage (`%`) and shows the first two significant decimal digits (`.2`).

❹ Passes our data dictionary into the `format` method called on the long string and uses `**` to *unpack* the dictionary. Unpacking a Python dictionary will send the key/value pairs in expanded form; here, the unpacked keys and values are sent to the `format` method.

For more advanced formatting, such as removing unnecessary spaces, aligning the data by length, and performing math equations in the `format` method, read the Python formatting documentation and examples (*http://bit.ly/format_string_syntax*).

Aside from strings and numbers, Python allows us to easily format dates. Python's `datetime` module has methods to format dates you already have (or generate) in Python as well as to read in any date formats and create Python date, datetime, and time objects.

The most commonly used methods to format dates in Python or make strings into dates are `strformat` and `strpformat`, and the formatting might be recognizable if you have used date formatting in other languages. For more information, read the "`strftime` and `strptime` Behavior" documentation (*http://bit.ly/strftime_strptime*).

The `datetime` module's `strptime` method allows you to use strings or numbers to create a Python datetime object. This is great if you want to save the date and time to a database or you need to modify the time zone or add an hour. By turning it into a Python object, you can harness the power of Python's date capabilities and easily turn it back into a human- or machine-readable string later.

Let's take a look at our data holding interview start and end times from our `zipped_data` list. To refresh our memories, let's print some of our first entry to make sure we know what data entries we need to use:

```
for x in enumerate(zipped_data[0][:20]): ❶
    print x
```

```
.....
(7, (['MWM6D', 'Day of interview', ''], '7'))
(8, (['MWM6M', 'Month of interview', ''], '4'))
(9, (['MWM6Y', 'Year of interview', ''], '2014'))
(10, (['MWM7', "Result of man's interview", ''], 'Completed'))
(11, (['MWM8', 'Field editor', ''], '2'))
(12, (['MWM9', 'Data entry clerk', ''], '20'))
(13, (['MWM10H', 'Start of interview - Hour', ''], '17'))
(14, (['MWM10M', 'Start of interview - Minutes', ''], '59'))
```

```
(15, (['MWM11H', 'End of interview - Hour', ''], '18'))
(16, (['MWM11M', 'End of interview - Minutes', ''], '7'))
```

❶ Utilizes Python's `enumerate` function to see which lines from the data we will need to evaluate.

We now have all the data we need to figure out exactly when the interview started and ended. We could use data like this to determine things whether interviews in the evening or morning were more likely to be completed, and whether the length of the interview affected the number of responses. We can also determine which was the first interview and the last interview and calculate average duration.

Let's try importing the data into Python datetime objects using `strptime`:

```
from datetime import datetime

start_string = '{}/{}/{} {}:{}'.format( ❶
    zipped_data[0][8][1], zipped_data[0][7][1], zipped_data[0][9][1], ❷
    zipped_data[0][13][1], zipped_data[0][14][1])

print start_string

start_time = datetime.strptime(start_string, '%m/%d/%Y %H:%M') ❸

print start_time
```

❶ Creates a base string to parse all of the data from the many entries. This code uses American-style date strings formatted with the month, day, year, and then hour and minute.

❷ Accesses the following format: `zipped_data[first data entry][data number row (derived from enumerate)][just the data itself]`. Using just the first entry to test, the row at index 8 is the month, the row at index 7 is the day, and the row at index 9 is the year. The second element (`[1]`) of each tuple is the data.

❸ Calls the `strptime` method with a date string and a pattern string using the syntax defined in the Python documentation (*http://bit.ly/strftime_strptime*). `%m/%d/%Y` is the month, day, year, and `%H:%M` is the hour and minute. The method returns a Python datetime object.

If you are using IPython to run code, you need not use `print` to show every line you are interested in viewing. It's common practice to instead just type the variable name and view the output in the interactive terminal. You can even use Tab to autocomplete.

With our code, we created a common date string and parsed it using datetime's `strptime` method. Because each element of the time data is a separate item in our dataset, we could also natively create Python datetime objects without using `strptime`. Let's take a look:

```
from datetime import datetime

end_time = datetime( ❶
    int(zipped_data[0][9][1]), int(zipped_data[0][8][1]), ❷
    int(zipped_data[0][7][1]), int(zipped_data[0][15][1]),
    int(zipped_data[0][16][1]))

print end_time
```

❶ Uses the `datetime` class in Python's `datetime` module to pass integers directly to form a date object. We pass them as arguments, using commas to separate the elements.

❷ Because `datetime` expects integers, this code converts all of our data to integers. The order `datetime` expects data in is year, month, day, hour, minute, so we must order the data accordingly.

As you can see, with fewer lines of code (in this case) we were able to get the end time of the interview in a Python datetime object. We now have two datetime objects, so let's do some math with them!

```
duration = end_time - start_time ❶

print duration ❷

print duration.days ❸

print duration.total_seconds() ❹

minutes = duration.total_seconds() / 60.0 ❺

print minutes
```

❶ Calculates duration by subtracting the start time from the end time.

❷ Prints a new Python date type. This is a `timedelta` object. As described in the `datetime` documentation (*http://bit.ly/python_datetime*), timedeltas show differences between two time objects and are used to change or alter time objects.

❸ Uses timedelta's built-in `days` attribute to see how many days the delta spans.

❹ Calls timedelta's `total_seconds` method to calculate the time difference in seconds. This also counts microseconds.

❺ Calculates the minutes, as timedelta has no minutes attribute.

In running our code, we saw the first interview lasted 8 minutes—but do we know if that is on average how long the interviews last? This is something we can figure out by parsing through the entire dataset using our new `datetime` skills. We've done some simple `datetime` math and figured out how to create Python datetime objects from our dataset. Now let's see if we can convert these new datetime objects back into formatted strings for use in a human-readable report:

```
print end_time.strftime('%m/%d/%Y %H:%M:%S')  ❶

print start_time.ctime()  ❷

print start_time.strftime('%Y-%m-%dT%H:%M:%S')  ❸
```

❶ `strftime` requires only one argument, the date pattern you would like to show. This line outputs the standard American time format.

❷ Python's datetime objects have a `ctime` method that outputs the datetime object according to C's `ctime` standard.

❸ Python's datetime objects can output the string in any way you might wish. This code uses a format often used by PHP. If you need to interact with APIs requiring a special string format, `datetime` can help.

Python's datetime objects are incredibly useful and very easy to manipulate, import, and export (via formatting). Depending on your dataset, you can use these new techniques to import and convert all of your string or Excel data into datetime objects, run statistics or averages on them, and then convert them back into strings for your reporting.

We've learned numerous formatting tips and tricks. Now let's begin some more intensive cleanup. We'll review how to easily find bad seeds in your data and what to do about them.

Finding Outliers and Bad Data

Identifying outliers and bad data in your dataset is probably one of the most difficult parts of data cleanup, and it takes time to get right. Even if you have a deep understanding of statistics and how outliers might affect your data, it's always a topic to explore cautiously.

You want to clean your data, not manipulate or change it, so spend some extra time determining how to handle outliers or bad records when considering their removal. You should be very explicit in your final conclusions if you removed outliers to help normalize your data.

We'll review more ways to find outliers in Chapter 9, but let's chat about some easy ways to check if you have bad data in your dataset.

Your first clues about data validity come from your source. As we talked about in Chapter 6, you want to ensure your source is properly vetted and you can trust the data. You'll want to have asked the source how the data was collected and if the data has already been cleaned or processed.

For the samples we are using here, we know that UNICEF surveys follow a standard format of questions. We know they perform these censuses at regular intervals. We also know they have a standard protocol for training their workers on how to properly conduct the interviews. These are all good signs that the data is a proper sample and not a pre-selected sample. If, instead, we found out that UNICEF only interviewed families in large cities and ignored the rural population, this might result in a selection bias or sampling error. Depending on your sources, you should determine what biases your dataset might have.

You can't always get perfect data. However, you should be aware of what sampling biases your data might have and ensure you don't make sweeping claims based on datasets that might not represent the entire story or population.

Moving on from source and data bias, you can find potential errors in your data by asking, "Do any of these data points not fit?" One easy way to tell if you have improper data values is to see if there are errors in the data values you have. For example, you can look through a dataset and see if an important value is missing. You can also look through a dataset and determine if the types (e.g., integer, date, string) don't properly match up. Let's take a look at some of these problems in our dataset by attempting to locate some missing data:

```
for answer in zipped_data[0]: ❶
    if not answer[1]: ❷
        print answer
```

❶ Iterates over all of the rows of our first entry.

❷ Tests whether a value "exists." We know the values are the second entries in the tuples, and we know we can use an `if not` statement to test this.

From the output of our code, we can see we don't have any *obvious* missing data in our first row. How can we test our entire dataset?

```
for row in zipped_data:  ❶
    for answer in row:  ❷
        if answer[1] is None:  ❸
            print answer
```

❶ This time, we loop over every row in our dataset instead of just the first entry.

❷ We remove the `[0]` from our previous example, as we have each row as its own loop.

❸ For example's sake, here we test if we see any `None` types. This will tell us if there are null data points, but won't tell us if we have zeros or empty strings.

We can see we don't have any obvious missing data in our entire dataset, but let's take a cursory look at some of our data to see if there are more difficult-to-discern bits of missing data. From our earlier `prints`, you might remember the usage of *NA* representing Not Applicable.

Although this is not missing data, we might want to know exactly how many *NA* answers we have, or if certain questions have an overrepresentation of these answers. If the sample is too small—i.e., if there is a preponderance of NA responses—we probably want to avoid making any larger conclusions based on the available data. If the majority of responses are *NA*, though, we might find that interesting (why was that question not applicable to the majority of the group?).

Let's see if there is a preponderance of *NA* answers for any specific questions:

```python
na_count = {} ❶

for row in zipped_data:
    for resp in row:
        question = resp[0][1] ❷
        answer = resp[1]
        if answer == 'NA': ❸
            if question in na_count.keys(): ❹
                na_count[question] += 1 ❺
            else:
                na_count[question] = 1 ❻

print na_count
```

❶ Defines a dictionary to keep track of questions with *NA* responses. Keeping the data in a hashed object (like a dictionary) allows Python to quickly and easily query the members. The questions will be the keys and the values will hold the count:

❷ Stores the second entry from the first part of the tuple (the description of the question) in `question`. The first entry (`[0]`) is the shorthand title and the last entry (`[2]`) is the question the surveyors asked, which is not always available.

❸ Uses Python's equivalency test to find *NA* responses. If we cared about more than one way to write *NA*, we might use something like `if answer in ["NA", "na", "n/a"]:` to accept a variety of written responses with the same meaning.

❹ Tests if this question is already in the dictionary by testing if it is in the keys of the dictionary.

❺ If the question is already in the keys, this code adds 1 to the value using Python's += method.

❻ If it is not a member of the dictionary yet, this code adds it to the dictionary and sets its count value to 1.

Wow! There are quite a few *NA* responses in our dataset. We have approximately 9,000 rows of data, and some of these questions have more than 8,000 *NA* responses. It's possible these questions are not relevant to the demographic or age group surveyed or don't resonate with the particular nation and culture. Regardless, there is little sense in using the *NA* questions to draw any sort of larger conclusions about the population surveys.

Finding things like the *NA* values in your dataset can be very useful in determining whether that dataset is appropriate for your research needs. If you find that the questions you need answered have an overwhelming amount of *NA*-style responses, you might have to keep looking for another source of data or rethink your questions.

We've covered missing data; now let's see if we can find any type outliers. A type outlier might be present, for example, if a year entry holds a string like `'missing'` or `'NA'`. If we see just a few data types that don't align, we might be dealing with outliers or a few instances of bad data. If we see that a large portion of them don't align, we might want to rethink using that data or determine why they seem to match a "bad data" pattern.

If we can easily account for the inconsistencies (e.g., because this answer only applies to women and the survey sample is mixed-gender), then we can include the data. If there is no clear explanation, and the question is significant and important to our result, we will have to keep investigating our current dataset or begin to look for other datasets that might explain the misalignment.

We'll talk more about finding outliers in Chapter 9, but for now let's take a quick look at analyzing data types and see if we can spot any obvious inconsistencies in our current dataset. For example, we should verify that answers we always expect to be numbers (like year of birth) are the right data type.

Let's take a quick look at the distribution of types in our responses. We'll use some of the same code we used for counting *NA* responses but this time we'll take a look at data types:

```python
datatypes = {} ❶

start_dict = {'digit': 0, 'boolean': 0,
              'empty': 0, 'time_related': 0,
              'text': 0, 'unknown': 0
              } ❷

for row in zipped_data:
    for resp in row:
        question = resp[0][1]
        answer = resp[1]
        key = 'unknown' ❸
        if answer.isdigit(): ❹
            key = 'digit'
        elif answer in ['Yes', 'No', 'True', 'False']: ❺
            key = 'boolean'
        elif answer.isspace(): ❻
            key = 'empty'
        elif answer.find('/') > 0 or answer.find(':') > 0: ❼
            key = 'time_related'
        elif answer.isalpha(): ❽
            key = 'text'
        if question not in datatypes.keys(): ❾
            datatypes[question] = start_dict.copy() ❿
```

```
datatypes[question][key] += 1 ⑪
```

```
print datatypes
```

❶ The first line initializes a dictionary, because it's a fast, reliable way to store data on a question-by-question level.

❷ This sets up a `start_dict` to ensure the same data exists for each question in our dataset. The dictionary will contain all of our possible guesses as to data type so we can easily compare.

❸ Here, we set a variable `key` with the default value *unknown*. If the `key` variable is not updated in one of the following `if` or `elif` statements, it remains *unknown*.

❹ Python's string class has many methods to help determine type. Here, we use the `isdigit` method: this line returns `True` if the string holds a digit.

❺ To determine if the data relates to Boolean logic, here we test if the answer is in the list of Boolean-based responses, including *Yes/No* and *True/False*. Although we could create a more comprehensive test, this is a good starting point.

❻ The Python string class's `isspace` method returns `True` if the string contains only spaces.

❼ The string's `find` method returns the index of the first match. If it finds no match in the string, it returns -1. This code tests for both / and :, which are commonly used in time strings. This is not a comprehensive check, but should give us an initial idea.

❽ The string's `isalpha` method returns `True` if the string contains only alphabetic characters.

❾ As in the code for counting *NA* responses, here we test if the question is in the keys of the `datatypes` dictionary.

❿ If the question is not in the `datatypes` dictionary, this code adds it and saves a copy of the `start_dict` as the value. The dictionary's `copy` method creates a separate dictionary object for each entry. If we assigned `start_dict` to each question, we would end up counting the lump sum in one dictionary, rather than starting with a new dictionary for every question.

⑪ This adds 1 to the value of the key we found. So, for each question and response, we have a "guess" about the type.

In our results, we can already see some variance! Some of the question and answer sets have significant representation in one "type", while others have a variety of type guesses. We can use these as a starting point, as these are just rough guesses.

One way we can start to use this new information is to find questions with a vast majority of digit-type responses and see what the values of the non-digit responses are. We would likely expect those to be either *NA* or improperly inserted values. We can move to normalize those values if they relate to questions we care about. One way to do that is to substitute *NA* values or erroneous values with *None* or null values. This can be useful if you are going to run statistical methods on the columns in question.

 As you continue to work with your dataset, you will find anomalies in data types or *NA* responses. How best to handle these inconsistencies depends on your knowledge of the topic and dataset as well as what questions you are trying to answer. If you are combining datasets, you can sometimes throw out these outliers and bad data patterns; however, be wary of overlooking minor trends.

Now that we've started recognizing outliers and outlier patterns in our data, let's work on eliminating bad data we may even have created ourselves—duplicates.

Finding Duplicates

If you are using more than one dataset with the same survey data or if you have used raw data that may have duplicate entries, removing duplicate data will be an important step in ensuring your data can be accurately used. If you have a dataset with unique identifiers, you can use those IDs to ensure you haven't accidentally inserted or acquired duplicate data. If you do not have an indexed dataset, you might need to figure out a good way to identify each unique entry (such as creating an indexable key).

Python has some great ways to identify uniques in the built-in library. Let's introduce some of the concepts here:

```
list_with_dupes = [1, 5, 6, 2, 5, 6, 8, 3, 8, 3, 3, 7, 9]

set_without_dupes = set(list_with_dupes)

print set_without_dupes
```

Your output should look something like this:

```
{1, 2, 3, 5, 6, 7, 8, 9}
```

What's happening here? Set and frozenset (*http://bit.ly/python_set*) are Python built-in types which allow us to take an iterable object (like a list, or a string, or a tuple) and create a set containing only the unique values.

 In order to use set and frozenset, the values need to be *hashable*. With hashable types, we can apply a hash method and the resulting value will *always* be the same. This means, for example, that we can trust a 3 is the same as every other 3 we see in code.

Most Python objects are hashable—only lists and dictionaries are not. We can create sets using `set` with any collection of hashable types (integers, floats, decimals, strings, tuples, etc.). The other neat thing about sets and frozensets is they have some fast comparison properties. Let's take a look at some examples:

```
first_set = set([1, 5, 6, 2, 6, 3, 6, 7, 3, 7, 9, 10, 321, 54, 654, 432])

second_set = set([4, 6, 7, 432, 6, 7, 4, 9, 0])

print first_set.intersection(second_set) ❶

print first_set.union(second_set) ❷

print first_set.difference(second_set) ❸

print second_set - first_set ❹

print 6 in second_set ❺

print 0 in first_set
```

❶ The `intersection` method of a set returns the intersection between two sets (i.e., the elements held in commom). A built-in Venn diagram!

❷ The `union` method of a set combines the values of the first set and the second set.

❸ The `difference` method shows the difference between the first set and the second set. Order of operations matters, as you'll see in the next line.

❹ Subtracting one set from another shows the difference between them. Changing the order of the difference sets changes the order of the result (just like in math).

❺ `in` tests set membership (with very fast performance).

Your output should look like this:

```
set([432, 9, 6, 7])
set([0, 1, 2, 3, 4, 5, 6, 7, 9, 10, 321, 432, 654, 54])
```

```
set([1, 2, 3, 5, 321, 10, 654, 54])
set([0, 4])
True
False
```

Sets have quite a lot of useful features for defining unique datasets and comparing sets. There are many times in data wrangling where we need to know the minimum and maximum of a series of values, or we need a union of unique keys. Sets can help us with those tasks.

Aside from sets, Python has several other libraries with easy ways to test uniqueness. One library you can use for uniqueness is numpy, a powerful mathmatics library for Python with scientific and statistical methods and classes. numpy has superior array, numerical, and mathematical capabilities compared to the core Python libraries. It also has a great method called unique used with a numpy array. You can install numpy like so:

```
pip install numpy
```

Let's take a look at how numpy's unique works:

```
import numpy as np

list_with_dupes = [1, 5, 6, 2, 5, 6, 8, 3, 8, 3, 3, 7, 9]

print np.unique(list_with_dupes, return_index=True)  ❶

array_with_dupes = np.array([[1, 5, 7, 3, 9, 11, 23], [2, 4, 6, 8, 2, 8, 4]])  ❷

print np.unique(array_with_dupes)  ❸
```

❶ Numpy's unique method keeps track of the indexes. Passing return_index=True results in a tuple of arrays: the first is an array of the unique values, and the second is a flattened array of the indexes—only the first occurrence of every number will be present.

❷ To show more numpy, this line creates a numpy matrix. This is an array of arrays (equally sized).

❸ unique creates a unique set out of a matrix.

Your output will look like this:

```
(array([1, 2, 3, 5, 6, 7, 8, 9]), array([ 0,  3,  7,  1,  2, 11,  6, 12]))
[ 1  2  3  4  5  6  7  8  9 11 23]
```

If you don't have unique keys, you can write a function to create a unique set. It can be as simple as using list comprehension. Let's try one using Python's sets for our dataset. First, we determine a unique number by taking a look at which data in our dataset is unique:

```
for x in enumerate(zipped_data[0]):
    print x

.....

(0, (['HH1', 'Cluster number', ''], '1'))
(1, (['HH2', 'Household number', ''], '17'))
(2, (['LN', 'Line number', ''], '1'))
(3, (['MWM1', 'Cluster number', ''], '1'))
(4, (['MWM2', 'Household number', ''], '17'))
(5, (['MWM4', "Man's line number", ''], '1'))
```

We see the first five elements of each row have some presumably unique identifiers. Assuming we are understanding the data properly, the cluster, household, and man's line numbers should create a unique combination. It's possible the line numbers are unique as well. Let's see if we are correct:

```
set_of_lines = set([x[2][1] for x in zipped_data])  ❶

uniques = [x for x in zipped_data if not set_of_lines.remove(x[2][1])]  ❷

print set_of_lines
```

❶ First, we make a set containing the line numbers of the survey. The line number is the third element in each response and the value is the second element of that row (x[2][1]). We use list comprehension to speed up our code.

❷ set_of_lines now holds the unique keys. We can use the set object's remove method to see if we have more than one of each of those keys in the dataset. If the line number is unique, it will remove each key only once. If we have duplicates, remove will throw a KeyError to let us know that key is no longer in our set.

Hmm. We did see an error when we ran the code, so we were wrong in our assumption the line numbers were unique. If we take a closer look at the set we made, it looks like line numbers go from 1–16 and then repeat.

 You'll often have to work with messy datasets, or datasets similar to this one with no obvious unique key. Our suggestion in times like these is to determine a good way to find a unique key and then use that as a comparison.

We have numerous options for creating a unique key. We could use the start time of the interview. However, we aren't sure whether UNICEF deploys many survey teams at once; and if so, we could remove items marked as duplicates which are actually not duplicates. We could use the birth date of the man combined with the time of the interview, as that's unlikely to have matches, but if we had any missing fields that could be problematic.

One nice solution is to see if a combination of the cluster, household, and line numbers creates a unique key. If so, then we could use this method across datasets—even ones without a start and end time. Let's give it a try!

```
set_of_keys = set([
    '%s-%s-%s' % (x[0][1], x[1][1], x[2][1]) for x in zipped_data]) ❶

uniques = [x for x in zipped_data if not set_of_keys.remove(
    '%s-%s-%s' % (x[0][1], x[1][1], x[2][1]))] ❷

print len(set_of_keys) ❸
```

❶ Makes a string out of the three parts we think are unique: the cluster number, the household number, and the line number. We are separating each with a - so we can differentiate between the three values.

❷ Re-creates the unique key we used, and uses the remove feature. This will remove those entries one by one, and the uniques list will hold every unique row. If there is a duplicate entry, our code will again throw an error.

❸ Evaluates the length our list of unique keys. This can show us how many unique entries we have in our dataset.

Super! This time we have no errors. We can see by the length of our list that each row is a unique entry. This is what we would expect from a processed dataset, as UNICEF does some data cleanup before publishing and ensures there are no duplicates. If we were combining this data with other UNICEF data, we might add M in our key because it's the men's group survey. We could then cross reference households that carry the same numbers.

Depending on your data, the unique key might not be obvious. Birth dates and addresses might be a good combination. The chances there are two 24-year-old women at the same address with the exact same date of birth are slim, although not out of the question if they are twins who live together!

Moving on from duplicates, we'll now take a look at fuzzy matching, a great way to find duplicates in particularly noisy datasets.

Fuzzy Matching

If you are using more than one dataset or unclean, unstandardized data, you might use fuzzy matching to find and combine duplicates. Fuzzy matching allows you to determine if two items (usually strings) are "the same." While not as in-depth as using natural language processing or machine learning to determine a match with big data-sets on language, fuzzy matching can help us relate "My dog & I" and "me and my dog" as having similar meaning.

There are many ways to go about fuzzy matching. One Python library, developed by SeatGeek (*http://bit.ly/fuzzy_string_matching*), uses some pretty cool methods internally to match tickets being sold online for different events. You can install it by using:

```
pip install fuzzywuzzy
```

So let's say you're dealing with some unclean data. Maybe it was input sloppily or is user-entered and contains misspellings and small syntactic errors or deviations. How might you account for that?

```
from fuzzywuzzy import fuzz

my_records = [{'favorite_book': 'Grapes of Wrath',
               'favorite_movie': 'Free Willie',
               'favorite_show': 'Two Broke Girls',
              },
              {'favorite_book': 'The Grapes of Wrath',
               'favorite_movie': 'Free Willy',
               'favorite_show': '2 Broke Girls',
              }]


print fuzz.ratio(my_records[0].get('favorite_book'),
                 my_records[1].get('favorite_book')) ❶

print fuzz.ratio(my_records[0].get('favorite_movie'),
                 my_records[1].get('favorite_movie'))

print fuzz.ratio(my_records[0].get('favorite_show'),
                 my_records[1].get('favorite_show'))
```

❶ Here we use the `fuzz` module's `ratio` function, which expects two strings to compare. It returns the similarity of the sequencing of the strings (a value between 1 and 100).

We can see from our own understanding of popular culture and English that these two entries have the same favorites; however, they have spelled them differently. FuzzyWuzzy helps us counter these unintentional mistakes. We can see our matches using `ratio` scored pretty high. This gives us some level of confidence the strings are similar.

Let's try another FuzzyWuzzy method and see our results. We'll use the same data for the sake of simplicity and comparison:

```
print fuzz.partial_ratio(my_records[0].get('favorite_book'),
                         my_records[1].get('favorite_book')) ❶

print fuzz.partial_ratio(my_records[0].get('favorite_movie'),
                         my_records[1].get('favorite_movie'))

print fuzz.partial_ratio(my_records[0].get('favorite_show'),
                         my_records[1].get('favorite_show'))
```

❶ Here we call the `fuzz` module's `partial_ratio` function, which expects two strings to compare. It returns the similarity of the sequencing of the closest matching substrings (a value between 1 and 100).

Wow, we can see we are getting much higher numbers! The `partial_ratio` function allows us to compare substrings, which means we don't need to worry if someone has forgotten a word (like in our book example) or used different punctuation. This means a closer match for all of our strings.

 If your data has some simple inconsistencies, these are some great functions to help find the mismatches. But if your data has some large differences in meaning with a few characters' difference, you might want to test similarity and difference. For example, "does" and "doesn't" are quite different in meaning but not very different in spelling. In the first `ratio` example, these two strings wouldn't score highly, but in the substring, we would have a match. Knowledge of your data and the complexities therein is a must!

FuzzyWuzzy also has some other cool options. Let's explore some of them, as they might pertain to your data cleanup needs:

```
from fuzzywuzzy import fuzz

my_records = [{'favorite_food': 'cheeseburgers with bacon',
               'favorite_drink': 'wine, beer, and tequila',
               'favorite_dessert': 'cheese or cake',
              },
              {'favorite_food': 'burgers with cheese and bacon',
               'favorite_drink': 'beer, wine, and tequila',
               'favorite_dessert': 'cheese cake',
              }]

print fuzz.token_sort_ratio(my_records[0].get('favorite_food'), ❶
                            my_records[1].get('favorite_food'))

print fuzz.token_sort_ratio(my_records[0].get('favorite_drink'),
                            my_records[1].get('favorite_drink'))

print fuzz.token_sort_ratio(my_records[0].get('favorite_dessert'),
                            my_records[1].get('favorite_dessert'))
```

❶ Here we call the `fuzz` module's `token_sort_ratio` function, which allows us to match strings despite word order. This is great for free-form survey data, where "I like dogs and cats" and "I like cats and dogs" mean the same thing. Each string is first sorted and then compared, so if they contain the same words in a different order, they will match.

From our output, we can see using tokens (here, words) gives us a pretty good chance at matching word order differences. Here we see the favorite drink options are the same, just in different orders. We can use this when the order of tokens doesn't change the meaning. For SeatGeek, "Pittsburgh Steelers vs. New England Patriots" is the same as "New England Patriots vs. Pittsburgh Steelers" (with the exception of home field advantage).

Let's take a look at another token-oriented function from FuzzyWuzzy, using our same data:

```
print fuzz.token_set_ratio(my_records[0].get('favorite_food'), ❶
                           my_records[1].get('favorite_food'))

print fuzz.token_set_ratio(my_records[0].get('favorite_drink'),
                           my_records[1].get('favorite_drink'))

print fuzz.token_set_ratio(my_records[0].get('favorite_dessert'),
                           my_records[1].get('favorite_dessert'))
```

❶ Here we use the `fuzz` module's `token_set_ratio` function, which uses the same token approach but compares sets of the tokens to see intersection and difference. The function attempts to find the best possible match of sorted tokens and returns the ratio of similarity for those tokens.

Here we can see an unintended side effect if we are not aware of similarities and differences in our dataset. One answer was improperly spelled. We know cheesecake and cheese are not the same thing, but using the token set approach, these resulted in a false positive. And sadly, we could not properly match our cheeseburger answer, even though it's the same. Can you do so using another method we've already learned?

One final matching method FuzzyWuzzy provides is the `process` module. This is great if you have a limited amount of choices or options and messy data. Let's say you know the answer has to be *yes*, *no*, *maybe*, or *decline to comment*. Let's take a look at how we can match these up:

```
from fuzzywuzzy import process

choices = ['Yes', 'No', 'Maybe', 'N/A']

process.extract('ya', choices, limit=2) ❶

process.extractOne('ya', choices) ❷
```

```
process.extract('nope', choices, limit=2)

process.extractOne('nope', choices)
```

❶ Uses FuzzyWuzzy's `extract` method to compare strings to the list of possible matches. The function returns two possible matches from the list of choices we have declared in our `choices` variable.

❷ Uses FuzzyWuzzy's `extractOne` method to return only the best match between our string and the list of available choices.

Aha! Given a variety of words we know "mean" the same thing, `process` can extract the best guess—and in these cases, the correct guess. With `extract` we get tuples with the ratios returned, and our code can parse through the string responses and compare how similar or different the matches are. The `extractOne` function just finds the best match and returns it along with its ratio as a tuple. Depending on your needs, you might opt for `extractOne` to help you simply find the best match and move along.

You've learned all about matching strings now, so let's talk a little about how to write some similar string matching functions on your own.

RegEx Matching

Fuzzy matching may not always fit your needs. What if you just need to identify a part of a string? What if you are only looking for a phone number or an email address? These are problems you'll encounter if you are scraping your data (as we will learn about in Chapter 11) or compiling raw data from numerous sources. For a lot of these problems, regular expressions can help.

Regular expressions allow computers to match, find, or eliminate patterns in strings or data defined in the code. Regular expressions, or regex, are often feared by developers since they can become complex and can be difficult to read and understand. However, they can be quite useful, and a basic introduction to them can help you read, write, and understand when regex can help solve your problem.

Despite their fearsome reputation, the basic regex syntax is fairly straightforward and easy to learn. Table 7-1 covers the fundamentals.

Table 7-1. Regex basics

Character/ Pattern	Legend	Example match
\w	Any alphanumeric character, including underscores	a or 0 or _
\d	Any digit	1 or 2 or 4
\s	Any whitespace character	' '
+	One or more (greedy) of the pattern or character	\d+ matches 476373
\.	The . character	.
*	Zero or more (greedy) of the character or pattern (think of this almost as an if)	\d* matches 03289 and ' '
|	Either the first pattern, or the next, or the next (like OR)	\d|\w matches 0 or a
[] or ()	Character classes (defining what you expect to see in one character space) and character groupings (defining what you expect to see in a group)	A matches [A-C] or (A|B|C)
-	Binds character groups	[0-9]+ matches \d+

For more examples, we recommend bookmarking a good regex cheat sheet (*http:// bit.ly/regex_cheat_sheet*).

 There's no need, especially as a Python developer, to memorize regex syntax; however, well-written regex can help you in some great ways. With Python's built-in regex module, re, you can easily search for basic matches and groupings.

Let's take a look at some of the possibilities regex gives us:

```
import re

word = '\w+'  ❶
sentence = 'Here is my sentence.'

re.findall(word, sentence)  ❷

search_result = re.search(word, sentence)  ❸

search_result.group()  ❹
```

```
match_result = re.match(word, sentence) ❺

match_result.group()
```

❶ Defines a basic pattern of a normal string. This pattern accounts for strings that contain letters and numbers but not spaces or punctuation. It will match until it doesn't match (i.e., the + makes it greedy! nomnom!).

❷ The re module's findall method locates all the pattern matches in a string. Every word we included in our sentence is found, but the period is missing. In this case, we used the pattern \w, so punctuation and spaces are not included.

❸ The search method allows us to search for a match throughout the string. If a match is found, a match object is returned.

❹ The match object's group method returns the matched string.

❺ The match method searches only from the beginning of the string. This operates differently from search.

We can easily match words in a sentence, and depending on our needs, we can vary how we find them. In this example, we saw findall return a list of all the matches. Let's say you only want to extract websites from a long text. You can use a regex pattern to find links and then use findall to extract all the links from the text. Or you can find telephone numbers, or dates. The findall method is your go-to tool if you can define what you are looking for in a simple pattern and apply it easily to your string data.

We also used search and match, which in this case, returned the same thing—they both matched the first word in the sentence. We returned a match object, and we were able to access the data using the group method. The group method will also take parameters. Try using .group(0) with one of your matches. What happened? What do you think the 0 means? (Hint: think of lists!)

search and match are actually quite different. Let's use them in a few more examples so we can see the differences:

```
import re

number = '\d+' ❶
capitalized_word = '[A-Z]\w+' ❷

sentence = 'I have 2 pets: Bear and Bunny.'

search_number = re.search(number, sentence)

search_number.group() ❸
```

```
match_number = re.match(number, sentence)

match_number.group() ❹

search_capital = re.search(capitalized_word, sentence)

search_capital.group()

match_capital = re.match(capitalized_word, sentence)

match_capital.group()
```

❶ Defines a numerical pattern. The plus sign makes it greedy, so it will gobble up all the digits it can until it reaches a non-digit character.

❷ Defines a capitalized word match. This pattern uses the square brackets to define a part of a longer pattern. These brackets tell our pattern the first letter we want is a capital letter. Following that, we are just looking for a continued word.

❸ What happens when we call group here? We see the match object returned from our search method.

❹ What result would you expect to see here? Likely the number, but instead we get an error. Our match returns None, not a match object.

Now we can see the differences between search and match more clearly. We were unable to find a good match with match, despite the fact that we had matches for each of the searches we tried. How come? As mentioned previously, match starts from the very beginning of the string, and if it doesn't find a match there, it returns None. In contrast, search will keep going until it finds a match. Only if it reaches the very end of the string without finding any matches will it return None. So, if you need to assert that a string matches or *begins with* an exact pattern, match is your friend. If you are only looking for the first occurrence or any match in the string, then search is the best option.

There was also a quick lesson on regex syntax here—did you catch it? What capitalized word did you expect to find first? Was it "I" or "Bear"? How come we didn't catch "I"? What pattern would have matched both of them? (Hint: refer to the table and take a look at what wildcard variables you can pass!)

Now that we have a better understanding of regex syntax and how to use it with match, search, and findall, let's see if we can create some patterns where we need to reference more than one group. In the previous examples, we only had one pattern group, so when we called the group method on a match, we only had one value. With regex, however, you can find more than one pattern, and you can give your found matched groups variable names so it's easier to read your code and you can be sure you have matched the proper group.

Let's try it out!

```
import re

name_regex = '([A-Z]\w+) ([A-Z]\w+)' ❶

names = "Barack Obama, Ronald Reagan, Nancy Drew"

name_match = re.match(name_regex, names) ❷

name_match.group()

name_match.groups() ❸

name_regex = '(?P<first_name>[A-Z]\w+) (?P<last_name>[A-Z]\w+)' ❹

for name in re.finditer(name_regex, names): ❺
    print 'Meet {}!'.format(name.group('first_name')) ❻
```

❶ Here we use the same capital word syntax twice, putting it in parentheses. Parentheses are used to define groups.

❷ Here we use the pattern with more than one regex group in our match method. This will now return more than one group if it finds a match.

❸ The groups method on our match shows a list of all the matches of groups we found.

❹ Naming our groups helps our code be clear and explicit. In this pattern, the first group is first_name and the second group is last_name.

❺ finditer is similar to findall, but it returns an iterator. We can view the matches in our string one by one using this iterator.

❻ Using our knowledge of string formatting, we print out our data. Here we only pull the first name out of each match.

Naming pattern groups using ?P<variable_name> creates code that's easy to understand. As our example shows, it's also quite easy to create groups to capture two (or more) particular patterns and their matching data. These techniques help take the guesswork out of reading someone else's (or your six-month-old) regex. Can you write another example to match middle initials, if there are any?

The power of regex lets you quickly discern what's in your strings and parse data from your strings easily. They're invaluable when it comes to parsing really messy datasets, like ones you get from web scraping. For more reading on regex, we recommend trying out the interactive regex parser at RegExr (*http://www.regexr.com/*) as well as walking through the free Regular-Expressions.info tutorial (*http://www.regular-expressions.info/tutorial.html*).

Now that you have many methods to match things, you can easily find duplicates. Let's review our choices when it comes to duplicates we find in our datasets.

What to Do with Duplicate Records

Depending on the state of your data, you may want to combine your duplicate records. If your dataset simply has duplicate rows, there is no need to worry about preserving the data; it is already a part of the finished dataset and you can merely remove or drop these rows from your cleaned data. If, however, you are combining different sets of data and you wish to preserve pieces of the duplicate entries, you will want to figure out how to best do so using Python.

We will review some comprehensive ways to join data in Chapter 9, using some new libraries. However, you can easily combine rows of data in the original way you parsed them. Let's walk through an example of how to do so if you are using `DictReader` to ingest your data. We'll combine some rows of our male dataset. This time, we want to combine the data based on household, so we can look at the surveys on a house-by-house basis rather than a man-by-man basis:

```python
from csv import DictReader

mn_data_rdr = DictReader(open('data/unicef/mn.csv', 'rb'))  ❶

mn_data = [d for d in mn_data_rdr]

def combine_data_dict(data_rows):  ❷
    data_dict = {}  ❸
    for row in data_rows:
        key = '%s-%s' % (row.get('HH1'), row.get('HH2'))  ❹
        if key in data_dict.keys():
            data_dict[key].append(row)  ❺
        else:
            data_dict[key] = [row]  ❻
    return data_dict  ❼

mn_dict = combine_data_dict(mn_data)  ❽

print len(mn_dict)
```

❶ We use the `DictReader` module so we can easily parse all of the fields we want.

❷ We define a function so we can reuse it with other UNICEF datasets. We are going to call it `combine_data_dict` because the function will take `data_rows`, combine them, and return a dictionary.

❸ This defines our new data dictionary to return.

❹ Like we did in our earlier example where we created a unique key from the cluster, household, and line numbers, this code sets a unique key. "HH1" represents the cluster number and "HH2" represents the household number. This code uses these to map unique households.

❺ If the household has already been added, this code extends the list representing the data by adding the current row to the list.

❻ If the household has not yet been added, this line adds a list with the current row of data.

❼ At the end of our function, this code returns the new data dictionary.

❽ Now we run the function by passing our rows of data and assigning the new dictionary to a variable we can use. This code sets the final dictionary to `mn_dict`, which we can now use to see how many unique households we have and how many surveys we have per household.

> If you forget the `return` at the end of a function, your function will return `None`. Be on the lookout for return errors as you begin to write your own functions.

We found approximately 7,000 unique households, meaning a little over 2,000 men who were interviewed shared a household. The average number of men per household for this interview was 1.3. Simple aggregations like this can give us some larger insights into our data and help us conceptualize what it means and what questions we can answer with the data we have available.

Summary

In this chapter, you learned the basics of data cleanup and why it's an essential step in your data wrangling process. You've seen some raw MICS data and interacted with it firsthand. You're now able to look at data and identify where you might have data cleanup issues. You can now also find and remove erroneous data and duplicates.

The new concepts and libraries introduced in this chapter are detailed in Table 7-2.

Table 7-2. New Python and programming concepts and libraries

Concept/Library	Purpose
List generators	Enable quick and easy list assembly using an iterator, a function, and/or an if statement to further clean and process your data.
Dictionary `values` method	Returns a list of the dictionary's values. Great for using to test membership.
`in` and `not in` statements	Test membership. Usually used with strings or lists. Return a Boolean value.
List `remove` method	Removes the first matching item passed from the list. Useful when you know exactly what you want out of an already-created list
`enumerate` method	Takes any iterable and returns a counter of what element you are on along with the value of that element as a tuple.
List `index` method	Returns the first matching index of the passed item in the list. If no match, returns None.
String `format` method	Enables you to easily make a readable string from a series of data. Uses { } as data placeholders and expects a matching number of data points to be passed. Can also be used with a dictionary using key names and can be used with a variety of string formatters.
String formatting (`.4f`, `.2%`, `,`)	Flags used to format numbers into easily readable strings.
`datetime` `strptime` and `strftime` methods	Enables you to easily format Python date objects into strings and create date objects out of strings.
`datetime` timedelta objects	Represents the difference between two Python date objects or modifies a date object (e.g., add or subtract time).
`if not` statements	Test whether the following statement is *not* True. Opposite Boolean logic from `if` statements.
`is` statements	Test if the first object is the same as the other object. Great for type testing (e.g., `is` None, `is list`). For more reading on `is`, check out Appendix E.
String `isdigit` and `isalpha` methods	Test if the string object contains only digits or only letters. Returns a Boolean.
String `find` method	Returns the index location of the passed substring in the string object. Will return -1 if it can't find a match.

Concept/Library	Purpose
Python set objects (*https:// docs.python.org/2/library/ sets.html*)	A collection class of only unique elements. Behaves much like a list but with no duplicate values. Has numerous methods for comparison (`union`, `intersection`, `difference`).
numpy package (*http:// www.numpy.org/*)	An essential mathematical Python library, used as part of the SciPy stack.
FuzzyWuzzy library (*https:// github.com/seatgeek/fuzzywuzzy*)	A library used for fuzzy matching of strings.
Regular expressions (*https:// en.wikipedia.org/wiki/Regu lar_expression*) and the Python `re` library (*https://docs.python.org/2/ library/re.html*)	Enable you to write patterns and find matches in strings.

As you move into the next chapter, you'll keep honing those cleanup and data analysis skills and use them to better organize and replicate your cleanup tasks. We'll review normalizing and standardizing data and how we can script and test our data cleanup.

## CHAPTER 8

Data Cleanup: Standardizing and Scripting

You've learned how to match, parse, and find duplicates in your data, and you've started exploring the wonderful world of data cleanup. As you grow to understand your datasets and the questions you'd like to answer with them, you'll want to think about standardizing your data as well as automating your cleanup.

In this chapter, we'll explore how and when to standardize your data and when to test and script your data cleanup. If you are managing regular updates or additions to the dataset, you'll want to make the cleanup process as efficient and clear as possible so you can spend more time analyzing and reporting. We'll begin by standardizing and normalizing your dataset and determining what to do if your dataset is not normalized.

Normalizing and Standardizing Your Data

Depending on your data and the type of research you are conducting, standardizing and normalizing your dataset might mean calculating new values using the values you currently have, or it might mean applying standardizations or normalizations across a particular column or value.

Normalization, from a statistical view, often has to do with calculating new values from a dataset to standardize the data on a particular scale. For example, you might need to normalize scores for a test to scale so you can accurately view the distribution. You might also need to normalize data so you can accurately see percentiles, or percentiles across different groups (or cohorts).

Say you want to see the distribution of a team's scores across a given season. You might first categorize them as wins, losses, and ties. You might then categorize those as points over, points under, and so on. You might also categorize minutes played and scores per minute. You have access to all of these datasets, and now you'd like to compare them across teams. If you wanted to normalize them, you might normalize total scores on a 0–1 scale. This would mean the outliers (top scores) would be close to 1 and the low scores would be close to 0. You could then use the distribution of that new data to see how many scores were in the middle, and if there were a lot in the low or high range. You could also identify outliers (i.e., if most of the scores are now between .3 and .4, then you know ones that don't fall into that range might be outliers).

What if you want to use standardization on that same data? For example, you could standardize the data and calculate the average number of scores per minute. Then you could chart your averages and see the distribution. What teams scored more per minute? Are there outliers?

You could also calculate the distribution by looking at standard deviations. We'll cover standardization more fully in Chapter 9, but you are basically asking, what is the normal range of the data and what is outside of that range? Does the data follow a pattern or not?

As you can see, normalization and standardization are not the same thing. However, they do often allow researchers or investigators to determine the distribution of their data and what that means for future research or calculations.

Sometimes standardizing and normalizing your data also requires removing outliers so you can better "see" the patterns and distribution of the data. Continuing with the same sports analogy, if you remove the top-scoring players' scores from the entire league, does it drastically change the way the teams perform? If one player is responsible for half of his or her team's scores, then yes, this could cause a dramatic shift.

Likewise, if one team always won by a significant number of points, removing that team from the league data might dramatically shift the distribution and averages. Depending on what problem you are trying to solve, you can use normalization, standardization, and removal of outliers (trimming your data) to help find the answers to your questions.

Saving Your Data

We've explored a few ways to save your data, so let's review them now that we have data we can use. If you are utilizing a database and already know how you'd like to format your tables and save the data you have already cleaned, you should continue to use the Python library modules we reviewed in Chapter 6 to connect and save your data. For many of these libraries, you can open a cursor and commit directly to the database.

We highly recommend adding failure messages and catches in your database scripts, in case you experience a network or database failure. We recommend committing frequently to help avoid network or latency issues affecting your script.

If you are using the SQLite example we reviewed in Chapter 6, you'll want to save your new clean data into your database. Let's take a look at how we can go about that:

```python
import dataset

db = dataset.connect('sqlite:///data_wrangling.db')  ❶

table = db['unicef_survey']  ❷

for row_num, data in enumerate(zipped_data):  ❸
    for question, answer in data:  ❹
        data_dict = {  ❺
            'question': question[1],  ❻
            'question_code': question[0],
            'answer': answer,
            'response_number': row_num,  ❼
            'survey': 'mn',
        }

    table.insert(data_dict)  ❽
```

❶ Here, we access our local database. If you stored the file in a different directory, make sure to change the file path to reflect the database file location in relation to your current file path (e.g., if it's stored in the parent directory: *file:///../datawrangling.db*).

❷ This line creates a new table, `unicef_data`. Because we know many UNICEF surveys follow this pattern, this is a safe, clear name for our database.

❸ We want to keep track of what row we are on so we have a number per response. This code uses the `enumerate` function so each entry (of each row/response) is easily linked in the database (they share a row number).

❹ We know our data is broken into tuples, with our headers as a list in the first entry in the tuple and the responses to those questions in the second part of the tuple. This code uses a `for` loop so we can parse and save the data contained therein.

❺ Each question and answer has its own entry in our database, so we can join together all of the responses for each row (i.e., interview). This code creates a dictionary with the necessary data for each response for each interview.

❻ The plainly written question is the second entry in the list of the headers. This code saves that data as `question` and the UNICEF short code as `question_code`.

❼ In order to keep track of each row of responses, or interview, this code includes the `row_num` from `enumerate`.

❽ Finally, we insert our newly assembled dictionary into our database using our new table's `insert` method.

We want to make sure our cleaned data is preserved in our SQLite database. We created a new database, using the `enumerate` function so we could join together each response (row). If we need to access our data, we can access our new table and use the functions described in Chapter 6 to see all of our records and retrieve them as needed.

If you instead would like to export the cleaned data to a simple file, it should be easy to do that as well. Let's take a look:

```
from csv import writer


def write_file(zipped_data, file_name):
    with open(file_name, 'wb') as new_csv_file:    ❶
        wrtr = writer(new_csv_file)    ❷
        titles = [row[0][1] for row in zipped_data[0]]    ❸
        wrtr.writerow(titles)    ❹
        for row in zipped_data:
            answers = [resp[1] for resp in row]    ❺
            wrtr.writerow(answers)


write_file(zipped_data, 'cleaned_unicef_data.csv')    ❻
```

❶ Uses `with...as` to assign the first output to the second variable name. This assigns the new file `open(file_name, 'wb')` creates to the variable `new_csv_file`. `'wb'` means write in binary mode.

❷ Initializes our CSV writer object by passing it an open file, and assigns the writer object to the `wrtr` variable.

❸ Creates a list of the titles for the header row, since the writer object needs a list of data to write row by row. The longer titles reside in the second element of the first part of our tuple, so the code uses `row[0][1]`.

❹ Uses the writer object's `writerow` method, which takes an iterable and turns it into a comma-separated row. This line writes the header row.

❺ Uses list comprehension to pull out the responses (the second value in the tuple).

❻ Writes each of the lists or responses created using list comprehension to our comma-separated data file.

Here we've used some new and some old syntax. We have learned how to use `with...` `as` to take the response of a simple function and assign it to a variable name. Here, we want to take our open file and assign it to our `new_csv_file` variable. This type of syntax is often used with files and other I/O objects, because once Python is done executing the code in the `with` block we created, it will close the file for us—bellissimo!

Additionally in this code, we've used our CSV writer, which operates similarly to our CSV reader. `writerow` helps us write a list containing each column of data to our CSV.

> The `writerow` method expects an iterable object, so make sure you always pass a list or a tuple. If you pass a string, don't be surprised to see some interesting CSVs ("l,i,k,e, ,t,h,i,s").

We've also used list comprehensions to help make lists of both titles and answers. Because we don't expect a new object or modified object from this function, we simply don't return anything. This function is good review of some of the concepts we've learned so far.

If you'd rather save it in another way, refer to the tips we gave in Chapter 6 on how to save your data. Once your cleaned data is saved, you can move onto securing the rest of your cleanup process and analyzing your data.

Determining What Data Cleanup Is Right for Your Project

Depending on the reliability of your data and how often you will be analyzing it, you might choose a different path for data cleanup. If the data you are working with is haphazard or has many different sources, you might not be able to accurately script your cleanup.

> You need to analyze how much time and effort it takes to completely script your cleanup and whether automating the cleanup will actually save you time.

If your cleanup is particularly onerous and involves many steps, you might want to create a repository of helper scripts. This can give you many functions to reuse throughout your data wrangling and enables you to process new data faster, even if you can't write a script that goes through all of the steps in order. For example, you can have some scripts to search a list or matrix for duplicates, and some functions to export or import data to/from CSVs or format strings and dates. With this type of solution, you can import those functions and use them as you wish with IPython or Jupyter (which we'll learn about in Chapter 10), or in other files in the repository.

If your cleanup code instead matches a determinate pattern and is unlikely to change, you can probably script the entire cleanup process.

Scripting Your Cleanup

As your Python knowledge deepens and grows, so will the Python you write. You are now able to write functions, parse files, import and use various Python libraries, and even store your data. It's about time to start really scripting your code—and by that, we mean deciding how to structure your code for future use, learning, and sharing.

Let's take our UNICEF data as an example. We know UNICEF will release these datasets every few years, and many of the data points will remain the same. It's unlikely the survey will change significantly—it's built on years of experience. Given these facts, we can likely depend on a fairly high level of consistency. If we are using UNICEF data again, we can probably reuse at least some of the same code we wrote for this first script.

We currently don't have a lot of structure and certainly are missing code documentation. On top of making our code hard to read, this makes it difficult to reuse. Although our functions make sense to us now, could we accurately read and understand them in a year? Could we pass them to a coworker and expect our notes to be understood? Until we can answer these questions affirmatively, we may as well not have written any code. If we can't read our code in a year's time, it will be of no use, and someone (probably us) will have to rewrite it again when the new reports are released.

The Zen of Python applies not only to how you write your code, but to how you organize your code; name your functions, variables, and classes; and so on. It's a good idea to take some time to consider your naming choices and determine what will be both clear to you and clear to others. Comments and documentation can help; however, your code should be somewhat legible on its own.

Python is often heralded as one of the easiest to read languages, even for those who can't read code! Keep your syntax readable and clean, and then your documentation will not have to go to great lengths to explain what your code is doing.

Zen of Python

It's always nice to refer to the Zen of Python (*https://www.python.org/dev/peps/pep-0020/*) (also easily accessible with an `import this`). The gist of it is that with Python (and many languages), it's always best to be explicit, clean, and as practical as possible.

As your skills grow, what seems explicit and practical might alter, but we can wholeheartedly recommend you err on the side of writing code that is clear, precise, and simple. Perhaps this will at times make your code a little slower or longer, but as you gain experience you will find ways to write code that is both fast and clear.

For now, always err on the side of making things overly obvious, so when you review the code later, you will understand what you intended.

Familiarize yourself with the PEP-8 Python Style Guide (*https://www.python.org/dev/peps/pep-0008/*) and stick to those rules. There are plenty of PEP-8 linters which read through your code and point out issues.

In addition to style standards and uses, you can use linters for evaluating code complexity. There are several that analyze code according to McCabe's theories and calculations on cyclomatic complexity (*http://bit.ly/cyclomatic_complexity*). Although you may not be able to break your code into simple chunks every time, you should aim to break down complex tasks into smaller, simpler ones and make your code less complicated and more explicit.

As you work to make your code clear and obvious, it's also useful to make reusable chunks more generic. Beware of becoming too generic (`def foo` will help no one), but if you build generic helper functions you will reuse often (like making a CSV from a list or making a set from a list of duplicates), your code will be more organized, clean, and simple.

If all of your reports use the same code to connect with your database or to open a data file, you can make this a function. As you write generic helper functions, your goal is to create simple code that is readable, usable, and doesn't repeat itself.

Table 8-1 summarizes some coding best practices to think about as you go forward. These best practices don't cover everything you'll end up doing with Python and coding, but they provide a good foundation for further scripting and learning.

Table 8-1. Python coding best practices

Practice	Description
Documentation	Include comments, function descriptions, and script clarifications throughout the code, as well as *README.md* files or any other necessary description in the repository structure.
Clear naming	All functions, variables, and files should have clear names that make their contents or intended use obvious.
Proper syntax	Variables and functions should follow proper Python syntax (generally lowercase with underscores between words, or CamelCase (*https://en.wikipedia.org/wiki/CamelCase*) for class names) and the code should follow PEP-8 standards.
Imports	Only import what you need and use, and follow PEP-8 guidelines for your import structure.
Helper functions	Create abstract helper functions to make your code clear and reusable (e.g., `export_to_csv` to take a list and write a CSV export).
Repository organization	Organize your repository into a logical and hierarchical structure, so code used together is organized together and follows normal logical patterns.
Version control	All code should be under version control, so you or your colleagues can create new branches, try out new features, and still have a working master version of the repository.
Fast but clear	Use the syntactic sugar of Python to write fast and efficient code, but err on the side of clarity if the two are opposed.
Use libraries	When you need to do something someone has already coded in Python, don't reinvent the wheel. Use good libraries and contribute to them to help the open source community.
Test your code	When applicable and possible, test your code by using test example data and writing tests for your individual functions.
Be specific	Use proper exceptions in your `try` blocks, be specific in your documentation, and use specific variable names.

Documenting your code is an essential part of writing any script. As Eric Holscher, Pythonista and cofounder of Write the Docs, aptly summarizes (*http://bit.ly/writing_docs*), there are many great reasons to document your code, the first being that you will probably need to use it again—or others may need to read and use it, or you may want to post it on GitHub, or you may want to use it in a future job interview, or you may want to send it to your mom. Whatever the reason, having documentation with, in, and throughout your code will save you hours of pain later. If you are a member of a team, it will save your team hundreds of hours of pain. The payoff is worth the effort of sitting down to analyze what your code is attempting to do and why.

There is a lot of great advice and help available from organizations like Read the Docs (*https://readthedocs.org/*) and Write the Docs (*http://www.writethedocs.org/*) to make writing documentation easier. A good rule of thumb is to have a *README.md* in the root of your project directory with a brief rundown of what the code does, how one can install and run it, what are the requirements, and where to find out more information.

 Sometimes a small code sample or example in your *README.md* is also useful, depending on how much interaction the user (reader) is going to have with the core components.

In addition to your *README.md* file, you'll want to add code comments. As we saw in Chapter 5, these can vary from quick notes to yourself to longer comments documenting how to use your scripts and functions.

 Thanks to PEP-350 (*https://www.python.org/dev/peps/pep-0350/*), the syntax and use of different types of commenting in Python are well documented. Following these standards will make your comments easy for everyone to understand.

Let's take a stab at documenting what we've been doing in our cleanup chapters. To get our creative documentation juices flowing, we'll start with a simple list of the tasks we set out to complete:

- Import data from UNICEF data files.
- Locate headers for data rows.
- Properly match headers we can read with cryptic built-in headers.
- Parse the data to see if we have dupes.
- Parse the data to see if we have missing data.
- Merge data with other rows based on household.
- Save data.

These are more or less in chronological order, and listing them takes some of the agony out of figuring out how to organize and script our code and how to document our new script.

One of the first things we need to do is organize all of the chunks of code we have written in this chapter and the previous chapter into one script. Once we have them all together, we can start to follow our rules for writing good code. Let's take a look at our script so far:

```python
from csv import reader
import dataset

data_rdr = reader(open('../../../data/unicef/mn.csv', 'rb'))
header_rdr = reader(open('../../../data/unicef/mn_headers_updated.csv', 'rb'))

data_rows = [d for d in data_rdr]
header_rows = [h for h in header_rdr if h[0] in data_rows[0]]

all_short_headers = [h[0] for h in header_rows]

skip_index = []
final_header_rows = []

for header in data_rows[0]:
    if header not in all_short_headers:
        print header
        index = data_rows[0].index(header)
        if index not in skip_index:
            skip_index.append(index)
    else:
        for head in header_rows:
            if head[0] == header:
                final_header_rows.append(head)
                break

new_data = []

for row in data_rows[1:]:
    new_row = []
    for i, d in enumerate(row):
        if i not in skip_index:
            new_row.append(d)
    new_data.append(new_row)

zipped_data = []

for drow in new_data:
    zipped_data.append(zip(final_header_rows, drow))

# look for missing

for x in zipped_data[0]:
    if not x[1]:
        print x

# look for dupes
```

```
set_of_keys = set([
    '%s-%s-%s' % (x[0][1], x[1][1], x[2][1]) for x in zipped_data])

uniques = [x for x in zipped_data if not
            set_of_keys.remove('%s-%s-%s' %
                                (x[0][1], x[1][1], x[2][1]))]

print len(set_of_keys)

# save to db

db = dataset.connect('sqlite:///../../data_wrangling.db')

table = db['unicef_survey']

for row_num, data in enumerate(zipped_data):
    for question, answer in data:
        data_dict = {
            'question': question[1],
            'question_code': question[0],
            'answer': answer,
            'response_number': row_num,
            'survey': 'mn',
        }

        table.insert(data_dict)
```

We can see most of our code is flat, meaning we don't have nested levels of importance. Much of the code and functions sit without indentation or documentation in
the file. It's not well abstracted, and the variable names are unclear. Let's start working
on parts of that, beginning at the top. The first two sets of lines repeat each other. Let's
write a function to do that instead:

```
def get_rows(file_name):
    rdr = reader(open(file_name, 'rb'))
    return [row for row in rdr]
```

Now we can use this function to shorten our file. Let's take a look at the next section
of code and see if we can improve it as well.

We are spending time rewriting our header_rows to align with headers from
data_rows; however, that bit of code is no longer needed. Because we create the
final_header_rows from matches between the two, we don't need to worry about
header_rows with no data_rows to match. We can remove that line.

Lines 14–27 all deal with creating the final_header_rows and skip_index lists. We
can summarize these as both working on eliminating nonmatching elements so we
can zip our final list. Let's put them together in one method:

```
def eliminate_mismatches(header_rows, data_rows):
    all_short_headers = [h[0] for h in header_rows]
    skip_index = []
    final_header_rows = []

    for header in data_rows[0]:
        if header not in all_short_headers:
            index = data_rows[0].index(header)
            if index not in skip_index:
                skip_index.append(index)
        else:
            for head in header_rows:
                if head[0] == header:
                    final_header_rows.append(head)
                    break
    return skip_index, final_header_rows
```

We have now combined *even more* sections of our cleanup into functions. This helps us delineate what each function does and documents our code so if (or should we say, when) we need to update it, we know exactly where to look.

Let's read on in our script and see if we have more contenders. It looks like the next section creates our zipped dataset. We could make this two functions: one to whittle down our data rows into just those that match the headers, and another that zips the two. We could also leave it as one function to create the zipped data. In the end, it's up to you to determine what might fit best. Here, we will keep it as one function with a smaller helper function, in case we need it again:

```
def zip_data(headers, data):
    zipped_data = []
    for drow in data:
        zipped_data.append(zip(headers, drow))
    return zipped_data


def create_zipped_data(final_header_rows, data_rows, skip_index):
    new_data = []
    for row in data_rows[1:]:
        new_row = []
        for index, data in enumerate(row):
            if index not in skip_index:
                new_row.append(data)
        new_data.append(new_row)
    zipped_data = zip_data(final_header_rows, new_data)
    return zipped_data
```

With our new functions, we were able to preserve our code, clear up some variable names, and add a helper function to zip headers with rows of data and return the list of zipped data. The code is clearer and broken up more appropriately. We're going to continue to apply the same logic to the rest of the file. Let's take a look at the result:

```python
from csv import reader
import dataset


def get_rows(file_name):
    rdr = reader(open(file_name, 'rb'))
    return [row for row in rdr]


def eliminate_mismatches(header_rows, data_rows):
    all_short_headers = [h[0] for h in header_rows]
    skip_index = []
    final_header_rows = []

    for header in data_rows[0]:
        if header not in all_short_headers:
            index = data_rows[0].index(header)
            if index not in skip_index:
                skip_index.append(index)
        else:
            for head in header_rows:
                if head[0] == header:
                    final_header_rows.append(head)
                    break
    return skip_index, final_header_rows


def zip_data(headers, data):
    zipped_data = []
    for drow in data:
        zipped_data.append(zip(headers, drow))
    return zipped_data


def create_zipped_data(final_header_rows, data_rows, skip_index):
    new_data = []
    for row in data_rows[1:]:
        new_row = []
        for index, data in enumerate(row):
            if index not in skip_index:
                new_row.append(data)
        new_data.append(new_row)
    zipped_data = zip_data(final_header_rows, new_data)
    return zipped_data


def find_missing_data(zipped_data):
    missing_count = 0
    for question, answer in zipped_data:
        if not answer:
            missing_count += 1
    return missing_count
```

```
def find_duplicate_data(zipped_data):
    set_of_keys = set([
        '%s-%s-%s' % (row[0][1], row[1][1], row[2][1])
        for row in zipped_data])

    uniques = [row for row in zipped_data if not
               set_of_keys.remove('%s-%s-%s' %
                                  (row[0][1], row[1][1], row[2][1]))]

    return uniques, len(set_of_keys)


def save_to_sqlitedb(db_file, zipped_data, survey_type):
    db = dataset.connect(db_file)

    table = db['unicef_survey']
    all_rows = []

    for row_num, data in enumerate(zipped_data):
        for question, answer in data:
            data_dict = {
                'question': question[1],
                'question_code': question[0],
                'answer': answer,
                'response_number': row_num,
                'survey': survey_type,
            }
            all_rows.append(data_dict)

    table.insert_many(all_rows)
```

Now we have a bunch of nice functions, but we've gutted how the program runs. If we run this script right now, no lines of code execute. It's just a set of written functions never called by anything.

We need to now work on re-creating how to use all these steps in a `main` function. The `main` function is often where Python developers will put code intended to run via the command line. Let's add our `main` function with the code to clean our datasets:

```
""" This section goes at the bottom of the script we've already written. """

def main():
    data_rows = get_rows('data/unicef/mn.csv')
    header_rows = get_rows('data/unicef/mn_headers_updated.csv')
    skip_index, final_header_rows = eliminate_mismatches(header_rows,
                                                        data_rows)
    zipped_data = create_zipped_data(final_header_rows, data_rows, skip_index)
    num_missing = find_missing_data(zipped_data)
    uniques, num_dupes = find_duplicate_data(zipped_data)
    if num_missing == 0 and num_dupes == 0:
```

```
            save_to_sqlitedb('sqlite:///data/data_wrangling.db', zipped_data)
    else:
        error_msg = ''
        if num_missing:
            error_msg += 'We are missing {} values. '.format(num_missing)
        if num_dupes:
            error_msg += 'We have {} duplicates. '.format(num_dupes)
        error_msg += 'Please have a look and fix!'
        print error_msg


if __name__ == '__main__':
    main()
```

Now we have an executable file we can run from the command line. What happens when you run this file? Do you get our newly created error message, or has your data been saved to your local SQLite database?

Making a File Command-Line Executable

Most Python files meant to be executed via the command line will have a few attributes in common. They will usually have a main function that utilizes smaller or helper functions, similar to what we built here for our cleanup.

That main function is usually called from a code block on the main indentation level of the file. The syntax used is if __name__ == '__main__':. This syntax uses global *private* variables (hence the double underscores around the names) and returns True when you are running the file from the command line.

Code in this if statement will *not* execute if the script is not being run from the command line. If we imported these functions into another script, the __name__ variable would not be '__main__' and the code would not execute. This is a widely used convention for Python scripts.

 If you run into any errors, try checking to make sure your code looks exactly like this and you are using the proper file paths to the data from the repository and the local database you created in Chapter 6.

Now let's put some work into documenting our code. We're going to add some docstrings to our functions, some inline notes so we can easily read the more complex bits of our script, and a larger explanation at the top of the script that we might move to a *README.md* file:

```
"""
Usage: python our_cleanup_script.py

This script is used to intake the male survey data from UNICEF
and save it to a simple database file after it has been checked
for duplicates and missing data and after the headers have been properly
matched with the data. It expects there to be a 'mn.csv' file with the
data and the 'mn_updated_headers.csv' file in a subfolder called 'unicef' within
a data folder in this directory. It also expects there to be a SQLite
file called 'data_wrangling.db' in the root of this directory. Finally,
it expects to utilize the dataset library
(http://dataset.readthedocs.org/en/latest/).

If the script runs without finding any errors, it will save the
cleaned data to the 'unicef_survey' table in the SQLite.
The saved data will have the following structure:
    - question: string
    - question_code: string
    - answer: string
    - response_number: integer
    - survey: string

The response number can later be used to join entire responses together
(i.e., all of response_number 3 come from the same interview, etc.).

If you have any questions, please feel free to contact me via ...
"""

from csv import reader
import dataset


def get_rows(file_name):
    """Return a list of rows from a given csv filename."""
    rdr = reader(open(file_name, 'rb'))
    return [row for row in rdr]


def eliminate_mismatches(header_rows, data_rows):
    """
    Return index numbers to skip in a list and final header rows in a list
    when given header rows and data rows from a UNICEF dataset. This
    function assumes the data_rows object has headers in the first element.
    It assumes those headers are the shortened UNICEF form. It also assumes
    the first element of each header row in the header data is the
    shortened UNICEF form. It will return the list of indexes to skip in the
    data rows (ones that don't match properly with headers) as the first element
    and will return the final cleaned header rows as the second element.
    """
    all_short_headers = [h[0] for h in header_rows]
    skip_index = []
    final_header_rows = []
```

```python
    for header in data_rows[0]:
        if header not in all_short_headers:
            index = data_rows[0].index(header)
            if index not in skip_index:
                skip_index.append(index)
        else:
            for head in header_rows:
                if head[0] == header:
                    final_header_rows.append(head)
                    break
    return skip_index, final_header_rows


def zip_data(headers, data):
    """
    Return a list of zipped data when given a header list and data list. Assumes
    the length of data elements per row and the length of headers are the same.

    example output: [(['question code', 'question summary', 'question text'],
                      'resp'), ....]
    """
    zipped_data = []
    for drow in data:
        zipped_data.append(zip(headers, drow))
    return zipped_data


def create_zipped_data(final_header_rows, data_rows, skip_index):
    """
    Returns a list of zipped data rows (matching header and data) when given a
    list of final header rows, a list of data rows, and a list of indexes on
    those data rows to skip as they don't match properly. The function assumes
    the first row in the data rows contains the original data header values,
    and will remove those values from the final list.
    """
    new_data = []
    for row in data_rows[1:]:
        new_row = []
        for index, data in enumerate(row):
            if index not in skip_index:
                new_row.append(data)
        new_data.append(new_row)
    zipped_data = zip_data(final_header_rows, new_data)
    return zipped_data


def find_missing_data(zipped_data):
    """
    Returns a count of how many answers are missing in an entire set of zipped
    data. This function assumes all responses are stored as the second element.
    It also assumes every response is stored in a list of these matched question,
```

```
    answer groupings. It returns an integer.
    """
    missing_count = 0
    for response in zipped_data:
        for question, answer in response:
            if not answer:
                missing_count += 1
    return missing_count


def find_duplicate_data(zipped_data):
    """
    Returns a list of unique elements and a number of duplicates found when given
    a UNICEF zipped_data list. This function assumes that the first three rows of
    data are structured to have the house, cluster, and line number of the
    interview and uses these values to create a unique key that should not be
    repeated.
    """

    set_of_keys = set([
        '%s-%s-%s' % (row[0][1], row[1][1], row[2][1])
        for row in zipped_data])

    #TODO: this will throw an error if we have duplicates- we should find a way
    #around this
    uniques = [row for row in zipped_data if not
                set_of_keys.remove('%s-%s-%s' %
                                    (row[0][1], row[1][1], row[2][1]))]

    return uniques, len(set_of_keys)


def save_to_sqlitedb(db_file, zipped_data, survey_type):
    """
    When given a path to a SQLite file, the cleaned zipped_data, and the
    UNICEF survey type that was used, saves the data to SQLite in a
    table called 'unicef_survey' with the following attributes:
        question, question_code, answer, response_number, survey
    """
    db = dataset.connect(db_file)

    table = db['unicef_survey']
    all_rows = []

    for row_num, data in enumerate(zipped_data):
        for question, answer in data:
            data_dict = {
                'question': question[1],
                'question_code': question[0],
                'answer': answer,
                'response_number': row_num,
                'survey': survey_type,
```

```
                }
            all_rows.append(data_dict)

        table.insert_many(all_rows)


    def main():
        """
        Import all data into rows, clean it, and then if
        no errors are found, save it to SQlite.
        If there are errors found, print out details so
        developers can begin work on fixing the script
        or seeing if there is an error in the data.
        """

        #TODO: we probably should abstract these files so that we can pass
        # them in as variables and use the main function with other surveys
        data_rows = get_rows('data/unicef/mn.csv')
        header_rows = get_rows('data/unicef/mn_updated_headers.csv')
        skip_index, final_header_rows = eliminate_mismatches(header_rows,
                                                             data_rows)
        zipped_data = create_zipped_data(final_header_rows, data_rows, skip_index)
        num_missing = find_missing_data(zipped_data)
        uniques, num_dupes = find_duplicate_data(zipped_data)
        if num_missing == 0 and num_dupes == 0:
            #TODO: we probably also want to abstract this
            # file away, or make sure it exists before continuing
            save_to_sqlite('sqlite:///data_wrangling.db', zipped_data, 'mn')
        else:
            #TODO: eventually we probably want to log this, and
            # maybe send an email if an error is thrown rather than print it
            error_msg = ''
            if num_missing:
                error_msg += 'We are missing {} values. '.format(num_missing)
            if num_dupes:
                error_msg += 'We have {} duplicates. '.format(num_dupes)
            error_msg += 'Please have a look and fix!'
            print error_msg


    if __name__ == '__main__':
        main()
```

Our code is now better documented, organized, and it has a clear set of reusable functions. This is a great start for our first script. Hopefully, we can use this code to import many sets of UNICEF data!

We've also put in some "TODO" notes for ourselves so we can improve the script over time. Which issues do you think are the most pressing? Why? Can you take a stab at fixing them?

We only have one file to run our code. However, as your code grows, your repository will as well. It's important to think about what you might add to your repository over time early on. Code and code structure are pretty similar. If you think this repository might be used for more than just UNICEF data parsing, you might want to organize it differently.

How so? For one thing, you might want to keep the data in a separate file. In fact, depending on how large your repository might grow, you might want the different data parsers and cleaners in separate folders.

 Don't worry too much about these decisions at the beginning. As you get better at Python and understanding your datasets, it will begin to be more obvious to you where to begin.

In terms of organizing your repository, it is fairly common to have a *utils* or *common* folder where you can store parts of the script shared among sections of code. Many developers store things like database connection scripts, commonly used API code, and communication or email scripts in such a folder, so they can be imported easily into any other script.

Depending on how the rest of your repository is managed, you might have several directories set up to contain different aspects of your project. One directory could be related only to UNICEF data. Another could contain web-scraping scripts or final reporting code. How you organize your repository is up to you. Always opt for being clear, obvious, and organized.

If you end up needing to reorganize your repository later, it will be far less awful if you took time to organize it in the first place. If, on the other hand, your repository is rife with 800-line files and no clear documentation, you'll have quite a task at hand. The best rule of thumb is to outline a good starting point for organization, and do occasional housekeeping as your repository grows and changes.

Outside of file organization, naming your directories, files, functions, and classes in clear and obvious ways will also help. In the *utils* folder, you might have half a dozen files. If you name them *utils1*, *utils2*, and so on, you will always need to look and see what they contain. However, if you have named them *email.py*, *database.py*, *twitter_api.py*, and so on, the filenames will give you more information.

Being explicit in every aspect of your code is a great start to a long and prosperous career in Python data wrangling. Let's think about our repository and organize how we might expect to find our files:

```
data_wrangling_repo/
|-- README.md
|-- data_wrangling.db
|-- data/
|    `-- unicef/
|        |-- mn.csv
|        |-- mn_updated_headers.csv
|        |-- wm.csv
|        `-- wm_headers.csv
|-- scripts/
|    `-- unicef/
|        `-- unicef_cleanup.py (script from this chp)
`-- utils/
     |-- databases.py
     `-- emailer.py
```

We haven't yet written a *databases* or *emailer* file, but we probably should. What else could we add to the structure? Why do you think we made two different *unicef* folders in our repository? Should developers separate their data files from the script files?

 While your project's folder structure may look like this, bear in mind that data is *not* usually stored or housed in a repository. Keep the data files for your project on a shared file server or somewhere on the local network. If you are working alone, make sure you have a backup somewhere. Don't check these large files into your repository. Not only will it slow down work if you need to check out the repository on a new device, but it's also not a smart way to manage your data.

We would advise against checking your *db* files or any *log* or *config* files into your repository. Do your best to build the structure in a convenient way. You can always add the expected structure of the files in your *README.md* and provide details about where to get the data files.

Git and .gitignore

If you're not already using Git (*https://git-scm.com/*) for your version control needs, you will be by the end of this book! Version control allows you to create a repository to manage and update your code and share it with your team or other colleagues.

We'll review Git in more depth in Chapter 14, but we wanted to call attention to *.gitignore* files (*https://github.com/github/gitignore*) while we are discussing repository structure. *.gitignore* files tell Git what it should ignore and not update or upload to the repository. It uses a simple pattern to match filenames, similar to the regex we learned about in Chapter 7.

In our repository structure, we could use a *.gitignore* file to tell Git we don't want any of the data files checked into the repository. We could then use the *README.md* to explain the structure of the repository and provide contact information for the data files. This keeps our repository clean and easy to download and allows us to still retain a nice structure for our code.

Creating a logical repository structure and using *README.md* and *.gitignore* files allows you to have an organized project folder with modular code and avoid storing large data files or potentially sensitive data (database or login data) in your repository.

Testing with New Data

Now that we've documented, scripted, and organized our code, we should write some tests or try it out using test data. This helps ensure we've properly executed what we'd like to see and keeps our code well defined. Because one of the reasons we scripted the data cleanup was so we could reuse it, testing it with new data proves our time and effort standardizing the code were appropriately spent.

One way we can test the script we have just written is to see how easily we can apply it to similar data we find on the UNICEF website. Let's take a look and see. You should have the *wm.csv* and *wm_headers.csv* files from the repository (*https://github.com/jack iekazil/data-wrangling*). These files are data for the women's survey from the Zimbabwe UNICEF data.

Let's try using those files in our script instead of the men's survey data. To do so, we change just those two filenames from our cleanup script to point to the two women's survey data files. We should also change the survey type to 'wm', so we can differentiate the data found in each set.

 The women's dataset is significantly larger than the men's. If you have unsaved data, we recommend saving it and closing other programs before proceeding. On that note, it's probably a good idea to start considering how we can improve memory usage in our script.

Let's take a look and see if it successfully imported our data:

```
import dataset

db = dataset.connect('sqlite:///data_wrangling.db')

wm_count = db.query('select count(*) from unicef_survey where survey="wm"') ❶

count_result = wm_count.next() ❷

print count_result
```

❶ We use a direct query so we can quickly see the number of rows we have where `survey='wm'`. This should only include rows from the second run, where we set the type to `'wm'`.

❷ This reads the result of our query, using the query reponse's `next` method to pull the first result. Because we used `count`, we should only have one response with the count.

So, we successfully imported more than 3 million questions and answers from our women's dataset. We know our script works, and we can see the results!

Testing your script using similar data is one way to go about ensuring it works as intended. It can also show your script is built generally enough for reuse. However, there are many other ways to test your code. Python has quite a few good testing libraries to help you write test scripts and utilize test data (and even test API responses) so you can ensure your code functions properly.

There are several testing modules built into Python's standard library. `unittest` (*https://docs.python.org/2/library/unittest.html*) provides unit tests for your Python code. It comes with some nice built-in classes with assert statements to test whether your code is working. If we were to write unit tests for our code, we could write one to assert the `get_rows` function returns a list. We could also assert the length of the list and the number of data lines in the file are the same. Each function can have these tests and assertions.

Another popular Python testing framework is `nose` (*https://nose.readthedocs.org/en/latest/*). `nose` is a very powerful testing framework with quite a lot of options in terms of extra plugins (*http://bit.ly/builtin_nose_plugins*) and configuration. It's great if you have a large repository with different testing requirements and many developers working on the same code.

Can't decide which one to start with? Then `pytest` (*http://pytest.org/latest/*) might be right for you. It allows you to write tests in either style and switch if need be. It also has a fairly active community for talks and tutorials (*http://bit.ly/pytest_talks_posts*), so it's a great place to start if you want to learn more and then start writing your tests.

 Normally, your test suite would be organized with a test file in each module (i.e., given our current repository structure, we would put a test file in each directory we have except for our data and configuration folders). Some people write a test file for every Python file in each folder, so that it's easy to see where the tests are for specific files. Others use a separate directory including the tests, with a structure that maps to the same Python files in the script part of the structure.

Whatever test style or organization you choose, make sure you are consistent and clear. That way you'll always know where to look for the tests, and you (and others) will be able to run them as needed.

Summary

In this chapter, we covered some basics in terms of standardizing your data, and when it might be useful to normalize your data or remove outliers. You were able to export your clean data (from your work in Chapter 6) into your database or a local file, and you began writing more coherent functions for those repetitive processes.

Additionally, you've worked on organizing your Python repository with nested folders and properly named files, and started to document and analyze your code. Finally, you had a basic introduction to testing, and some of the tools you'll have at your disposal when you start writing your tests.

Table 8-2 lists the Python concepts covered in this chapter.

Table 8-2. New Python and programming concepts and libraries

Concept/Library	Purpose
Dataset `insert` method	Allows you to easily store your data into your SQLite database using an `insert` command.
CSV writer object	Lets you store your data in a CSV using the `csv writer` class.
Zen of Python (`import this`)	A philosophy for how to write and think like a Python programmer.
Python best practices	A basic outline of some best practices to follow as a new Python developer.
Python command-line execution (`if __name__ == '__main__':`)	Formatting a script with this block allows you to run your `main` function from the command line.
TODO notation	Allows you to easily see what needs to be done for your script via commenting.
Git (*https://git-scm.com/*)	Version control system to help track changes in your code. Absolutely essential for code you want to deploy or use with others, but also incredibly useful on a local solo project. More on Git in Chapter 14.

In the next chapter, you'll keep honing those cleanup and data analysis skills and use them to help prep a new dataset, as we move on to analyzing your data.

## CHAPTER 9

Data Exploration and Analysis

Now that you've spent time acquiring and cleaning your data, you are ready to start analyzing! It's important to approach your data exploration with very few expectations for outcomes. Your question could be too broad for a singular answer, or it might not have a conclusive answer. Recall learning about hypotheses and conclusions in your first science course? It's best to approach your data exploration with those same methods in mind—and with an understanding that you may not find a clear conclusion.

That said, just exploring the data and finding there *are* no trends or the trends don't match your expectations is part of the fun. If everything was how we expected it to be, data wrangling would be a bit boring. We've learned to expect little and explore a lot.

 As you begin to analyze and explore your data, you might realize you need more data or different data. That's all part of the process and should be embraced as you further define the questions you aim to answer and examine what the data is telling you.

Now is also a great time to revisit the initial questions you had when you found your dataset(s). What do you want to know? Are there other related questions to aid your exploration? Those questions might point you in a direction where you find a story. If not, they might lead to other interesting questions. Even if you can't answer your initial question, you can reach a greater understanding of the topic and discover new questions to explore.

In this chapter, we will learn about some new Python libraries for data exploration and analysis, and continue to apply what we've learned about cleaning our data from the previous two chapters. We'll take a look at how to join datasets, explore the data, and come to statistical conclusions about relationships in our datasets.

Exploring Your Data

You learned how to parse and clean your data in the preceding chapters, so you should be familiar with interacting with your data in Python. Now we will take a more in-depth look at exploring data with Python.

To begin with, we will install a helper library, `agate` (*http://agate.readthedocs.org/*), that will allow us to start looking at some basic features of our data. It's a data-analysis library built by Christopher Groskopf (*https://github.com/onyxfish*), an accomplished data journalist and Python developer, and it can help us *get to know* our data. To install the library, use pip:

```
pip install agate
```

This chapter is compatible with `agate` 1.2.0. Because `agate` is a relatively young library, it's possible some of this functionality will change as the library matures. To ensure you install a particular version of a library, you can set that as you use `pip`. For this book, you can install `agate` using: `pip install agate==1.2.0`. We recommend you also test the latest and feel free to keep track of code changes on the book's repository.

We want to investigate some of the features of the `agate` library. To do that, we'll be using the data we acquired from UNICEF's annual report (*http://data.unicef.org/child-protection/child-labour.html*) on child labor.

Importing Data

To begin, we'll take a look at our first dataset—UNICEF's child labor summary data. The data we downloaded was an Excel file containing listings of different percentages of child labor around the world. We can use what we learned about Excel files and data cleaning from Chapters 4 and 7 to get the data into a format accepted by the `agate` library.

As we work through the Excel sheet, we recommend having the sheet open in your preferred Excel viewer. This makes it easier to compare what Python "sees" with what you see in the sheet, facilitating navigation and extraction.

First, we want to import the libraries we anticipate needing and get the Excel file into an `xlrd` notebook:

```
import xlrd
import agate

workbook = xlrd.open_workbook('unicef_oct_2014.xls')

workbook.nsheets

workbook.sheet_names()
```

We now have our Excel data in a variable called workbook. This worksheet contains one sheet, named *Child labour*.

If you're running this in your IPython terminal (recommended, as you'll see more output), you should see the following:

```
In [6]: workbook.nsheets
Out[6]: 1

In [7]: workbook.sheet_names()
Out[7]: [u'Child labour  ']
```

Try selecting the sheet so you can import it into the agate library. According to the agate library documentation (*http://bit.ly/agate_tutorial*), it can import data with a list of titles, a list of types for the columns of data, and a data reader (or an iterable list of the data). So, we'll need the data types so we can properly import the data from the sheet into the agate library:

```
sheet = workbook.sheets()[0]

sheet.nrows ❶

sheet.row_values(0) ❷

for r in range(sheet.nrows):
    print r, sheet.row(r) ❸
```

❶ nrows identifies how many rows are in our sheet.

❷ row_values allows us to select a single row and display its values. In this case, it shows the title, as it is on the first line of the Excel file.

❸ By using range and a for loop to iterate over every row, we can see each line as Python sees it. The sheet's row method will return some information on the data and data type for each row.

We know from Chapter 3, the csv library takes an open file and turns it into an *iterator*. An iterator is an object we can *iterate* or loop over, returning each of its values one at a time. In code, an iterator is a more efficient way of unpacking data than a list, as it has speed and performance advantages.

Because we're working with a relatively small dataset, we can create a list and pass it in place of an iterator. Most libraries that require an iterator work fine with any iterable object (like a list). This way, we're still complying with what our xlrd and agate libraries expect.

First, let's get the titles of our columns. From our previous output, we can see the titles are in 4 and row 5. We will use zip to grab our title rows:

```
title_rows = zip(sheet.row_values(4), sheet.row_values(5))

title_rows
```

Now we can see the value of our `title_rows` variable is:

```
[('', u'Countries and areas'),
 (u'Total (%)', ''),
 ('', ''),
 (u'Sex (%)', u'Male'),
 ('', u'Female'),
 (u'Place of residence (%)', u'Urban'),
 ('', u'Rural'),
 (u'Household wealth quintile (%)', u'Poorest'),
 ('', u'Second'),
 ('', u'Middle'),
 ('', u'Fourth'),
 ('', u'Richest'),
 (u'Reference Year', ''),
 (u'Data Source', '')]
```

Using both rows retains extra information we would lose if we chose only one. It's a perfect match and we could spend some extra time improving this, but for an initial exploration of the data, it's a good first start. The title data is currently in a list of tuples. We know the agate library expects a tuple list where the first value is the title strings, so we should turn our titles into a list of strings:

```
titles = [t[0] + ' ' + t[1] for t in title_rows]

print titles

titles = [t.strip() for t in titles]
```

In this code, we use two list generators. In the first one, we pass our `title_rows` list, which is a list of tuples. In those tuples, we have strings from the Excel file's title rows.

The first list generator takes both parts of the tuple (using indexing) to create one string. We add each of those tuple values together, using ' ' for readability. Now our titles list is just a list of strings—the tuples are gone! We've made the titles a bit messier though, as not every tuple has two values. By adding the space, we created some titles with leading spaces, like ' Female'.

To remove the leading spaces, in the second iterator we use the `strip` string method, which removes leading and trailing spaces. Now our `titles` variable has a clean list of strings for use with the `agate` library.

Our titles are sorted out, so now we need to choose which lines to use from our Excel file. Our sheet has both country and continent data, but let's focus on the country data. We want to avoid accidentally mixing in the totals with our data. We know from our previous code output that lines 6–114 have the data we want to use. We will use the `row_values` method to return the values of the rows from the `xlrd` sheet object:

```
country_rows = [sheet.row_values(r) for r in range(6, 114)]
```

Now we have our titles and our data list, so we only need to define the types to import it into the `agate` library. According to the documentation on defining columns (*http://bit.ly/agate_tutorial*), we have text, Boolean, number, and date columns, and the library's authors advise us to use text if we are unsure of the type. There is also a built-in `TypeTester` (*http://bit.ly/agate_typetester*) we can use to guess the types. To begin, we are going to use some of the `xlrd` built-ins to help define our columns:

```
from xlrd.sheet import ctype_text
import agate

text_type = agate.Text()
number_type = agate.Number()
boolean_type = agate.Boolean()
date_type = agate.Date()

example_row = sheet.row(6)

print example_row ❶

print example_row[0].ctype ❷
print example_row[0].value

print ctype_text ❸
```

❶ By performing a visual check on this row, we see we have good data. Other than one empty column, `xlrd` is identifying all of the data.

❷ In these lines, we call the `ctype` and `value` attributes to get the type and value attributes of each cell.

You can easily find new methods and attributes when using IPython by creating a new object out of something you're curious to see and adding a period at the end and pressing Tab. This will populate a list of attributes and methods you can further explore.

❸ Using the `ctype_text` object from the `xlrd` library, we can match up the integers returned by the `ctype` method and map them to something readable. This is a great alternative to mapping types by hand.

This code gives us a better idea of the tools we have available to define types. The `ctype` method and `ctype_text` object can be used to order and show data types given the example row.

 Although it can seem like a lot of work to create lists this way, they provide reusability that will save you time. Reusing code snippets will save you countless tedious hours later and is a fun aspect of writing your own code.

Now we know what functions we can use to investigate Excel column types, so we need to try to make a list of types for our `agate` library. We will need to iterate over our example row and use `ctype` to match the column types:

```
types = []

for v in example_row:
    value_type = ctype_text[v.ctype]  ❶
    if value_type == 'text':  ❷
        types.append(text_type)
    elif value_type == 'number':
        types.append(number_type)
    elif value_type == 'xldate':
        types.append(date_type)
    else:
        types.append(text_type)  ❸
```

❶ Maps the integers we found when we explored the `ctype` attribute of each row with the `ctype_text` dictionary to make them readable. Now `value_type` holds the column type string (i.e., text, number, etc.).

❷ Uses `if` and `elif` statements with the `==` operator to match `value_type` with the `agate` column types. Then, the code appends the proper type to the list and moves on to the next column.

❸ As advised by the library's documentation, if there is no type match, we append the text column type.

Now we've constructed a function to take an empty list, iterate over the columns, and create a full list of all of the column types for our dataset. After running the code we have our types, our titles, and a list of our data. We can zip the titles with the types and try importing the result into our `agate` table by running the following line of code:

```
table = agate.Table(country_rows, titles, types)
```

When you run the code you should see a `CastError`, with the message `Can not convert value "-" to Decimal for NumberColumn.`

As we covered in Chapters 7 and 8, learning how to clean your data is an essential part of data wrangling. Writing well-documented code allows you to save time in the future. By reading this error message, we realize we have some bad data lying around in one of our number columns. Somewhere in our sheet, the data is placing `'-'` instead of `''`, which would be properly processed as null. We can write a function to handle this problem:

```
def remove_bad_chars(val): ❶
    if val == '-': ❷
        return None ❸
    return val

cleaned_rows = []

for row in country_rows:
    cleaned_row = [remove_bad_chars(rv) for rv in row] ❹
    cleaned_rows.append(cleaned_row) ❺
```

❶ Defines a function to remove bad characters (like `'-'` in an integer column)

❷ If the value is equal to `'-'`, selects this value to be replaced

❸ If the value is `'-'`, returns `None`

❹ Iterates through `country_rows` to create newly cleaned rows with the proper data

❺ Creates a `cleaned_rows` list holding the clean data (using the `append` method)

 When we write functions to modify values, keeping a default return outside of the main logic (like in this example) ensures we always return a value.

By using this function, we can make sure our integer columns have `None` types instead of `'-'`. `None` tells Python that it's null data, and to ignore it when analyzing it in comparison with other numbers.

Because it seems like this type of cleaning and changing might be something we'll want to reuse, let's take some of the code we have already written and make it into a more abstract and generic helper function. When we created our last cleaning function, we made a new list, iterated over all of the rows, and then iterated over each individual row to clean the data and return a new list for our `agate` table. Let's see if we can take those concepts and abstract them:

```python
def get_new_array(old_array, function_to_clean):  ❶
    new_arr = []
    for row in old_array:
        cleaned_row = [function_to_clean(rv) for rv in row]
        new_arr.append(cleaned_row)
    return new_arr  ❷

cleaned_rows = get_new_array(country_rows, remove_bad_chars)  ❸
```

❶ Defines our function with two arguments: the old data array, and the function to clean the data.

❷ Reuses our code with more abstract names. At the end of the function, returns the new clean array.

❸ Calls the function with the `remove_bad_chars` function and saves it in `cleaned_rows`.

Now let's retry our code to create the table:

```python
In [10]: table = agate.Table(cleaned_rows, titles, types)

In [11]: table
Out[11]: <agate.table.Table at 0x7f9adc489990>
```

Hooray! We have a `table` variable holding a `Table` object. We can now look at our data using the `agate` library functions. If you're curious what the table looks like, have a quick look by using the `print_table` method like so:

```python
table.print_table(max_columns=7)
```

 If you've been following along using IPython and you'd like to ensure you have these variables in your next session, use `%store` (*http://bit.ly/storemagic*). If we want to save our `table` we can simply type `%store table`. In our next IPython session we can restore `table` by typing `%store -r`. This will be useful to "save" your work as you analyze your data.

Next, we'll take a deeper look at our table using some built-in research tools.

Exploring Table Functions

The `agate` library gives us many functions to investigate our data. First, we'll try out the sorting methods (*http://agate.readthedocs.org/en/latest/tutorial.html?#sorting-and-slicing*). Let's try ordering our table so we can see the most egregious nations by ordering using the total percentage column. We will use the `limit` (*http://bit.ly/agate_table_limit*) method to see the top 10 offenders:

```
table.column_names ❶

most_egregious = table.order_by('Total (%)', reverse=True).limit(10) ❷

for r in most_egregious.rows: ❸
    print r
```

❶ Checks the column names so we know what column to use.

❷ Chains the `order_by` and `limit` methods to create a new table. Because `order_by` will order from least to greatest, we are using the `reverse` argument to say we'd like to see the largest numbers first.

❸ Using the new table's `rows` attribute, iterates through the top 10 worst countries for child labor.

Running the code returns a list of the 10 countries with the highest incidence of child labor. In terms of percentages of children working, there are a high number of African countries at the top of the list. It's our first interesting find! Let's keep exploring. To investigate which countries have the most girls working, we can use the `order_by` and `limit` functions again. This time, we need to apply them to the *Female* percentage column:

```
most_females = table.order_by('Female', reverse=True).limit(10)
for r in most_females.rows:
    print '{}: {}%'.format(r['Countries and areas'], r['Female'])
```

 When first exploring your data, use the Python `format` function to make your output easier to read rather than simply printing out each row. This means you can remain focused on the data instead of struggling to read it.

We see we have some `None` percentages. That isn't what we expected! We can remove those using the `agate` table's `where` method, as shown in the following code. This method is similar to a SQL `WHERE` statement or a Python `if` statement. `where` creates another table including only the fitting rows:

```
female_data = table.where(lambda r: r['Female'] is not None)
most_females = female_data.order_by('Female', reverse=True).limit(10)

for r in most_females.rows:
    print '{}: {}%'.format(r['Countries and areas'], r['Female'])
```

First, we created the `female_data` table, which uses the Python `lambda` function to ensure each row has a value for the *Female* column. The `where` function takes the Boolean value from the `lambda` function and separates out only the rows where it returns `True`. Once we've separated out the rows with only female child labor values, we use the same sorting, limiting, and formatting technique to see the countries with the highest incidence of female child labor.

---

lambda

The Python `lambda` function allows us to write a one-line function and pass in one variable. It's incredibly useful for situations like the one we're exploring in this section, where we want to pass a singular value through a simple function.

When writing a `lambda` function, as in the example shown here, we want to first write `lambda` and the variable we are using to represent the data we will pass to the function. In our example, the variable was `r`. After the variable name, we place a colon (`:`). This is similar to how we define functions with `def` and end the line with a colon.

After the colon, we give Python the logic we wish our `lambda` to compute so it will return a value. In our example, we return a Boolean value telling us whether the *Female* value of the row is not None. You don't have to return a Boolean; `lambda` can return any type (integers, strings, lists, etc.).

You can also use `lambda` functions with an `if else` clause, allowing you to return a value based on some simple logic. Try this code in your Python interpreter:

```
(lambda x: 'Positive' if x >= 1 else 'Zero or Negative')(0)  ❶
(lambda x: 'Positive' if x >= 1 else 'Zero or Negative')(4)
```

❶ Passes the `lambda` function via the first parentheses pair and the variable to use as x in the second parentheses pair. This `lambda` tests if a value is equal to or greater than one. If it is, it returns `Positive`. If it's not, it returns `Zero or Negative`.

`lambda` functions are incredibly useful, but can also make your code less readable. Make sure you follow the rules of good programming and use them only in obvious and clear situations.

In reviewing the data, we see many of the same countries we saw in our overall percentages. We've reviewed a bit of filtering and sorting, so let's take a look at some of the built-in statistical functions in the `agate` library. Say we wanted to find the average percentage of child labor in cities. To do so, we would pull the mean out of the column *Place of residence (%) Urban*:

```
table.aggregate(agate.Mean('Place of residence (%) Urban'))
```

In this code snippet, we call the table's `aggregate` method, using the `agate.Mean()` statistical method and the column name to return the numerical mean of that column. You can see other statistical aggregates you can use on columns in the *agate* documentation (*http://bit.ly/agate_stats*).

When you run the code, you should receive a `NullComputationWarning`. As you can probably guess from the name and our previous experience, this means we likely have some null rows in the *Place of residence (%) Urban* column. We can again use the `where` method to focus on the urban averages:

```
has_por = table.where(lambda r: r['Place of residence (%) Urban'] is not None)

has_por.aggregate(agate.Mean('Place of residence (%) Urban'))
```

You'll notice you get the same value—this is because `agate` just does the same thing (removing null columns and computing the average of what's left) behind the scenes. Let's take a look at some of the other math we can do with the place of residence table. We can see the minimum (`Min`), maximum (`Max`), and average (`Mean`) of the place of residence columns.

Say we want to find one of the rows with more than 50% of rural child labor. The `agate` library has a `find` method that uses a conditional statement to find the first match. Let's try writing out our question in code:

```
first_match = has_por.find(lambda x: x['Rural'] > 50)

first_match['Countries and areas']
```

The row returned is the first match, and we can see the name as we would in a normal dictionary. One nice final step we'd like to do in our first exploration of the `agate` library is to use the `compute` method alongside the `agate.Rank()` statistical method (*http://bit.ly/agate_rank*) to add a ranked column based on the values from another column.

Ranking your data based on one column is a great way to do a good "gut check" when you're comparing datasets.

To see the ranks of the worst offenders in terms of child labor percentages, we can use the *Total (%)* column and rank the data accordingly. Before we join this data with other datasets, we'll want an easy-to-see rank column to help us compare the joined data. Because we want the countries with the highest percentages to appear at the top of the list, we need to rank descending order by using the `reverse=True` argument (*http://bit.ly/agate_rank_descending*):

```
ranked = table.compute([('Total Child Labor Rank',
                          agate.Rank('Total (%)', reverse=True)), ])

for row in ranked.order_by('Total (%)', reverse=True).limit(20).rows:
    print row['Total (%)'], row['Total Child Labor Rank']
```

If we wanted to calculate the rank in another way, we could create a column with the inverse percentages. Instead of having the total percentage of children involved in child labor in each country, we could have the percentage of children not involved in child labor. This would then allow us to use the `agate.Rank()` method without `reverse`:

```
def reverse_percent(row): ❶
    return 100 - row['Total (%)']

ranked = table.compute([('Children not working (%)',
                          agate.Formula(number_type, reverse_percent)),
                        ]) ❷

ranked = ranked.compute([('Total Child Labor Rank',
                          agate.Rank('Children not working (%)')),
                        ]) ❸

for row in ranked.order_by('Total (%)', reverse=True).limit(20).rows:
    print row['Total (%)'], row['Total Child Labor Rank']
```

❶ Creates a new function to calculate and return the inverse percentage if given a row.

❷ Uses the `agate` library's `compute` method, which adds new columns when passed a list. Each list item should be a tuple whose first item contains the column name and whose second item computes the new column. Here, we are using the `For mula` class, which also requires an `agate` type, alongside the function to create that column value.

❸ Creates the *Total Child Labor Rank* column with a proper ranking using our *Children not working (%)* column.

As you can see, `compute` is a great tool to calculate a new column based on another column (or a few other columns). Now that we have our ranking, let's see if we can join some new data to our child labor dataset.

Joining Numerous Datasets

When investigating datasets to join with our child labor data, we hit a lot of dead ends. We tried to compare agricultural versus service economies using WorldBank data (*http://data.worldbank.org/*), but didn't find any good links. We did more reading and found some people correlated child labor with HIV rates. We took a look at those datasets but did not find a compelling overall trend. Along those same lines, we wondered if homicide rates had an effect on child labor rates—but again, we found no clear link.[1]

After many such dead ends, an errant thought occurred while perusing the data and reading some more articles. Would government corruption (or perceived government corruption) affect child labor rates? When reading stories about child labor, there are often links with antigoverment militias, schools, and industries. If a populace doesn't trust the government and must create non-state-sanctioned spaces, this could be a reason to enlist all those willing to work and help (even children).

We located Transparency International's Corruption Perceptions Index (*https://www.transparency.org/cpi2013/results*) and decided to compare this dataset with our UNICEF child labor data. First, we needed to import the data into Python. Here is how to do that:

```python
cpi_workbook = xlrd.open_workbook('corruption_perception_index.xls')
cpi_sheet = cpi_workbook.sheets()[0]

for r in range(cpi_sheet.nrows):
    print r, cpi_sheet.row_values(r)

cpi_title_rows = zip(cpi_sheet.row_values(1), cpi_sheet.row_values(2))
cpi_titles = [t[0] + ' ' + t[1] for t in cpi_title_rows]
cpi_titles = [t.strip() for t in cpi_titles]

cpi_rows = [cpi_sheet.row_values(r) for r in range(3, cpi_sheet.nrows)]

cpi_types = get_types(cpi_sheet.row(3))
```

We are again using `xlrd` to import the Excel data and reusing the code we've written to parse our titles and get the data ready to import in our **agate** library. But before you can run the last item, which calls a new function, **get_types**, we need to write some code to help define types and create a table:

```python
def get_types(example_row):
    types = []
    for v in example_row:
        value_type = ctype_text[v.ctype]
        if value_type == 'text':
```

---

1 To take a look at some of those explorations, see the book's repository.

```
            types.append(text_type)
        elif value_type == 'number':
            types.append(number_type)
        elif value_type == 'xldate':
            types.append(date_type)
        else:
            types.append(text_type)
    return types


def get_table(new_arr, types, titles):
    try:
        table = agate.Table(new_arr, titles, types)
        return table
    except Exception as e:
        print e
```

We are using the same code we wrote earlier to create the function get_types, which takes an example row and outputs a list of the types for our agate library. We've also built a get_table function, which uses Python's built-in exception handling.

Exception Handling

Throughout this book, we've encountered errors and dealt with them as they arose. Now we have more experience and can begin anticipating potential errors and making conscious decisions about how to handle them.

Being specific with your code (especially with your exceptions) will allow you to communicate what errors you anticipate in your code. It will also make sure any unforeseen errors actually *do* raise exceptions and will end up in your error logs and halt execution.

When we use try and except we tell Python, "Please try to execute this code. If you run into an error, please stop running the previous section of code and run the code in the except block". Here's an example:

```
try:
    1 / 0
except Exception:
    print 'oops!'
```

This example is a generic exception. Usually we would want to use a specific exception we know the code might raise. For example, if we have code we know turns strings into integers, we know we might run into a ValueError exception. We could handle this as follows:

```
def str_to_int(x):
    try: ❶
        return int(x) ❷
    except ValueError: ❸
```

```
            print 'Could not convert: %s' % x ❹
        return x
```

❶ Begins the try block, which defines the code that might throw an error. The try keyword is always followed by a colon and appears on its own line. The next line or lines, a Python try block, are indented another four spaces.

❷ Returns the value of the argument passed into the function as an integer. When the arguments are values like 1 or 4.5, this will be no problem. If the value is - or foo, this throws a ValueError.

❸ Begins the except block, which defines the type of exception to catch. This line also ends with a colon, and specifies we are awaiting a ValueError (so, this except block will only catch ValueError exceptions). This block and the following lines of code execute only if the code in the try clause throws the error defined with this line of code.

❹ Prints lines to give us information about the exception. We can use this information if we need to update and change our code.

Generally, we want to build really concise and specific try and except blocks. This makes our code readable, predictable, and specific.

You may be asking, why then do we have except Exception in the get_table function we have written? This is a great question! We *always* want to be specific in our code; however, when you are first experimenting with a library or a dataset, you might not know what errors to anticipate.

To write specific exceptions, you need to predict what types of exceptions your code might throw. There are built-in Python exception types, but also special library exceptions that are unfamiliar to you. If you are using an API library, the authors might write a RateExceededException indicating you are sending too many requests. When a library is new to us, using an except Exception block with print or logging will help us learn more about these errors.

 When you write an except block, you can store the exception in a variable e by adding as e at the end of your exception line (before the colon). Because we are printing the e variable holding the exception, we can learn more about the raised exceptions. Eventually we will rewrite the except Exception block with more specific exceptions, or a series of exception blocks, so our code runs smoothly and predictably.

Now we have a `get_table` function to track our `agate` library exceptions and anticipate ways to improve our code. We can use our new functions to get the perceived corruption index data into our Python code. Try running this:

```
cpi_types = get_types(cpi_sheet.row(3))

cpi_table = get_table(cpi_rows, cpi_types, cpi_titles)
```

Payoff! When you run the code, instead of the function breaking completely, our new `get_table` function allows you to see the thrown errors. Duplicate titles probably mean we have some bad titles in our title list. Check it out by running this:

```
print pci_titles
```

We can see the problem: we have two of the *Country Rank* columns. By looking at the Excel data in the spreadsheet, we see we do indeed have duplicate columns. For expediency, we're not going to worry about removing the duplicate data, but we do need to handle the duplicate column names. We should add *Duplicate* to one of them. Here's how to do that:

```
cpi_titles[0] = cpi_titles[0] + ' Duplicate'

cpi_table = get_table(cpi_rows, cpi_types, cpi_titles)
```

We are replacing the first title with *Country Rank Duplicate* and trying again to make our new `pci_table`:

```
cpi_rows = get_new_array(cpi_rows, float_to_str)

cpi_table = get_table(cpi_rows, cpi_types, cpi_titles)
```

Now we have our `cpi_table` without any errors. We can work on joining it with our child labor data and see what connections we can make between the two datasets. In the `agate` library, we have an easy-to-use method for joining tables: the `join` (*http://bit.ly/agate_table_join*) method. This `join` method emulates SQL by joining two tables together based on one shared key. Table 9-1 summarizes the different joins and their functionality.

Table 9-1. Table joins

Join type	Function
Left outer join	Preserves all rows from the left table (or first table in the `join` statement), binding on the shared key(s). If there are rows with no match in the right (or second) table, these rows will hold *null* values.
Right outer join	Uses the right table (second table in the `join` statement) as the table to begin matching keys. If there is no match in the first (or left) table, these rows will hold null values.
Inner join	Returns only the rows matching both tables using the shared key(s).

Join type	Function
Full outer join	Preserves all rows from both tables, still combining rows on the shared key(s) when they align properly.

If your data doesn't exactly match up or have a one-for-one relationship and you are using an outer join, you will have rows with null values. When the tables don't match up, an outer join keeps the data from the tables intact and replaces missing data with null values. This is great if you'd like to keep the mismatched data because it's essential for your reporting.

If we wanted to join `table_a` and `table_b` but make sure we didn't lose any `table_a` data, we would write something like this:

```
joined_table = table_a.join(
    table_b, 'table_a_column_name', 'table_b_column_name')
```

In the resulting `joined_table`, we will have all of the `table_a` values that match with the `table_b` values based on the column names we passed. If there are values in `table_a` that don't match `table_b`, we will keep those rows, but they will have null values for the `table_b` columns. If there are values in `table_b` not matched in `table_a`, they will be excluded from our new table. Choosing which table to place first and specifying what type of join to use is important.

What we want, however, is not to have null values. Our questions revolve around how the values correlate, so for that, we want to use an inner join. The `agate` library's `join` method allows us to pass `inner=True`, which will make an inner join retaining only matching rows, with no null rows from the join.

We'll try a join with our child labor data and our newly formed `cpi_table`. When looking at our two tables, we can likely match them up on the names of the countries/territories. In our `cpi_table` we have the column *Country / Territory*, and in the child labor data we have the *Countries and areas* column. To join the two tables, run the following line of code:

```
cpi_and_cl = cpi_table.join(ranked, 'Country / Territory',
                            'Countries and areas', inner=True)
```

Our new table, `cpi_and_cl`, has our matching rows. We can see this by printing out a few of the values and investigating the new joined columns, like so:

```
cpi_and_cl.column_names

for r in cpi_and_cl.order_by('CPI 2013 Score').limit(10).rows:
    print '{}: {} - {}%'.format(r['Country / Territory'],
                                r['CPI 2013 Score'], r['Total (%)'])
```

When you look at the column names, you can see we now have all of the columns from both tables. A simple count of the data returns 93 rows. We don't need all of the data points (pci_table has 177 rows, ranked has 108), especially since we really want to see the data correlated together. Did you notice anything else when you printed out the new joined table after sorting by CPI score? We only took the top 10 rows, but some interesting information is becoming clear:

```
Afghanistan: 8.0 - 10.3%
Somalia: 8.0 - 49.0%
Iraq: 16.0 - 4.7%
Yemen: 18.0 - 22.7%
Chad: 19.0 - 26.1%
Equatorial Guinea: 19.0 - 27.8%
Guinea-Bissau: 19.0 - 38.0%
Haiti: 19.0 - 24.4%
Cambodia: 20.0 - 18.3%
Burundi: 21.0 - 26.3%
```

With the exception of Iraq and Afghanistan, there are some pretty high child labor rates among the countries with very low CPI scores (i.e., high perception of corruption). Using some of the agate library's built-in methods, we can investigate such correlations in our datasets.

Identifying Correlations

The agate library has some great tools for simple statistical analysis of your datasets. These are a good first toolset—you can often start with the agate library tools and then move on to more advanced statistical libraries, including pandas, numpy, and scipy, as needed.

We want to determine whether perceived government corruption and child labor rates are related. The first tool we'll use is a simple Pearson's correlation (*http://bit.ly/ pearson-correlation*). agate is at this point in time working on building this correlation into the agate-stats library (*https://github.com/onyxfish/agate-stats*). Until then, you can correlate using numpy. Correlation coefficients (like Pearson's) tell us if data is related and whether one variable has any effect on another.

If you haven't already installed numpy, you can do so by running pip install numpy. Then, calculate the correlation between child labor rates and perceived government corruption by running the following line of code:

```
import numpy

numpy.corrcoef(cpi_and_cl.columns['Total (%)'].values(),
            cpi_and_cl.columns['CPI 2013 Score'].values())[0, 1]
```

We first get an error which looks similar to the `CastError` we saw before. Because numpy expects floats, not decimals, we need to convert the numbers back to floats. We can use list comprehension for this:

```
numpy.corrcoef(
    [float(t) for t in cpi_and_cl.columns['Total (%)'].values()],
    [float(s) for s in cpi_and_cl.columns['CPI 2013 Score'].values()])[0, 1]
```

Our output shows a slight negative correlation:

```
-0.36024907120356736
```

A negative correlation means as one variable increases, the other variable decreases. A positive correlation means the numbers increase or decrease together. Pearson's correlation values range from –1 to 1, with 0 meaning no correlation and –1 and 1 meaning very strong correlations.

Our value of –.36 indicates a weak correlation, but a correlation nevertheless. We can use this knowledge to dive deeper into these datasets and what they mean.

Identifying Outliers

As your data analysis progresses, you will want to use some other statistical methods to interpret your data. One starting point is to identify outliers.

Outliers occur when particular rows of data signficantly differ from other parts of the dataset. Outliers usually tell us part of the story. Sometimes removing them will show a significant trend. Other times they tell a story in and of themselves.

With the `agate` library, finding outliers is easy. There are two different methods: one uses standard deviations, and the other uses median absolute deviations. If you have studied some statistics and would like to rely on one or the other, feel free to do so! If not, analyzing both measures of variance and deviation in your datasets may unveil different revelations.[1]

---

[1] For more reading on median absolute deviations and standard deviations, check out a great writeup by Matthew Martin on why we still use standard deviations (*http://bit.ly/why_std_deviation*) and Stephen Gorad's academic paper on why and when to use mean deviations (*http://bit.ly/mean_deviation_uses*).

If you already know the distribution of your data, you can apply the right ways to determine variance; but when you first explore your data, try looking at more than one method to determine the distribution and to learn more about how your data's composition.

We're going to use the `agate` table's standard deviation outlier (*http://bit.ly/iden tify_outliers*) method. This method returns a table of values at least three deviations above or below the mean. Here is how you can see the standard deviation outliers using your `agate` table.

If you are working with data in IPython and need to install a new library, you can use IPython's magic `%autoreload` to reload your Python environment after installing the library in a different terminal. Try `%load_ext autoreload` and then `%autoreload`. Violà! You have the new library without losing your progress.

First, you will need to install the `agate-stats` library by running `pip install agate-stats`. The run the following code:

```
import agatestats
agatestats.patch()

std_dev_outliers = cpi_and_cl.stdev_outliers(
    'Total (%)', deviations=3, reject=False) ❶

len(std_dev_outliers.rows) ❷

std_dev_outliers = cpi_and_cl.stdev_outliers(
    'Total (%)', deviations=5, reject=False) ❸

len(std_dev_outliers.rows)
```

❶ Uses our child labor *Total (%)* column and the `agate-stats stdev_outliers` method to see if our child labor data has easy-to-find standard deviation outliers. We assign the output of this method to a new table, `std_dev_outliers`. We use the argument `reject=False` to specify we want to see the outliers. If we set `reject` to `True`, we would get just the values that are not outliers.

❷ Checks how many rows of outliers were found. (The table has 94 rows total.)

❸ Increases the number of deviations to find fewer outliers. (`deviations=5`).

We can see from the output that we don't have a good grip on the distribution of the data. When we used the *Total (%)* column to try to identify outliers using three standard deviations, we got a table matching our current table. This is not what we want.

When we used five deviations, we did not see a change in the result. This is telling us our data is not very regularly distributed. In order to figure out the actual variance in our data, we are going to have to investigate further and determine if we need to refine our data to a subset of the countries we are investigating.

We can test the varience of the Total (%) column using the mean absolute deviation:

```
mad = cpi_and_cl.mad_outliers('Total (%)')

for r in mad.rows:
    print r['Country / Territory'], r['Total (%)']
```

Interesting! We did indeed identify a much smaller table of outliers, but we got a strange list of results:

```
Mongolia 10.4
India 11.8
Philippines 11.1
```

When we look at the list, we don't see any of the top or bottom of our sample. This means that our dataset likely doesn't play by the normal statistical rules for identifying outliers.

 Depending on your dataset and the distribution of data, these two methods often do a great job of showing your data's story in a meaningful way. If they don't, as in the case of our dataset, move on and figure out what relationships and trends your data *can* tell you about.

Once you've explored the distribution of your data and the trends that distribution reveals, you'll want to explore grouped relationships in your data. The following section explains how to group your data.

Creating Groupings

To further explore our dataset, we are going to create groupings and investigate their relationships. The `agate` library provides several tools to create groupings and other methods which allow us to aggregate those groupings and determine connections between them. Earlier we had continental data intact for our child labor dataset. Let's try grouping the data geographically by continent and see if this reveals any connections with our perceived corruption data or allows us to draw any conclusions.

First, we need to figure out how to get the continent data. In this book's repository (*https://github.com/jackiekazil/data-wrangling*), we have provided a *.json* file listing every country by continent. Using this data, we can add a column showing each country's continent allowing us to group by continent. Here's how we do that:

```
import json

country_json = json.loads(open('earth.json', 'rb').read()) ❶

country_dict = {}

for dct in country_json:
    country_dict[dct['name']] = dct['parent'] ❷


def get_country(country_row):
    return country_dict.get(country_row['Country / Territory'].lower()) ❸

cpi_and_cl = cpi_and_cl.compute([('continent',
                                  agate.Formula(text_type, get_country)),
                                ]) ❹
```

❶ Uses the `json` library to load the *.json* file. If you take a look at the file, you'll see it's a list of dictionaries.

❷ Loops through the `country_dict` and adds the `country` as the key and the `continent` as the value.

❸ Creates a function that, when given a country row, returns the continent. It uses the Python string's `lower` method, which replaces capital letters with lowercase ones. The *.json* file has all lowercase country names.

❹ Creates a new column, *continent*, using the `get_country` function. We keep the same table name.

Now we have continents with our country data. We should do a quick check to make sure we didn't miss anything. To do so, run this code:

```
for r in cpi_and_cl.rows:
    print r['Country / Territory'], r['continent']
```

Hmm, it looks like we have some missing data because we can see `None` types for some of our countries:

```
Democratic Republic of the Congo None
...
Equatorial Guinea None
Guinea-Bissau None
```

We'd rather not lose this data, so let's take a look at why these rows aren't matching. We want to only print out the lines that have no match. We can use `agate` to help us find them by running this code:

```
no_continent = cpi_and_cl.where(lambda x: x['continent'] is None)
```

```
for r in no_continent.rows:
    print r['Country / Territory']
```

Your output should be:

```
Saint Lucia
Bosnia and Herzegovina
Sao Tome and Principe
Trinidad and Tobago
Philippines
Timor-Leste
Democratic Republic of the Congo
Equatorial Guinea
Guinea-Bissau
```

There's only a short list of countries with no continent data. We recommend just cleaning up the *earth.json* data file, as this will make it easier to use the same data file for joining this same data at a future time. If you instead use code to find the exceptions and match them, it will be hard to repeat with new data and you'll need to change it every time.

In order to fix our matching in the *.json* file, we should figure out why the countries were not found. Open up the *earth.json* file and find a few of the countries from our no_continent table. For example:

```
{
    "name": "equatorial Guinea",
    "parent": "africa"
},
....
{
    "name": "trinidad & tobago",
    "parent": "north america"
},
...
{
    "name": "democratic republic of congo",
    "parent": "africa"
},
```

As we can see from looking at our *.json* file, there are some small differences preventing us from properly finding the continents for these countries. This book's repository also contains a file called *earth-cleaned.json*, which is the *earth.json* file with the necessary changes made, such as adding *the* to the DRC entry and changing *&* to *and* for several countries. We can now rerun our code from the beginning of this section with the new file as our country_json data. You will need to start by rejoining the table so you don't have duplicate columns (using the same code we used earlier to join the two tables). After you've rerun those two pieces of code you should have no unmatched countries.

Let's try to group our now-complete continent data by contintent and see what we find. The following code does just that:

```
grp_by_cont = cpi_and_cl.group_by('continent')

print grp_by_cont ❶

for cont, table in grp_by_cont.items(): ❷
    print cont, len(table.rows) ❸
```

❶ Uses the `agate` library's `group_by` method, which returns a dictionary where the keys are the continent names and the values are new tables containing rows for that continent.

❷ Iterates over the dictionary items to see how many rows are in each table. We are assigning the key/value pairs from `items` to the `cont` and `table` variables, so `cont` represents the key or continent name and `table` represents the value or table of matching rows.

❸ Prints our data to review our groupings. We are using Python's `len` function to count the number of rows we have for each table.

When we run that code, we get the following (note you may have a different order):

```
north america 12
europe 12
south america 10
africa 41
asia 19
```

We can see a numerical concentration in Africa and Asia compared to the other continents. This interests us, but `group_by` doesn't easily give us access to aggregate data. If we want to start aggregating our data and creating summed columns, we should take a look at the aggregation methods in the `agate` library.

We notice the `agate` table's `aggregate` method (*http://bit.ly/aggregate_stats*), which takes a grouped table and a series of aggregate operations (like a sum) to calculate new columns based on the grouping.

After looking at the `aggregate` documentation, we are most interested in how the continents compare across perceived corruption and child labor. We want to use some statistical methods to take a look at the group as a whole (using `Median` and `Mean`) but also to identify the most egregious (`Min` for the CPI score and `Max` for the total child labor percentage). This should give us some nice comparisons:

```
agg = grp_by_cont.aggregate([('cl_mean', agate.Mean('Total (%)')),
                             ('cl_max', agate.Max('Total (%)')),
                             ('cpi_median', agate.Median('CPI 2013 Score')),
                             ('cpi_min', agate.Min('CPI 2013 Score'))]) ❶
```

```
        agg.print_table() ❷
```

❶ Calls the **aggregate** method on our grouped table and passes a list containing tuples of new aggregate column names and **agate** aggregation methods (which utilize column names to compute the values for the new columns). We want the mean and max of the child labor percentage column and the median and min of the corruption perception score. You can use different aggregate methods depending on your questions and data.

❷ Prints the new table so we can visually compare our data.

When you run that code, you should see this result:

```
|---------------+----------------------------------+--------+------------+---------|
| continent     |                          cl_mean | cl_max | cpi_median | cpi_min |
|---------------+----------------------------------+--------+------------+---------|
| south america | 12,710000000000000000000000000   |   33,5 |       36,0 |      24 |
| north america | 10,333333333333333333333333333   |   25,8 |       34,5 |      19 |
| africa        | 22,348780487804878048780487      |   49,0 |       30,0 |       8 |
| asia          |  9,589473684210526315789473      |   33,9 |       30,0 |       8 |
| europe        |  5,625000000000000000000000000   |   18,4 |       42,0 |      25 |
|---------------+----------------------------------+--------+------------+---------|
```

If we wanted to take a closer look at some other charts surrounding our data, we could use the **agate** table's **print_bars** method, which takes a label column (here, *continent*) and a data column (here, *cl_max*) to chart the child labor maximum in our iPython session. Its output is as follows:

```
In [23]: agg.print_bars('continent', 'cl_max')
```

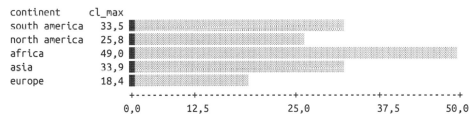

Now we have several easy-to-compare outputs of our continent data, and the picture is showing some trends. We notice Africa has the highest mean of the total child labor percentage column. It also has the highest maximum value, followed by Asia and South America. The comparatively low means for Asia and South America suggest that there are one or more outliers in these regions.

We see a fairly even median across our perceived corruption data, with Europe scoring the highest (i.e., least amount of corruption perceived). However, when we look at the minimums (or worst perceived corruption scores), we can see that Africa and Asia again represent the "worst" scores.

This shows there are several stories we can investigate further in these datasets. We were able to see a link (albeit weak) between perceived corruption and child labor. We were also able to investigate which countries and which continents are the worst offenders for child labor and perceived corruption. We can see Africa has a high rate of child labor and fairly high perceived corruption. We know in Asia and South America one or two countries might stand out in terms of child labor compared to their neighbors.

Our aggregation and exploration have only taken us so far. We can continue to use the tables we've created to tell more stories and investigate further.

Further Exploration

There are some other powerful features in the `agate` library, and some other interesting statistical libraries that you can use to experiment with your own datasets.

 Depending on your data and what your questions are, you may find some of these features and libraries more useful than others, but we strongly encourage you to find ways to experiment with a variety of tools. It will deepen your understanding of Python and data analysis libraries as well as your data analysis itself.

The `agate-stats` library has some interesting statistical methods we haven't yet investigated. You can keep track of the new releases and functionality on GitHub (*https://github.com/onyxfish/agate-stats*).

In addition, we recommend continuing to play around using `numpy`. You can use `numpy` to calculate percentiles (*http://bit.ly/numpy_percentile*). You can also expand into using the `scipy` library and play around with the z score statistical methods for determining outliers (*http://bit.ly/scipy_zscore*).

If you have time-sensitive data, `numpy` has the ability to calculate column-by-column changes between data (*http://bit.ly/numpy_diff*) to investigate changes over time. `agate` can also compute change columns (*http://bit.ly/computing_new_columns*) with time-sensitive data. Don't forget to use the date type when forming your date columns, as this will enable you to do some interesting date analysis (such as percent change over time or time series mapping).

If you want to investigate with even more statistics, install the `latimes-calculate` library (*http://bit.ly/latimes-calculate*). This library has many statistical methods as well as some interesting geospatial analysis tools. If you have access to geospatial data, this library can provide you with some valuable tools to better understand, map, and analyze your data.

If you'd like to take your statistics one step further, we highly recommend Wes McKinney's book *Python for Data Analysis* (O'Reilly). It introduces you to some of the more robust Python data analysis libraries, including `pandas`, `numpy`, and the `scipy` stack.

Take time to play around and explore your data with some of the methods and lessons we've already reviewed. We will now move on to analyzing our data further and determining some ways we can draw conclusions and share our knowledge.

Analyzing Your Data

Once you've played with a few more examples from the `agate` library's Cookbook (*http://agate.readthedocs.org/en/latest/cookbook.html*) (an assortment of different methods and tools to use for investigation), you probably have enough familiarity with your data to begin your analysis.

 What is the difference between data exploration and analysis? When we analyze data, we ask questions and attempt to answer them using the data at our disposal. We might combine and group datasets to create a statistically valid sampling. With exploration, we simply want to investigate trends and attributes of our datasets without trying to answer specific questions or come to conclusions.

With some basic analysis, we can attempt to determine the answers to the questions we uncovered in our exploration:

- Why do there seem to be higher frequencies of child labor in Africa?
- What child labor outliers exist in Asia and South America?
- How do perceived corruption and child labor tie together?

For your dataset, you will have different questions, but try to follow our examples and find trends you'd like to investigate. Any statistical outliers or aggregation tendencies can point you to interesting questions to research.

To us, the most interesting question for our particular dataset concerns the connection between perceived corruption and child labor in Africa. Does government corruption, or the perception of government corruption, affect how communities are able to prohibit child labor?

Depending on the datasets you are using and what your data exploration has shown, you may have a variety of questions you are interested in pursuing. Try to focus on a specific question and answer it using your analysis. Repeat this for as many specific questions as you'd like. Focusing will help you determine good answers and keep your analysis clear.

Answering this question will require more investigation and more datasets. We might want to read more articles to see what's been written on the topic. We might also want to call and interview experts in the field. Finally, we might want to focus and choose a particular region in Africa or series of countries to better evaluate the story of child labor. The next section explains how to do that.

Separating and Focusing Your Data

For further analysis, we first need to separate out our data for African nations and investigate this subset of data more fully. We already know a lot of ways to filter with our **agate** library, so let's start there. Here's how to separate out the African data from the other data:

```
africa_cpi_cl = cpi_and_cl.where(lambda x: x['continent'] == 'africa') ❶

for r in africa_cpi_cl.order_by('Total (%)', reverse=True).rows:
    print "{}: {}% - {}".format(r['Country / Territory'], r['Total (%)'],
                                r['CPI 2013 Score']) ❷

import numpy
print numpy.corrcoef( ❸
    [float(t) for t in africa_cpi_cl.columns['Total (%)'].values()],
    [float(c) for c in africa_cpi_cl.columns['CPI 2013 Score'].values()])[0, 1]

africa_cpi_cl = africa_cpi_cl.compute([('Africa Child Labor Rank',
                                        agate.Rank('Total (%)', reverse=True)),
                                       ])

africa_cpi_cl = africa_cpi_cl.compute([('Africa CPI Rank',
                                        agate.Rank('CPI 2013 Score')),
                                       ]) ❹
```

❶ Uses the **where** table method to filter only rows where the continent is *africa*.

❷ Prints the rows with some formatting so we can view our data for a "gut check." We want to make sure we have only African countries and we can see our total child labor percentages and CPI scores.

❸ Shows whether the Pearson's correlation has changed after separating out the most interesting data.

---

❹ Adds a new ranking to show how the countries within our subset of data rank up just against one another.

With this subset of the data, we calculated a new Pearson's correlation:

```
-0.404145695171
```

Our Pearson's correlation decreased, showing a slightly stronger relationship between child labor and perceived corruption in our African data than in the global data.

Now let's see if we can identify good stories and find data points we'd like to investigate. We are going to find the mean values for perceived corruption and child labor percentages and show the countries with the highest child labor and worst perceived corruption (i.e., where the values are worse than the mean). Here's how to do that:

```
cl_mean = africa_cpi_cl.aggregate(agate.Mean('Total (%)'))
cpi_mean = africa_cpi_cl.aggregate(agate.Mean('CPI 2013 Score')) ❶


def highest_rates(row):
    if row['Total (%)'] > cl_mean and row['CPI 2013 Score'] < cpi_mean: ❷
        return True
    return False

highest_cpi_cl = africa_cpi_cl.where(lambda x: highest_rates(x)) ❸

for r in highest_cpi_cl.rows:
    print "{}: {}% - {}".format(r['Country / Territory'], r['Total (%)'],
                                r['CPI 2013 Score'])
```

❶ Pulls out the column averages we are most interested in: corruption score and child labor percentages.

❷ Creates a function to identify countries with high child labor rates and low CPI scores (i.e., high corruption).

❸ Returns True or False from our highest_rates function, which selects a row. This lambda asks whether the country has higher than average child labor rates and perceived corruption.

When we run the code we see some interesting output. Of particular interest are these rows:

```
Chad: 26.1% - 19.0
Equatorial Guinea: 27.8% - 19.0
Guinea-Bissau: 38.0% - 19.0
Somalia: 49.0% - 8.0
```

Our output shows some data in the "middle" that is not too far off the mean, but then these worst offenders with lower corruption scores and higher child labor percentages. Because we are interested in why there are high child labor rates and how corruption affects child labor, these would be our best case studies.

As we continue our research, we want to identify what is happening in these specific countries. Are there films or documentaries related to young people or child labor in these countries? Are there articles or books written on the topic? Are there experts or researchers we can contact?

When we look more deeply into these countries, we see some stark realities: child trafficking, sexual exploitation, maliciously acting religious groups, street and domestic labor. Are these realities connected to disenfranchisement? To a public who cannot trust the government? Can we trace commonalities among these countries and their neighbors? Can we determine elements or actors helping ease the problems?

It would be interesting to look into the effects of political and generational changes over time. We could peruse the backlog of UNICEF data or focus in one country and utilize UNICEF's Multiple Indicator Cluster Survey (*http://bit.ly/unicef_mics*) data to understand changes through the decades.

For your own dataset, you need to determine what possibilities you have for future exploration. Can you find more data for your investigation? Are there people you can interview or trends you can identify over a long period of time? Are there books, movies, or articles on the topic that can shed more light? Your analysis is the beginning of future research.

What Is Your Data Saying?

Now that we've explored and analyzed our data, we can begin figuring out what the data is telling us. As we experienced when we first started looking at our child labor data, sometimes your data has no connections, it tells no story, and it's not correlated. That's OK to find out!

 Sometimes finding no correlation tells you to keep researching to find actual existing connections. Sometimes *not* finding a connection is a revelation in and of itself.

In data analysis, you search for trends and patterns. Most of the time, as we saw with our child labor data, analysis is a starting poing for further research. As much as your numbers tell a story, adding a human voice or another angle is a great way to expand on the connections and questions revealed by your analysis.

If you find some connections, even weak ones, you can dig deeper. Those connections lead to better questions and more focused research. As we saw with our child labor data, the more focused we became in our research, the easier it was to see connections. It's great to start broad, but important to finish with a more refined view.

Drawing Conclusions

Once you've analyzed your data and understand the connections, you can start determining what you can conclude. It's essential you have a real understanding of your datasets and the topic, so you can have a firm backing for your ideas. With your data analysis, interviews, and research completed, your conclusions are formed, and you simply need to determine how to share them with the world.

 If you have trouble finding a definitive conclusion, it's OK to include open questions in your findings. Some of the biggest stories start with just a few simple questions.

If you can cast light on the topic and point out the need for more documentation, research, and action in order to draw complete conclusions, that is an important message itself. As we found with our investigation, it's hard to say if government corruption causes high child labor rates, but we can say there is a weak correlation between the two, and we'd like to research and analyze the way they are linked—particularly in certain African nations.

Documenting Your Conclusions

Once you've found some conclusions and more questions you'd like to research, you should begin documenting your work. As part of your documentation and final presentation, you should be clear about what sources you used and how many data points you analyzed. In our subset, we investigated only ~90 data points, but they represented the segment we wanted to study.

You may find the dataset you focus on is smaller than anticipated. As long as you are clear about your methods and the reasons for the smaller subset, you will not lead your audience or reporting astray. In the next chapter, we'll dive deeper into reporting our findings, documenting our thoughts and processes as we share our conclusions with the world.

Summary

In this chapter, we explored and analyzed our datasets using some new Python libraries and techniques. You were able to import datasets, join them, group them, and create new datasets based on the findings.

You can now utilize statistical methods to find outliers and measure correlation. You can determine solid, answerable questions to investigate by separating out interesting groupings and diving deeper into your exploration. If you've been using IPython and `%store` to save your variables, we will be interacting more with them in the next chapter.

You should now feel comfortable:

- Evaluating your data using the `agate` library
- Determining what, if anything, is significant in your data
- Finding holes in your data or parts of the data you'd need to further investigate to come to conclusions
- Challenging your assumptions by analyzing and exploring your data

The new concepts and libraries we've covered are summarized in Table 9-2.

Table 9-2. New Python and programming concepts and libraries

Concept/Library	Purpose
agate library	Data analysis made easy with the ability to easily read in data from a CSV, make tables for analysis, run basic statistical functions, and apply filters to gain insight into your dataset.
xlrd ctype and ctype_text objects	Allow you to easily see what cell type your data is in when using xlrd to analyze Excel data.
isinstance function	Tests the type of a Python object. Returns a Boolean value if the types match.
lambda functions	One-line functions in Python, great for simple filtering or parsing of your dataset. Be careful not to write a lambda that can't be easily read and understood. If it's too complex, write a small function instead.
Joins (inner, outer, left, right)	Allow you to join two different datasets on one or more matching fields. Depending on how you join your data (inner/outer and left/right), you will get different datasets. Take time to think about what join fits your needs.
Exception handling	Enables you to anticipate and manage Python exceptions with code. It's always better to be specific and explicit, so you don't disguise bugs with overly general exception catches.
numpy coerrcoef	Uses statistical models like Pearson's correlation to determine whether two parts of a dataset are related.
agate mad_outliers and stdev_outliers	Use statistical models and tools like standard deviations or mean average deviations to determine whether your dataset has specific outliers or data that "doesn't fit."

Concept/Library	Purpose
`agate group_by` and `aggregate`	Group your dataset on a particular attribute and run aggregation analysis to see if there are notable differences (or similarities) across groupings.

In the next chapter, you will learn how to use visualizations and storytelling tools to share your conclusions on the Web and in numerous other formats.

## CHAPTER 10

Presenting Your Data

You've learned how to analyze your data, and now you'd like to present it. Depending on the audience you have in mind, the presentation can differ greatly. We'll learn about all different types in this chapter: from simple presentations you can make on your computer to interactive website presentations.

Depending on what you'd like to present, your visualization, with charts, maps, or graphs, might be a major part of the story you are trying to tell. We will cover how to get your own site up and running to share your findings. We'll also show you how to share a Jupyter notebook, where folks can see your code along with the charts, graphs, and conclusions.

To begin, we'll explore how to think about your audience and begin telling the stories you have found via your data analysis.

Avoiding Storytelling Pitfalls

Storytelling is not an easy job. Depending on your topic, you might have a difficult time determining solid conclusions from your data. You might encounter inconsistent or inconclusive data. This is OK! We recommend continuing to explore—maybe the story is in the disparate examples you find in your datasets.

 Some of the difficulties you face in storytelling will be due to personal biases you bring to your data analysis. As economist and journalist Allison Schranger aptly discusses in her article "The Problem with Data Journalism" (*http://bit.ly/data_journalism_prob lems*), we bring biases to our analyses that we can't adequately counter. Her sage advice is to admit those biases and attempt to get to know your data to such a degree you cannot misconstrue it for the purpose of your story.

Don't presume the story you want to tell and the data are congruous. Attempt to learn the data first, then tell the story you learn from the data. Don't spend too much time manipulating the data. If you have to alter the data too much (by standardizing, normalizing, and removing outliers), you probably should find another story or different data.

With that in mind, storytelling is a powerful part of becoming an area expert. With the knowledge you have gained by exploring the data you have, you can help illuminate new topics and ideas. With the humility you learn by understanding your biases, the story will be effective and enlightening.

How Will You Tell the Story?

Deciding what story you'd like to tell is just as important as deciding how to tell it. You can use charts, graphs, timelines, maps, videos, words, and interactives. You can publish it online or present it at a meeting or conference. You can upload it to a video sharing site. Whatever you choose, make sure the way you are telling the story enhances your findings. There is nothing more disheartening than seeing a presentation so poor it actually nullifies the story it attempts to tell.

In the next few sections, we will evaluate how your audience, your story, and the platforms available affect your presentation choices. We recommend reading through all of them, even if you already have an idea of how you'd like to present your findings. This will give you a greater understanding of what's available even if you stick with your initial choice. A combination of several formats can be the best option for those trying to reach a larger audience.

Determining how often you plan to update the data in the future is another part of how you tell the story. Is this an ongoing series? Can your audience expect to hear more about this story soon, or in an annual report? Can you tell them clearly when and how it will be updated? Keeping an audience waiting is only a good idea if you can clarify their expectations.

Know Your Audience

Who you are writing for is almost as important as what you are writing. By identifying your target audience, you can determine what they already know about a topic, what is of most interest to them, and how they learn best. Missing the mark in terms of communicating with your audience creates a story without an interested party.

If your reporting or presentation is part of your job, it should be fairly easy to determine your audience. Whether it's a small group at work, an executive team, or a daily or annual publication, you know exactly who will be reading your reporting.

If you are interested in publishing your data for a wider audience, you should research what has already been written and who was interested in learning more. Becoming familiar with the corpus of work in your target field will help you determine whether there's an existing or new audience to whom you can speak.

If you're not sure which audience to target, one good strategy is to approach different people you know who have markedly different levels of interest in your chosen topic, say, a parent or mentor, a peer, and a mentee (in terms of exposure to the world and your topic). Is one part of the story more interesting to different people, depending on their level of knowledge about the topic? Do different questions come up depending on the age and experience of your audience? Observe their questions and reactions once you explain your topic and amend your target audience interpretation based on these observations.

Once you've determined your target audience, you can find out more about them. Use the tips in the following sidebar to help refine how you might tell the story depending on your audience.

Talking to Your Audience

When thinking about how to tell your story to your audience, it's important to address how they learn, and understand the world, and your topic in particular. These questions should guide your storytelling to best communicate your findings to your target audience:

- How does your audience learn about new things? Online? Word of mouth? In a publication?
- How much prior knowledge does your audience have on the topic? Are there words and ideas that may be unfamiliar?
- Can your audience explore data on their own?
- How much time and attention does your audience have for the story?
- How engaged will your audience be in speaking with you and one another about the story?
- Will your audience want to be alerted and updated if new information is released?

These are just some of many questions you can ask yourself to determine who your *real* audience is and how they might best consume your story. Use these questions as an initial prompt, and let them lead you to more questions and realizations about how to share your findings.

Once you've found your audience and taken some time to begin your storytelling, you can start investigating ways to tell your data's story through visualization.

Visualizing Your Data

When working with data, it's likely you'll want to use some kind of visualization to tell your story. Depending on what your story is, your visualization might be a chart, a graph, or a timeline. Regardless of how you present your data, the first step is to determine what visual data is both useful and relevant.

With visual storytelling, it's incredibly important to determine how to show your findings. As Alberto Cairo writes in his blog post on data visualizations (*http://www.thefunctionalart.com/2014/08/to-make-visualizations-that-are.html*), if you don't show all the relevant data, you might leave the audience questioning your methods and findings.

 Similar to our documentation detailing our data analysis and methodology, we need to document and defend our visual exploration and representation of the data and ensure we are not omitting important parts of the story.

In this section, we will explore how to use charts, time series and timelines, maps, mixed media, words, images, and video to share findings. Depending on the audience you have in mind, there might be a mixture of these types that are relevant to your story. Each of these formats has its pros and cons, and we'll review these as we explore.

Charts

Charts are a great way to share numeric data, especially when comparing divergent datasets or different groupings. If you have a clear trend in your data or your data shows specific outliers, charts help communicate those observations to your audience.

You can use a stacked or bar chart to show a large number of figures alongside one another. For example, in his *Washington Post* story on infant mortality (*http://www.washingtonpost.com/blogs/wonkblog/wp/2014/09/29/our-infant-mortality-rate-is-a-national-embarrassment/*), Christopher Ingraham uses a bar chart to compare countries alongside one another.

To show trends over time, one usually employs a line chart. Ingraham also uses a line chart to compare infant mortality rates at different ages. The bar graph helps us see that the United States lags behind most other countries in infant care. The line chart allows us to compare mortality rates in different countries over time, giving us another way to observe the data.

You will note the author chose to only show a few countries on the line chart rather than all of the countries represented in the bar graph. Why do you think he made this decision? It's possible he reviewed the data and found including more countries made the chart hard to read.

These are the types of decisions you will need to make when visualizing your findings. In order to better determine whether a chart is right for you and what kind of chart is most useful, first define what you'd like to show with your charts. The easy-to-use flowchart available on the Extreme Presentation blog (*http://bit.ly/abela-choosing*) is one place to start when first thinking about these issues. Juice Labs has built an interactive chart selector (*http://labs.juiceanalytics.com/chartchooser*) showing some of the same concepts.

 Different charts have their own strengths and weaknesses. If you'd like to show relationships, you can use a scatter plot, bubble chart, or line chart, all of which can show data correlations. Bar charts better compare many subjects. If you want to show composition or factors, you can make a stacked chart. To show distribution, you can use a time series plot or histogram.

Let's think about the data we've investigated so far and use some built-in `agate` features to chart the data.

Charting with matplotlib

One of the main Python charting and imaging libraries is `matplotlib`, which helps chart and plot datasets. It's a great way to generate simple charts, and the more parts of the plotting library you learn, the more advanced your graphs and charts will be. First, we need to install it by running `pip install matplotlib`.

Let's show our perceived corruption scores compared to the child labor percentages. Here's how we'd do that:

```
import matplotlib.pyplot as plt

plt.plot(africa_cpi_cl.columns['CPI 2013 Score'],
         africa_cpi_cl.columns['Total (%)'])  ❶

plt.xlabel('CPI Score - 2013')  ❷
plt.ylabel('Child Labor Percentage')
plt.title('CPI & Child Labor Correlation')  ❸

plt.show()  ❹
```

❶ Uses pylab's `plot` method to pass the x and y label data. The first variable passed is the x-axis and the second variable is the y-axis. This creates a Python chart plotting those two datasets.

❷ Calls the `xlabel` and `ylabel` methods to label our chart axes.

❸ Calls the `title` method to title our chart.

❹ Calls the `show` method to draw the chart. Everything we set up with our chart before we call `show` will be displayed in the system's default image program (like Preview or Windows Photo Viewer). Our title, axis labels, and any other attributes we set via the `matplotlib` library will be displayed in the chart.

And voilà! Python renders the chart shown in Figure 10-1.[1]

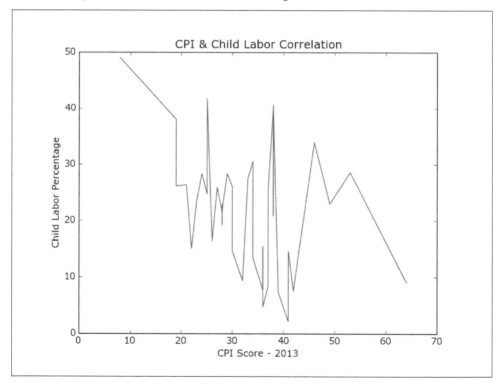

Figure 10-1. Child labor and CPI chart

---

1 If a chart doesn't show up for you, follow the instructions on Stack Overflow (*http://bit.ly/matplot_lib_settings*) to identify where your `matplotlib` settings are and to set your backend to one of the defaults (*Qt4Agg* for Mac/Linux or *GTKAgg* for Windows). For Windows, you may need to also `pip install pygtk`.

We can indeed see the overall downward trend, but we can also see the data in the middle does not follow a particular trend. In fact, the data varies greatly, telling us there is not a connection between child labor and perceived corruption for all of the countries, but only for some of them.

Let's make the same chart using only the worst offenders. We already separated out these worst offenders, in "Separating and Focusing Your Data" on page 244. When we run the previous code again with our highest_cpi_cl table, we see the chart shown in Figure 10-2.

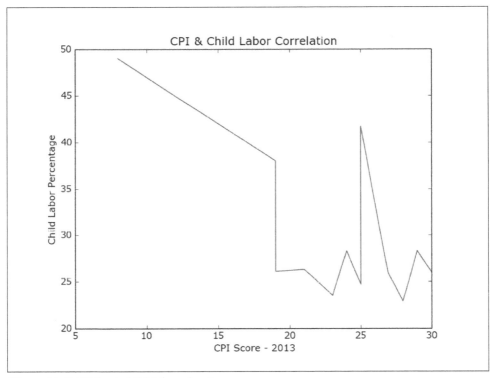

Figure 10-2. Highest child labor chart

Now we can see a clear downward trend for the worst offenders, followed by some anomalies as the child labor rates and perceived corruption scores decrease.

There are many chart types available from pylab, including histograms, scatter charts, bar graphs, and pie charts. We strongly recommend taking a look at matplotlib.org's introduction to pyplot (*http://bit.ly/pyplot_tutorial*), covering how to change different aspects of your charts (color, labels, size) and use multiple figures, subplots, and more chart types.

Charting your data can give you a good idea of anomalies or outliers within your dataset. Using the different charting methods available to you in the Python charting libraries can help you research your data's story and interrelatedness.

The more you play with the library's charting toolset, the easier it will be to understand which charts work best with your dataset.

Charting with Bokeh

Bokeh (*http://bokeh.pydata.org/*) is a Python charting library with fairly simple commands for more complex chart types. If you want to create a stacked chart, scatter chart, or time series, we recommend playing around with Bokeh and seeing if it's right for you. Let's try making a scatter chart with Bokeh for our CPI and child labor data on a country-by-country basis. Install Bokeh by running this command:

```
pip install bokeh
```

Then build a scatter chart with some simple commands using the `agate` table:

```
from bokeh.plotting import figure, show, output_file


def scatter_point(chart, x, y, marker_type):    ❶
    chart.scatter(x, y, marker=marker_type, line_color="#6666ee",
                  fill_color="#ee6666", fill_alpha=0.7, size=10)    ❷


chart = figure(title="Perceived Corruption and Child Labor in Africa")    ❸
output_file("scatter_plot.html")    ❹
for row in africa_cpi_cl.rows:
    scatter_point(chart, float(row['CPI 2013 Score']),
                  float(row['Total (%)']), 'circle')    ❺
show(chart)    ❻
```

❶ Defines a function, `scatter_point`, which takes a chart, x-axis and y-axis values, and marker type (circle, square, rectangle) and adds the point to the chart.

❷ The chart's `scatter` method takes two required arguments (x- and y-axis) and a variety of keyword arguments to style those points (including the color, opacity, and size). This line passes some line colors and fill colors as well as size and opacity settings.

❸ Creates the chart using the `figure` function and passes a title.

❹ Defines what file to output using the `output_file` function. This will create the file *scatter_plot.html* in the folder where you run the code.

❺ For each row, adds a point using the CPI score as the x-axis and the child labor percentage as the y-axis.

❻ Shows the chart in a browser window.

When you run the code, it opens a tab in your browser containing the chart (Figure 10-3).

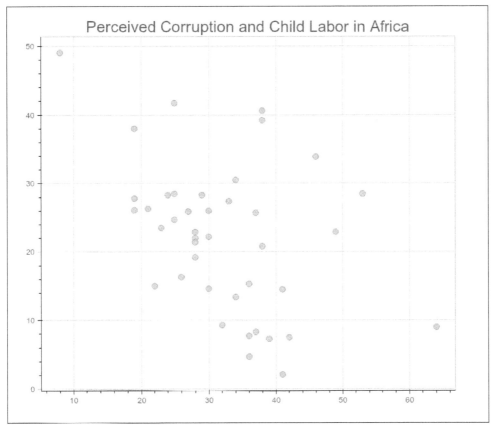

Figure 10-3. CPI and child labor scatter plot

That's pretty nice, but we can't see much about what those dots mean. Bokeh can add interactive elements in our charts. Let's try adding some:

```
from bokeh.plotting import ColumnDataSource, figure, show, output_file
from bokeh.models import HoverTool ❶

TOOLS = "pan,reset,hover" ❷


def scatter_point(chart, x, y, source, marker_type): ❸
```

```
        chart.scatter(x, y, source=source,
                      marker=marker_type, line_color="#6666ee",
                      fill_color="#ee6666", fill_alpha=0.7, size=10)

    chart = figure(title="Perceived Corruption and Child Labor in Africa",
                   tools=TOOLS) ❹
    output_file("scatter_int_plot.html")
    for row in africa_cpi_cl.rows:
        column_source = ColumnDataSource(
            data={'country': [row['Country / Territory']]}) ❺
        scatter_point(chart, float(row['CPI 2013 Score']),
                      float(row['Total (%)']), column_source, 'circle')

    hover = chart.select(dict(type=HoverTool)) ❻

    hover.tooltips = [
        ("Country", "@country"), ❼
        ("CPI Score", "$x"),
        ("Child Labor (%)", "$y"),
    ]

    show(chart)
```

❶ Imports the main libraries we have been using and adds the `ColumnDataSource`
    and `HoverTool` classes.

❷ Defines the tools you'd like to use (*http://bit.ly/specifying_tools*) for the final prod-
    uct. This code adds `hover` so we can use the hover methods.

❸ Adds `source` to the required variables. This will hold our country name
    information.

❹ Passes the `TOOLS` variable to our figure upon initialization.

❺ `column_source` now holds a data source dictionary with the country name. This
    line passes the name as a list because the values must be iterable objects.

❻ Selects the `HoverTool` object from the chart.

❼ Uses the `tooltips` method of the hover object to show different data attributes.
    `@country` selects the data passed via the column source, whereas `$x` and `$y` selects
    the x and y points on the chart.

Now your chart should look like Figure 10-4.

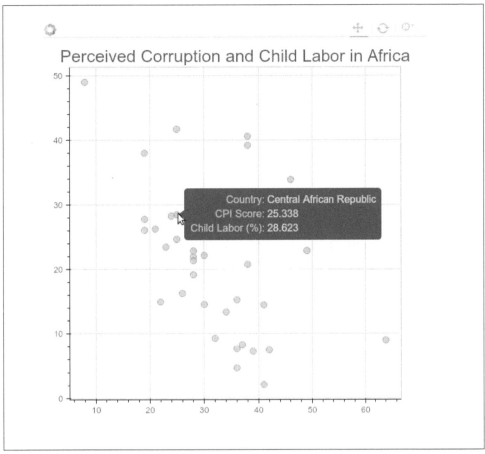

Figure 10-4. CPI and child labor interactive scatter plot

As you move your cursor over each point, the data for x and y change. To improve the chart, try adding the exact values for our two data points to the `column_source` object by entering new keys and values into the `data` dictionary.

Bokeh has a great gallery of examples (*http://bokeh.pydata.org/en/latest/docs/gallery.html*) and code available to help you get started. We recommend taking time with your charts and giving Bokeh a try.

Time-Related Data

Time series and timeline data help represent your findings over time. Time series charts show data changing over time (usually as a line chart, bar chart, or histogram).

Timelines allow you to visually tell the story of the data by marking events, occurrences, and changes over time.

Time series data

Time series display trends over time, and work especially well when focusing on one factor. *The Wall Street Journal* produced a great time series on vaccines and disease rates (*http://graphics.wsj.com/infectious-diseases-and-vaccines/*). The interactive element allows for exploration, and the built-in time-lapse animation feature makes for an easy-to-read visual. The vaccination introduction markers add clarity for the readers.

We haven't investigated changes over time with our dataset. A good next step would be to collect the same datasets for previous years. Such data can answer questions like: Where is child labor increasing over time? Can we see a clear regional trend over time? Can we see another trend over time if we join with another dataset (e.g., does child labor increase alongside agriculture exports)?

There's a great answer on Stack Overflow (*http://bit.ly/plot_time_series_python*) providing more information on using `matplotlib` to chart time series. Remember the `agate` table's `rows` and `columns` methods, covered in Chapter 9, which allow you to select a column or row of data when given a selection? The lists returned by these methods can be passed to any of the `matplotlib` functions to pass the data to the chart.

If you'd like to take a look at time-related data using Bokeh, check out some of their excellent examples (*http://bit.ly/high-level_charts*).

Timeline data

Timeline data can help introduce your audience to important moments in your topic's history or a breakdown of recent developments. For example, the timeline on the History of Vaccines website (*http://bit.ly/history_of_vaccines*) shows the history of the measles vaccine and recent developments in California so the audience can quickly understand the topic via historical data.

If we wanted to present a timeline for our child labor story, we would look for important moments in international child labor history. We could research questions that would help point out timeline events, like: When were the first laws to protect child safety implemented? When did public opinion shift against children labor? What public incidents and scandals involved child labor?

For the visualization, TimelineJS (*http://timeline.knightlab.com/*) by Knight Lab takes a data spreadsheet and creates simple interactive timelines.

Maps

If your findings focus on geography, a map is a great way to present your data. Maps help people identify the impact of a topic on people and regions they know. Depending on how much your audience knows about the area or region you are discussing, you might need to include extra information and context with your map to help relate the story to more familiar regions.

If it's a local audience, you might include references to locally known monuments and street names. If it's an international audience and the story covers a particular region (e.g., Amazon deforestation), first reference continental maps and then focus in on your target area.

Maps can be a difficult form of data visualization. Not only are you beholden to the geographical knowledge of your audience, but maps don't always show patterns in a clear or digestible way. It's very important when using a map to be quite familiar with the geography of the region you are showing, so you can both display the important geolocation elements to orient your audience and showcase the findings.

One example of a newsworthy map is *The New York Times*'s vaccinations in California map (*http://bit.ly/cali_vaccination_rates*). Published during the recent measles outbreak in California, it gives the readers the ability to zoom in and out for more details, provides short anecdotes, and shows differences between personal belief exemptions and other causes for low vaccination rates (such as poverty or lack of access). By focusing only on California, the map is able to show a level of detail that on a nationwide or regional scale could be too cluttered or complicated.

When preparing your map, you may want to utilize ColorBrewer (*http://colorbrewer2.org/*), which allows you to compare different map color schemas side by side. You want colors that both tell the story and allow for contrast so the reader can clearly see distinctions between groups and group levels.

One example of a larger geographic area map is *The Economist*'s global debt clock (*http://www.economist.com/content/global_debt_clock*). This map shows public debt on a country-by-country basis with an interactive timeline to examine changes in public debt over time. Its complementary color scheme makes the map easy to read, and one can easily differentiate between heavily indebted countries and those with little or no debt.

The authors of the global debt clock map normalized debt to use the US dollar as a common currency so users can compare different countries and debt ratios side by side. These small normalizations aid audience understanding and enhance the impact of the findings.

There is a very easy-to-use chart and mapping Python library called pygal (*http:// pygal.org/*) with great built-in mapping features. pygal has documentation for everything from pie charts and scatter plots to world and country maps. We can use pygal with our agate table to show the worldwide child labor rates. First, we need to install the library and its dependencies by running these commands:

```
pip install pygal
pip install pygal_maps_world
pip install cssselect
pip install cairosvg
pip install tinycss
pip install lxml
```

In the pygal world map documentation (*http://bit.ly/pygal_world_map*), we see the two-character ISO codes for every country are necessary to properly map using the world map. We can add these to our ranked table using methods we already know:

```
import json

country_codes = json.loads(open('iso-2.json', 'rb').read()) ❶
country_dict = {}

for c in country_codes:
    country_dict[c.get('name')] = c.get('alpha-2') ❷

def get_country_code(row):
    return country_dict.get(row['Countries and areas']) ❸

ranked = ranked.compute([('country_code',
                         agate.Formula(text_type, get_country_code)), ])

for r in ranked.where(lambda x: x.get('country_code') is None).rows: ❹
    print r['Countries and areas']
```

❶ Loads the string from the *iso-2.json* file we downloaded from @lukes on GitHub (*https://github.com/lukes/ISO-3166-Countries-with-Regional-Codes*). This file is available in the book's repository.

❷ Creates a country dictionary where the keys are the country names and the values are the ISO codes.

❸ Defines a new function get_country_code which will take a row of data and return the country code using the country_dict object. If there is no match, it will return None.

❹ Evaluates which ones we couldn't find matches for so we can further investigate.

You should see output like this:

```
Bolivia (Plurinational State of)
Cabo Verde
Democratic Republic of the Congo
Iran (Islamic Republic of)
Republic of Moldova
State of Palestine
The former Yugoslav Republic of Macedonia
United Republic of Tanzania
Venezuela (Bolivarian Republic of)
```

We found most matches, but there are still a few missing. As we did with our *earth.json* file in the previous chapter, we corrected the matches manually by modifying the names in the data file for the mismatched countries. The cleaned file, *iso-2-cleaned.json*, is also available in the repository. Now we can use the preceding code with the new, cleaned JSON to make a complete table. Note, you will have to either rename your columns or use the new column name country_code_complete so you don't run into duplicate column name issues. We will utilize the table to create our own world map using the pygal mapping methods:

```
import pygal

worldmap_chart = pygal.maps.world.World()  ❶
worldmap_chart.title = 'Child Labor Worldwide'

cl_dict = {}
for r in ranked.rows:
    cl_dict[r.get('country_code_complete').lower()] = r.get('Total (%)')  ❷

worldmap_chart.add('Total Child Labor (%)', cl_dict)  ❸
worldmap_chart.render()  ❹
```

❶ The pygal library's World class in the maps.world module returns our map object.

❷ cl_dict holds a dictionary where the keys are the country codes and the values are the child labor percentages.

❸ Following the pygal documentation, this code passes the label for the data and a data dictionary.

❹ We call the map's render method to display the map.

We can see that render outputs the *.svg* to the terminal as a long, complicated string. If we want to save it in a file, we need to call a different method. pygal gives us a few options for different file types:

```
worldmap_chart.render_to_file('world_map.svg')
```

```
worldmap_chart.render_to_png('world_map.png')
```

Now when we open up our *.svg* or *.png*, we'll see the chart shown in Figure 10-5.

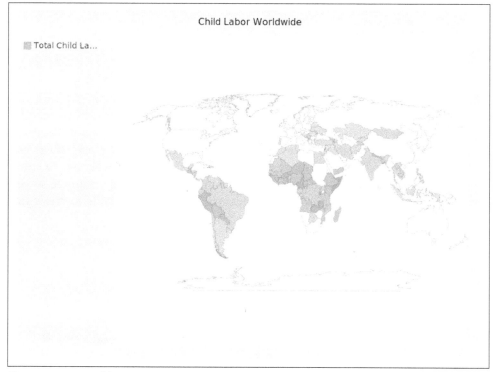

Figure 10-5. World map

 If you have any trouble with the map rendering, make sure you have all dependency libraries installed. If you don't have an *.svg* file viewer on your computer, you can always open up your *.svg* files in a browser, as shown in Figure 10-5.

We strongly encourage you to check out the many other *.svg* options pygal provides. The documentation is full of examples, both advanced and simple, and it's a very accessible *.svg* library for beginners.

Interactives

Interactives tell a story through website interactions or simulations. Because users can click around and explore via the browser, they can take in the topic at their own pace and seek out their own conclusions from the data. This can be particularly powerful for topics which require more research to fully understand.

In response to the recent measles outbreak in the United States, *The Guardian* created an outbreak interactive (*http://bit.ly/vaccination_effects*) allowing users to see and replay effects of potential measles outbreaks with different vaccination rates. This interactive displays different scenarios *The Guardian* staff researched and coded. Not every simulation turns out with the same outcome, allowing users to understand there is an element of chance, while still showing probability (i.e., less chance of infection with higher vaccination rates). This takes a highly politicized topic and brings out real-world scenarios using statistical models of outbreaks.

Although interactives take more experience to build and often require a deeper coding skillset, they are a great tool, especially if you have frontend coding experience.

As an example, for our child labor data we could build an interactive showing how many people in your local high school would have never graduated due to child labor rates if they lived in Chad. Another interactive could show goods and services available in your local mall that are produced using child labor. These take hard-to-visualize information and present it to your audience so they can understand the data and connect with the story.

Words

Telling the story with words comes naturally for writers and reporters. Regardless of what visual methods you use, any writing or words you include should be useful and appropriate for your intended audience. You might want to interview or speak with topic experts. Including their words, ideas, and conclusions on the findings will help your audience synthesize the information.

If you are researching how a local school board is determining budgeting for upcoming school years, you could speak to board members and perhaps get inside information regarding proposed changes. If you are researching upcoming product releases for your company, you might want to talk to some of the key decision makers to determine what may be on the horizon.

For more information on interviewing and choosing quotes to accompany your story, Poynter has some great tips (*http://bit.ly/better_interviews*) on how to become a better interviewer, and Columbia University's Interview Principles (*http://bit.ly/interviewing_principles*) shares insights on how to prepare for your interview and determine how to use different interviews for your projects' needs.

If you are an area expert and use technical or unfamiliar jargon, you might want to break down those topics into bite-sized chunks, depending on your audience. A simple glossary can be useful. This is common practice in scientific, technical, and medical writing when aimed at a larger audience.

Images, Video, and Illustrations

If your story has a strong visual element, images and video can enhance the storytelling. For example, videotaping interviews with people related to your topic can show a personal side of the data and may uncover other perspectives or future avenues of investigation.

As with videos, images paint a picture for your audience. As we've all experienced with graphic images of war or other gruesome current events, they can impact our interpretation of a story. However, using images to simply shock your audience takes away from the careful research you put into your work. Use your discretion to find a good compromise for your storytelling.

If you don't have access to photos and videos related to your topic or the ability to collect your own, illustrations can be used for visual storytelling. A *Washington Post* interactive on healthy vs. unhealthy office spaces (*http://bit.ly/unhealthy_offices*) uses an illustration to show the story concepts.

For our child labor data, it's unlikely we'll have a chance to collect videos and photos ourselves of the greatest violations uncovered in our data analysis. However, we can use photos from past child labor exposés (with permission and attribution) as a representation of children still affected by the issue worldwide.

Presentation Tools

If you don't want to publish your data, but you'd like to present it to a smaller (or internal) group, creating a slide presentation is easier than ever. With many options for how to display your data, you can create a slick presentation without much extra work.

One top-rated tool for creating professional-looking slides is Prezi (*https://prezi.com/*). Prezi gives you the ability to create free publicly available slide decks and has a variety of desktop clients (if you'd like to have private presentations, you'll need to sign up for a paid account). Haiku Deck (*https://www.haikudeck.com/*) is another online-only option allowing for free public slideshows and private ones for a fee. You can also use Google Slides as a free and easy alternative, particularly if you are presenting to an internal audience and your company uses Google Apps.

Publishing Your Data

You've spent time researching, exploring, and presenting your data, and now you want to share your reporting with the world online. When publishing your data online, you should first determine whether the data should be publicly accessible.

 If your presentation includes private data or data pertinent only to your company (proprietary data), you should publish it on a password-protected site, or on an internal network site.

If you want to share your data with the world, publishing it via one of the many different available web platforms should be no problem. In this section, we'll cover how to publish your data on free and easy-to-use blogging platforms or on your own site.

Using Available Sites

Many of the websites designed for publishing data cater to writers and investigators like you, who want to share reporting or ideas and easily distribute them on the Web. Here are some of the best options.

Medium

On Medium (*https://medium.com/*), you can create an account, start writing your post and easily embed comments, quotes, photos, and charts. Because it's a social media platform, others on Medium can recommend your post, share it, bookmark it, and follow your future articles.

 Using a hosted site like Medium allows you to focus on writing and reporting without spending time figuring out how to build and maintain your own site.

Medium's team maintains some nice charting tools, including Charted.co (*https://github.com/mikesall/charted*), which uses simple CSV or TSV files to render an interactive chart. As of the writing of this book, they have not yet enabled embedding of these charts directly into posts, but it's likely they will add that feature.

Medium makes it easy to embed a variety of social media, videos, photos, and other media (*http://bit.ly/medium_embed_media*) directly into your post. You can get great storytelling ideas by reading through some of the top Medium posts of the month (*https://medium.com/top-100/*).

We recommend reading and searching Medium posts in your topic area and connecting with other topic area authors to get a feel for how people tell stories.

Medium is a great way to blog on a social network and share your ideas with the world. But what if you want to run your own blog? Read on for some great options to get your site up and running.

Easy-to-start sites: WordPress, Squarespace

If you'd rather have more control over the layout and access to your content, you might start your own blog on Squarespace (*http://www.squarespace.com/*) or WordPress (*https://wordpress.com/*). These platforms give you a maintained website for free (WordPress) or for a relatively small fee (Squarespace), and let you customize the look and feel of your site. You can set up a domain so your writing is hosted on your own URL.

Most web hosting providers give you a one-click install for WordPress. You'll need to choose a username and some site titles and ensure you have a strong and secure password. With WordPress, you have a great selection of themes (*https://wordpress.org/themes/browse/popular/*) and plug-ins (*https://wordpress.org/plugins/browse/popular/*) available to customize the look, feel, and functionality of your site. To protect your site, we recommend installing one of the popular security plug-ins and reading WordPress's sage advice around security (*http://codex.wordpress.org/Hardening_Word Press*).

Getting set up with Squarespace is a matter of signing up on their site and choosing a layout. You can customize your connected social media, your domain, and whether you'd like to have an ecommerce shop.

Once your site is up and running, adding content is straightforward. You'll want to post new pages or posts, add text and images using the built-in editors (or, if you're using WordPress, you can install extra editor plug-ins with more features), and then publish your content.

You can make your posts easier to find by taking the time to fill out a description and keywords to increase your visibility via search engine optimization (SEO). There are WordPress plug-ins and Squarespace features to do so for each post.

Your own blog

If you run your own website or blog, you already have a great platform for sharing your reporting. You need to ensure you can properly embed your visual storytelling.

Most of the charts we have been working with can be easily embedded into the HTML on your site.

If you are on a platform other than WordPress or Squarespace, you might need to research how to share charts, videos, and photos on your site. We recommend reaching out to the platform's community or creators or reading through the site's how-tos and documentation to determine how to best embed images, charts, and interactives.

Open Source Platforms: Starting a New Site

We've mentioned options for getting a new site up and running using free or low-cost platforms like Squarespace and WordPress; but if you'd like to launch, run, and maintain your own site, you can pick from a wealth of great open source platforms.

Ghost

One easy platform to run is Ghost (*https://github.com/tryghost/Ghost*). Ghost uses Node.js (*https://nodejs.org/*), an open source JavaScript asynchronous server, which is fun to use and learn if you're interested in JavaScript. Because it's asynchronous, it has great performance and can handle a lot of traffic. Ghost also offers the ability to set up a hosted site (*https://ghost.org/*), similar to WordPress or Squarespace, for a small fee.

If you'd like to host your own Ghost blog, DigitalOcean and Ghost have partnered to create an easy-to-use and install server image (*http://bit.ly/digitalocean_ghost*) to get up and running with Ghost on your server in less than an hour. If it's your first time setting up a server, we highly recommend this route, as some of the initial work is completed for you.

If you have your own servers and you'd like to install Ghost from scratch or on a different platform, Ghost provides some how-tos (*http://support.ghost.org/deploying-ghost/*). The main steps you will need to take are:

1. Download and install the latest source code.
2. Get node running. (We recommend using nvm (*https://github.com/creationix/nvm*).)
3. Install node dependencies using npm (the node version of pip).
4. Get pm2 (*https://github.com/Unitech/pm2*) running to manage your Ghost processes.
5. Set up nginx to talk to the running Ghost processes using a gateway.
6. Get blogging!

If you run into any issues, you can hop into the Ghost slack channel (*https://ghost.org/slack/*) and see if someone can help you, or search for more information on Stack Overflow (*http://stackoverflow.com/*).

GitHub Pages and Jekyll

If you are using GitHub for your code, you can also use it to host your website. Git-Hub Pages (*https://pages.github.com/*), a GitHub-run website hosting tool, gives you flexibility for deployment and eases content creation. With GitHub Pages, you can deploy static content directly to your GitHub page by pushing to your repository. If you'd like to use a framework, you can use Jekyll (*http://jekyllrb.com/*), a Ruby-based static page generator with GitHub Page's integration.

Jekyll's documentation (*http://jekyllrb.com/docs/home/*) has an explanatory overview covering how to get Jekyll up and running locally, but we recommend reading Barry Clark's article for *Smashing Magazine* (*http://bit.ly/jekyll_github_blogs*), where he lays out how to fork an existing repository, get your site up, and modify Jekyll settings and features. If you'd rather not use Jekyll but still want to use GitHub Pages, you can generate static HTML files with a library or by hand and push those files to your GitHub Pages repository.

> One easy-to-use Python HTML generator is Pelican (*https://github.com/getpelican/pelican*), which takes AsciiDoc, Markdown, or reStructuredText files and turns them into static content. It has easy steps to enable commenting and analytics tracking and fairly thorough instructions on getting started with GitHub pages (*http://bit.ly/publishing_to_github*).

There are plenty of other static site generators, and many write-ups on how to integrate them with GitHub Pages. One option for setting up a GitHub Pages blog is Hexo, a Node.js-based framework (*http://bit.ly/hexo_setup*). Octopress (*https://github.com/octopress/octopress*) is another great option; it's built on Jekyll, so you can easily use GitHub Pages and Ruby to publish and deploy your site.

One-click deploys

If you'd like to stick with a bigger blogging or website framework such as WordPress, DigitalOcean has many one-click installs (*https://www.digitalocean.com/features/one-click-apps/*) enabling you to set up your server and install all the necessary libraries and databases in a very short time period. It also provides a handy tutorial describing how to set up WordPress on a droplet (*http://bit.ly/one-click_wordpress_install*).

In addition to large-scale hosting providers, you can also use Python, Ruby, and other open source platforms with Heroku, a cloud-based application host (*https://devcen*

ter.heroku.com/start). If you are using or learning an open source framework, you can use Heroku to deploy your website; it offers great documentation and tech support.

No matter what framework or hosting solution you use, it's important to focus on an easy way to publish your content or code online. Choose something straightforward and simple and focus your attention on getting your content properly displayed, published, and shared with the world.

Jupyter (Formerly Known as IPython Notebooks)

We've covered how to share your findings, but what if you'd also like to share your code, data, and process? Depending on your audience, it may be appropriate to share your code and allow people to interact directly with it. If you are sharing with colleagues or peers, this is a great way to show how you went about your research.

Jupyter notebooks (*https://jupyter.org/*) (formerly known as IPython notebooks (*http://ipython.org/notebook.html*)) are a great way to share your Python code and charts generated by your code. These notebooks combine the ease of using a browser with IPython's interactive features. Notebooks are also tremendously useful for iterative code design and data exploration.

Learning a new library or playing around with some new data? Save your work in a Jupyter notebook. Once you've iterated on and improved your code, you can move the important bits of the code into a repository and properly structure, document, and synthesize them in one place.

Getting Jupyter up and running locally is simple; just run this command:

```
pip install "ipython[notebook]"
```

To start your notebook server, run:

```
ipython notebook
```

You should see some terminal output like:

```
[NotebookApp] Using MathJax from CDN: https://cdn.mathjax.org/mathjax/latest/
    MathJax.js
[NotebookApp] Terminals not available (error was No module named terminado)
[NotebookApp] Serving notebooks from local directory: /home/foo/my-python
[NotebookApp] 0 active kernels
[NotebookApp] The IPython Notebook is running at: http://localhost:8888/
[NotebookApp] Use Control-C to stop this server and shut down all kernels.
Created new window in existing browser session.
```

This is the notebook server starting up. You will also see a new browser window (or tab) open to an empty notebook.

Depending on what folder you are running your notebook in, you might see some files in your browser. The notebook server runs directly from whatever folder you are in and displays that folder's contents. We recommend creating a new folder for your notebooks. To stop the server so you can create a new folder, press Ctrl-C (Windows and Linux) or Cmd-C on a Mac in the running terminal. Make a new directory, change into it, and restart your server, like so:

```
mkdir notebooks
cd notebooks/
ipython notebook
```

Let's begin using Jupyter by starting a new notebook. To do that, click the New drop-down menu and choose "Python 2" under the Notebooks heading. Once you have created a new notebook, give it a useful name. To do so, click on the title section (it should currently say "Untitled") and enter a new name. Naming your notebooks will save you hours of searching later.

In Jupyter, each text area is called a cell. Notebooks support many different cell types. It's a great idea to have some Markdown (*https://daringfireball.net/projects/mark down/syntax*) cells at the top or between sections of code to explain and document your code. Figure 10-6 shows an example of adding a header.

Figure 10-6. Adding a Markdown title

To start writing Python, simply click on the next available cell and start typing. When you are done with whatever statement or function you are writing, hit Shift+Enter. Your code will execute and a new cell will appear for your next Python code. As you can see in Figure 10-7 and your own notebook, you can see any and all outputs you'd expect in a normal Python interpreter.

```
                Data Exploration -- Unicef Child Labor

In [1]:  1 == 1
Out[1]:  True

In [2]:  def test_function(x, y):
             return int(x) + int(y)

In [3]:  test_function(1, 2)
Out[3]:  3

In [4]:  test_function(foo, bar)
         -------------------------------------------------------------
         NameError                       Traceback (most recent call last)
         <ipython-input-4-c9ed7bdf68f5> in <module>()
         ----> 1 test_function(foo, bar)

         NameError: name 'foo' is not defined

In [ ]:
```

Figure 10-7. Working in Jupyter

There are a ton of great Jupyter (and IPython) notebook tutorials available, but a good starting point might be to retry some code we've been using in this book.

 We recommend organizing your notebooks similar to your repository. You might want to have a *data* folder containing your data in the root directory of your notebook folder, and a *utils* folder with scripts you can import into your notebooks. Your notebook is like another script, only it's interactive and in your browser.

When you are done using a notebook, hit the Save button (to make sure it creates a new checkpoint so your files are updated). If you are done with a particular notebook but still using other notebooks, it's a good idea to stop the old notebook process. To do so, navigate to the *Running* tab in your server and click the Shutdown button. When you are done with all of your notebooks, save them all and shut down your server in the running notebook terminal using Ctrl-C or Cmd-C.

Shared Jupyter notebooks

Now that you are familiar with using Jupyter notebooks, you can set one up to share your code with others using a shared server. This will allow others to access your notebook on the normal Internet (not just localhost, like the notebook run from your terminal).

There are some great tutorials available on how to set up a notebook server using DigitalOcean (*http://calebmadrigal.com/ipython-notebook-vps/*), Heroku (*https://*

github.com/mietek/instant-ipython), Amazon Web Services (*http://bit.ly/html_note book_aws*), Google DataLab (*https://cloud.google.com/datalab/*), or whatever server you'd like (*http://bit.ly/notebook_server*).

 Remember to use secure passwords with your notebook server to ensure your notebooks are being used only by those with the password. This will keep your server and data safe.

We recommend setting up a version control system like Git (explored in more depth in Chapter 14) for your Jupyter notebooks as well, so you can have a history of your notebooks on a daily or weekly basis. This way, you can revert them if anything gets removed, and it helps you store and organize your code.

 If you are using a shared notebook server, make sure people know how to run all of the code if the kernel has been interrupted, which can happen if the server is restarted or if someone stops or restarts the kernel in a notebook. To run all notebook code, select the Cell drop-down in the notebook's toolbar and click "Run All." You should also advise users to use Shutdown to stop notebooks when they are done working so you don't have useless running processes on your server.

Jupyter notebooks, both local and shared, are a great tool for presenting your data and workflow. They are also incredibly useful to run locally as you iterate through your data exploration and analysis. As your Python knowledge grows, you can migrate your scripts to Python 3 and run JupyterHub (*https://github.com/jupyter/jupy terhub*), a multiuser notebook server that runs many different languages (including Python) and is currently under active development.

Whether you choose to publish on a notebook server or an open source platform, you now possess the skills to analyze how to best present and publish your findings, data, and code.

Summary

You've learned how to get your data into a presentable form and distribute it via the Web. You have many publishing options with varying levels of privacy and maintenance requirements. You can set up a site for your reporting and create beautiful graphs and charts to tell your story. With the power of Jupyter, you can easily share and present the code you've written and teach others a bit of Python in the process.

You've also been introduced to the libraries and concepts listed in Table 10-1.

Table 10-1. New Python and programming concepts and libraries

Concept/Library	Purpose
`matplotlib` library for charting	Allows you to generate simple charts with two charting libraries. You can use labels and titles for your charts to show your data in a concise way.
Bokeh library for more complex charts	Allows you to easily generate more complex charts, along with charts using more interactive features.
`pygal` library for SVG charts and maps	For a slicker view and the ability to generate SVGs, `pygal` gives you the ability to pass your data using simple functions.
Ghost blogging platform	A Node.js-backed blogging platform to quickly set up a blog on your own server (or hosted on Ghost's infrastructure) to share stories on your own site.
GitHub Pages and Jekyll	A simple publishing platform utilizing GitHub to share your posts and presentations via a simple repository push.
Jupyter notebooks	An easy way to share your code with other developers or colleagues, as well as a nice way to get started developing your own code using an agile (i.e., trial and error) approach.

Next, we'll move on to how to gather even more data via web scraping and API usage. The lessons you've learned in this chapter can be used with the data you'll collect from this point forward, so keep reading and take your new presentation skills with you. In the following chapters, you will acquire more advanced Python data skills, allowing you to better collect, evaluate, store, and analyze data with Python. The storytelling tools you learned in this chapter will aid you in your bright future of Python data wrangling and sharing what you learn with your audience and the world.

## CHAPTER 11

Web Scraping: Acquiring and Storing Data from the Web

Web scraping is an essential part of data mining in today's world, as you can find nearly everything on the Web. With web scraping, you can use Python libraries to explore web pages, search for information, and collect it for your reporting. Web scraping lets you crawl sites and find information not easily accessible without robotic assistance.

This technique gives you access to data not contained in an API or a file. Imagine a script to log into your email account, download files, run analysis, and send an aggregated report. Imagine testing your site to make sure it's fully functional without ever touching a browser. Imagine grabbing data from a series of tables on a regularly updated website. These examples show how web scraping can assist with your data wrangling needs.

Depending on what you need to scrape—local or public websites, XML documents— you can use many of the same tools to accomplish these tasks. Most websites contain data in HTML code on the site. HTML is a markup language, and uses brackets (like our XML example in Chapter 3) to hold data. In this chapter, we will use libraries that understand how to parse and read markup languages like HTML and XML.

There are many sites that use internal APIs and embedded JavaScript to control the content on their pages. Because of these new ways to build the Web, not all of the information can be found using page-reading scrapers. We'll also learn how to use some screen-reading web scrapers for sites with multiple data sources. Depending on the makeup of the site, you might also be able to connect to an API, which you'll learn more about in Chapter 13.

What to Scrape and How

Web scraping opens up a wide world of possibilities for data collection. There are millions of websites on the Internet with a huge variety of content and data you might use for your projects. Being a conscientious web scraper, you'll want to inform yourself about each site and what content you can scrape.

Copyright, Trademark, and Scraping

When scraping on the Web, you should think about the data you collect and its use as you would any media you find (from a newspaper, magazine, book, or blog). Would you download someone else's photo and post it as your own? No—that would be unethical and, in some cases, illegal.

Learning about aspects of media law like copyright (*http://www.dmlp.org/legal-guide/copyright*) and trademark (*http://www.dmlp.org/legal-guide/trademark*) can inform your decisions, particularly if you are scraping data considered to be someone's intellectual property (*http://www.dmlp.org/legal-guide/intellectual-property*).

Investigate the domain and look for legal notices about what is allowed and disallowed, and peruse the robots file (*http://www.robotstxt.org/robotstxt.html*) to better understand the site owner's wishes. If you have a question about whether the data can be scraped, reach out to a lawyer or the site itself. Depending on where you live and what you use the data for, you might want to find a digital media legal organization to contact in case you have any questions surrounding the precedents and laws in your country.

For most web scraping, it makes sense to scrape text rather than links, images, or charts. If you also need to save links, images, or files, most of these can be downloaded using simple bash commands (like `wget` or `curl` (*http://bit.ly/wget_v_curl*)), which require no Python. You could simply save a list of the file URLS and write a script with to download your files.

We will start with simple text scraping. Most web pages are built with a similar structure defined in proper HTML standards. Most sites have a *head* where most of the JavaScript and styles for the page are defined along with other extra information, like meta tags for services like Facebook and Pinterest and descriptions for search engine usage.

After the head comes the *body*. The body is the main section of the site. Most sites use *containers* (which are markup nodes similar to our XML nodes) to organize the site and allow the site's content management system to load content into the page. Figure 11-1 shows how a typical web page is organized.

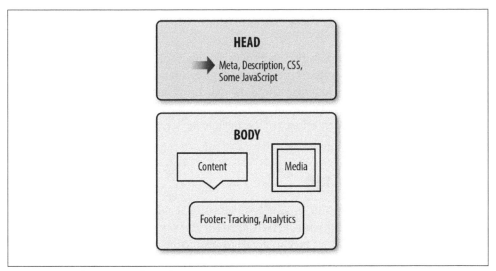

Figure 11-1. Anatomy of a web page

For many sites, the top section of the page contains navigation and links to the major site sections or related topics. Links or ads often appear down the sides of the page. The middle of the page usually contains the content you want to scrape.

> Becoming familiar with the structure of most web pages (in terms of where the elements are visually and where they exist in the markup of the page) will help you scrape data from the Internet. If you can spot where to look for the data, you'll be able to quickly build scrapers.

Once you know what you are looking for on the page, and you've analyzed the markup by studying the construction of the page source, you can determine how you'd like to gather the important parts of the page. Many web pages offer content on first page load, or serve a cached page with the content already loaded. For these pages, we can use a simple XML or HTML parser (which we'll learn about in this chapter) and read directly from the first HTTP response (what your browser loads when you request a URL). It's similar to reading documents, just with an initial page request.

If you need to first interact with the page to get the data (i.e., enter some data and push a button) and it's not just a simple URL change, you will need to use a browser-based scraper to open the page in a browser and interact with it.

If you need to traverse an entire site looking for data, you'll want a *spider*: a robot that crawls pages and follows rules to identify good content or more pages to follow. The library we will work with for spidering is incredibly fast and flexible, and makes writing these types of scripts much easier.

Before we start writing our scraper code, we'll take a look at a few websites and get used to analyzing which scraper type to use (page reader, browser reader, or spider) and how difficult or easy scraping the data will be. There will be times when it's important to determine what level of effort the data is worth. We'll give you some tools to determine how much effort will be needed to scrape the data and how much time it's worth putting into that work.

Analyzing a Web Page

Most of your time web scraping will be spent staring at markup in your browser and figuring out how to interact with it. Getting used to your favorite browser's debugging or development tools is an essential part of becoming an advanced web scraper.

Depending on what browser you use, the tools might have different names and functionality, but the concepts are the same. You'll want to educate yourself on your favorite browser's tools, be it Internet Explorer (*http://bit.ly/f12_dev_tools*), Safari (*https://developer.apple.com/safari/tools/*), Chrome (*https://developer.chrome.com/devtools*), or Firefox (*http://bit.ly/ff_developer_toolbar*).

The basics of every browser debugger are similar. You'll have an area where you can see the requests and page load data (usually called Network or something similar). You'll have another area where you can analyze the markup of the page and see the styles and content in each tag (usually called Inspection or Elements or DOM). You'll have a third area where you can see JavaScript errors and interact with the JavaScript on the page, usually called Console.

Your browser's developer tools may have other tabs, but we really only need these three to get a good idea of how the page is built and how to easily scrape the content.

Inspection: Markup Structure

When you want to scrape a site, first analyze the site structure and markup. As we learned in Chapter 3, XML has a structure of nodes and content, keys and values. HTML is quite similar. If you open your browser's developer tools and navigate to the Inspection, Elements, or DOM tab, you'll notice you can see a series of nodes and their values. The nodes and data contained therein are a bit different from what we saw in our XML examples—they are HTML tags (some basics are outlined in Table 11-1). The HTML tag used tells you about the content. If you were trying to find all the photos on a page, you would look for img tags.

Table 11-1. Basic HTML tags

Tag	Description	Example
head	Used to hold metadata and other essential information for the document	`<head> <title>Best Title Ever</title> </head>`
body	Used to hold the majority of the content on the page	`<body> <p>super short page</p> </body>`
meta	Used to hold metadata such as a short description of the site or keywords	`<meta name="keywords" content="tags, html">`
h1, h2, h3…	Used to hold header information; the smaller the number, the larger the header	`<h1>Really big one!</h1>`
p	Used to hold text paragraphs	`<p>Here's my first paragraph.</p>`
ul, ol	Used to hold both unordered lists (ul: think bullets) and ordered (ol: think numbers)	`<ul><li>first bullet</li></ul>`
li	Used to hold list items; should always be inside a list (ul or ol)	`<ul><li>first</li> <li>second</li></ul>`
div	Used to section or divide content	`<div id="about"><p>This div is about things.</p></div>`
a	Used to link content; called "anchor tags"	`<a href="http://oreilly.com">Best Ever</a>`
img	Used to insert an image	`<img src="/flying_cows.png" alt="flying cows!" />`

For a more robust and complete introduction to HTML tags and their uses, take a look at the Mozilla Developer Network's HTML reference, guide, and introduction (*https://developer.mozilla.org/en-US/docs/Web/HTML*).

Aside from tags used and content structure, the placement of tags in relation to one another is important. Similar to XML, HTML has *parents* and *children*. There is a hierarchy of relationships in the structure. The parent nodes have child nodes, and learning how to traverse the family tree structure will help you get the content you want. Knowing the relationship of the elements to one another, whether they are parents or children or siblings, will help you write more efficient, fast, and easy-to-update scrapers.

Let's take a closer look at what these relationships mean in an HTML page. Here is a mock-up of a basic HTML site:

```
<!DOCTYPE HTML>
<html>
<head>

  <title>My Awesome Site</title>
  <link rel="stylesheet" href="css/main.css" />

</head>
<body>
    <header>
        <div id="header">I'm ahead!</div>
    </header>
    <section class="main">
     <div id="main_content">
        <p>This site is super awesome! Here are some reasons it's so awesome:</p>
            <h3>List of Awesome:</h3>
            <ul>
                <li>Reason one: see title</li>
                <li>Reason two: see reason one</li>
            </ul>
        </div>
    </section>
    <footer>
        <div id="bottom_nav">
          <ul>
                <li><a href="/about">About</a></li>
                <li><a href="/blog">Blog</a></li>
                <li><a href="/careers">Careers</a></li>
          </ul>
        </div>
    <script src="js/myjs.js"></script>
    </footer>
</body>
</html>
```

If we start with the very first tag of this page (below the document type declaration), we can see all of the content of the entire page lives in the html tag. The html tag is the root tag for the entire page.

Inside the html tag, we have the head and the body. The vast majority of the page is in the body, but the head has some content as well. The head and body tags are the children of the html element. In turn, those tags contain their respective children and descendants. The head and body tags are siblings.

Looking inside the main body tag, we can see other sets of familial relationships. All of our list items (li tags) are children of unordered lists (ul tags). The header, section, and footer tags are all siblings. The script tag is a child of the footer tag and a sibling of the div tag in the footer that holds links. There are many complex relationships, and this is just one simple page!

To further investigate, the following code shows a page with slightly more compli-cated relationships (when we are dealing with web scraping we will rarely have a *per-fect* page with everything properly organized and the relationships always intact):

```html
<!DOCTYPE html>
<html>
    <head>
        <title>test</title>
        <link ref="stylesheet" href="/style.css">
    </head>
    <body>
        <div id="container">
            <div id="content" class="clearfix">
                <div id="header">
                    <h1>Header</h1> ❶
                </div>
                <div id="nav"> ❷
                    <div class="navblock"> ❸
                        <h2>Our Philosophy</h2>
                        <ul>
                            <li>foo</li>
                            <li>bar</li>
                        </ul>
                    </div>
                    <div class="navblock"> ❹
                        <h2>About Us</h2> ❺
                        <ul>
                            <li>more foo</li> ❻
                            <li>more bar</li>
                        </ul>
                    </div>
                </div>
                <div id="maincontent"> ❼
                    <div class="contentblock">
                        <p>Lorem ipsum dolor sit amet...</p>
                    </div>
                    <div class="contentblock">
                        <p>Nunc porttitor ut ipsum quis facilisis.</p>
                    </div>
                </div>
            </div>
        </div>
        <style>...</style>
    </body>
</html>
```

❶ First child of previous sibling of the current element's parent

❷ Parent/ancestor of current element

❸ Sibling of current element

❹ Current element

❺ First child/descendant of current element

❻ Child/descendant of current element

❼ Next sibling of current element's parent

For the purpose of our discussion, the "current element" is the second div with the navblock class. We can see it has two children, a heading (h2), and an unordered list (ul), and there are list items (li) inside that list. They are descendants (and depending on what library you use could be included in "all children"). The current element has one sibling, the first div with the navblock class.

The div with ID nav is the parent of our current element, but our element has other ancestors. How could we navigate from our current element to the div with ID header? Our parent element is a sibling of that header element. To get the header element content, we could find the previous sibling of our parent element. The parent element also has another sibling, the div with ID maincontent.

All together these relationships are described as the *Document Object Model* (DOM) structure. HTML has rules and standards for organizing the content on a page (also known as a document). The HTML element nodes are "objects," and they have a particular model/standard they must follow to be displayed properly.

The more time you spend understanding the relationships between nodes, the easier it will be to traverse the DOM quickly and efficiently with code. Later in this chapter, we'll cover XPath, which uses familial relationships to select content. For now, with our improved understanding of HTML structure and the relationships between DOM elements, we can take a closer look at locating and analyzing the content we wish to scrape on our selected site(s).

Depending on your browser, you might be able to search the markup using the developer tools. This is a great way to see the element structure. For example, if we are looking for a particular section of content, we can search for those words and find their location. Many browsers also allow you to right-click on an element on the page and select "Inspect." This usually opens your developer tools to the selected element.

We'll use Chrome for our examples, but follow along using your favorite browser. When researching child labor in Africa, we came across data connecting child labor practices with conflicts. This led us to organizations working to stop conflict zones and conflict mining across Africa. Open up a page for one of those organizations: the Enough Project's Take Action page (*http://www.enoughproject.org/take_action*).

When we first open our developer tools—select Tools→Developer Tools in Chrome, press F12 in Internet Explorer, choose Tools→Web Developer→Inspector in Firefox, or enable the Develop menu in Safari's advanced preferences—we will see markup in one panel, CSS rules and styles in another small panel, and the actual page in a panel above the tools. Depending on your browser, the layout might be different, but the tools should be similar enough to see these features (displayed in Figure 11-2).

Figure 11-2. Enough Project Take Action page

 If you move your cursor over an element in the markup section (Inspection tab) of the developer tools, you will probably see different areas of the page highlight. This is a great feature to help you see the different elements in the markup and page structure.

If you click on the arrows next to the div's and main elements of the page, you can see elements located within them (child elements). For example, on the Enough Project's page, we can investigate the right sidebar (circled in Figure 11-3) by clicking to open the main-inner-tse div and other internal div's.

Figure 11-3. Exploring the sidebar

We can see the sidebar's images are located inside links, which are inside a paragraph, inside a div—the list goes on and on. Understanding when images are inside links (or vice versa), determining which content is located in paragraph tags, and figuring out other page structure elements are essential to locating and scraping page content.

Another great use of developer tools is to investigate elements. If you right-click on a part of the page, you should see a menu including some useful tools for web scraping. Figure 11-4 shows an example of such a menu.

If we click the "Inspect element" option, the developer tools should open to that element in the source markup. This is a tremendously useful feature for interacting with the content and seeing where it's located in the code.

In addition to being able to interact with elements in the browser portion of the window, you can also interact with elements in the source code portion. Figure 11-5 shows the type of menu you get by right-clicking on an element in the markup area. We can see options to copy CSS selectors or XPath selectors (both of which we will use in this chapter to locate and extract content from websites).

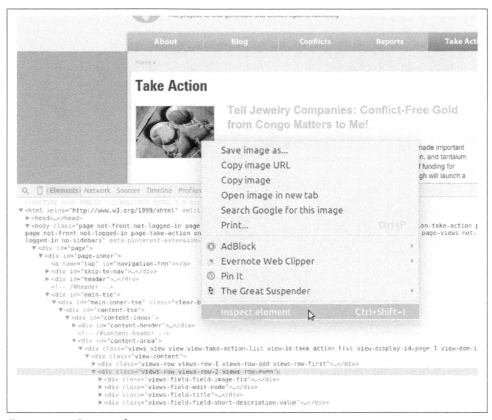

Figure 11-4. Inspect element

 Depending on your browser, the language and interaction of your tools might vary, but the menu options should be similar to the ones described here, and this should give you some idea of how to access this data and these interactions.

In addition to finding elements and content, your developer tools show you quite a lot about the node structure and family relationships on the page. There will often be a section of the Inspection tab in your developer tools showing you a list of the parent elements of your current element. The elements in this list can usually be clicked on or selected, so you can traverse the DOM with a single click. In Chrome, this list is in the gray section between the developer tools and the page above.

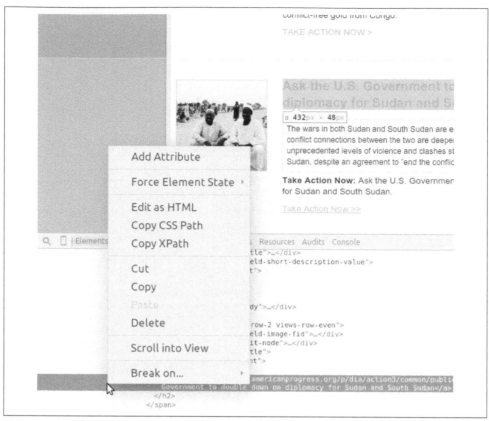

Figure 11-5. Element options

We've taken a look at how web pages are structured and how we can interact with them to better understand where our content lies. We will now investigate the other powerful tools in our web browser that make our web scraping easier.

Network/Timeline: How the Page Loads

Analyzing the Timeline and/or Network tabs in your developer tools will give you great insights into how the content on the page loads, and in what order. The timing and way a page loads can greatly influence how you decide to scrape the page. Understanding where the content comes from can sometimes give you a "shortcut" to the content you wish to scrape.

The Network or Timeline tab shows you what URLs were loaded, in what order, and how long each of them took to load. Figure 11-6 shows what the Network tab looks like in Chrome for the Enough Project page. Depending on your browser, you may need to reload the page to see the Network tab's page assets.

Figure 11-6. Network tab with one page

We can see the entire page is loaded in one call since we only have one request in our Network tab. This is great news as a web scraper, because it means everything is available in only one request.

If we click on the request, we can see more options, including the source code of the response (Figure 11-7). Viewing each request's content will be essential to locating the content you need when pages are loaded via many different requests. You can investigate headers and cookies by clicking on the Headers tab of your Network tab, in case you need extra data to load the site.

Let's take a look at a similar organization's page with a complex Network tab. Open your Network tab and navigate your browser to the #WeAreFairphone page (*http://www.fairphone.com/we-are-fairphone/*) on the Fair phone initiative's site (Figure 11-8).

You can immediately see this page is processing more requests. By clicking on each request, you can see the content each request loads. The request order is indicated in the timeline on your Network tab. This can help you understand how to scrape and process the page to get to your desired content.

Figure 11-7. Network response

Figure 11-8. Network tab with lots of pages

By clicking on each of the requests, we can see most of the content is loaded after the initial page load. When we click on the initial page request, it is quite empty. The first question we want to ask is, is there a JavaScript call or some other call loading the content using JSON? If so, this might be an apt "shortcut" for our script.

 You know how to parse and read JSON (Chapter 3), so if you find a URL in your Network tab with a JSON response holding the data you need, you can use that URL to get the data and then parse the data directly from the response. You should be aware of any headers (shown in the Headers section of your Network tab) you might need to send with your request in order to get the proper response.

If there is no easy JSON URL matching the information you need, or if the information is scattered over several different requests and would require maneuvering to put it together, you can now be certain you should use a browser-based approach to scrape the site. Browser-based web scraping allows you to read from the page you *see*, not each request. This can also be useful if you need to interact with a drop-down or perform a series of browser-based actions before you can scrape the content properly.

The Network tab helps you figure out what requests hold your desired content and if there are any good alternative data sources. We'll look at JavaScript next, to see if that can give us some ideas for our scraper as well.

Console: Interacting with JavaScript

You've now analyzed the markup and structure of the page and the timing of the page load and network requests, so let's move on to the JavaScript console to see what we can learn from interacting with the JavaScript running on the page.

If you're already familiar with JavaScript, this is fairly easy to use; if you've never interacted with JavaScript, it might be useful to take a look at an easy introduction to JavaScript course (*http://www.codecademy.com/en/tracks/javascript*). You only need to understand JavaScript's basic syntax, giving you the ability to interact with elements of the page via the console. We'll begin by reviewing JavaScript and style basics to see how to use the console view.

Style basics

Every web page uses some style elements to help organize, size, color, and visually modify its content. When browsers began developing HTML standards, style standards also came into existence. The result was Cascading Style Sheets, or CSS, which gives us a standard way of styling pages. For example, if you want all titles to use a different font or all photos to be centered on the page, you would write those rules in CSS.

CSS allows styles to cascade, or inherit from parent styles and style sheets. If we define one set of styles for the entire site, it's quite easy for our content management system to make one page look like every other page. Even if we have a complex site with many different page types, we can define a major CSS document and several minor ones, which are loaded if the page requires extra styles.

CSS works because it defines rules that allow DOM elements to be grouped together (or separately defined) by attributes within the tags. Remember when we explored XML in Chapter 3 and looked at nested attributes? CSS also uses these nested attributes. Let's take a look using our element inspection tools. Because you are likely still on the Fairphone site, let's take a look at some of the CSS on the page. When we highlight an element in our bottom toolbar, we see some text displayed next to the corresponding element on the page (Figure 11-9).

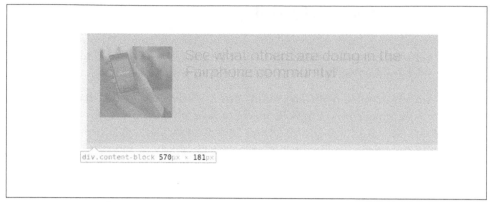

Figure 11-9. Introduction to CSS

In this case, we already know what div means, but what is content-block? Let's take a look at the HTML, using our inspection techniques (right-click on the element on the page and select "Inspect element").

We see content-block is the CSS class (as shown in Figure 11-10 in the nested attribute class="content-block"). It's defined in the opening div tag, and that div holds all of the other child tags. Speaking of CSS classes, how many classes can you see just on this section of the page? There are plenty!

```
▶ <header role="navigation">…</header>
▼ <div id="weAreFairphone">
  ▼ <div class="container content">
      ::before
    ▼ <div class="topContent">
      ▶ <div class="row">…</div>
      ▼ <div class="row movement-header">
          ::before
        ▼ <div class="content-block">     ⬉
          ▼ <div class="incentive">
              ::before
            ▼ <div class="row">
                ::before
              ▼ <div class="col-sm-3">
                ▼ <div class="image">
                    <img src="http://www.fairphone.com/wp-content/uploads/2014/09/social-mc
                  </div>
                </div>
              ▶ <div class="col-sm-9">…</div>
                ::after
              </div>
```

Figure 11-10. CSS class

Similar to classes, there are also CSS IDs. Let's find one (shown in Figure 11-11) and see how it looks different from classes.

```
 ▶ <header role="navigation">…</header>
 ▼ <div id="weAreFairphone">
   ▼ <div class="container content">
       ::before
     ▼ <div class="topContent">
       ▶ <div class="row">…</div>
       ▼ <div class="row movement-header">
           ::before
         ▼ <div class="content-block">
           ▼ <div class="incentive">
               ::before
             ▼ <div class="row">
                 ::before
               ▼ <div class="col-sm-3">
                 ▼ <div class="image">
                     <img src="http://www.fairphone.com/wp-content/uploads/
                     </div>
                   </div>
               ▶ <div                                div#weAreFairphone
 ...   div#weAreFairphone   div.container.content   div.topContent   div.row.movement-header
```

Figure 11-11. CSS ID

The HTML looks very similar, but the notation in our navigation uses a hash or
pound sign. The # is a proper CSS selector for IDs. With classes, we use . (as shown
in div.content-block).

 CSS structure and syntax state that ids should be unique, but you
can have many elements with the same class. Pages don't always
follow this structure, but it's noteworthy. A CSS id has a greater
specificity than a class. Some elements have more than one class
so they can have many styles applied to them.

Using our right-click menu, it's fairly easy to copy CSS selectors from the page. If you
already know CSS, this knowledge will help with your web scraping. If you don't
know much about CSS but would like to explore it further, take a look at Codecademy's introduction to CSS course (*http://bit.ly/css_codecademy*) or walk through the
Mozilla Developer Network's reference and tutorial (*https://developer.mozilla.org/en-
US/docs/Web/CSS*).

Now we have a better grip on CSS and how it styles the page; but what, you may ask,
does CSS have to do with the browser console? Good question! Let's review some
jQuery and JavaScript basics so we can see how CSS relates to interacting with content on the web page.

jQuery and JavaScript

The evolution of JavaScript and jQuery is a much longer story than HTML and CSS,
in part because JavaScript developed without a whole lot of standards for quite a long
time. In one sense, JavaScript was (and on some level still is) the Wild West of the
website landscape.

Although JavaScript has changed quite a bit in the past 10 years, decade-old scripts can often still run on quite a few browsers, meaning the push to standardize exactly how to write JavaScript and what things are disallowed has been a bit slower than for HTML and CSS.

JavaScript is *not* markup; it's a scripting language. Because Python is also a scripting language, you can apply some of the things you've learned—functions, objects and classes, methods—to your understanding of JavaScript. As with Python, there are extra libraries and packages to help you write clean, simple, and efficient JavaScript code that can be understood by browsers and humans.

jQuery (*https://jquery.com/*) is a JavaScript library used by many large websites to make JavaScript easier to read and simpler to write, while still allowing browsers (and their varied JavaScript engines) to parse the scripts.

 Started back in 2005–2006, jQuery introduced ideas to simplify and standardize JavaScript and give JavaScript developers tools so they don't have to write all their code from scratch. jQuery really pushed JavaScript development forward, creating a more object-oriented approach with powerful and easy-to-interpret methods and a closer link to CSS rules when selecting page elements.

Since jQuery was developed, JavaScript and CSS have had a much closer relationship, and many newer JavaScript frameworks build on this object-oriented approach. If a site is running jQuery, it's easy to interact with elements on the page using their CSS identifiers. Say we want to grab content from the content-block class we were taking a look at on the #WeAreFairphone page (Figure 11-12). How can we do that using our JavaScript console?

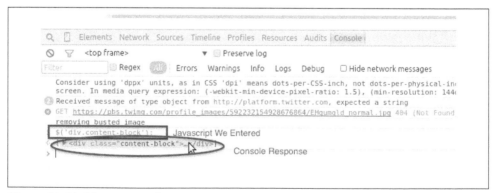

Figure 11-12. jQuery console

Since the site is running JQuery, we simply type the following code onto our first line in the Console tab:

```
$('div.content-block');
```

When we hit Enter, the console responds with the element. Click on the response in the console and you will see subelements and children of that element. We can use our CSS selectors with some jQuery basics (e.g., $(elem);) to select other elements on the page. Using the $ and parentheses tells jQuery we are looking for an element that matches the selector we pass in a string inside the parentheses.

Can you use the console to select the div with the ID weAreFairphone? Can you select only the anchor (a) tags on the page? Try it out in your console. The console and jQuery give us an easy way to use CSS selectors or tag names to interact with the actual elements on the page and pull content from those elements. But what does this have to do with Python?

Because jQuery changed the way people view the usefulness of CSS selectors, Python scraping libraries now use these same selectors to traverse and find elements in web pages. In the same way you can use a simple jQuery selector in your browser console, you can use it in your Python scraper code. If you are interested in learning more jQuery, we recommend visting the jQuery Learning Center (*https://learn.jquery.com/*) or taking the courses at Codecademy (*http://www.codecademy.com/en/tracks/jquery*) or Code School (*https://www.codeschool.com/courses/try-jquery*).

If you come across a site that doesn't use jQuery, then jQuery won't work in your console. To select elements by class using only JavaScript, run:

```
document.getElementsByClassName('content-block');
```

You should see the same div and be able to navigate the same way in your console. Now you know a little about the tools at our disposal, so let's take a closer look at how to determine the best way to scrape the page for interesting content. First, we will take a look at how to investigate all parts of the page.

In-Depth Analysis of a Page

One great way to go about developing a web scraper is to first play around with the content in your browser. Begin by selecting the content you are most interested in and viewing it in your browser's Inspection or DOM tab. How is the content formed? Where are the parent nodes? Is the content wrapped in many elements, or just a few?

 Before scraping a page, always check if you *can* scrape the page by looking at restrictions on the content and the site's *robots.txt* file. You can find the file by typing the domain name and then */robots.txt* (e.g., *http://oreilly.com/robots.txt*).

Then, move on to the Network and/or Timeline tab (see Figure 11-6). What does the first page load look like? Is JSON used in the page load, and if so what do those files look like? Is most of the content loaded after the initial request? All of these answers can help you determine what type of scraper to use and how challenging it will be to scrape the page.

Next, open up your Console tab. Try using some of the information from your inspection to interact with the elements containing important content. How easy is it to write a jQuery selector for that content? How reliably does your selector perform across the entire domain? Can you open a similar page, use that selector, and get similar results?

If your content is easy to interact with in a JavaScript console using jQuery or JavaScript, it's likely going to be just as easy with Python. If it's difficult to select an element with jQuery or if what works on one page doesn't work on another similar page, it's likely going to be more difficult in Python as well.

There is rarely a page on the Web that can't be properly parsed using the Python tools at your disposal. We'll teach you some tricks for messy pages, inline JavaScript, poorly formatted selectors, and all of the awful choices you can find in code across the World Wide Web, and outline some best practices along the way. To begin, we'll take a look at loading and reading a web page.

Getting Pages: How to Request on the Internet

The first step of any web scraper is…(drumroll)…connecting to the Web. Let's go over some basics of how this works.

When you open up a browser and type in a site name or search term(s) and hit Enter, you are making a *request*. Most often, this is an HTTP (HyperText Transfer Protocol) request (or HTTPS—the secure version). You are likely making a GET request, which is one of many *request methods* (*http://bit.ly/http_request_methods*) used on the Internet. Your browser handles all of this for you, along with parsing what you typed to determine whether you are requesting a website or a search term. Depending on what it determines, it will send you to either the search results or the website you were requesting.

Let's take a look at the built-in Python libraries for URL requests: urllib (*https://docs.python.org/2/library/urllib.html*) and urllib2 (*https://docs.python.org/2/library/urllib2.html*). These are Python's two standard libraries for URL requests. Using urllib2 is a good idea, but there are a few useful methods in urllib. Take a look:

```
import urllib
import urllib2

google = urllib2.urlopen('http://google.com') ❶

google = google.read() ❷

print google[:200] ❸

url = 'http://google.com?q='
url_with_query = url + urllib.quote_plus('python web scraping') ❹

web_search = urllib2.urlopen(url_with_query)
web_search = web_search.read()

print web_search[:200]
```

❶ Uses the `urlopen` method to open the request. This returns a buffer, where you can read the contents of the web page.

❷ Reads the contents of the entire page into the `google` variable.

❸ Prints the first 200 characters so we can see the beginning of the web page.

❹ Uses the `quote_plus` method to escape strings with plus signs. This is useful when crafting website query strings—we want to search Google for web results, and we know Google expects a query string with plus signs between the words.

See? It's pretty easy to reach out to a URL, or a service (e.g., Google Search), receive a response, and read that response. `urllib` and `urllib2` both have some extra request methods and the ability to add headers, send basic authentication, and assemble more complicated requests.

Depending on the complexities of your request, you can also use the `requests` library (*http://docs.python-requests.org/en/latest/*). `requests` uses `urllib` and `urllib2` and makes the complex requests easier to format and send. If you need to format a complicated post of a file (*http://bit.ly/complicated_post_requests*) or see what cookies you have in your session (*http://bit.ly/quickstart_cookies*) or check the response status code (*http://bit.ly/response_status_codes*), `requests` is a great option.

 As we reviewed in our Network (or Timeline) tab, you will sometimes find pages utilizing specific HTTP headers (*http://en.wikipedia.org/wiki/List_of_HTTP_header_fields*), cookies or other authentication methods. You can send these along with your request using `urllib2`, `urllib`, or the `requests` library.

Let's take a look at some of the `requests` tools in action:

```
import requests

google = requests.get('http://google.com')  ❶

print google.status_code  ❷

print google.content[:200]

print google.headers  ❸

print google.cookies.items()  ❹
```

❶ Calls the `requests` library's `get` method to send a GET request to the URL.

❷ Calls the `status_code` attribute to make sure we have a 200 response (properly completed request). If we don't have a 200, we could decide to operate our script logic differently.

❸ Checks the response's `headers` attribute to see what headers Google sends back. We can see the `headers` attribute is a dictionary.

❹ Reads the cookies Google sends in a response using the `cookies` attribute and calls the `items` method on that dictionary to show the key/value pairs.

Using the `requests` library, we can make different code decisions based on the response and its attributes. It's easy to use and has great documentation. Whether you use `urllib` or `requests`, you can make simple and complex requests with only a few lines of Python. We now know the basics of requesting a web page, so we can start parsing responses. We'll first learn about *Beautiful Soup* (*http://bit.ly/beauti ful_soup_docs*), a simple Python web page parser.

Reading a Web Page with Beautiful Soup

Beautiful Soup is one of the most popular and simple libraries for Python web scraping. Depending on your needs, it may provide everything you're looking for in a web scraper. It is simple, straightforward, and fairly easy to learn. Let's take a look at parsing a page using Beautiful Soup. First, install the library using pip (we use `beauti fulsoup4` as the previous version is no longer being supported and developed):

```
pip install beautifulsoup4
```

Let's take another look at one of the simple pages we inspected earlier, the Enough Project's Take Action page (*http://www.enoughproject.org/take_action*). We want to see if we can properly parse all of the calls to action on the page and save them. Here's how to import the page into Beautiful Soup so we can start reading it:

```
from bs4 import BeautifulSoup ❶
import requests

page = requests.get('http://www.enoughproject.org/take_action') ❷

bs = BeautifulSoup(page.content) ❸

print bs.title

print bs.find_all('a') ❹

print bs.find_all('p')
```

❶ First, we import the parser directly from the beautifulsoup4 library.

❷ Using the requests library to grab the content of the page, this line assigns the response (and its content) to the page variable.

❸ To start parsing with Beautiful Soup, this line passes the HTML of the page into the BeautifulSoup class. We can grab the response's page source using the content attribute.

❹ Once we have parsed the page object, we can use its attributes and methods. This line asks Beautiful Soup to find all a tags (or links) on the page.

We can open a page, read the response into a Beautiful Soup object, and use the attributes of that object to see the title, all of the paragraphs on the page, and all of the links on the page.

Because we've learned about family relationships in HTML, let's take a look at some relationships on the page:

```
header_children = [c for c in bs.head.children] ❶

print header_children

navigation_bar = bs.find(id="globalNavigation") ❷

for d in navigation_bar.descendants: ❸
    print d

for s in d.previous_siblings: ❹
    print s
```

❶ We use a list comprehension to create a list of all of the children from the header of the page. By stringing together the Beautiful Soup page object along with .head, which calls the head of the page, and then .children, we can view all of the nodes contained in the header. If we wanted to, we could use this to parse the header's meta content, including the page description.

❷ If you inspect the page using the developer tools, you'll see the navigation bar is defined by using a CSS selector ID of `globalNavigation`. This line uses the page object's `find` method, passes an ID, and locates the navigation bar.

❸ We iterate over the descendants of the navigation bar using the navigation bar's `descendants` method.

❹ With the final descendant from our navigation bar, this line uses `.previous_sib lings` to iterate over the siblings of our navigation elements.

The family trees let us navigate using the built-in attributes and methods in the Beautiful Soup library's `page` class. As we can see from our header and navigation bar examples, it's easy to select an area of the page and navigate the children, descendants, or siblings. Beautiful Soup's syntax is very simple and chains together elements and their attributes (like `.head.children`). With this in mind, let's focus on the main sections of the page and see if we can pull out some of the content we may be interested in viewing.

If we inspect the page using our developer tools, we notice a few things. First, it looks like each of the action items are located in a `views-row` div. These `divs` have many different classes, but they *all* have the `views-row` class. It's a good place to start parsing them. The headline is located in an h2 tag and the link is also in that h2 tag, inside an anchor tag. The calls to action are in paragraphs in `divs` that are children of the `views-row` div. We can now parse the content using Beautiful Soup.

First, we want to find the pieces of content using what we know about Beautiful Soup and what we understand about the page structure and how to navigate it. Here's how to do that:

```
from bs4 import BeautifulSoup
import requests

page = requests.get('http://www.enoughproject.org/take_action')

bs = BeautifulSoup(page.content)

ta_divs = bs.find_all("div", class_="views-row") ❶

print len(ta_divs) ❷

for ta in ta_divs:
    title = ta.h2 ❸
    link = ta.a
```

```
about = ta.find_all('p')  ❹
print title, link, about
```

❶ Uses Beautiful Soup to find and return all of the divs with a class containing the string views-row.

❷ Prints to check if we have the same number here as the number of rows of stories we can see on the website, indicating we've properly matched our rows.

❸ Iterates over the rows and grabs the tags we want based on our page investigation. The title is in an h2 tag, and it's the only h2 tag in the row. The link is the first anchor tag.

❹ Matches all paragraph tags to get the text, as we're not sure how many there are per row. Because we use the .find_all method, Beautiful Soup returns a list rather than the first matching element.

You should see something similar to:

```
<h2><a href="https://ssl1.americanprogress.org/o/507/p/dia/action3/common/public/
?action_KEY=391">South Sudan: On August 17th, Implement "Plan B" </a></h2> <a
href="https://ssl1.americanprogress.org/o/507/p/dia/action3/common/public/
?action_KEY=391">South Sudan: On August 17th, Implement "Plan B" </a>
[<p>During President Obama's recent trip to Africa, the international community
set a deadline of August 17 for a peace deal to be signed by South Sudan's
warring parties.....]
```

The content may change as the site is updated, but you should see an h2 element, then an anchor (a) element, and then a list of paragraphs for each node.The current output is messy—not only because we are using a print, but also because Beautiful Soup prints out the entire element and its contents. Instead of the entire element, we'd like to hone in on the essential parts, namely the title text, link hrefs, and paragraph text. We can use Beautiful Soup to take a closer look at these pieces of data:

```
all_data = []

for ta in ta_divs:
    data_dict = {}
    data_dict['title'] = ta.h2.get_text()  ❶
    data_dict['link'] = ta.a.get('href')  ❷
    data_dict['about'] = [p.get_text() for p in ta.find_all('p')]  ❸
    all_data.append(data_dict)

print all_data
```

❶ We use the get_text method to extract all strings from the HTML element. This gives us the title text.

❷ To get an attribute of an element, we use the get method. When we see `<a href="http://foo.com">Foo</a>` and we want to extract the link, we can call `.get("href")` to return the href value (i.e., foo.com).

❸ To extract the paragraph text, we use the get_text method and iterate over the paragraphs returned by the find_all method. This line uses list comprehension to compile a list of strings with the call to action content.

Now the data and output show a more organized format. We have a list of all the data in our all_data variable. Each of our data entries is now in its own dictionary with matching keys. We have scraped the data from the page in a cleaner way using some new methods (get and get_text), and the data now resides in data dictionaries. Our code is more clear and precise, and we can make it clearer by adding helper functions (like we covered in Chapter 8).

In addition, we could automate the script to check if there are new calls to action. If we saved our data to SQLite and used it for a monthly review of labor practices in the Congo, we could automate our reporting. With each new report, we could extract this data and raise more interest in fighting conflict mining and child labor.

Beautiful Soup is an easy-to-use tool, and the documentation (*http://bit.ly/beauti ful_soup_docs*) is rife with examples of how to use the many other methods available. The library is great for beginners and has many simple functions; however, compared with some other Python libraries, it's oversimplified.

Because Beautiful Soup's parsing is regex-based, it's great to use with really broken pages lacking proper tag structure. But if you're going to traverse more complicated pages, or you'd like your scraper to run faster and navigate pages quickly, there are far more advanced Python libraries you can use. Let's take a look at a favorite library for many talented web scraper developers: lxml.

Reading a Web Page with LXML

One of the more advanced web scrapers (and one that other advanced tools use as a parser) is lxml (*http://lxml.de/*). It's incredibly powerful and fast, with a lot of great features, including the ability to generate HTML and XML and clean up poorly written pages. Additionally, it has a variety of tools for traversing the DOM and family relationships.

Let's take a quick look at the main lxml features we'll use for web scraping by rewriting the Beautiful Soup code to use lxml:

```
from lxml import html

page = html.parse('http://www.enoughproject.org/take_action') ➊
root = page.getroot() ➋

ta_divs = root.cssselect('div.views-row') ➌

print ta_divs

all_data = []

for ta in ta_divs:
    data_dict = {}
    title = ta.cssselect('h2')[0] ➍
    data_dict['title'] = title.text_content() ➎
    data_dict['link'] = title.find('a').get('href') ➏
    data_dict['about'] = [p.text_content() for p in ta.cssselect('p')] ➐
    all_data.append(data_dict)

print all_data
```

➊ Here we use lxml's parsing method, which can parse from a filename, an open buffer, or a valid URL. It returns an `etree` object.

➋ Because `etree` objects have far fewer possible methods and attributes than HTML element objects, this line accesses the root (top of the page and HTML) element. The root contains all of the possible branches (children) and twigs (descendants) within reach. From this root we can parse down to each link or paragraph and back up to the `head` or `body` tags of the entire page.

➌ Using the root element, this line finds all of the `div`s with class `views-row`. It uses the `cssselect` method with a CSS selector string and returns a list of matching elements.

❹ To grab the titles, we use `cssselect` to find the h2 tag. This line selects the first element of that list. `cssselect` returns a list of all matches, but we only want the first match.

❺ Similar to Beautiful Soup's `get_text` method, `text_content` returns text from within the tag (and any child tags) for `lxml` HTML element objects.

❻ Here we use chained methods to get the anchor tag from the `title` element and pull the `href` attribute from the anchor tag. This returns only the value of that attribute, similar to Beautiful Soup's `get` method.

❼ We use list comprehension to pull out text content from each paragraph in the Take Action `div` in order to get the full text.

You should see the same data extracted as before, when we were using Beautiful Soup. What looks different is the syntax and the way the page is loaded. While Beautiful Soup uses regex to parse the document as a large string, `lxml` uses Python and C libraries to recognize page structure and traverse it in a more object-oriented way. `lxml` looks at the structure of all of the tags and (depending on your computer and how you installed it) uses the fastest method to parse the tree and return data in an `etree` object.

We can use the `etree` object itself, or we can call `getroot`, which will return the highest element of the tree—normally `html`. With this element, we can use many different methods and attributes to read and parse the rest of the page. Our solution highlights one way: using the `cssselect` method. This method takes CSS selector strings (similar to our jQuery examples) and uses those strings to identify DOM elements.

`lxml` also has `find` and `findall` methods. What are the main differences between `find` and `cssselect`? Let's take a look at some examples:

```
print root.find('div') ❶

print root.find('head')

print root.find('head').findall('script') ❷

print root.cssselect('div') ❸

print root.cssselect('head script') ❹
```

❶ Uses `find` on the root element to find `divs`, which returns empty. From inspecting with our browser, we know the page is full of `divs`!

❷ Uses the `find` method to look at the header tag and the `findall` method to locate the script elements in the header section.

❸ Uses `cssselect` instead of `find` and properly locates all `divs` contained in the document. They are returned as a large list.

❹ Using `cssselect`, locates the script tags within the header section by nesting CSS selectors. Using `head script` returns the same list as chaining together our `find` commands from the root.

So, `find` and `cssselect` operate very differently. `find` utilizes the DOM to traverse the elements and find them based on ancestry and familial relationships, whereas the `cssselect` method employs CSS selectors to find all possible matches within the page or the element's descendants, much like jQuery.

 Depending on your needs, `find` or `cssselect` may be more useful. If the page is well organized with CSS classes, IDs and other identifiers, `cssselect` is a great choice. But if the page is disorganized or doesn't use many of those identifiers, traversing the DOM can help you identify the location of the content via ancestry.

We want to explore other useful `lxml` methods. As you learn and grow as a developer, you might feel the need to express your progress through emojis. For that reason, let's write a quick parser of an emoji cheat sheet (*http://www.emoji-cheat-sheet.com/*) to keep an up-to-date list of emojis you can use on Basecamp, GitHub and many other tech-related sites. Here's how to do that:

```
from lxml import html
import requests

resp = requests.get('http://www.emoji-cheat-sheet.com/')
page = html.document_fromstring(resp.content) ❶

body = page.find('body')
top_header = body.find('h2') ❷

print top_header.text

headers_and_lists = [sib for sib in top_header.itersiblings()] ❸

print headers_and_lists

proper_headers_and_lists = [s for s in top_header.itersiblings() if
                            s.tag in ['ul', 'h2', 'h3']] ❹

print proper_headers_and_lists
```

❶ This code pulls in the body of the HTML document using the `requests` library and then uses the `html` module's `document_fromstring` method to parse the data into an HTML element.

❷ By viewing the page structure, we see it's a series of headers with matching lists. This line locates the first header so we can use familial relationships to find the other useful sections.

❸ This line uses list comprehension along with the `itersiblings` method, which returns an iterator, to view all of the siblings.

❹ The previous `print` shows our initial `itersiblings` list comprehension returned more data than we needed, including some of the lower sections on the page with `div` and `script` elements. Using page inspection, we determined the only tags we want are `ul`, `h2`, and `h3`. This line uses list comprehension with an `if` to ensure we return only our target content.

The `itersiblings` method and `tag` attributes help us easily locate the content we want to select and parse. In this example, we haven't used any CSS selectors. We know our code won't break if a new section is added, as long as the page keeps the content in the header and list tags.

 Why would we want to build a parser using only HTML elements? What are the advantages of not relying on CSS classes? If a site's developers change its design or make mobile-friendly updates, it's likely they will use CSS and JavaScript to do so, rather than rewriting the page structure. If you can use basic page structure to power your scrapers, they will likely have longer lives and greater long-term success than those using CSS.

In addition to `itersiblings`, `lxml` objects can iterate over children, descendants, and ancestors. Using these methods to traverse the DOM is a great way to get acquainted with how the page is organized and write longer-lasting code. You can also use family relationships to write meaningful XPath—a structured pattern for XML-based documents (like HTML). Although XPath is not the easiest way to parse a web page, it's a fast, efficient, and *nearly* foolproof way to do so.

A Case for XPath

Although using CSS selectors is an easy way to find elements and content on the page, we would also recommend you learn and use XPath (*https://en.wikipedia.org/wiki/XPath*). XPath is a markup pattern selector combining the power of CSS selectors with the ability to traverse the DOM. Understanding XPath is a great way to learn web scraping and website structure. With XPath, you can access content that is not easily read using only CSS selectors.

 XPath can be used with all of the major web scraping libraries and is much faster than most other ways to identify and interact with content on the page. In fact, most of the selector methods you use to interact with the page are translated into XPath within the libraries themselves.

To practice XPath, you need not look further than your browser's tools. Many browsers come with the ability to see and copy XPath elements in the DOM. Microsoft also has a great writeup on XPath (*http://bit.ly/xpath_examples*), and there are many great tools and examples on the Mozilla Developer Network (*http://bit.ly/mdn_xpath*) for furthering your XPath education.

XPath follows a specific syntax to define the type of element, where it might be found in the DOM, and what attributes it might have. Table 11-2 reviews some of the XPath syntax patterns we can use in our web-scraping code.

Table 11-2. XPath syntax

Expression	Description	Example
//node_name	Selects all nodes with matching node_name from the document	//div (select all div items in the document)
/node_name	Selects all nodes with matching node_name from the current or preceding element	//div/ul (select ul item(s) located in any div)
@attr	Selects an attribute of an element	//div/ul/@class (select the class of the ul item(s) in any div)
../	Selects the parent element	//ul/../ (select the parent elements of all ul elements)
[@attr="attr_value"]	Selects elements with specific attributes	//div[@id="mylists"] (select the div that has the ID "mylists")
text()	Selects text from a node or element	//div[@id="mylists"]/ul/li/text() (select text from the elements in the list in the div with ID "mylists")

Expression	Description	Example
`contains(@attr, "value")`	Selects elements with attributes containing particular values	`//div[contains(@id, "list")]` (select all `div` items that have "list" in the ID)
`*`	Wildcard character	`//div/ul/li/*` (select all descendants that are in the list items in a `ul` in any `div`)
`[1,2,3…]`, `[last()]`, or `[first()]`	Selects elements by the order that they appear in the node	`//div/ul/li[3]` (select the third list item in a `ul` in any `div`)

There are many more expressions, but these should get us started. Let's investigate how to parse familial relationships between HTML elements using XPath with our super-awesome HTML page we created earlier in this chapter. To follow along, you might want to pull it up in your browser from the book's code repository (*https:// github.com/jackiekazil/data-wrangling*) (file: *awesome_page.html*).

OK, say we want to select the links in our footer section. We can see by using our "Inspect element" option (Figure 11-13) that the bottom bar shows a list of the elements and their ancestors. The anchor links are inside `li` tags inside a `ul` inside a `div` with a CSS `id` inside the `footer` inside the body inside the `html` tag (whew! thought I was going to run out of breath there!).

Figure 11-13. Finding elements on the page

How could we write the XPath to select this? Well, there are many ways. Let's start with a fairly obvious path, and use the `div` with the CSS `id` to write the XPath. We could select that `div` by using the XPath syntax we already know:

```
'//div[@id="bottom_nav"]'
```

We can test this using our browser's JavaScript console. To test XPath in your console, simply put it inside $x();, which is a jQuery console implementation for browsing the page with XPath. Let's take a look in our console (see Figure 11-14).[1]

Figure 11-14. Using the console to write XPath

We know we have valid XPath for selecting the navigation because our console returned an object (similar to our jQuery selectors). But what we really want are the links. Let's take a look at how we might navigate to them from this div. We know they are descendants, so let's write out the family relationship:

```
'//div[@id="bottom_nav"]/ul/li/a'
```

Here we are saying we want any divs with id bottom_nav, with an unordered list inside of them, and then the list items inside of those matches, and then the anchor tags inside of those matches. Let's try this again in our console (Figure 11-15).

We can see from the output in our console that we have selected those three links. Now, we want to grab just the web addresses themselves. We know every anchor tag has an href attribute. Let's use our XPath to write a selector for just those attributes:

```
'//div[@id="bottom_nav"]/ul/li/a/@href'
```

When we run that selector in our console, we see we've properly selected only the web addresses of our footer links (see Figure 11-16).

---

1 If you want to use XPath on a site that doesn't use JQuery, you'll need to use different syntax as documented by Mozilla (*http://bit.ly/xpath_in_js*). The syntax for this element would be document.evaluate('//div[@id="bottom_nav"]', document);.

Figure 11-15. XPath subelements

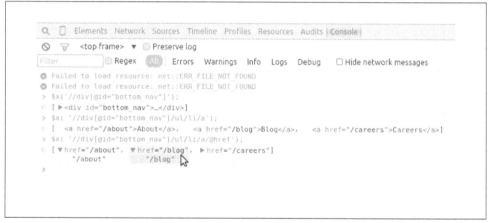

Figure 11-16. Finding XPath attributes

Knowing the page structure can help us get at content we might have trouble accessing otherwise by using XPath expressions instead.

With the power and speed of XPath comes a learning curve. For one, if there are spaces in the classes or IDs for the page you are interacting with, you should use the `contains` pattern rather than `=`. Elements can have more than one class, and XPath assumes you are including the entire class string; using `contains` helps you find any element with that substring.

Finding parent elements of elements you are interested in can also be useful. Say you are interested in a list of items on the page. Let's also say you can easily locate one or more of the list items using a CSS class or a piece of text contained in the list. You can use that information to build an XPath selector locating that element and then find the parent element, giving you access to the entire list. We'll be exploring these types of XPath selectors in "Building a Spider with Scrapy" on page 336, as Scrapy utilizes XPath for speedy parsing.

One reason to utilize XPath is you will find the CSS classes via CSS selectors might not always properly select your element, especially when you are using several different drivers to process the page (e.g., Selenium with many browsers). XPath is inherently more specific, making it a more trustworthy way to parse pages properly.

If you are scraping a site for a long period of time and want to reuse the same code, XPath will be less prone to break over time due to small code changes and development on the site. It's a lot more common for someone to rewrite a few CSS classes or styles than the entire site and page structure. For this reason, XPath is a safer bet than using CSS (although not foolproof!).

Now that you've learned some XPath, we can try rewriting the emoji processor using XPath syntax to properly store all of the emojis and headers for each section. Here's what that looks like:

```
from lxml import html

page = html.parse('http://www.emoji-cheat-sheet.com/')

proper_headers = page.xpath('//h2|//h3') ❶
proper_lists = page.xpath('//ul') ❷

all_emoji = []

for header, list_cont in zip(proper_headers, proper_lists): ❸
    section = header.text
    for li in list_cont.getchildren(): ❹
        emoji_dict = {}
        spans = li.xpath('div/span') ❺
        if len(spans):
            link = spans[0].get('data-src') ❻
            if link:
                emoji_dict['emoji_link'] = li.base_url + link ❼
            else:
                emoji_dict['emoji_link'] = None
            emoji_dict['emoji_handle'] = spans[1].text_content() ❽
        else:
            emoji_dict['emoji_link'] = None
            emoji_dict['emoji_handle'] = li.xpath('div')[0].text_content() ❾
        emoji_dict['section'] = section
        all_emoji.append(emoji_dict)

print all_emoji
```

❶ This line finds the headers related to the emoji content. It uses XPath to grab all of the h2 and h3 elements.

➋ Each of the headers located has a ul element to match. This line gathers all the ul elements in the entire document.

➌ We use the zip method to zip headers with their appropriate lists, which returns a list of tuples. This line then unpacks those tuples, using a for loop to pull each part (header and list content) into separate variables to use in the for loop.

➍ This code iterates through the ul element's children (li elements holding the emoji information).

➎ From page inspection, we know most li elements have a div containing two span elements. These spans contain the image links for the emojis and the text needed to evoke the emojis on the service. This line uses the XPath div/span to return any span elements in a child div element.

➏ To find a link for each element, this line calls the data-src attribute of the first span. If the link variable is None, the code sets the emoji_link attribute in our data dictionary to None.

➐ Because data-src holds a relative URL, this line uses the base_url attribute to make a full absolute URL.

➑ In order to get the handle, or what text is needed to evoke the emoji, this line grabs the second span's text. Unlike with the logic for links, we don't need to test whether this exists or not, because every emoji has a handle.

➒ For the part of the site including Basecamp sounds, there is one div for each list item (you can easily see this by inspecting the page using your browser's developer tools). This code selects the div and grabs the text content from it. Because this code is in the else block, we know these are only the sound files because they do not use spans.

By rewriting our emoji code to use XPath relationships, we found the last block of tags are sounds and the data in them is stored differently. Instead of having a link in a span, there is only a div with the text to evoke the sound. If we only wanted emoji links, we could skip adding them to our list item iteration. Depending on what data you are interested in, your code will vary greatly, but you can always easily utilize if...else logic to specify what content you're after.

In less than 30 lines of code we have created a scraper to request the page, parse it by traversing the DOM relationships with XPath, and grab the necessary content using the appropriate attribute or text content. It's a fairly resilient block of code, and if the authors of the page add more sections of data, as long as the structure doesn't change drastically, our parser will continue to pull content from the page and we'll have tons of emojis at our fingertips!

There are many other useful lxml functions. We've summarized a few and their uses in Table 11-3.

Table 11-3. LXML features

Method or attribute name	Description	Documentation
clean_html	A function used to attempt to clean up poorly formed pages so they can be properly parsed	*http://lxml.de/lxmlhtml.html#cleaning-up-html*
iterlinks	An iterator to access every anchor tag on a page	*http://lxml.de/lxmlhtml.html#working-with-links*
[x.tag for x in root]	All etree elements can be used as simple iterators that support child element iteration	*http://lxml.de/api.html#iteration*
.nsmap	Provides easy access to namespaces, should you ever have the pleasure of working with them	*http://lxml.de/tutorial.html#namespaces*

You should now feel pretty confident investigating markup on web pages and deciphering how to extract content from a page using lxml, Beautiful Soup, and XPath. In the next chapter, we'll be moving on to other libraries you can use for different types of scraping, such as browser-based parsing and spidering.

Summary

You've learned a lot about web scraping. You should now feel comfortable writing a scraper in many formats. You know how to write jQuery, CSS, and XPath selectors and how to easily match content using your browser and Python.

You should also feel comfortable analyzing how a web page is built using your developer tools. You've sharpened your CSS and JavaScript skills, and you've learned how to write valid XPath to interact directly with the DOM tree.

Table 11-4 outlines the new concepts and libraries introduced in this chapter.

Table 11-4. New Python and programming concepts and libraries

Concept/Library	Purpose
robots.txt file usage, copyright and trademark investigation	From a site's *robots.txt* file as well as Terms of Service or other published legal warnings on the page, you can determine whether you can legally and ethically scrape site content.
Developer tools usage: Inspection/DOM	Used to investigate where on the page the content lies and how to best find it using your knowledge of page hierarchy and/or CSS rules.
Developer tools usage: Network	Used to investigate what calls the page makes to fully load. Some of these requests may point to APIs or other resources so you can easily ingest the data. Knowledge of how the page loads can help you determine whether to use a simple scraper or a browser-based one.
Developer tools usage: JavaScript Console	Used to investigate how to interact with the elements on the page using their CSS or XPath selectors.
`urllib` and `urllib2` stdlib libraries	Help you make simple HTTP requests to visit a web page and get the content via the Python standard library.
`requests` library	Helps you more easily make complex requests for pages, particularly those requiring extra headers, complex POST data, or authentication credentials.
`BeautifulSoup` library	Allows you to easily read and parse web pages. Great for exceptionally broken pages and initial web scraping.
`lxml` library	Allows you to parse pages easily, using DOM hierarchy and tools like XPath syntax.
XPath usage	Gives you the ability to write patterns and matches using regex and XPath syntax to quickly find and parse web page content.

In the next chapter, you'll be learning even more ways to scrape data from the Web.

Advanced Web Scraping: Screen Scrapers and Spiders

You've begun your web scraping skills development, learning how to decipher what, how, and where to scrape in Chapter 11. In this chapter, we'll take a look at more advanced scrapers, like browser-based scrapers and spiders to gather content.

We'll also learn about debugging common problems with advanced web scraping and cover some of the ethical questions presented when scraping the Web. To begin, we'll investigate browser-based web scraping: using a browser directly with Python to scrape content from the Web.

Browser-Based Parsing

Sometimes a site uses a lot of JavaScript or other post-page-load code to populate the pages with content. In these cases, it's almost impossible to use a normal web scraper to analyze the site. What you'll end up with is a very empty-looking page. You'll have the same problem if you want to interact with pages (i.e., if you need to click on a button or enter some search text). In either situation, you'll want to figure out how to *screen read* the page. Screen readers work by using a browser, opening the page, and reading and interacting with the page after it loads in the browser.

Screen readers are great for tasks performed by walking through a series of actions to get information. For this very reason, screen reader scripts are also an easy way to automate routine web tasks.

The most commonly used screen reading library in Python is Selenium (*http://bit.ly/selenium_intro*). Selenium is a Java program used to open up a browser and interact with web pages through screen reading. If you already know Java, you can use the Java IDE to interact with your browser. We will be using the Python bindings to interact with Selenium using Python.

Screen Reading with Selenium

Selenium is a powerful Java-based engine to interact directly with a website through any of the Selenium-supported browsers. It's a very popular framework for user testing, allowing companies to build tests for their sites. For our purposes, we will use Selenium to scrape a site we need to interact with or one where not all content is loaded on the first request (refer to our Figure 11-6 example, where most content is loaded after the initial request is complete). Let's take a look at that page and see if we can read it with Selenium.

First, we need to install Selenium (*http://bit.ly/selenium_install*) using `pip install`:

```
pip install selenium
```

Now, let's get started writing Selenium code. First, we need to open the browser. Selenium supports many different browsers, but ships with a built-in driver for Firefox. If you don't have Firefox installed, you can either install it, or install the Selenium driver for Chrome (*https://code.google.com/p/selenium/wiki/ChromeDriver*), Internet Explorer (*https://code.google.com/p/selenium/wiki/InternetExplorerDriver*), or Safari (*https://code.google.com/p/selenium/wiki/SafariDriver*). Let's see if we can open a web page using Selenium (in our examples, we'll be using Firefox, but it's very easy to switch and use a different driver):

```
from selenium import webdriver ❶

browser = webdriver.Firefox() ❷
browser.get('http://www.fairphone.com/we-are-fairphone/') ❸

browser.maximize_window() ❹
```

❶ Imports the `webdriver` module from Selenium. This module is used to call any installed drivers.

❷ Instantiates a Firefox browser object by using the `Firefox` class from the `web driver` module. This should open a new Firefox window on your computer.

❸ Accesses the URL we want to scrape by using the `get` method and passing a URL. The open browser should now start to load the page.

❹ Maximizes the open browser by using the `maximize_browser` method. This helps Selenium "see" more of the content.

We now have a browser object (variable `browser`) with a page loaded and ready. Let's see if we can interact with the elements on the page. If you use your browser's Inspection tab, you'll see the social media content bubbles are div elements with a class of content. Let's see if we can see them all using our new `browser` object:

```
content = browser.find_element_by_css_selector('div.content')  ❶

print content.text  ❷

all_bubbles = browser.find_elements_by_css_selector('div.content')  ❸

print len(all_bubbles)

for bubble in all_bubbles:  ❹
    print bubble.text
```

❶ The `browser` object has a function `find_element_by_css_selector` that uses CSS selectors to select HTML elements. This line of code selects the first div with class content, which returns the first match (an `HTMLElement` object).

❷ This line will print the text in that first match element. We expect to see the first chat bubble.

❸ This line uses the `find_elements_by_css_selector` method to pass a CSS selector and find all matches. This method returns a list of `HTMLElement` objects.

❹ We iterate over the list and print out the content for each.

Hmm, that's odd. It looks like there are only two matches for the elements we want to find (because we saw an output of 2 when we printed the length of `all_bubbles`), and yet we see plenty of content bubbles on the page. Let's take a deeper look at the HTML elements on the page and see if we can figure out why we aren't matching more elements (see Figure 12-1).

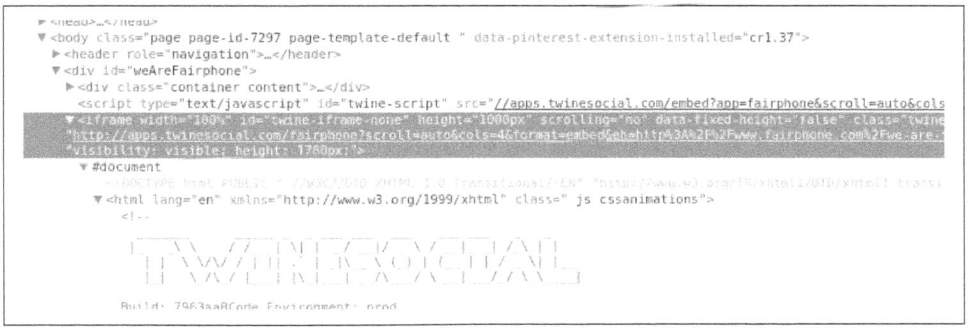

Figure 12-1. iframe

Aha! When we look at the parent element for our content, we see it is an `iframe` (*http://bit.ly/mdn_iframe*) in the middle of our page. An `iframe` (inline frame) is an HTML tag that embeds another DOM structure into the page, essentially allowing a page to load to another page inside itself. Our code will likely not be able to parse it, because parsers expect to traverse only *one* DOM. Let's see if we can get the `iframe` loaded into a new window, so we don't have to go through the pain of traversing two DOMs:

```
iframe = browser.find_element_by_xpath('//iframe')  ❶

new_url = iframe.get_attribute('src')  ❷

browser.get(new_url)  ❸
```

❶ Uses the `find_element_by_xpath` method, which returns the first element that matches an `iframe` tag

❷ Gets the `src` attribute, which should contain the URL to the page in the `iframe`

❸ Loads the `iframe`'s URL in our browser

We figured out how to load the content we wanted. Now we can see if we can load all of the content bubbles:

```
all_bubbles = browser.find_elements_by_css_selector('div.content')

for elem in all_bubbles:
    print elem.text
```

Now we have the bubble content—excellent! Let's collect some information: we'll want to retrieve the person's name, what content they shared, the photo if there is one, and the links to the original content.

In looking through the HTML on the page, it looks like for each content element we have `fullname` and `name` elements to identify the person, and a `twine-description` element with the text. We see there's a `picture` element, and a `when` element with the time data. The `when` element also has the original link. Let's break it down:

```
from selenium.common.exceptions import NoSuchElementException  ❶

all_data = []

for elem in all_bubbles:  ❷
    elem_dict = {}

    elem_dict['full_name'] = \
        elem.find_element_by_css_selector('div.fullname').text  ❸
    elem_dict['short_name'] = \
        elem.find_element_by_css_selector('div.name').text
```

```
elem_dict['text_content'] = \
    elem.find_element_by_css_selector('div.twine-description').text
elem_dict['timestamp'] = elem.find_element_by_css_selector('div.when').text
elem_dict['original_link'] = \
    elem.find_element_by_css_selector('div.when a').get_attribute('href')  ❹
try:
    elem_dict['picture'] = elem.find_element_by_css_selector(
            'div.picture img').get_attribute('src')  ❺
except NoSuchElementException:
    elem_dict['picture'] = None  ❻
all_data.append(elem_dict)
```

❶ This line imports `NoSuchElementException` from Selenium's exception classes. When using exception classes in a `try...except` block, make sure you import and use the library's exceptions to properly handle expected errors. We know not every item has a photo, and Selenium will throw this exception if it can't find the `picture` HTML element we are looking for, so we can use this exception to differentiate the bubbles with photos and those without.

❷ In our `for` loop, we iterate over the content bubbles. For each of these `elem` objects, we can find elements within them by traversing further down the tree.

❸ For each of our text elements, this line calls the `HTMLElement`'s `text` attribute, which strips away tags in the text and returns just the text content of that element.

❹ The `HTMLElement`'s `get_attribute` method expects a nested attribute and returns the value of that attribute. This line passes the `href` attribute to get the URL, using nested CSS to look for an anchor tag in a `div` element with a class of `when`.

❺ In a `try` block, this code looks for a photo in the `div`. If there isn't a photo, the next line catches the `NoSuchElementException` Selenium throws since there is no matching element.

❻ If we don't find a matching element, this line adds a `None` value. This ensures all items in our new list have a `picture` key.

We're running into a problem pretty early in our script. You should see an exception containing the following text:

```
Message: Unable to locate element:
  {"method":"css selector","selector":"div.when"}
```

This tells us there are some issues finding the `when` element. Let's take a closer look in our Inspection tab and see what's going on (see Figure 12-2).

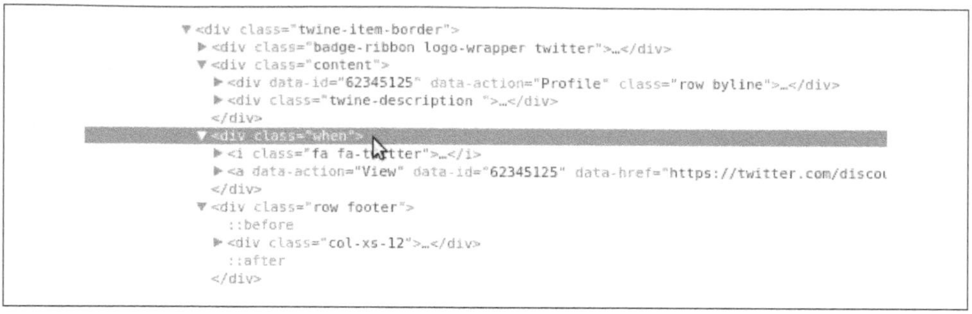

```
▼<div class="twine-item-border">
  ▶<div class="badge-ribbon logo-wrapper twitter">…</div>
  ▼<div class="content">
    ▶<div data-id="62345125" data-action="Profile" class="row byline">…</div>
    ▶<div class="twine-description ">…</div>
    </div>
    ▼<div class="when">
      ▶<i class="fa fa-twitter">…</i>
      ▶<a data-action="View" data-id="62345125" data-href="https://twitter.com/disco
      </div>
    ▼<div class="row footer">
      ::before
      ▶<div class="col-xs-12">…</div>
      ::after
      </div>
    </div>
```

Figure 12-2. Sibling divs

Upon closer inspection, we can see the content divs and when divs are actually siblings, not parent and child in the DOM structure. This presents a problem because we are iterating over only the content divs, not the parent div. If we take a closer look, we can see that the twine-item-border element is the parent of both the content and when elements. Using the code we have written, we can see if iterating over the parent works. You will need to change what we use for all_bubbles by loading the parent element, like so:

```
all_bubbles = browser.find_elements_by_css_selector('div.twine-item-border')
```

Rerun the previous code with that change. What happens? You will see more NoSuchElementException errors. Because we aren't sure every single element has the same attributes, let's assume they are all different and rewrite the code to account for exceptions:

```
from selenium.common.exceptions import NoSuchElementException

all_data = []
all_bubbles = browser.find_elements_by_css_selector(
    'div.twine-item-border')

for elem in all_bubbles:
    elem_dict = {'full_name': None,
                 'short_name': None,
                 'text_content': None,
                 'picture': None,
                 'timestamp': None,
                 'original_link': None,
                 } ❶
    content = elem.find_element_by_css_selector('div.content') ❷
    try:
        elem_dict['full_name'] = \
            content.find_element_by_css_selector('div.fullname').text
    except NoSuchElementException:
        pass ❸
    try:
        elem_dict['short_name'] = \
```

```
            content.find_element_by_css_selector('div.name').text
    except NoSuchElementException:
        pass
    try:
        elem_dict['text_content'] = \
            content.find_element_by_css_selector('div.twine-description').text
    except NoSuchElementException:
        pass
    try:
        elem_dict['timestamp'] = elem.find_element_by_css_selector(
            'div.when').text
    except NoSuchElementException:
        pass
    try:
        elem_dict['original_link'] = \
            elem.find_element_by_css_selector(
                'div.when a').get_attribute('href')
    except NoSuchElementException:
        pass
    try:
        elem_dict['picture'] = elem.find_element_by_css_selector(
            'div.picture img').get_attribute('src')
    except NoSuchElementException:
        pass
    all_data.append(elem_dict)
```

❶ For each iteration through our items, this line adds a new dictionary and sets all of the keys to None. This gives us a clean dictionary setup so every item has the same keys and we can add data to the keys as we discover it.

❷ We pull out the content div so we can select from that div. This makes our code more specific in case there are other divs with similar names.

❸ We use Python's pass (*http://bit.ly/pass_statements*) to move past exceptions. Because all of our keys are already set to None, we don't need to do anything here. Python's pass keeps the code moving through the exception so execution continues with the following code block.

Once you've collected the data in all_data, you can print it to have a look at what you've collected. Here is some example output (it's a social media timeline, so yours will look different than what's shown here):

```
[{'full_name': u'Stefan Brand',
  'original_link': None,
  'picture': u'https://pbs.twimg.com/media/COZlle9WoAE5pVL.jpg:large',
  'short_name': u'',
  'text_content': u'Simply @Fairphone :) #WeAreFairphone http://t.co/vUvKzjX2Bw',
  'timestamp': u'POSTED ABOUT 14 HOURS AGO'},
 {'full_name': None,
  'original_link': None,
```

```
 'picture': None,
 'short_name': u'',
 'text_content': None,
 'timestamp': None},
{'full_name': u'Sietse/MFR/Orphax',
 'original_link': None,
 'picture': None,
 'short_name': u'',
 'text_content': u'Me with my (temporary) Fairphone 2 test phone.
 # happytester #wearefairphone @ Fairphone instagram.com/p/7X-KXDQzXG/',
 'timestamp': u'POSTED ABOUT 17 HOURS AGO'},...]
```

The data looks to be in varied states of disarray. Our for loop is messy and hard to read and understand. Also, it seems like we could improve some of the ways we go about our data collection—our date objects are just strings, when they should probably be dates. We should play around with Selenium's ability to interact with the page, too, which may allow us to load more content.

We also need to debug errors we are seeing. We can't find the short name properly; our code seems to be returning an empty string. After some page investigation, it appears the name div is hidden. With Selenium, hidden elements often can't be read, so we'll need to use the innerHTML attribute of that element, which will return content inside the tags. We also notice the timestamp data is stored in the title attribute and the URL is actually stored in data-href, not the href attribute.

 Over time, it becomes easier to write scraper code that works on the first try. It also becomes easier to anticipate what might be troublesome. Investigating with your browser's developer tools and debugging with IPython lets you play around with the variables and test what might work.

On top of finding all of the data, we want to make sure our script is formed properly. We want to create functions and better abstract our data extraction. Instead of parsing the URL from the initial page, we should simplify our code and load the page directly. Through trial and error in our browser, we find we can remove the long query strings for the iframe URL (i.e., *?scroll=auto&cols=4&format=embed&eh=...*) and still load the whole page with the embedded content from social media. Let's take a look at the cleaned-up and simplified script:

```
from selenium.common.exceptions import NoSuchElementException, \
    WebDriverException
from selenium import webdriver


def find_text_element(html_element, element_css):  ❶
    try:
        return html_element.find_element_by_css_selector(element_css).text  ❷
```

```
        except NoSuchElementException:
            pass
        return None


    def find_attr_element(html_element, element_css, attr):  ❸
        try:
            return html_element.find_element_by_css_selector(
                element_css).get_attribute(attr)  ❹
        except NoSuchElementException:
            pass
        return None


    def get_browser():
        browser = webdriver.Firefox()
        return browser


    def main():
        browser = get_browser()
        browser.get('http://apps.twinesocial.com/fairphone')

        all_data = []
        browser.implicitly_wait(10)  ❺
        try:
            all_bubbles = browser.find_elements_by_css_selector(
                'div.twine-item-border')
        except WebDriverException:
            browser.implicitly_wait(5)
            all_bubbles = browser.find_elements_by_css_selector(
                'div.twine-item-border')
        for elem in all_bubbles:
            elem_dict = {}
            content = elem.find_element_by_css_selector('div.content')
            elem_dict['full_name'] = find_text_element(
                content, 'div.fullname')
            elem_dict['short_name'] = find_attr_element(
                content, 'div.name', 'innerHTML')
            elem_dict['text_content'] = find_text_element(
                content, 'div.twine-description')
            elem_dict['timestamp'] = find_attr_element(
                elem, 'div.when a abbr.timeago', 'title')  ❻
            elem_dict['original_link'] = find_attr_element(
                elem, 'div.when a', 'data-href')
            elem_dict['picture'] = find_attr_element(
                content, 'div.picture img', 'src')
            all_data.append(elem_dict)
        browser.quit()  ❼
        return all_data  ❽
```

```
if __name__ == '__main__':
    all_data = main()
    print all_data
```

❶ Creates a function to take an HTML element and CSS selector and return the text element. In our last code example, we had to repeat our code again and again; now we want to create a function so we can reuse it without needing to rewrite code throughout our script.

❷ Uses the abstracted function variables to return the text of the HTML element. If we don't find a match, returns None.

❸ Creates a function to find and return attributes, similar to our text element function. It requires the HTML element, the CSS selector, and the attribute we want to pull from the selector and returns the value for that selector or None.

❹ Uses the abstracted function variables to find the HTML element and return the attribute.

❺ Uses the Selenium browser class's implicitly_wait method, which takes as an argument the number of seconds you want the browser to implicitly wait before moving to the next line of code. This is a great method to use if you aren't sure the page will load immediately. There is a lot of great Selenium documentation on using implicit and explicit waits (*http://bit.ly/selenium_waits*).

❻ Passes CSS selectors to grab the title attribute of the abbr element located in an anchor tag inside the when div, in order to capture the timestamp data.

❼ Closes the browser using the quit method when we are done scraping our data.

❽ Returns the collected data. The __name__ == '__main__' block allows us to print the data when running from command line, or we can import the function into IPython and run main to return our data.

Try running the script from the command line or importing it into IPython and then running the main function. Did your data look more complete this time? You'll also notice we added another try...except block. We noticed that sometimes the interactions Selenium uses were interfering with the JavaScript on the page and made Selenium throw a WebDriverException. Allowing the page more time to load and trying again fixed the problem.

If you visit the URL in your browser, you can see you're able to load more data as you scroll down the page. With Selenium, we can do those things as well! Let's take a look at some of the other neat things Selenium can do. We can try searching Google for Python web scraping libraries and use Selenium to interact with the search results:

```python
from selenium import webdriver
from time import sleep


browser = webdriver.Firefox()
browser.get('http://google.com')

inputs = browser.find_elements_by_css_selector('form input')  ❶
for i in inputs:
    if i.is_displayed():  ❷
        search_bar = i  ❸
        break

search_bar.send_keys('web scraping with python')  ❹

search_button = browser.find_element_by_css_selector('form button')
search_button.click()  ❺

browser.implicitly_wait(10)
results = browser.find_elements_by_css_selector('div h3 a')  ❻

for r in results:
    action = webdriver.ActionChains(browser)  ❼
    action.move_to_element(r)  ❽
    action.perform()  ❾
    sleep(2)

browser.quit()
```

❶ We need to find an input. Google, like many sites, has inputs all over the place, but usually only one big search bar visible. This line locates all form inputs so we have a good starting batch.

❷ This line iterates over the inputs to see if they are hidden or displayed. If is_displayed returns True, we have a visible element. Otherwise, this loop will keep iterating.

❸ When a displayed input is found, we assign the value to the search_bar variable and break out of the loop. This will find the first visible input, which is probably the one we want.

❹ This line sends keys and strings to the selected element using the send_keys method (in this case, it sends keys to the search bar). It's like typing on your keyboard, but with Python!

❺ Selenium can also `click` on visible elements on the page. This line tells Selenium to click on the search form submit button to view our search results.

❻ To view all the search results, this line selects header elements in `div`s with a link, which is how Google result pages are structured.

❼ This code loops over each result, utilizing Selenium's ActionChains to formulate a series of actions, and tells the browser to perform those actions.

❽ This line uses the `move_to_element` method of the ActionChain, passing the element we want the browser to move to.

❾ This line calls `perform`, meaning the browser will move to highlight each search result. We used a `sleep`, which tells Python to wait a certain number of seconds (here, 2) before the next line executes, so your browser doesn't move so fast you miss the fun.

Voilà! We can now go to a site, fill out a form, submit it, and use Selenium Action-Chains to scroll through the results. As you have seen, ActionChains (*http://bit.ly/action_chains*) are a powerful way to perform a series of actions in the browser. There are more great features you can explore in Selenium's Python bindings documentation (*http://selenium-python.readthedocs.org/*), including explicit waits (*http://bit.ly/explicit_waits*) (where the browser can wait until a particular element is loaded, not just for the page to be complete), handling alerts (*http://bit.ly/selenium_alerts*), and saving screenshots (*http://bit.ly/save_screenshot*), which is great for debugging purposes.

Now that you've seen some of the power of Selenium, can you rewrite the code we have for the #WeAreFairphone site and scroll through the first 100 entries? (Hint: if you don't want to use ActionChains to scroll through each element, you can always use JavaScript! The Selenium driver's `execute_script` method (*http://bit.ly/execute_script*) allows you to execute JS just like in your browser console. You can use JavaScript's `scroll` method (*http://bit.ly/window_scroll*). Selenium element objects also have a `location` attribute (*http://bit.ly/selenium_location*), which returns the x and y values for the element on the page.)

We have learned how to manipulate and use our browser for web scraping with Selenium, but we aren't done yet! Let's take a look at using Selenium with a headless browser.

Selenium and headless browsers

One of the most popular headless browser kits is PhantomJS (*http://phantomjs.org/*). If you are a proficient JavaScript developer, you can build your scrapers directly in

PhantomJS. If, however, you'd like to give it a try using Python, you can use Selenium with PhantomJS. PhantomJS works with GhostDriver (*https://github.com/detro/ghost driver*) to open pages and navigate across the Web.

Why use a headless browser? Headless browsers (*http://en.wikipedia.org/wiki/Head less_browser*) can be run on servers. They also run and parse pages faster than normal browsers and can be used on more platforms than normal browsers. If you eventually want to run your browser-based web scraping script on a server, you'll likely use a headless browser. You can install one and be running in 10 minutes or less, as opposed to most other browsers, which take time to load and get running properly (depending on the stack you are using and how you intend to deploy).

Screen Reading with Ghost.Py

Ghost.py (*http://jeanphix.me/Ghost.py/*) is a WebKit implementation for screen reading implemented to interact directly with Qt WebKit (*http://doc.qt.io/qt-5/qtwebkit-index.html*). This is a WebKit implementation on top of Qt (*http://bit.ly/qt_wikipedia*), a cross-platform application development framework built in C++.

To begin working with Ghost.py, you're going to need to install some pretty hefty libraries. It works best if you are able to install PySide (*https://pypi.python.org/pypi/PySide*), which allows Python to connect with Qt and gives Python access to a wider range of programs and interactions. The process can take a while, so feel free to go make yourself a sandwich after you begin running this installation:[1]

```
pip install pyside
pip install ghost.py --pre
```

Let's use Ghost.py to search the Python home page (*http://python.org*) for new scraping documentation. You start a new Ghost.py instance very simply:

```
from ghost import Ghost


ghost = Ghost() ❶
with ghost.start() as session:
    page, extra_resources = session.open('http://python.org') ❷

    print page
    print page.url
    print page.headers
    print page.http_status
    print page.content ❸
```

---

[1] If you have trouble installing PySide, take a look at the project's documentation specific to your operating system. You can alternatively install PyQt (*http://bit.ly/install_pyqt5*). You can also check for updates in the Installation documentation on GitHub (*https://github.com/jeanphix/Ghost.py#installation*).

```
print extra_resources

for r in extra_resources:
    print r.url ❹
```

❶ This line calls the `Ghost` class's session object and instantiates a Ghost object to interact with pages.

❷ The `open` method for the `Ghost` class returns two objects, so this line captures those objects in two separate variables. The first object is the page object used to interact with the HTML elements. The second is a list of other resources the page loads (the same list you'd see in your Network tab).

❸ Our page object has many attributes, such as headers, content, URLs, and content from the page. This line looks at the content.

❹ This code loops through the page's extra resources and prints them to see if these are useful. Sometimes these URLs are API calls we can use to get easier access to data.

Ghost.py gives us insight into the resources the page uses (given in a tuple, as we can see when we first open the page using the `open` method) and numerous features of the actual page. We can also load the content of the page by using the `.content` attribute, so if we wanted to parse it using one of our page parsers, like LXML, we could do so and still proceed to interact with the page using Ghost.py.

 Currently, much of Ghost.py's power lies in executing JavaScript (not jQuery) on the page, so you might want to have the Mozilla Developer Network's JavaScript guide (*http://bit.ly/moz-dev-js*) open. This will help you easily search for and find JavaScript to use with Ghost.py.

As we are interested in searching the Python home page for scraping libraries, let's see if we can locate the input box:

```
print page.content.contains('input') ❶

result, resources = session.evaluate(
    'document.getElementsByTagName("input");') ❷

print result.keys()
print result.get('length') ❸
print resources
```

❶ Tests whether an `input` tag exists on the page (most search boxes are simply input elements). This returns a Boolean.

❷ Uses some simple JavaScript to find all the elements on the page with "input" as a tag name.

❸ Prints to see the length of the JavaScript array in the response.

According to the JavaScript results, we only have two inputs on the page. To determine which one to use, let's take a look at the first one's and see if it looks appropriate:

```
result, resources = session.evaluate(
    'document.getElementsByTagName("input")[0].getAttribute("id");') ❶

print result
```

❶ Indexes our list of results and asks for the id attribute. JavaScript gives us CSS attributes directly from elements, so this is a useful way to see the CSS related to the elements you have selected.

Similar to how we can index results in Python, we can index them in JavaScript. We want the first input element. Then, we need to grab the CSS id of the input.

 We could even write a JavaScript for loop (*http://bit.ly/js_for_mdn*) to iterate over the list returned by the getElementsByTagName function and evaluate the attributes that way. If you'd like to try out the JavaScript in your browser, you can do so using the console (see Figure 11-12).

By the name of the id (`id-search-field`) we can tell we've located our search field element, so now let's send some data to it:

```
result, resources = ghost.set_field_value("input", "scraping")
```

This code uses the `set_field_value` method, which takes a selector (here simply "`input`") and sends it a string ("`scraping`"). Ghost.py also has a `fill` method (*http://jeanphix.me/Ghost.py/#form*) which allows you to send a dictionary of values to fill out a series of matching form fields. This is useful if you have more than one field to fill. Now we have our search term filled in; let's see if we can submit our query. We see it's in a form, so we can try a simple form submit:

```
page, resources = session.fire("form", "submit", expect_loading=True) ❶

print page.url
```

❶ This line calls Ghost.py's `fire` method, which fires a JavaScript event. We want to send the form element a signal for the submit event, so it submits our search and navigates to the next page. We also set `expect_loading` equal to `True` so Ghost.py knows we are waiting for a page to load.

Did it work? In our testing, we received timeouts when we ran this code. We'll be talking about timeouts a bit later in this chapter, but this means Ghost.py stopped waiting for a response because it was taking too long. When you are dealing with scrapers submitting data, finding the right timeout is essential to keeping your script going. Let's try a different way to submit. Ghost.py can interact with and click on page elements, so let's try that:

```
result, resources = session.click('button[id=submit]')  ❶

print result

for r in resources:
    print r.url  ❷
```

❶ Ghost.py's `click` method clicks on an object using a JavaScript selector. This code clicks on the button with `id="submit"`.

❷ With most interactions via Ghost.py, you will receive a result and a list of resources. This line looks at the resources returned from the code interactions.

Hmm—when we click on the submit button, we get a URL that looks like a console. Let's see if we can see what Qt WebKit is seeing. Similar to Selenium's `save_screen shot` method, Ghost.py allows us to take a look at the page.

 With headless or WebKit browsers we can't use without code, the page sometimes appears different than it does in a normal browser. When using Ghost.py or PhantomJS, you'll want to utilize screenshots to "see" the page the headless or kit browser is using.

We can use Ghost.py's `show` method to "see" the page:

```
session.show()
```

You should see a new window open showing you the site as the scraper sees it. It should look similar to Figure 12-3.

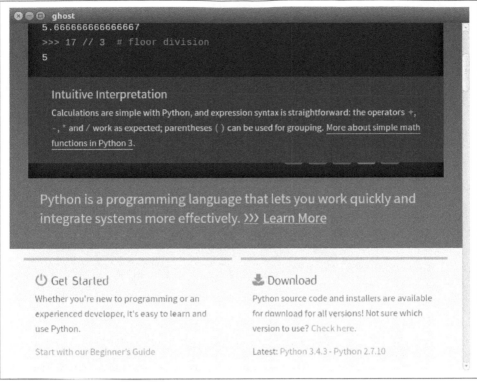

Figure 12-3. Ghost page

Whoops! We are in the middle of the page. Let's try scrolling up and having another look:

```
session.evaluate('window.scrollTo(0, 0);')
```

```
session.show()
```

Now it should look like Figure 12-4.

This view helps us understand our error. The page has not opened as wide as it did in our normal browser, and the search and submit inputs are not readily available. One solution would be to reopen the page using a larger viewport; or we could set a longer timeout for our submit.

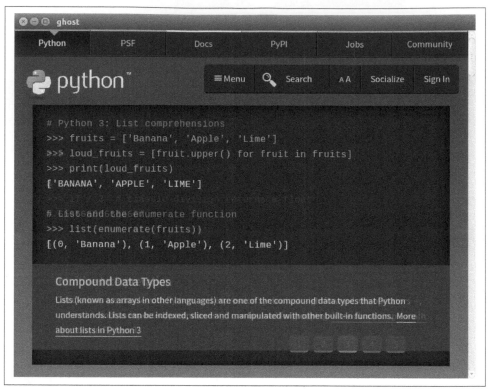

Figure 12-4. Ghost top of page

 As you can see from the documentation (*http://bit.ly/ ghost_py_docs*), the first Ghost object we create can take arguments like `viewport_size` and `wait_timeout`. If you'd like to restart the browser and set a larger viewport or a longer timeout, those are valid fixes.

For now, though, we'll see if we can use some JavaScript to get it to submit:

```
result, resources = session.evaluate(
    'document.getElementsByTagName("input")[0].value = "scraping";') ❶
result, resources = session.evaluate(
    'document.getElementsByTagName("form")[0].submit.click()') ❷
```

❶ Sets the input value equal to "scraping" using pure JavaScript.

❷ Calls the submit element of the form and actively clicks on it using the JavaScript function.

Now if you run `show` again, you should see something like Figure 12-5.

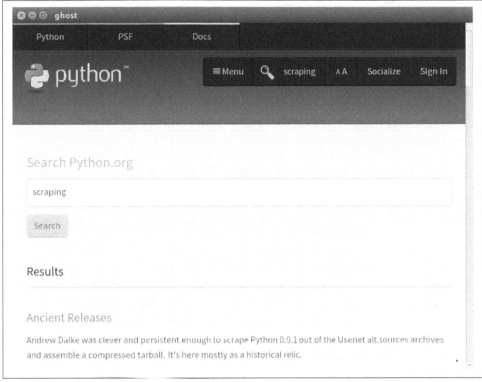

Figure 12-5. Ghost search

We have successfully searched using a Qt browser. Some of the functions are not yet as smooth as with Selenium, but Ghost.py is still a fairly young project.

You can see how old a project is by evaluating its version numbers. Ghost.py, as of the writing of this book, is still below 1.0 (in fact, this book is likely only compatible with 0.2 releases). It will probably change a lot in the next few years, but it's a very interesting project. We encourage you to help it by submitting ideas to the creators and by investigating and fixing bugs!

Now that we've taken a look at several ways to interact with a browser in Python, let's do some spidering!

Spidering the Web

If you need to capture data from more than one page on a site, a spider likely is the best solution. Web spiders (or robots) are great for finding information across an entire domain or site (or series of domains or sites).

You can think of a spider as an advanced scraper, where you can utilize the power of page-reader scrapers (like the ones we learned about in Chapter 11) and apply rules allowing you to match URL patterns to follow across the entire site.

Spiders give you power to learn how a site is structured. For example, a site could contain an entire subsection you weren't aware of that contains interesting data. With a spider traversing the domain, you can find subdomains or other useful linked content for your reporting.

When building a spider, you first investigate the site you're interested in and then build the page-reader piece to identify and read content. Once that is built, you can set a list of *follow rules* the spider will use to find other interesting pages and content, and your parser will collect and save content using the page-reader scraper you built.

With a spider, you should either have a clear definition of what you want to find up front, or use a broad approach to first explore the site and then rewrite it to be more specific. If you choose the broad approach, you might need to do a lot of data cleanup afterward to narrow down what you have found into a usable dataset.

We'll start building our first spider with Scrapy.

Building a Spider with Scrapy

Scrapy (*http://scrapy.org/*) is the most powerful Python web spider. It lets you use the power of LXML (see "Reading a Web Page with LXML" on page 304) with the power of Python's asynchronous network engine, Twisted (*http://twistedmatrix.com/trac/*). If you need an exceptionally fast scraper which also handles a large amount of tasks, we highly recommend Scrapy.

Scrapy comes with some nice built-in features, including the ability to export results in several formats (CSV, JSON, etc.), an easy-to-use server deployment structure to run multiple on-demand scrapers, and a bunch of other neat features like using middleware to handle proxy requests or retry bad status codes. Scrapy logs errors it encounters so you can update and modify your code.

To use Scrapy appropriately, you need to learn the Scrapy class system. Scrapy uses several different Python classes to parse the Web and return good content. When you define a spider class, you also define rules and other class attributes. These rules and attributes are used by the spider when it begins to crawl the Web. When you define a new spider, you are using something called *inheritance*.

Inheritance

Inheritance gives you the ability to use a class as a base and build extra attributes or methods on top of that class.

With Scrapy, when you inherit from one of the spider classes you inherit useful built-in methods and attributes. You'll then want to change a few of the methods and attributes so they are specific to your spider.

Python's inheritance is obvious: you begin defining a class and place another class name in the parentheses of the class definition (e.g., class NewAwesomeRo bot(OldRobot):). The new class (here, NewAwesomeRobot) is inheriting from the class within the parentheses (here, OldRobot). Python gives us the ability to use this direct inheritance so we can actively reuse code when writing new classes.

Inheritance allows us to use the wealth of scraping knowledge in the Scrapy library while only redefining a few methods and some initial spider attributes.

Scrapy uses inheritance to define content to scrape on the page. For each Scrapy project you have, you will collect a series of items and likely create a few different spiders. The spiders will scrape the page and return items (i.e., data) in whatever format you define in your settings.

Using Scrapy spiders requires more organization than the other libraries we have used to scrape the Web, but it's fairly intuitive. The scraper organization makes your projects easy to reuse, share, and update.

There are a few different types of Scrapy spiders, so let's investigate the major similarities and differences. Table 12-1 provides a summary.

Table 12-1. Spider types

Spider name	Main purpose	Documentation
Spider	Used to parse a particular list number of sites and pages	*http://doc.scrapy.org/en/latest/topics/spiders.html#scrapy.spider.Spider*
Crawl Spider	Used to parse a domain given a set of regex rules on how to follow links and identify good pages	*http://doc.scrapy.org/en/latest/topics/spiders.html#crawlspider*
XMLFeed Spider	Used to parse XML feeds (like RSS) and pull content from nodes	*http://doc.scrapy.org/en/latest/topics/spiders.html#xmlfeedspider*

Spider name	Main purpose	Documentation
CSVFeed Spider	Used to parse CSV feeds (or URLs) and pull content from rows	http://doc.scrapy.org/en/latest/topics/spiders.html#csvfeedspider
SiteMap Spider	Used to parse site maps for a given list of domains	http://doc.scrapy.org/en/latest/topics/spiders.html#sitemapspider

For normal web scraping, you can use the Spider class. For more advanced scraping to traverse the whole domain, use the CrawlSpider class. If you have feeds or files in XML and CSV format, especially if they are quite large, use the XMLFeedSpider and CSVFeedSpider to parse them. If you need to take a look at site maps (for your own sites or elsewhere), use the SiteMapSpider.

To become more acquainted with the two major classes (Spider and CrawlSpider), let's build a few different crawlers. First, we'll create a scraper to crawl our same emoji page (*http://www.emoji-cheat-sheet.com*) using a Scrapy spider. For this we will want to use the normal Spider class. Let's begin by installing Scrapy using pip:

```
pip install scrapy
```

It's also recommended to install the *service_identity* module, which provides some nice features for security integration as you crawl the Web:

```
pip install service_identity
```

To start a project with Scrapy, you use a simple command. You want to make sure you are in the directory you'd like to use for your spider, as this command will create a bunch of folders and subfolders for the spider:

```
scrapy startproject scrapyspider
```

If you list the files in your current folder, you should see a new parent folder with numerous subfolders and files. As documented on the Scrapy site (*http://bit.ly/ scrapy_creating_project*), there are a few different files for configuration (*scrapy.cfg* in the main folder and *settings.py* in the project folder, as well as a folder to put your spider files in and a file used to define your items).

Before we build our scraper, we need to define the items we want to collect with the page's data. Let's open up our *items.py* file (located inside the nested project folder) and modify it to store the page data:

```
# -*- coding: utf-8 -*-

# Define here the models for your scraped items
#
# See documentation in:
# http://doc.scrapy.org/en/latest/topics/items.html

import scrapy


class EmojiSpiderItem(scrapy.Item):  ❶
    emoji_handle = scrapy.Field()  ❷
    emoji_image = scrapy.Field()
    section = scrapy.Field()
```

❶ We create our new class via inheritance from the `scrapy.Item` class. This means we have the built-in methods and attributes of that class.

❷ To define each field or data value, we add a new line to our class, set the attribute name, and initialize it by setting it as a `scrapy.Field()` object. These fields support any normal Python data structure, including dictionaries, tuples, lists, floats, decimals, and strings.

You probably noticed your *items.py* file was mainly prebuilt. This is a really great feature to quickstart your development and ensure you have the project structured the right way. The `startproject` command supplies all of this tooling and is the best way to begin new Scrapy projects. You can also see how easy it is to set up a new class to collect data. With only a few lines of Python, we are able to define the fields we care about and have our items ready to use with our spider.

To get started on your spider class, you'll want to create a new file in the *spiders* folder in your new project directory structure. Let's call it *emo_spider.py*:

```
import scrapy
from scrapyspider.items import EmojiSpiderItem  ❶


class EmoSpider(scrapy.Spider):  ❷
    name = 'emo'  ❸
    allowed_domains = ['emoji-cheat-sheet.com']  ❹
    start_urls = [
        'http://www.emoji-cheat-sheet.com/',  ❺
    ]

    def parse(self, response):  ❻
        self.log('A response from %s just arrived!' % response.url)  ❼
```

① All Scrapy imports use the root project folder as the starting module point, so you'll want to include the parent folder in the import. This line imports the `Emo jiSpiderItem` class from the `emojispider.items` module.

② We define our `EmoSpider` class using inheritance, basing the new class on the simple `scrapy.Spider` class. This means our spider will need certain initialization attributes (*http://bit.ly/scrapy_spiders*), so it knows which URLs to scrape and what to do with scraped content. We define these attributes on the next few lines (`start_urls`, `name`, and `allowed_domains`).

③ The spider name is what we will use when we want to identify the spider in command-line tasks.

④ `allowed_domains` tells the spider what domains to scrape. If it comes across a link to a domain not included in this list, it will ignore it. This attribute is useful when writing a crawl scraper so your scraper doesn't end up attempting to scrape all of Twitter or Facebook if it follows a link there. You can also pass subdomains.

⑤ The `Spider` class uses the `start_urls` attribute to iterate through a listing of URLs to scrape. With a `CrawlSpider`, these are used as a jumping-off point for finding more matching URLs.

⑥ This line redefines the spider's `parse` method to *do* something by defining a method within the class using `def` and the method name. When you are defining methods for classes, you will almost always begin by passing `self`. This is because the object calling the method is the first argument (i.e., `list.append()` first passes the list object itself, then passes the argument within the parenthesis). The next argument for `parse` is the response. As covered in the documentation (*http://bit.ly/scrapy_parse*), the `parse` method will be passed a response object. We end the line with a colon, just as we would when defining any function.

⑦ To begin testing our spider, this line from the Scrapy tutorial uses the spider's `log` method to send a message to our log. We use the response's URL attribute to show the response's location.

To run this Scrapy spider, we need to ensure we are in the proper directory (*scrapy-spider* with the *scrapy.cfg* file in it), and then run the command-line argument to parse the page:

```
scrapy crawl emo
```

The log should show your spider opening and show what middleware it's running. Then, near the end, you should see something like this:

```
2015-06-03 15:47:48+0200 [emo] DEBUG: A resp from www.emoji-cheat-sheet.com
    arrived!
2015-06-03 15:47:48+0200 [emo] INFO: Closing spider (finished)
2015-06-03 15:47:48+0200 [emo] INFO: Dumping Scrapy stats:
    {'downloader/request_bytes': 224,
     'downloader/request_count': 1,
     'downloader/request_method_count/GET': 1,
     'downloader/response_bytes': 143742,
     'downloader/response_count': 1,
     'downloader/response_status_count/200': 1,
     'finish_reason': 'finished',
     'finish_time': datetime.datetime(2015, 6, 3, 13, 47, 48, 274872),
     'log_count/DEBUG': 4,
     'log_count/INFO': 7,
     'response_received_count': 1,
     'scheduler/dequeued': 1,
     'scheduler/dequeued/memory': 1,
     'scheduler/enqueued': 1,
     'scheduler/enqueued/memory': 1,
     'start_time': datetime.datetime(2015, 6, 3, 13, 47, 47, 817479)}
```

Our scraper parsed one page in about a second. We can also see the logging from our parse method. Cool! We successfully defined our first item and class and were able to set them up and run them.

Our next step is actually parsing the page and pulling out the content. Let's try out another built-in feature, the Scrapy shell. It is similar to our Python or command-line shell, but with all the available spider commands. With the shell, it's very easy to investigate the page and determine how to get to page content. To launch a Scrapy shell, simply run:

```
scrapy shell
```

You should see a listing of available options or functions you can call. One of them should be fetch. Let's test it out:

```
fetch('http://www.emoji-cheat-sheet.com/')
```

You now should see some output similar to your scraping output. It will have some message indicating that the URL was crawled, then give you a new listing with objects available to you. One of them is the response object from the request. The response is the same response object your parse method will use. Let's see if we can determine some of the ways to interact with the response object:

```
response.url
response.status
response.headers
```

Each of these should return some data. The url is the same URL we used to write our log message. The status tells us the HTTP status code of the response. The headers should give us a dictionary of the headers the server returned with the response.

If you type `response.` and hit Tab, you should see the full list of methods and attributes available with your response object. You can also do this with any other Python object in your IPython terminal.[1]

Each response object will also have an `xpath` and a `css` method. These are similar to the selectors we have been working with throughout this chapter and in Chapter 11. As you may have already guessed, `xpath` expects you to send an XPath string and `css` expects a CSS selector. Let's have a look at selecting using the XPath we've already written for this page:

```
response.xpath('//h2|//h3')
```

When you run that command, you should see a list similar to this:

```
[<Selector xpath='//h2|//h3' data=u'<h2>People</h2>'>,
 <Selector xpath='//h2|//h3' data=u'<h2>Nature</h2>'>,
 <Selector xpath='//h2|//h3' data=u'<h2>Objects</h2>'>,
 <Selector xpath='//h2|//h3' data=u'<h2>Places</h2>'>,
 <Selector xpath='//h2|//h3' data=u'<h2>Symbols</h2>'>,
 <Selector xpath='//h2|//h3' data=u'<h3>Campfire also supports a few sounds<'>]
```

Now let's see if we can read just the text content from those headers. When using Scrapy, you'll want to extract the exact element you are looking for; there are (as of the writing of this book) no `get` or `text_content` methods. Let's see if we can use our XPath knowledge to select the text from the headers:

```
for header in response.xpath('//h2|//h3'):
    print header.xpath('text()').extract()
```

You should get output similar to this:

```
[u'People']
[u'Nature']
[u'Objects']
[u'Places']
[u'Symbols']
[u'Campfire also supports a few sounds']
```

We can see our `extract` method will return a list of the matching elements. We can use the `@` symbol to represent attributes and `text()` to pull out text. We'll need to rewrite some of the code, but we should now be able to use a lot of the same LXML logic we wrote in "A Case for XPath" on page 308:

---

1 If you have IPython installed, you should also be seeing this tab completion on most Python shells you use. If you aren't seeing this, you can add a *.pythonrc* file to your computer (*http://bit.ly/py_tab_completion*) and set it as your *PYTHONSTARTUP* environment.

```
import scrapy
from scrapyspider.items import EmojiSpiderItem


class EmoSpider(scrapy.Spider):
    name = 'emo'
    allowed_domains = ['emoji-cheat-sheet.com']
    start_urls = [
        'http://www.emoji-cheat-sheet.com/',
    ]

    def parse(self, response):
        headers = response.xpath('//h2|//h3')
        lists = response.xpath('//ul')
        all_items = [] ❶
        for header, list_cont in zip(headers, lists):
            section = header.xpath('text()').extract()[0] ❷
            for li in list_cont.xpath('li'):
                item = EmojiSpiderItem() ❸
                item['section'] = section
                spans = li.xpath('div/span')
                if len(spans):
                    link = spans[0].xpath('@data-src').extract() ❹
                    if link:
                        item['emoji_link'] = response.url + link[0] ❺
                    handle_code = spans[1].xpath('text()').extract()
                else:
                    handle_code = li.xpath('div/text()').extract()
                if handle_code:
                    item['emoji_handle'] = handle_code[0] ❻
                all_items.append(item) ❼
        return all_items ❽
```

❶   Because we know we are going to have more than one item per page, this line starts a list at the beginning of the parse method to keep a list of found items as we go through the page.

❷   Instead of calling header.text as we do in the LXML script, this line locates the text section (.xpath("text()")) and extracts it using the extract function. Because we know that method will return a list, this code selects the first and only item for each list and sets it equal to section.

❸   This line defines the item. For each list item, we create a new EmojiSpiderItem object by calling the class name with empty parentheses.

❹   To extract data attributes, this line uses the XPath @ selector. This code selects the first span and extracts the @data-src attribute, which will return a list.

❺ To create our full path `emoji_link` attribute, this line takes the response URL and adds the first list item from the `@data-src` attribute. To set item fields, we use dictionary syntax, setting the keys (i.e., field names) equal to the values. This line will not execute if there is no `@data-src` from the previous code.

❻ To combine some code and not repeat ourselves, this code finds the handle strings for the emojis and sounds, and sets the `emoji_handle` field.

❼ At the end of each loop for the list elements, this line appends the new item to our `all_items` list.

❽ At the end of our `parse` method, this line returns the list of all found items. Scrapy will use a returned item or list of items to proceed with the scraping (usually by saving, cleaning, or outputting the data in a format we can read and use).

We have now added in our Scrapy `extract` calls and identified more specifically the text and attributes to pull from the page. We removed some of the `None` logic, as our Scrapy item will automatically know which fields it has and doesn't have. For this reason, if we export the output to CSV or JSON, it will show both null and found values. Now that we've updated the code to work with Scrapy, let's run it by calling our `crawl` method again:

```
scrapy crawl emo
```

You should see some output similar to our first scrape, except this time with quite a few more lines! Scrapy will log every item it finds as it parses the Web. At the end, you'll see the same summary output showing errors, debugging, and how many items were scraped:

```
2015-06-03 18:13:51+0200 [emo] DEBUG: Scraped from
    <200 http://www.emoji-cheat-sheet.com/>
    {'emoji_handle': u'/play butts',
     'section': u'Campfire also supports a few sounds'}
2015-06-03 18:13:51+0200 [emo] INFO: Closing spider (finished)
2015-06-03 18:13:51+0200 [emo] INFO: Dumping Scrapy stats:
    {'downloader/request_bytes': 224,
     'downloader/request_count': 1,
     'downloader/request_method_count/GET': 1,
     'downloader/response_bytes': 143742,
     'downloader/response_count': 1,
     'downloader/response_status_count/200': 1,
     'finish_reason': 'finished',
     'finish_time': datetime.datetime(2015, 6, 3, 16, 13, 51, 803765),
     'item_scraped_count': 924,
     'log_count/DEBUG': 927,
     'log_count/INFO': 7,
     'response_received_count': 1,
     'scheduler/dequeued': 1,
```

```
        'scheduler/dequeued/memory': 1,
        'scheduler/enqueued': 1,
        'scheduler/enqueued/memory': 1,
        'start_time': datetime.datetime(2015, 6, 3, 16, 13, 50, 857193)}
  2015-06-03 18:13:51+0200 [emo] INFO: Spider closed (finished)
```

Scrapy helped us parse more than 900 items in about a second—impressive! As we look through our logs, we see all of our items have been parsed and added. We did not experience any errors; if there were any, we would see a count for them in the final output similar to the DEBUG and INFO output lines.

We don't yet have an actual file or output from our script. We can set one using a built-in command-line argument. Try rerunning the crawl with some extra options:

```
scrapy crawl emo -o items.csv
```

At the end of the scrape you should have an *items.csv* file in your project root directory. If you open it, you should see all of your data has been exported into CSV format. You can also export *.json* and *.xml* files, so feel free to try those out by simply changing the filename.

Congratulations, you've built your first web spider! With only a few files and less than 50 lines of code you're able to parse an entire page—more than 900 items—in less than a minute and output those findings to a simple-to-read and easy-to-share format. Scrapy, as you can see, is a truly powerful and incredibly useful tool.

Crawling Whole Websites with Scrapy

We've explored using the Scrapy shell and crawl for a normal page, but how can we use the power and speed of Scrapy to crawl an entire website? To investigate the CrawlSpider's capabilities, we must first determine what to crawl. Let's try finding Python packages related to scraping on the PyPI home page (*http://pypi.python.org*). To begin, take a look at the page and figure out what data we want. Performing a quick search for the term "scrape" (*http://bit.ly/scrape_packages*) shows a whole list of results and each of those pages has more information, including documentation, a link to the related package, a list of what Python versions are supported, and the number of recent downloads.

We can build an item model around that data. Normally, we would start a new project for each scraper if it is not related to the same data; but for ease of use, we'll use the same folder as for our emoji scraper. Begin by modifying the *items.py* file:

```
# -*- coding: utf-8 -*-

# Define here the models for your scraped items
#
# See documentation in:
# http://doc.scrapy.org/en/latest/topics/items.html

import scrapy


class EmojiSpiderItem(scrapy.Item):
    emoji_handle = scrapy.Field()
    emoji_link = scrapy.Field()
    section = scrapy.Field()


class PythonPackageItem(scrapy.Item):
    package_name = scrapy.Field()
    version_number = scrapy.Field()
    package_downloads = scrapy.Field()
    package_page = scrapy.Field()
    package_short_description = scrapy.Field()
    home_page = scrapy.Field()
    python_versions = scrapy.Field()
    last_month_downloads = scrapy.Field()
```

We define our new item class directly underneath our old class. You should keep a few lines of space in between the classes so it's easy to read the file and see class distinctions. Here, we added some fields we are interested in from the Python package pages, including how many downloads there have been in the last month, the package home page, what Python versions it supports, and the version number.

With our items defined, we can use the Scrapy shell to investigate content on the Scrapely page. Scrapely is a project from the authors of Scrapy that uses Python to screen-read HTML. If you haven't already, we also recommend installing IPython, which will ensure your input and output looks like ours and give you some extra shell tools. In the shell (started using `scrapy shell`), we need to first fetch content using the following command:

```
fetch('https://pypi.python.org/pypi/scrapely/0.12.0')
```

We can try fetching the version number from the breadcrumbs at the top of the page. We see they are in a div with the ID `"breadcrumb"`. We can write some XPath to find that:

```
In [2]: response.xpath('//div[@id="breadcrumb"]')
Out[2]: [<Selector xpath='//div[@id="breadcrumb"]'
         data=u'<div id="breadcrumb">\n                <a h'>]
```

The IPython `Out` message shows we have properly found the breadcrumb `div`. By inspecting the element in the browser's inspection tab, we see the text is located in an anchor tag in that `div`. We need to be specific with XPath, so we tell it to find the text inside the child anchor tag with the following line of code:

```
In [3]: response.xpath('//div[@id="breadcrumb"]/a/text()')
Out[3]:
[<Selector xpath='//div[@id="breadcrumb"]/a/text()' data=u'Package Index'>,
 <Selector xpath='//div[@id="breadcrumb"]/a/text()' data=u'scrapely'>,
 <Selector xpath='//div[@id="breadcrumb"]/a/text()' data=u'0.12.0'>]
```

We can now see the version number is in the last of those `div`s, and we can grab the last one when we extract. We can also do some testing and ensure the version data is a number using regex (see "RegEx Matching" on page 183) or testing with Python's `is_digit` (like we did back in "Finding Outliers and Bad Data" on page 169).

Now let's take a look at how to grab a slightly more complex part of the page: last month's downloads. If you inspect the element in your browser, you'll see it's in an unordered list in a list item in a span. You'll notice none of those elements have a CSS ID or class. You'll also notice the `span` does not include the actual word "month" (for easy searching). Let's see if we can get a selector that works:

```
In [4]: response.xpath('//li[contains(text(), "month")]')
Out[4]: []
```

Bummer, no dice on finding it easily using an XPath text search. However, one nice trick you'll notice with XPath is sometimes it behaves differently if you change the query slightly and parse something similar. Try running this command:

```
In [5]: response.xpath('//li/text()[contains(., "month")]')
Out[5]: [<Selector xpath='//li/text()[contains(., "month")]'
         data=u' downloads in the last month\n    '>]
```

See? How come one works and not the other? Because the element is a `span` inside an `li` element and the other text sits after the `span`, it's confusing the hierarchy of the XPath pattern search. The messier the page structure, the more difficult it is to write a perfect selector. What we asked for in the second pattern is a bit different—we said "show me text residing in an `li` that has the word *month* somewhere in it," rather than "show me an `li` that has the text *month* in it." It's a small difference, but when dealing with messy HTML, it can be useful to work around difficult sections of content by trying several selectors.

But what we really want is the `span` containing the download number. We can use the beauty of XPath relationships to navigate up the chain and locate that `span`. Try out this code:

```
In [6]: response.xpath('//li/text()[contains(., "month")]/..')
Out[6]: [<Selector xpath='//li/text()[contains(., "month")]/..' data=u'<li>\n
         <span>668</span> downloads in t'>]
```

By using the `..` operator, we have essentially moved back up to the parent node, so now we have both the text after the span and the span itself. Our final step will be selecting the span, so we don't have to worry about stripping text:

```
In [7]: response.xpath('//li/text()[contains(., "month")]/../span/text()')
Out[7]: [<Selector xpath='//li/text()[contains(., "month")]/../span/text()'
    data=u'668'>]
```

Super! Now we have the number we were looking for, and it should work across all of our pages as we've based it on page hierarchy and not on attempting to "guess" where the content might lie.

 Use the shell to debug and locate the elements you want using your XPath skills. As you gain experience, it will become easier to write selectors that work on the first try, so we encourage you to write more web scrapers and experiment by testing many different selectors.

We'll begin with a scraper we know properly parses the Scrapely page using the `Spider` class and then transform it to use the `CrawlSpider` class. It's always good to approach two- or three-factor problems step by step, successfully completing one part of the task before moving on to the next one. Because we have to debug two parts with a `CrawlSpider` (the crawl rules to find matching pages and scraping the page itself), it's good to test it by first ensuring one of the parts works. We recommend starting by building a scraper which works on one or two of the matching pages and then writing the crawl rules to test the crawling logic.

Here's a look at our completed `Spider` for the Python package pages. You will want to include it as a new file in your *spiders* folder, alongside your *emo_spider.py* file. We have called it *package_spider.py*:

```
import scrapy
from scrapyspider.items import PythonPackageItem


class PackageSpider(scrapy.Spider):
    name = 'package'
    allowed_domains = ['pypi.python.org']
    start_urls = [
        'https://pypi.python.org/pypi/scrapely/0.12.0',
        'https://pypi.python.org/pypi/dc-campaign-finance-scrapers/0.5.1',  ❶
    ]

    def parse(self, response):
        item = PythonPackageItem()  ❷
        item['package_page'] = response.url
        item['package_name'] = response.xpath(
            '//div[@class="section"]/h1/text()').extract()
```

```
item['package_short_description'] = response.xpath(
    '//meta[@name="description"]/@content').extract() ❸
item['home_page'] = response.xpath(
    '//li[contains(strong, "Home Page:")]/a/@href').extract() ❹
item['python_versions'] = []
versions = response.xpath(
    '//li/a[contains(text(), ":: Python ::")]/text()').extract()
for v in versions:
    version_number = v.split("::")[-1] ❺
    item['python_versions'].append(version_number.strip()) ❻
item['last_month_downloads'] = response.xpath(
    '//li/text()[contains(., "month")]/../span/text()').extract()
item['package_downloads'] = response.xpath(
    '//table/tr/td/span/a[contains(@href,"pypi.python.org")]/@href' ❼
).extract()
return item ❽
```

❶   This line adds an extra URL we haven't investigated. Using more than one URL is a great way to quickly see if you have clean and reusable code as you move from a Spider to a CrawlSpider.

❷   For this scraper, we only have one item per page. This line creates the item at the beginning of our parse method.

❸   One great way to get easy-to-read descriptions of pages while you are parsing is to learn a bit about search engine optimization (SEO). Most sites will create short descriptions, keywords, titles, and other meta tags for Facebook, Pinterest, and other sharing sites. This line pulls in that description for our data collection.

❹   The package's "Home Page" URL is located in a strong tag in an li. Once we find that element, this line selects just the link from the anchor element.

❺   If we take a look at the version number links, we see they come in a list item that uses :: to separate Python and the version number. The version numbers always come last, so this line splits our string using :: as the delimiter and takes the last element.

❻   This line appends the version text (stripped of extra spaces) to the Python version array. The item's python_versions key will now hold all Python versions.

❼   We can see in the table that links to package downloads rather than their MD5 checksums use the *pypi.python.org* domain. This line tests to make sure the link has the proper domain and grabs only those links that do.

❽   At the end of our parse method, Scrapy expects us to return an item (or a list of items). This line returns the item.

When you ran the code (scrapy crawl *package*) you should have gotten two items and no errors. You will notice, however, we have varying data. For example, our package data has no good listing of supported Python versions for each download. If we wanted to, we could parse from the *PyVersion* field in the table and match it with each download. How might you go about doing that? (Hint: it's in the third column of each table row, and XPath allows you to pass element indexes.) We also notice the data is a bit messy, as the following output (formatted to fit the page; your output will look a little different!) shows:

```
2015-09-10 08:19:34+0200 [package_test] DEBUG: Scraped from
    <200 https://pypi.python.org/pypi/scrapely/0.12.0>
    {'home_page': [u'http://github.com/scrapy/scrapely'],
     'last_month_downloads': [u'668'],
     'package_downloads':
     [u'https://pypi.python.org/packages/2.7/s/' + \
       'scrapely/scrapely-0.12.0-py2-none-any.whl',
      u'https://pypi.python.org/packages/source/s/' + \
       'scrapely/scrapely-0.12.0.tar.gz'],
     'package_name': [u'scrapely 0.12.0'],
     'package_page': 'https://pypi.python.org/pypi/scrapely/0.12.0',
     'package_short_description':
     [u'A pure-python HTML screen-scraping library'],
     'python_versions': [u'2.6', u'2.7']}
```

We have a few fields where we might expect a string or integer, but instead we have an array of strings. Let's build a helper method to clean up our data before we define our crawl spider rules:

```
import scrapy
from scrapyspider.items import PythonPackageItem


class PackageSpider(scrapy.Spider):
    name = 'package'
    allowed_domains = ['pypi.python.org']
    start_urls = [
        'https://pypi.python.org/pypi/scrapely/0.12.0',
        'https://pypi.python.org/pypi/dc-campaign-finance-scrapers/0.5.1',
    ]

    def grab_data(self, response, xpath_sel):        ❶
        data = response.xpath(xpath_sel).extract()   ❷
        if len(data) > 1:                            ❸
            return data
        elif len(data) == 1:
            if data[0].isdigit():
                return int(data[0])                  ❹
            return data[0]                           ❺
        return []                                    ❻

    def parse(self, response):
```

```
item = PythonPackageItem()
item['package_page'] = response.url
item['package_name'] = self.grab_data(
    response, '//div[@class="section"]/h1/text()') ❼
item['package_short_description'] = self.grab_data(
    response, '//meta[@name="description"]/@content')
item['home_page'] = self.grab_data(
    response, '//li[contains(strong, "Home Page:")]/a/@href')
item['python_versions'] = []
versions = self.grab_data(
    response, '//li/a[contains(text(), ":: Python ::")]/text()')
for v in versions:
    item['python_versions'].append(v.split("::")[-1].strip())
item['last_month_downloads'] = self.grab_data(
    response, '//li/text()[contains(., "month")]/../span/text()')
item['package_downloads'] = self.grab_data(
    response,
    '//table/tr/td/span/a[contains(@href,"pypi.python.org")]/@href')
return item
```

❶ This line defines a new method to take our **self** object (so the spider can then call it like a normal method), our response object, and the long XPath selector to find the content.

❷ This line uses the new function variables to extract the data.

❸ If the length of the data is greater than 1, this line returns the list. We probably want all of the data, so we return it as is.

❹ If the length of the data is equal to 1 and the data is a digit, this line returns the integer. This would be the case for our downloads number.

❺ If the length of the data is equal to 1 and is not a digit, this line returns just the data. This will match strings containing links and simple text.

❻ If this function hasn't returned yet, this line returns an empty list. We use a list here because you would expect **extract** to return empty lists if no data was found. If you used None types or empty strings, you might have to modify other code to save it to a CSV.

❼ This line calls our new function and invokes **self.grab_data** with the arguments: the response object and the XPath selection string. r use the other built-in export features.

Now we have pretty clean data and code and are repeating ourselves less often. We could further improve it, but for the sake of your eyes not rolling to the back of your head, let's move on to defining our crawling rules. Crawling rules, denoted by regular expressions, tell your spider where to go by defining what types of URLs to follow from what parts of the page. (Isn't it great that we covered regexes in Chapter 7? You're a pro now!) If we take a look at the package links (*https://pypi.python.org/pypi/dc-campaign-finance-scrapers/0.5.1* and *https://pypi.python.org/pypi/scrapely/0.12.0*), we can see some similarities:

- They both have the same domain, *pypi.python.org*, and they both use *https*.
- They both have the same pattern for the path in the URL: */pypi/ <name_of_the_library>/<version_number>*.
- The name of the library uses lowercase letters and dashes, and the version number is digits and periods.

We can use these similarities to define regex rules. Before we write them in our spider, let's try them in our Python console:

```
import re

urls = [
    'https://pypi.python.org/pypi/scrapely/0.12.0',
    'https://pypi.python.org/pypi/dc-campaign-finance-scrapers/0.5.1',
]

to_match = 'https://pypi.python.org/pypi/[\w-]+/[\d\.]+' ❶

for u in urls:
    if re.match(to_match, u):
        print re.match(to_match, u).group() ❷
```

❶ This line finds a link with *https*, the *pypi.python.org* domain, and the path from our investigation. The first block is *pypi*, the next block is lowercase word-like text with - symbols (matched easily with [\w-]+), and the last part looks for numbers with or without periods ([\d\.]+).

❷ This line prints out the matching group. We are using the regex `match` method, because that is the regex Scrapy crawl spiders use.

We have a match (two, to be exact!). Now, let's have one last look at where we need to start. What the Scrapy crawl spider will do is look at a list of start URLs and use those pages to find URLs to follow. If we take another look at our search results page (*http://bit.ly/scrape_packages*), we notice the page uses relative URLs, so we only need to match the URL path. We also see the links are all in a table, so we can restrict where Scrapy looks to find links to crawl. With this knowledge, let's update the file by adding the crawl rules:

```
from scrapy.contrib.spiders import CrawlSpider, Rule ❶
from scrapy.contrib.linkextractors import LinkExtractor ❷
from scrapyspider.items import PythonPackageItem
```

```python
class PackageSpider(CrawlSpider):  ❸
    name = 'package'
    allowed_domains = ['pypi.python.org']
    start_urls = [
        'https://pypi.python.org/pypi?%3A' + \
                'action=search&term=scrape&submit=search',
        'https://pypi.python.org/pypi?%3A' + \
                'action=search&term=scraping&submit=search',  ❹
    ]

    rules = (
        Rule(LinkExtractor(
            allow=['/pypi/[\w-]+/[\d\.]+', ],  ❺
            restrict_xpaths=['//table/tr/td', ],  ❻
        ),
            follow=True,  ❼
            callback='parse_package',  ❽
        ),
    )

    def grab_data(self, response, xpath_sel):
        data = response.xpath(xpath_sel).extract()
        if len(data) > 1:
            return data
        elif len(data) == 1:
            if data[0].isdigit():
                return int(data[0])
            return data[0]
        return []

    def parse_package(self, response):
        item = PythonPackageItem()
        item['package_page'] = response.url
        item['package_name'] = self.grab_data(
            response, '//div[@class="section"]/h1/text()')
        item['package_short_description'] = self.grab_data(
            response, '//meta[@name="description"]/@content')
        item['home_page'] = self.grab_data(
            response, '//li[contains(strong, "Home Page:")]/a/@href')
        item['python_versions'] = []
        versions = self.grab_data(
            response, '//li/a[contains(text(), ":: Python ::")]/text()')
        for v in versions:
            version = v.split("::")[-1]
            item['python_versions'].append(version.strip())
        item['last_month_downloads'] = self.grab_data(
            response, '//li/text()[contains(., "month")]/../span/text()')
        item['package_downloads'] = self.grab_data(
            response,
```

```
          '//table/tr/td/span/a[contains(@href,"pypi.python.org")]/@href')
     return item
```

❶ This line imports both our `CrawlSpider` class and our `Rule` class, as we need them both for our first crawl spider.

❷ This line imports our `LinkExtractor`. The default link extractor uses LXML (we know how to write for that!).

❸ This line redefines our `Spider` so it inherits from the `CrawlSpider` class. Because we're changing this inheritance, we must define a `rules` attribute.

❹ We include search pages for the terms *scrape* and *scraping* to see if we can find even more Python packages. You can add a long list here if you have different starting points where you'd like your spider to begin searching.

❺ This line sets `allow` to match the regex for the links on the page. Because we only need relative links, we start with just the path. `allow` accepts a list, so you could add more than one `allow` rule here if you have more than one type of URL you are looking to match.

❻ This line restricts our crawl spider to the results table. This means it is only going to look for matching links in columns inside rows of a table.

❼ This tells the rule to follow (i.e., load) the matching links. Sometimes you might have pages you want to parse to give you content but whose links you don't need to follow. If you want the spider to follow the page links and open them, you need to use `follow=True`.

❽ Gives the rule a callback and renames the `parse` method to ensure we don't mess with the normal parsing methods Scrapy `CrawlSpiders` use that are different from the Scrapy `Spiders`. Now our parse method is called `parse_package`, and the spider will call this method once it has followed a matching URL to a page we want to scrape.

You can run the crawl spider the same way you would a normal spider:

```
scrapy crawl package
```

You've officially built your first crawl spider! Are there things that can be improved? There is one easy-to-fix bug we've left in this code. Can you spot what it is, and how to fix it? (Hint: look at your Python versions and see what's going on, then take a look at the way versions are expected to be returned (i.e., always in a list) compared to how we might return some of them with `grab_data`.) See if you can fix this issue in the crawl spider script. If you get stuck, you can check the book's repository (*https://github.com/jackiekazil/data-wrangling*) for the completely fixed code.

Scrapy is a powerful, fast, and easy-to-configure tool. There is a lot more to explore, which you can do by reading the library's excellent documentation (*http://doc.scrapy.org/en/latest/*). It's fairly easy to configure your scripts to use databases and special feed extractors, and have them all running on your own server using Scrapyd (*http://scrapyd.readthedocs.org/en/latest/*). We hope this was the first of many Scrapy projects to come!

You now understand screen readers, browser readers, and spiders. Let's review some other things you should know as you build more complex web scrapers.

Networks: How the Internet Works and Why It's Breaking Your Script

Depending on how often your scraping script runs and how essential it is that every scrape works, you will probably run into network problems. Yes, the Internet is trying to break your script. Why? Because it assumes if you actually care, you will retry. Dropped connections, proxy problems, and timeout issues are rife within the web scraping world. However, there are a few things you can do to mitigate these issues.

In your browser, if something doesn't load properly, you merely hit refresh, sending another request immediately. For your scraper, you can mimic this type of behavior. If you are using Selenium, it's incredibly simple to refresh your content. The Selenium `webdriver` object has a `refresh` function just like your browser. If you've just filled out a form, you might need to resubmit the form to move to the next page (this is similar to how your browser behaves at times). If you need to interact with an alert or pop-up, Selenium gives you the tools necessary to accept or decline the message (*http://bit.ly/selenium_common_alert*).

If you are using Scrapy, it has built-in retry middleware. To enable it, you merely need to add it to the list of middleware in your project's *settings.py* file. The middleware (*http://bit.ly/downloader_middleware*) expects you to set some default values in your settings so it knows what HTTP response codes to retry (e.g., should it retry only 500s?) as well as how many retries to pursue.

 If you don't specify those values, it will still work with the default options listed in the documentation. We recommend starting with 10 retries if you are seeing network errors and then either increasing the download wait time (another global settings variable) or checking the error codes you are receiving to see if you are overloading the site with your script.

If you are using your own Python script with LXML or BeautifulSoup, it's a good idea to catch those errors and determine a good method to deal with them. Most of the time, you'll notice a preponderance of urllib2.HTTPError exceptions (*http://bit.ly/ httperror_exceptions*) or, if you are using requests, your code will not load content and fail. Using a try...except block in Python, your code could look something like this:

```python
import requests
import urllib2


resp = requests.get('http://sisinmaru.blog17.fc2.com/')

if resp.status_code == 404: ❶
    print 'Oh no!!! We cannot find Maru!!'
elif resp.status_code == 500:
    print 'Oh no!!! It seems Maru might be overloaded.'
elif resp.status_code in [403, 401]:
    print 'Oh no!! You cannot have any Maru!'


try:
    resp = urllib2.urlopen('http://sisinmaru.blog17.fc2.com/') ❷
except urllib2.URLError: ❸
    print 'Oh no!!! We cannot find Maru!!'
except urllib2.HTTPError, err: ❹
    if err.code == 500: ❺
        print 'Oh no!!! It seems Maru might be overloaded.'
    elif err.code in [403, 401]:
        print 'Oh no!! You cannot have any Maru!'
    else:
        print 'No Maru for you! %s' % err.code ❻
except Exception as e: ❼
    print e
```

❶ When using the requests library to find network errors, check the status_code of your response. This attribute returns an integer representing the code received in the HTTP response. This line tests for 404 errors.

❷ If using urllib2, put your request in a try statement (as on this line).

❸ One of the exceptions we might see from urllib2 is the URLError. Writing a catch is a good idea. If it can't resolve the domain, it will probably throw this error.

❹ One of the other exceptions we might see is an HTTPError. Any bad response linked to HTTP request errors will raise this error. By adding the comma and err here, we catch the error and put it in the variable err so we can log our errors.

❺ Now that we have caught the error and set it equal to err in the previous line of code, this line tests the code attribute to see the HTTP error code.

❻ For all other HTTP errors, this line uses an else to show the code of the error by formatting it into a string.

❼ This line catches any other errors we might run into and shows the error. Here we again assign the exception to e and print it so we can read the exception messages.

Intelligently designing your scripts to be as failure-resistant as possible is an important step we'll talk more about in Chapter 14, and ensuring you have proper try... except blocks throughout your code to account for errors is one important part of that process. Other than HTTP errors, sometimes the page takes too long to load. For our scraper, we might adjust the timeout if we find we are getting slow responses or experiencing latency problems.

 What is *latency*? In a networking sense, it's the amount of time it takes for data to be sent from one place to another. *Round-trip latency* is the time it takes to send a request from your computer to the server and get a response. Latency happens because data has to be transferred, sometimes thousands of miles, to complete your request.

It's good to think about latency when writing and scaling your script. If you have a script connecting to a site hosted in another country, you are going to experience network latency. You will likely want to adjust your timeouts accordingly, or set up a server closer to your desired endpoint. If you need to add timeouts to your Selenium and Ghost.py scripts, you can do so directly when starting your scraping. For Selenium, use the set_page_load_timeout (*http://bit.ly/set_page_load_timeout*) method or use implicit or explicit waits (*http://bit.ly/selenium_waits_docs*), where the browser will wait for particular sections of code to load. For Ghost.py, you may pass the wait_timeout argument as defined in the Ghost class documentation (*http://bit.ly/ghost_class*).

For Scrapy, the asynchronous nature of the scrapers and ability to retry a particular URL numerous times makes timeouts a somewhat trivial issue. You can, of course, alter the timeout directly in Scrapy settings using the DOWNLOAD_TIMEOUT (*http://doc.scrapy.org/en/latest/topics/settings.html#download-timeout*) setting.

If you are writing your own Python script and using LXML or BeautifulSoup to parse the page, adding a timeout to your calls will be your responsibility. If you use requests or urllib2, you can do so directly as you call the page. In requests, you simply add it as an argument to your `get` request (*http://bit.ly/quickstart_timeouts*). For `urllib2`, you'll want to pass the timeout as an argument in your `urlopen` method (*http://bit.ly/urlopen*).

If you are experiencing continuous network-related issues, and it's essential that your script run on a steady schedule, we recommend setting up some logging, attempting to run it on another network (i.e., not your home network, to see if these are issues with your home Internet connection), and testing whether running it at non-peak hours helps.

 Does it matter whether the script updates every day at 5 p.m. or at 5 a.m.? It's likely 5 p.m. will be pretty busy on your local ISP's network, while 5 a.m. will probably be quiet. If you notice it's hard to do anything on your home network at those peak times, it's highly unlikely your script will be able to do anything then either!

Aside from network problems, you'll probably find other issues that break your scraping script—like the fact that the Internet is a changing thing.

The Changing Web (or Why Your Script Broke)

As you know, web redesigns, updated content management systems, and changes in page structure (a new ad system, a new referral network, etc.) are a normal part of the Internet landscape. The Web grows and changes. For that reason, your web scraping scripts *will* break. The good news is, there are a lot of sites that only change annually, or once every few years. There are also some changes that may not even affect page structure (sometimes style updates or ad updates don't change the content and structure of the code). Don't lose all hope; it's possible your script will work for quite some time!

However, we don't want to give you *false* hope. Your script will break eventually. One day, you'll go to run it and you will realize it no longer works. When this happens, give yourself a big hug, pour yourself some tea or coffee, and begin again.

Now you know more about how to examine the content on a site and figure out the most useful bits for your reporting. You already have quite a lot of code written which will still mainly work. You are in a good debugging stage, and you now have tons of tools at your disposal to find that new `div` or table with the data you seek.

A (Few) Word(s) of Caution

When scraping the Web, it's important to be conscientious. You should also inform yourself about laws in your country pertaining to content on the Web. Generally, how to be conscientious is pretty clear. Don't take someone else's content and use it as your own. Don't take content that says it's not supposed to be shared. Don't spam people or websites. Don't hack websites or maliciously scrape sites. Basically, don't be a jerk! If you couldn't share with your mom or a close friend what you are doing and feel good about yourself, don't do it.

There are a few ways to be clear about what you are doing on the Internet. Many of the scraping libraries allow you to send User-Agent strings. You can put your information or your company's information in those strings so it's clear who is scraping the site. You also want to make sure to take a look at the site's *robots.txt* file (*http://www.robotstxt.org/robotstxt.html*), which tells web spiders what parts of the site are off-limits.

 Before building a spider to traverse a site, see if the parts of the site you are interested in are included in the Disallow section of the *robots.txt* file. If they are, you should find another way to get the data, or contact the site owner and see if they can get it to you in a different way.

Be a force of good on the Internet and do the right thing when you build scrapers. This means you can be proud of your work; stay out of trouble with lawyers, companies, and the government; and freely use the information you gather.

Summary

You should now feel comfortable writing a scraper for difficult-to-parse content. You can use Selenium or Ghost.py to open a browser, read a web page, interact with the page, and extract data. You can use Scrapy to crawl and spider an entire domain (or series of domains) and extract large quantities of data. You also practiced regex syntax and wrote your own Python class (with the help of Scrapy).

On top of that, your Python code is coming along. You have explored some bash commands. You are gaining some great experience interacting with shell scripts, and you are well on your way to being a professional data wrangler. Table 12-2 lists the new concepts and tools introduced in this chapter.

Table 12-2. New Python and programming concepts and libraries

Concept/ Library	Purpose
Selenium library	Library used to interact directly with web pages and their elements using a browser of your choice, as well as with headless browsers. Great if you need to click on elements, enter information in forms, and interact with pages that require quite a few requests to load the content.
PhatomJS library	JavaScript library used as a headless browser for web scraping on a server or other browserless machine. Can also be used to write a web scraper using only JavaScript.
Ghost.py library	Library used to interact with web pages through Qt WebKit, rather than a traditional browser. Can be used in similar situations to where one would use a browser, with the ability to write native JavaScript.
Scrapy library	Library used to spider or crawl many pages across a domain or several domains. Great if you need to investigate more than one domain or more than one type of page to collect your data.
Scrapy crawl rules	Crawl rules instruct your spider to match URL structures and identify parts of the page where the spider might find such links. This enables your spider to navigate and find more content.

Finally, for scrapers, make sure you follow some basic logic (see Table 12-3).

Table 12-3. Which scraper to use

Scraper type	Libraries	Use case
Page-reader scraper	BeautifulSoup, LXML	Simple page scraping where all the data you want exists on one page loaded in one request.
Browser-based scraper	Selenium, PhantomJS, Ghost.py	Browser-based scraping where you need to interact with elements on the page or the page requires many different requests to load.
Web spider/ crawler	Scrapy	Following links across many pages or parsing similar pages in a fast and asynchronous way. Great for if you know you need many matches across an entire domain or series of domains.

In the next few chapters, we'll look at expanding your web skills using APIs, as well as scaling and automating your data. These are the final stages in bringing all of your learning together into a series of repeatable, executable scripts—some of which run without you having to do anything. Remember all those rote tasks you thought about when you first started this book? Well, they are soon to be rote no more—read on!

## CHAPTER 13

APIs

An application programming interface (API) sounds like a fancy concept, but it is not. An API is a standardized way of sharing data on the Web. Many websites share data through API endpoints. There are too many available APIs to list in this book, but here are some you might find useful or interesting:

- Twitter (*https://dev.twitter.com/overview/api*)
- US Census (*http://www.census.gov/data/developers/data-sets.html*)
- World Bank (*http://data.worldbank.org/node/9*)
- LinkedIn (*https://developer.linkedin.com/docs/rest-api*)
- San Francisco Open Data (*https://data.sfgov.org/*)

All of these are examples of APIs that return data. You make a request to the API, and the API returns data. APIs can also serve as a way to interact with other applications. For example, we could use the Twitter API to get data from Twitter and build another application that interacts with Twitter (e.g., an application that posts Tweets using the API). The Google API list (*https://developers.google.com/apis-explorer/#p/*) is another example—most APIs allow you to interact with the company's services. With the LinkedIn API, you can retrieve data, but also post updates to LinkedIn without going through the web interface. Because an API can do many different things, it should be considered a service. For our purposes, the service provides data.

In this chapter, you will request API data and save it to your computer. APIs usually return JSON, XML, or CSV files, which means after the data is saved locally to your computer, you just need to apply the skills you learned in the early chapters of this book to parse it. The API we will be working with in this chapter is the Twitter API.

We chose the Twitter API as an example for a number of reasons. First, Twitter is a well-known platform. Second, it has a lot of data (tweets) that folks are interested in analyzing. Finally, the Twitter API allows us to explore many API concepts, which we will discuss along the way.

Twitter data has been used both as an informal information collection tool, like in the One Million Tweet Map (*http://onemilliontweetmap.com/*), and as a more formal research tool, such as for predicting flu trends (*http://bit.ly/flu_trends_twitter*) and detecting real-time events like earthquakes (*http://bit.ly/social_sensors*).

API Features

An API can be as simple as a data response to a request, but it's rare to find APIs with only that functionality. Most APIs have other useful features. These features may include multiple API request methods (REST or streaming), data timestamps, rate limits, data tiers, and API access objects (keys and tokens). Let's take a look at these in the context of the Twitter API.

REST Versus Streaming APIs

The Twitter API is available in two forms: REST and streaming. Most APIs are REST-ful, but some real-time services offer streaming APIs. *REST* stands for *Representational State Transfer* and is designed to create stability in API architecture. Data from REST APIs can be accessed using the `requests` library (see Chapter 11). With the `requests` library, you can `GET` and `POST` web requests—which is what REST APIs use to return matching data. In the case of Twitter, the REST API allows you to query tweets, post tweets, and do most things Twitter allows via its website.

 With a REST API, you can often (but not always) preview your query in a browser by using the API request as a URL. If you load the URL in your browser and it looks like a text blob, you can install a format previewer for your browser. For example, Chrome has plug-ins to preview JSON files in an easy-to-read way.

A *streaming API* runs as a real-time service and listens for data relating to your query. When you encounter a streaming API, you will likely want to use a library built to help manage data intake. To learn more about how Twitter's streaming API works, see the overview on the Twitter website (*https://dev.twitter.com/streaming/overview*).

Rate Limits

APIs often have rate limits, which restrict the amount of data a user can request over a period of time. Rate limits are put in place by the API providers for several different reasons. In addition to rate limiting, you may also encounter an API with limited access to data, particularly if the data relates to business interests. For infrastructure and customer service purposes, the API provider will want to limit the number of requests so the servers and architecture can manage the amount of data transferred. If everyone was allowed to have 100% of the data 100% of the time, this could cause the API servers to crash.

If you encounter an API requiring payment for extra access, you'll need to determine if you can pay and how much the data is worth for your research. If you encounter an API with rate limiting, you'll want to determine if a subset of the data is sufficient. If the API has rate limits, it may take you quite a long time to collect a representative sample, so be sure to estimate the level of effort you're willing and able to expend.

APIs will often have a rate limit for all users, as it's easier to manage. Twitter's API was once limited in such a way; however, with the launch of the Streaming API, the usage changed. Twitter's Streaming API provides a constant stream of data, while the REST API limits the number of requests you can make per 15-minute period. To help developers understand the rate limits, Twitter has published a chart (*https://dev.twitter.com/rest/public/rate-limits*).

For our exercise, we will use the item called GET search/tweets. This query returns tweets containing a certain search term. If you refer to the documentation (*http://bit.ly/get_search_tweets*) you will find the API returns JSON responses and is rate limited to 180 or 450 requests per 15 minutes, depending on whether you are querying the API as a user or an application.

 When you save data files from API responses, you can save many files *or* you can write the data to one file. You can also save the tweet data to a database, as we covered in Chapter 6. No matter what way you choose to save your data, ensure you do so regularly so you don't lose what you've already requested.

In Chapter 3, we processed one JSON file. If we maximize our API usage for every 15 minutes, we can collect 180 JSON files. If you hit the rate limit and need to optimize your requests to Twitter or other APIs, read the section on "Tips to Avoid Being Rate Limited" in Twitter's "API Rate Limits" article (*https://dev.twitter.com/rest/public/rate-limiting*).

Tiered Data Volumes

So far, we have been talking about Twitter data freely available via its API. But maybe you want to know, how do I get *all* the data? In the case of Twitter, there are three access tiers you may have heard of before: firehose, gardenhose, and Spritzer. The spritzer is the free API. Table 13-1 describes differences between these tiers.

Table 13-1. Twitter feed types

Feed type	Coverage	Availability	Cost
Firehose	All tweets	Available through a partner - DataSift (*http://datasift.com/*) or Gnip (*https://gnip.com/*)	$$$
Gardenhose	10% of all tweets	New access is no longer available	N/A
Spritzer	1% of tweets, or up to it	Available through the public API	Free

You might look at these options and think, "I need the firehose, because I have to have it all!" But there are some things you should know before attempting to purchase access:

- The firehose is a *lot* of data. When handling massive data, you need to scale your data wrangling. It will require numerous engineers and servers to even begin to query the dataset the firehose provides.

- The firehose costs money—a few hundred thousand dollars a year. This doesn't include the cost of the infrastructure you need to consume it (i.e., server space and database costs). Consuming the firehose is not something individuals do on their own—usually, a larger company or institution supports the costs.

- Most of what you really need, you can get from the *Spritzer*.

We will be using the *Spritzer* feed, which is the free public API from Twitter, where we can access Tweets within the bounds of the rate limits. To access this API, we will use API keys and tokens.

API Keys and Tokens

API keys and *tokens* are ways of identifying applications and users. Twitter API keys and tokens can be confusing. There are four components you need to be aware of:

API key
  Identifies the application

API secret
  Acts as a password for the application

Token
  Identifies the user

Token secret
  Acts as a password for the user

The combination of these elements gives you access to the Twitter API. Not all APIs have two layers of identifiers and secrets, however. Twitter is a good "best case" (i.e., more secure) example. In some cases, APIs will have no key or only one key.

Creating a Twitter API key and access token

Continuing our child labor research, we will collect chatter around child labor on Twitter. Creating a Twitter API key is easy, but it requires a few steps:

1. If you don't have a Twitter account, sign up (*https://twitter.com/signup*).

2. Sign in to *apps.twitter.com*.

3. Click the "Create New App" button.

4. Give your application a name and description. For our example, let's set the name to "Child labor chatter" and the description to "Pulling down chatter around child labor from Twitter."

5. Give your application a website—this is the website hosting the app. The instructions say, "If you don't have a URL yet, just put a placeholder here but remember to change it later." We don't have one, so we are also going to put the Twitter URL in the box. Make sure you include *https*, like this: *https://twitter.com*.

6. Agree to the developer agreement, and click "Create Twitter Application."

After you create the application, you will be taken to the application management page. If you lose this page, you can find it by going back to the application landing page (*https://apps.twitter.com/*).

At this point, you need to create a token:

1. Click on the "Keys and Access Tokens" tab. (This is where you can reset your key as well as create an access token.)

2. Scroll to the bottom and click on "Create my access token." Once you do this, the page will refresh with an update at the top. If you scroll to the bottom once again, you will see the access token.

Now you should have a consumer (API) key and a token. These are what ours look like:

- Consumer key: `5Hqg6JTZ0cC89hUThySd5yZcL`

- Consumer secret: `Ncp1oi5tUPbZF19Vdp8Jp8pNHBBfPdXGFtXqoKd6Cqn87xRj0c`

- Access token: `3272304896-ZTGUZZ6QsYKtZqXAVMLaJzR8qjrPW22iiu9ko4w`

- Access token secret: `nsNY13aPGWdm2QcgOl0qwqs5bwLBZ1iUVS2OE34QsuR4C`

Never share your keys or tokens with anyone! If you share your key with a friend, they can electronically represent you. If they abuse the system, you might lose access and be liable for their behavior.

Why did we publish ours? Well, for one, we generated new ones. In the process of generating new keys and tokens, the one included in this book was disabled—which is what you should do if you accidentally expose your key or token. If you need to create a new key, go to the "Keys and Access Tokens" tab and click "Regenerate." This will generate a new API key and token.

Now that we have a key, let's access the API!

A Simple Data Pull from Twitter's REST API

With a set of keys, we can now start to access data from Twitter's API. In this section, we will put together a simple script to pull data from the API by passing a search query. The script in this section is based on a snippet of Python code (*http://bit.ly/single-user_oauth*) provided by Twitter as an example. This code uses Python OAuth2, which is a protocol for identifying and connecting securely when using APIs.

The current best practice for authentication is to use OAuth2. Some APIs might still use OAuth1, which will function differently and is a deprecated protocol. If you need to use OAuth1, you can use Requests-OAuthlib (*https://requests-oauthlib.readthedocs.org/en/latest/*) in conjunction with `requests`. When authenticating via an API, make sure to identify which protocol to use. If you use the wrong one, you will receive errors when trying to connect.

To start, we need to install Python OAuth2:

```
pip install oauth2
```

Open a new file and start by importing `oauth2` and assigning your key variables:

```
import oauth2

API_KEY = '5Hqg6JTZ0cC89hUThySd5yZcL'
API_SECRET = 'Ncp1oi5tUPbZF19Vdp8Jp8pNHBBfPdXGFtXqoKd6Cqn87xRj0c'
TOKEN_KEY = '3272304896-ZTGUZZ6QsYKtZqXAVMLaJzR8qjrPW22iiu9ko4w'
TOKEN_SECRET = 'nsNY13aPGWdm2QcgOl0qwqs5bwLBZ1iUVS20E34QsuR4C'
```

Then add the function to create the OAuth connection:

```
def oauth_req(url, key, secret, http_method="GET", post_body="",
              http_headers=None):
    consumer = oauth2.Consumer(key=API_KEY, secret=API_SECRET)       ❶
```

```
token = oauth2.Token(key=key, secret=secret)                    ❷
client = oauth2.Client(consumer, token)                         ❸
resp, content = client.request(url, method=http_method,         ❹
                        body=post_body, headers=http_headers)
return content                                                  ❺
```

❶ Establishes the consumer of the oauth2 object. The consumer is the owner of the keys. This line provides the consumer with the keys so it can properly identify via the API.

❷ Assigns the token to the oauth2 object.

❸ Creates the client, which consists of the consumer and token.

❹ Using the url, which is a function argument, executes the request using the OAuth2 client.

❺ Returns the content received from the connection.

Now we have a function that allows us to connect to the Twitter API. However, we need to define our URL and call the function. The Search API documentation (*https://dev.twitter.com/rest/public/search*) tells us more about what requests we want to use. Using the web interface, we can see that if we search for *#childlabor*, we end up with the following URL: *https://twitter.com/search?q=%23childlabor*. The documentation instructs us to reformat the URL so we end up with the following: *https://api.twitter.com/1.1/search/tweets.json?q=%23childlabor*.

Then, we can add that URL as a variable and call the function using our previously defined variables:

```
url = 'https://api.twitter.com/1.1/search/tweets.json?q=%23childlabor'
data = oauth_req(url, TOKEN_KEY, TOKEN_SECRET)

print(data)                                                     ❶
```

❶ Add a print statement at the end, so you can see the output.

When you run the script, you should see the data printed as a long JSON object. You may remember a JSON object looks like a Python dictionary, but if you were to rerun the script with print(type(data)), you would find out that the content is a string. At this point we could do one of two things: we could convert the data into a dictionary and start parsing it, or we could save the string to a file to parse later. To continue parsing the data in the script, add import json at the top of the script. Then, at the bottom, load the string using json and output it:

```
data = json.loads(data)
print(type(data))
```

The data variable will now return a Python dictionary. If you want to write the data to a file and parse it later, add the following code instead:

```
with open('tweet_data.json', 'wb') as data_file:
    data_file.write(data)
```

Your final script should look like the following:

```
import oauth2

API_KEY = '5Hqg6JTZ0cC89hUThySd5yZcL'
API_SECRET = 'Ncp1oi5tUPbZF19Vdp8Jp8pNHBBfPdXGFtXqoKd6Cqn87xRj0c'
TOKEN_KEY = '3272304896-ZTGUZZ6QsYKtZqXAVMLaJzR8qjrPW22iiu9ko4w'
TOKEN_SECRET = 'nsNY13aPGWdm2QcgOl0qwqs5bwLBZ1iUVS20E34QsuR4C'


def oauth_req(url, key, secret, http_method="GET", post_body="",
              http_headers=None):
    consumer = oauth2.Consumer(key=API_KEY, secret=API_SECRET)
    token = oauth2.Token(key=key, secret=secret)
    client = oauth2.Client(consumer, token)
    resp, content = client.request(url, method=http_method,
                                   body=post_body, headers=http_headers)
    return content


url = 'https://api.twitter.com/1.1/search/tweets.json?q=%23popeindc'
data = oauth_req(url, TOKEN_KEY, TOKEN_SECRET)

with open("data/hashchildlabor.json", "w") as data_file:
    data_file.write(data)
```

From here you can refer back to the section "JSON Data" on page 52 in Chapter 3 to parse the data.

Advanced Data Collection from Twitter's REST API

Pulling a single data file from Twitter is not terribly useful, because it only returns about 15 tweets. We are looking to execute multiple queries in a row, so we can collect as many tweets as possible related to our topic. We are going to use another library to do some of the heavy lifting for us—Tweepy. Tweepy can help us manage a series of requests as well as OAuth using Twitter. Start by installing tweepy:

```
pip install tweepy
```

At the top of your script, import tweepy and set your keys again:

```
import tweepy

API_KEY = '5Hqg6JTZ0cC89hUThySd5yZcL'
API_SECRET = 'Ncp1oi5tUPbZF19Vdp8Jp8pNHBBfPdXGFtXqoKd6Cqn87xRj0c'
```

```
TOKEN_KEY = '3272304896-ZTGUZZ6QsYKtZqXAVMLaJzR8qjrPW22iiu9ko4w'
TOKEN_SECRET = 'nsNY13aPGWdm2QcgOl0qwqs5bwLBZ1iUVS2OE34QsuR4C'
```

Then pass your API key and API secret to `tweepy`'s `OAuthHandler` object, which will manage the same OAuth protocol covered in the last example. Then set your access token:

```
auth = tweepy.OAuthHandler(API_KEY, API_SECRET)          ❶
auth.set_access_token(TOKEN_KEY, TOKEN_SECRET)           ❷
```

❶ Creates an object to manage the API authentication via `tweepy`

❷ Sets token access

Next, pass the authorization object you just created to `tweepy.API`:

```
api = tweepy.API(auth)
```

The `tweepy.API` object can take a variety of arguments to give you customized control over how `tweepy` behaves when requesting data. You can directly add retries and delays between requests using parameters like `retry_count=3, retry_delay=5`. Another useful option is `wait on_rate_limit`, which will wait until the rate limit has been lifted to make the next request. Details on all of these niceties and more are included in the `tweepy` documentation (*http://docs.tweepy.org/en/latest/api.html*).

We want to create a connection to the Twitter API using `tweepy.Cursor`. We can then pass the cursor the API method to use, which is `api.search` (*http://docs.tweepy.org/en/latest/api.html#API.search*), and the parameters associated with that method:

```
query = '#childlabor'                                    ❶
cursor = tweepy.Cursor(api.search, q=query, lang="en")   ❷
```

❶ Creates the query variable

❷ Establishes the cursor with the query, and limits it to just the English language

 While the term `Cursor` might not feel intuitive, it's a common programming term in reference to database connections. Although an API is not a database, the class name `Cursor` was probably adopted from this usage. You can read more about cursors on Wikipedia (*https://en.wikipedia.org/wiki/Cursor_(databases)*).

According to `tweepy`'s documentation (*http://tweepy.readthedocs.org/en/latest/api.html*), `cursor` can return an iterator on a per-item or per-page level. You can also define limits (*http://bit.ly/tweepy_limits*) to determine how many pages or items the cursor grabs. If you look at `print(dir(cursor))`, you'll see there are three methods:

['items', 'iterator', 'pages']. A page returns a bunch of items, which are individual tweets from your query. For our needs, we are going to use pages.

Let's iterate through the pages and save the data. Before we do that, we need to do two things:

1. Add `import json` to the top of the script.
2. Create a directory called *data* in the same directory as the script. To do this, run `mkdir data` on the command line.

Once you've done those two things, run the following code to iterate through and save the tweets:

```
for page in cursor.pages():                                  ❶
    tweets = []                                              ❷
    for item in page:                                        ❸
        tweets.append(item._json)                            ❹

with open('data/hashchildlabor.json', 'wb') as outfile:      ❺
    json.dump(tweets, outfile)
```

❶ For each page returned in `cursor.pages()`...

❷ Creates an empty list to store tweets.

❸ For each item (or tweet) in a page...

❹ Extracts the JSON tweet data and saves it to the tweets list.

❺ Opens a file called *hashchildlabor.json* and saves the tweets.

You will notice not many tweets are being saved to the file. There are only 15 tweets per page, so we'll need to figure out a way to get more data. Options include:

- Open a file and never close it, or open a file and append the information at the end. This will create one massive file.
- Save each page in its own file (you can use timestamps to ensure you have different filenames for each file).
- Create a new table in your database to save the tweets.

Creating one file is dangerous, because at any moment the process could fail and corrupt the data. Unless you have a small data pull (e.g., 1000 tweets) or are doing development testing, you should use one of the other options.

There are a couple of ways to save the data in a new file every time, the most common ones being creating a filename by using a date and timestamp (*https://docs.python.org/2/library/datetime.html*), or just by incrementing a number and appending it to the end of the filename.

We'll go ahead and add our tweets to our simple database. To do so, we'll use this function:

```python
def store_tweet(item):
    db = dataset.connect('sqlite:///data_wrangling.db')
    table = db['tweets']                               ❶
    item_json = item._json.copy()
    for k, v in item_json.items():
        if isinstance(v, dict):                        ❷
            item_json[k] = str(v)
    table.insert(item_json)                            ❸
```

❶ Creates or accesses a new table called `tweets`

❷ Tests if there are any dictionaries in our tweet item values. Since SQLite doesn't support saving Python dictionaries, we need to convert dictionaries into strings.

❸ Inserts the cleaned JSON item.

We will also need to add `dataset` into our import. We will then need to add the use of this function where we were previously storing the pages. We'll also want to make sure we iterate over every tweet. Your final script should look like the following:

```python
import json
import tweepy
import dataset

API_KEY = '5Hqg6JTZ0cC89hUThySd5yZcL'
API_SECRET = 'Ncp1oi5tUPbZF19Vdp8Jp8pNHBBfPdXGFtXqoKd6Cqn87xRj0c'
TOKEN_KEY = '3272304896-ZTGUZZ6QsYKtZqXAVMLaJzR8qjrPW22iiu9ko4w'
TOKEN_SECRET = 'nsNY13aPGWdm2QcgOl0qwqs5bwLBZ1iUVS2OE34QsuR4C'

def store_tweet(item):
    db = dataset.connect('sqlite:///data_wrangling.db')
    table = db['tweets']
    item_json = item._json.copy()
    for k, v in item_json.items():
        if isinstance(v, dict):
            item_json[k] = str(v)
    table.insert(item_json)

auth = tweepy.OAuthHandler(API_KEY, API_SECRET)
auth.set_access_token(TOKEN_KEY, TOKEN_SECRET)

api = tweepy.API(auth)
```

```
query = '#childlabor'
cursor = tweepy.Cursor(api.search, q=query, lang="en")

for page in cursor.pages():
    for item in page:
        store_tweet(item)
```

Advanced Data Collection from Twitter's Streaming API

Early in this chapter, we mentioned there are two types of Twitter APIs available: REST and Streaming.

How does the Streaming API differ from the REST API? Here's a brief rundown:

- The data is live, while the REST API returns only data that has already been tweeted.

- Streaming APIs are less common, but will become more available in the future as more live data is generated and exposed.

- Because up-to-date data is interesting, many people are interested in the data, which means you can find lots of resources and help online.

Let's create a script to collect from the Streaming API. Such a script builds on all the concepts we've covered in this chapter. We'll first add the basics—imports and keys:

```
from tweepy.streaming import StreamListener                         ❶
from tweepy import OAuthHandler, Stream                             ❷

API_KEY = '5Hqg6JTZ0cC89hUThySd5yZcL'
API_SECRET = 'Ncp1oi5tUPbZF19Vdp8Jp8pNHBBfPdXGFtXqoKd6Cqn87xRj0c'
TOKEN_KEY = '3272304896-ZTGUZZ6QsYKtZqXAVMLaJzR8qjrPW22iiu9ko4w'
TOKEN_SECRET = 'nsNY13aPGWdm2QcgOl0qwqs5bwLBZ1iUVS2OE34QsuR4C'
```

❶ Imports `StreamListener`, which creates a streaming session and listens for messages

❷ Imports `OAuthHandler`, which we used before, and `Stream`, which actually handles the Twitter stream

In this script, we are doing our `import` statements slightly differently than we did in the last script. Both of these are valid approaches and a matter of preference. Here's a quick comparison of the two approaches:

Approach 1

```
import tweepy
...
auth = tweepy.OAuthHandler(API_KEY, API_SECRET)
```

Approach 2

```
from tweepy import OAuthHandler
...
auth = OAuthHandler(API_KEY, API_SECRET)
```

Usually the first approach is used when the library is not used much in the script. It is also good when you have a longer piece of code and want to be explicit. However, when the library is used a lot it gets tiresome to type this out: also, if the library is the cornerstone of the script, it should be fairly obvious to people what modules or classes are imported from the library.

Now we are going to subclass (a concept you learned about in Chapter 12) the Stream Listener class we imported because we want to override the on_data method. To do this, we redefine it in our new class, which we call Listener. When there is data, we want to see it in our terminal, so we are going to add a print statement:

```
class Listener(StreamListener):            ❶

    def on_data(self, data):               ❷
        print data                         ❸
        return True                        ❹
```

❶ Subclasses StreamListener.

❷ Defines the on_data method.

❸ Outputs tweets.

❹ Returns True. StreamListener has an on_data method, which also returns True. As we're subclassing and redefining it, we must repeat the return value in the subclassed method.

Next, add your authentication handlers:

```
auth = OAuthHandler(API_KEY, API_SECRET)
auth.set_access_token(TOKEN_KEY, TOKEN_SECRET)
```

Finally, pass the Listener and auth to the Stream and start filtering with a search term. In this case, we are going to look at *child labor* because it has more traffic than *#childlabor*:

```
stream = Stream(auth, Listener())          ❶
stream.filter(track=['child labor'])       ❷
```

❶ Sets up the stream by passing auth and Listener as arguments

❷ Filters the stream and returns only items with the terms *child* and *labor*

Your final script should look like this:

```
from tweepy.streaming import StreamListener
from tweepy import OAuthHandler, Stream


API_KEY = '5Hqg6JTZ0cC89hUThySd5yZcL'
API_SECRET = 'Ncp1oi5tUPbZF19Vdp8Jp8pNHBBfPdXGFtXqoKd6Cqn87xRj0c'
TOKEN_KEY = '3272304896-ZTGUZZ6QsYKtZqXAVMLaJzR8qjrPW22iiu9ko4w'
TOKEN_SECRET = 'nsNY13aPGWdm2QcgOl0qwqs5bwLBZ1iUVS20E34QsuR4C'


class Listener(StreamListener):

    def on_data(self, data):
        print data
        return True

auth = OAuthHandler(API_KEY, API_SECRET)
auth.set_access_token(TOKEN_KEY, TOKEN_SECRET)

stream = Stream(auth, Listener())
stream.filter(track=['child labor'])
```

From here, you would add a way to save tweets to your database, file, or other storage using your on_data method as we did earlier in the chapter.

Summary

Being able to interact with application programming interfaces is an important part of data wrangling. In this chapter, we covered some of the API basics (see Table 13-2 for a summary) and processed data from the Twitter API.

Table 13-2. API concepts

Concept	Usage
REST APIs (vs. streaming)	Return data and expose static endpoints
Streaming APIS (vs. REST)	Return live data to query
OAuth and OAuth2	Authenticate given a series of keys and tokens
Tiered data volumes	Various layers of rate limits/availability of data; some cost $
Keys and tokens	Unique IDs and secrets to identify the user and application

We reused many Python concepts we already knew and learned a few new Python concepts in this chapter. The first was the usage of tweepy, a library to handle interactions with the Twitter API. You also learned about authentication and OAuth protocols.

As an extension of interacting with an API, Chapter 14 will help you learn about techniques enabling you to run your API scripts while you are away.

## CHAPTER 14

Automation and Scaling

You've scraped large amounts of data from APIs and websites, you've cleaned and organized your data, and you've run statistical analysis and produced visual reports. Now it's time to let Python take the wheel and automate your data wrangling. In this chapter, we'll cover how to automate your data analysis, collection, and publication. We will learn how to create proper logging and alerting so you can fully automate your scripts and get notifications of success, failure, and any issues your work encounters along the way.

We will also take a look at scaling your automation using Python libraries designed to help you execute many tasks and monitor their success and failure. We'll analyze some libraries and helper tools for fully scaling your data in the cloud.

Python gives us plenty of options for automation and scaling. There are some simple, straightforward tasks that lend themselves to Python automation on almost any machine without much setup, and there are some larger, more complex ways to automate. We'll cover examples of both, as well as how to scale your data automation as a data wrangler.

Why Automate?

Automation gives you a way to easily run your scripts without needing to do so on your local machine—or even be awake! The ability to automate means you can spend time working on other more thought-intensive projects. If you have a well-written script to perform data cleanup for you, you can focus on working with the data to produce better reporting.

Here are some great examples of tasks where automation can help:

- Every Tuesday a new set of analytics comes out; you compile a report and send it to the interested parties.
- Another department or coworker needs to be able to run your reporting tool or cleanup tool without your guidance and support.
- Once a week, you have to download, clean, and send data.
- Every time a user requests a new report, the reporting script should run and alert the user once the report is generated.
- Once a week, you need to clean erroneous data from the database and back it up to another location.

Each of these problems has myriad solutions, but one thing is certain: they are good tasks to automate. They are clear in their outcomes and steps. They have a limited but specific audience. They have a certain time or event that sets them into motion. And they are all things you can script and run when the particular circumstances apply.

Automation is easiest when the task is clear and well defined and the outcomes are easy to determine. However, even if the outcome is not always easy to test or predict, automation can help complete a part of a task and leave the rest for your (or someone else's) closer inspection and analysis. You can think of automation here similarly to the ways you automate other things in your life. You might have a favorite saved pizza order or an auto-reply on your email. If a task has a fairly clear outcome and occurs regularly, then it is a good task to automate.

But when should you not automate? Here are some criteria to indicate if a task isn't a good candidate for automation:

- The task occurs so rarely and is so complex, it's better to do it yourself (e.g., filing your taxes).
- A successful outcome for the task is difficult to determine (e.g., group discussion, social research, or investigation).
- The task requires human interaction to determine the proper way to complete it (e.g., navigating traffic, translating poetry).
- It is imperative the task succeeds.

Some of these examples—particularly things that require human input—are ripe for some level of automation. Some we can partially automate by allowing machines to find recommendations, which we can then determine are right or wrong (machine learning with human feedback). Others, like when a task is rare and complex or is business critical, might end up becoming automated, or partially automated, as they become familiar. But you can see the overall logic to guide when automation fits best and when it's not a good idea.

If you're not sure automation is right for you, you can always try automating something small you do on a regular interval and see how it works. Chances are you'll find more applicable solutions over time, and the experience of automating one thing will make it easier to automate more things in the future.

Steps to Automate

Because automation begins with a clear and simple focus, your steps to automate should also be clear and simple. It is particularly helpful to begin automation by documenting the following (in a list, on a whiteboard, in drawings, in a storyboard):

- When must this task begin?
- Does this task have a time limit or maximum length? If so, when must it end?
- What are the necessary inputs for this task?
- What constitutes success, or partial success, for this task?
- If this task fails, what should happen?
- What does the task produce or provide? To whom? In what way?
- What, if anything, should happen after this task concludes?

If you can answer five or more of these questions, you are in a good place. If you can't, it might be worth doing some more research and clarification before you begin. If you are asked to automate something you have never done before, or haven't done often, try documenting it as you perform the task and then determine if you can answer the questions listed here.

 If your project is too large or vague, try breaking it up into smaller tasks and automate a few of those tasks. Perhaps your task involves a report which downloads two datasets, runs cleanup and analysis, and then sends the results to different groups depending on the outcome. You can break this task into subtasks, automating each step. If any of these subtasks fail, stop the chain and alert the person(s) responsible for maintaining the script so it can be investigated and restarted after the bug or issue is resolved.

So, our basic steps for automation are as follows (note that these will vary depending on the types of tasks you are completing):

1. Define your problem set and break it into smaller chunks of work.
2. Describe exactly what each subtask needs as input, what it needs to do, and what it needs to be marked complete.
3. Identify where you can get those inputs and when the tasks need to run.

4. Begin coding your task and testing with real or example data.

5. Clean up your task and your script, and add documentation.

6. Add logging, with a focus on debugging errors and recording successful completion.

7. Submit your code to a repository and test it manually. Make changes as needed.

8. Get your script ready for automation, by replacing manual tasks with automated ones.

9. Watch your logs and alerts as the task begins automation. Correct any errors or bugs. Update your testing and documentation.

10. Develop a long-term plan for how often the logs are checked for errors.

The first step toward automation is always to better define your tasks and subtasks and make them small enough chunks, so they can easily be completed and their success or failure determined.

The next few steps align well with our process throughout this book. You should identify how you can begin to solve the problem with Python. Search for libraries or tools to help fix the problem or complete the request, and begin coding. Once your script is working, you'll want to test it with a few different possible datasets or inputs. After successful testing, you'll want to simplify and document it. You will likely set it up in a repository (on Bitbucket or GitHub) so you can document changes and additions over time.

Once you have a completed script, first run it by hand (rather than the automated way). When the new data arrives or the time comes to run it, do so manually and keep watch over its output. There might be unforeseen errors or extra logging and debugging you'll need to add.

Depending on what type of automation fits your needs, you might set up a simple cron task where the script is executed at certain intervals. (You'll learn all about cron later in this chapter.) You might need to slightly modify the script so it has the ability to run autonomously by using argument variables, databases, or particular files on the system. You might add it to a task queue to manage when it runs. Whichever fits, your job is not yet over.

When your script is first automated, it's essential you take time to review it every time it runs. Look through your logs and monitor what is happening. You will likely find small bugs, which you can then fix. Again, refresh any necessary logging and documentation.

After about five successes or properly logged failures, you can likely scale back your manual review. However, it's still a great idea to `grep` (*http://bit.ly/practi cal_grep_examples*) your logs monthly or quarterly and see what's happening. If you are using a log aggregator, you can actually automate this step and have the task send you error and warning reports. How meta is that?

Automation is no small process, but an early investment in time and attention will pay dividends. A well-running set of automation tasks takes time to complete, but the result is often far better than haphazard scripts requiring constant attention, care, and monitoring. Pay close attention now and take time to automate your script the right way. Only then can you really move on to whatever is next at hand, rather than constantly having one part of your work tied to monitoring and administering support for a few unruly tasks.

What Could Go Wrong?

There are quite a few things that can go wrong with your automation. Some of them are easy to correct and account for, while others are more nebulous and might never have a true fix. One of the important lessons in automation is figuring out what types of errors and issues are worth taking the time and energy to fix and what ones are better to just plan for and work through another way.

Let's take, for example, the types of errors we talked about in Chapter 12: our network errors for web scraping. If you are running into significant network errors, you have only a few good options. You can change who hosts your tasks and see if the performance improves (which may be costly and time consuming, depending on your setup). You can call your network provider and ask for support. You can run the tasks at a different time and see if there is a different outcome. You can expect the problems to happen and build your script around these expectations (i.e., run more than you need and expect some percentage to fail).

There are many possible errors you will encounter when running your tasks by automation:

- Database connection errors leading to lost or bad data
- Script bugs and errors where the script does not properly complete
- Timeout errors or too many request errors from websites or APIs
- Edge cases, where the data or parts of the reporting don't conform and break the script
- Server load issues or other hardware problems

- Poor timing, race conditions (*https://en.wikipedia.org/wiki/Race_condition*) (if scripts depend on previous completion of other tasks, race conditions can invalidate the data)

 There are naturally far more potential issues than you can anticipate. The larger the team you work with, the greater the chance that poor documentation, poor understanding, and poor team communication can hurt automation. You will not be able to prevent every error, but you can try through the best communication and documentation you can provide. Still, you will also need to accept your automation will sometimes fail.

To prepare for eventual failure, you will want to be alerted when issues arise. You should determine what percentage of error is acceptable. Not every service performs well 100% of the time (hence the existence of status pages); however, we can strive for perfection and determine how many hours and how much effort our automation is worth.

Depending on your automation and its weaknesses, there are some ways to combat those issues. Here are some ways to build a more resilient automation system:

- Retry failed tasks at a specific interval.
- Ensure your code has numerous `try...except` blocks allowing it to work through failures.
- Build special exception blocks around code handling connections to other machines, databases, or APIs.
- Regularly maintain and monitor machines you use for your automation.
- Test your tasks and automation on a regular basis using test data and ensure they run properly.
- Make yourself aware of dependencies, race conditions, and API rules in your script's domain and write code according to this knowledge.
- Utilize libraries like `requests` and `multiprocessing` to make difficult problems easier and attempt to take some of the mystery out of problems that plague many scripts.

We'll be reviewing some of these techniques and ideas as we walk through how to best go about monitoring and automating your scripts. For now, let's move on to tools we can use for automation to make our lives as data wranglers easier and simpler and determine a few tips on where and how you should implement these tools.

Where to Automate

Depending on the needs of your script, deciding where it runs will be an important first step. No matter where it first runs, you can move it elsewhere, but this will likely require some rewriting. At the beginning, you will probably need it to run locally. To run a script or task *locally* is to run it on your own computer.

To run something *remotely* means to run it on another machine—likely a server somewhere. Once your script succeeds and is well tested, you will want to move it to run remotely. If you manage or have servers, or work for an organization with servers, it can be relatively easy to port your scripts to those servers. This allows you to work on your own machine (laptop or desktop) and not worry about when you turn it off and on. Running your scripts remotely also means you are not dependent on your ISP.

If you don't have access to a server, but you have an old desktop or laptop you don't use anymore, you can essentially turn it into your server. If it's running an old operating system, you can upgrade it so you can properly run Python on it, or you can wipe it and install Linux.

Using a home computer as your remote device means it should always be turned on and plugged into your home Internet. If you'd like to also install an OS you haven't used before, like Linux, this is an easy way to learn a new operating system and can help transition you to managing your own servers. If you're just getting started with Linux, we recommend you choose one of the popular distributions, such as Ubuntu (*http://bit.ly/ubuntu_guide*) or LinuxMint (*http://linuxmint.com/*).

If you'd like to manage your own server but you're just getting started, don't panic! Even if you've never managed or helped manage a server, increased competition among cloud service providers has made it a lot easier. Cloud providers allow you to spin up new machines and run your own server without needing to know a lot of technical knowledge. One such provider, DigitalOcean, has several nice writeups on how to get started, including introductions to creating your first server (*http://bit.ly/droplet_virtual_server*) and getting your server set up (*https://www.digitalocean.com/help/getting-started/setting-up-your-server/*).

Whether you host your scripts locally or remotely, there are a variety of tools to keep your computer or your server well monitored and updated. You'll want to ensure your scripts and tasks are fairly easy to manage and update, and that they run to completion on a regular basis. Finally, you'll want to be able to configure them and document them easily. We'll cover all of those topics in the following sections, starting off with Python tools you can use to help make your scripts more automation-friendly.

Special Tools for Automation

Python gives us many special tools for automation. We'll take a look at some of the ways we can manage our automation using Python, as well as using other machines and servers to do our bidding. We'll also discuss how we can use some built-in Python tools to manage inputs for our scripts and automate things that seem to require human input.

Using Local Files, argv, and Config Files

Depending on how your script works, you may need arguments or input that cannot always or shouldn't always be in a database or an API. When you have a simple input or output, you can use local files and arguments to pass the data.

Local files

When using local files for input and output, you'll want to ensure the script can run on the same machine every day, or can be easily moved with the input and output files. As your script grows, it's possible you will move and change it along with the files you use.

We've used local files before, but let's review how to do so from a more functional code standpoint. This code gives you the ability to open and write files using standard data types, and is very reusable and expandable depending on your script's needs:

```python
from csv import reader, writer


def read_local_file(file_name):
    if '.csv' in file_name:  ❶
        rdr = reader(open(file_name, 'rb'))
        return rdr
    return open(file_name, 'rb')  ❷


def write_local_file(file_name, data):
    with open(file_name, 'wb') as open_file:  ❸
        if type(data) is list:  ❹
            wr = writer(open_file)
            for line in data:
                wr.writerow(line)
        else:
            open_file.write(data)  ❺
```

❶ This line tests whether the file might be a good candidate to open with the csv module. If it ends in *.csv*, then it's likely we might want to open it using our CSV reader.

---

❷ If we haven't returned with our CSV reader, this code returns the open file. If we wanted to build a series of different ways to open and parse files based on the file extension, we could do that as well (e.g., using the `json` module for JSON files, or `pdfminer` for PDFs).

❸ This code uses `with...as` to return the output of the `open` function, assigning it to the `open_file` variable. When the indented block ends, Python will close the file automatically.

❹ If we are dealing with a list, this line uses the CSV writer to write each list item as a row of data. If we have dictionaries, we might want to use the `DictWriter` class.

❺ We want a good backup plan in case it's not a list. For this reason, write the raw data to file. Instead of this option, we could write different code depending on the data type.

Let's look at an example where we need the most recent file in a directory, which is often useful if you need to parse log files going back in time or look at the results of a recent web spider run:

```
import os

def get_latest(folder):
    files = [os.path.join(folder, f) for f in os.listdir(folder)] ❶
    files.sort(key=lambda x: os.path.getmtime(x), reverse=True) ❷
    return files[0] ❸
```

❶ Uses Python's built-in `os` module to list each file (`listdir` method), then uses the `path` module's `join` method to make a long string representing a full file path. This is an easy way to get a list of all of the files in a folder just by passing a string (the folder's path).

❷ Sorts files by last-modified date. Because `files` is a list, we can call the `sort` method and give it a key on which to sort. This code passes the full file paths to `getmtime`, which is the `os` module's "get modified time" method. The `reverse` argument makes sure the more recent files are on the top of the list.

❸ Returns only the most recent file.

This code returns the most recent folder, but if we wanted to return the whole list of files starting with the most recent we could simply modify the code to not return the first index, but instead the whole list or a slice.

There are many powerful tools to look up, modify, and alter files on your local (or your server's local) machine using the os library. A simple search on Stack Overflow returns educated answers as to how to find the only file modified in the last seven days or the only *.csv* file modified in the last month, and so on. Using local files, particularly when the data you need is already there (or easily put there with a wget), is a great way to simplify your automation.

Config files

Setting up local config files for your sensitive information is a must. As asserted in the Twelve-Factor App (*http://12factor.net/config*), storing your configuration (such as passwords, logins, email addresses, and other sensitive information) outside of your code base is part of being a good developer. If you connect to a database, send an email, use an API, or store payment information, that sensitive data should be stored in a configuration file.

Usually, we store config files in a separate folder within the repository (e.g., *config/*). All the code in the repository has access to these files, but by using *.gitignore* files, we can keep the configuration out of version control. If you have other developers or servers who need those files, you should copy them over manually.

We recommend having a section of the repository's *README.md* cover where and how to get hold of special configuration files so new users and collaborators know who to ask for the proper files.

Using a folder rather than one file allows you to have different configurations depending on what machine or environment the script runs in. You might want to have one configuration file for the test environment with test API keys, and a production file. You might have more than one database depending on what machine the script uses. You can store these specific pieces of information using a *.cfg* file, like the following example:

```
# Example configuration file
[address] ❶
name = foo ❷
email = myemail@bar.com
postalcode = 10177
street = Schlangestr. 4
city = Berlin
telephone = 015745738292950383

[auth_login]
user = test@mysite.com
pass = goodpassword
```

```
[db]
name = my_awesome_db
user = script_user
password = 7CH+89053FJKwjker)
host = my.host.io

[email]
user = script.email@gmail.com
password = 788Fksjelwi&
```

❶ Each section is denoted by square brackets with an easy-to-read string inside of them.

❷ Each line contains a *key* = *value* pair. The `ConfigParser` interprets these as strings. Values can contain any characters, including special characters, but keys should follow PEP-8 easy-to-read syntax and structure.

Having sections, keys, and values for our configuration lets us use the names of the sections and keys to access configuration values. This adds clarity to our Python scripts, without being insecure. Once you have a config file like the previous example set up, it's quite easy to parse with Python and use in your script and automation. Here's an example:

```
import ConfigParser
from some_api import get_client  ❶


def get_config(env):
    config = ConfigParser.ConfigParser()  ❷
    if env == 'PROD':
        return config.read(['config/production.cfg'])  ❸
    elif env == 'TEST':
        return config.read(['config/test.cfg'])
    return config.read(['config/development.cfg'])  ❹


def api_login():
    config = get_config('PROD')  ❺
    my_client = get_client(config.get('api_login', 'user'),
                           config.get('api_login', 'auth_key'))  ❻
    return my_client
```

❶ Here's an example of an API client hook we could import.

❷ This code instantiates a config object by calling the `ConfigParser` class. This is now an empty configuration object.

❸ This line calls the configuration parser object's `read` method and passes a list of configuration files. Here, we store them in a directory in the root of the project in a folder called *config*.

❹ If the environment variable passed does not match production or testing, we will always return the development configuration. It's a good idea to have catches like this in your configuration code, in case of a failure to define environment variables.

❺ We'll assume our example needs the production API, so this line asks for the PROD configuration. You can also save those types of decisions in the bash environment and read them using the built-in `os.environ` method (*http://bit.ly/ process_parameters*).

❻ This line calls the section name and key name to access the values stored in the configuration. This will return the values as strings, so if you need integers or other types, you should convert them.

The built-in `ConfigParser` library gives us easy access to our sections, keys, and values stored in our config file. If you'd like to store different pieces of information in different files and parse a list of them for each particular script, your code might look like this:

```
config = ConfigParser.ConfigParser()
config.read(['config/email.cfg', 'config/database.cfg', 'config/staging.cfg'])
```

It's up to you to organize your code and configuration depending on your needs. The syntax to access the configuration values simply uses the section name in your config (i.e., [*section_name*]) and the name of the key. So, a config file like this one:

```
[email]
user = test@mydomain.org
pass = my_super_password
```

can be accessed like this:

```
email_addy = config.get('email', 'user')
email_pass = config.get('email', 'pass')
```

 Config files are a simple tool to keeping all of your sensitive information in one place. If you'd rather use *.yml* or other extension files, Python has readers for those file types as well. Make sure you use *something* to keep your authentication and sensitive information stored separately from your code.

Command-line arguments

Python gives us the ability to pass command-line arguments to use for automation. These arguments pass information regarding how the script should function. For example, if we need the script to know we want it to run with the development configuration, we could run it like so:

```
python my_script.py DEV
```

We are using the same syntax to run a file from the command line, calling python, then the script name, and then adding DEV to the end of the line. How can we parse the extra argument using Python? Let's write code that does just that:

```
from import_config import get_config
import sys


def main(env):
    config = get_config(env)
    print config


if __name__ == '__main__':
    if len(sys.argv) > 1: ❶
        env = sys.argv(1) ❷
    else:
        env = 'TEST'
    main(env) ❸
```

❶ The built-in sys module helps with system tasks, including parsing command-line arguments. If the command-line argument list returned has a length greater than 1, there are extra arguments. The first argument always holds the name of the script (so if it has a length of 1, that's the only argument).

❷ To get the value of an argument, pass the index of that argument to the sys module's argv method. This line sets env equal to that value. Remember, the 0-index of argv will always be the Python script name, so you start parsing with the argument at the 1-index.

❸ This line uses the parsed arguments to modify your code according to the command-line arguments.

If we wanted to parse more than one extra variable, we could test the length to ensure we have enough, and then continue parsing. You can string together as many arguments as you'd like, but we recommend keeping it to under four. If you need more than four arguments, consider writing some of the logic into your script (e.g., on Tuesdays we only run testing, so if it's a Tuesday, use the test section of code, etc.).

Argument variables are great if you need to reuse the same code to perform different tasks or run in different environments. Maybe you have a script to run either collection *or* analysis, and you'd like to switch which environments you use. You might run it like so:

```
python my_script.py DEV ANALYSIS
python my_script.py PROD COLLECTION
```

Or you might have a script that needs to interact with a newly updated file folder and grab the latest logs—for example, to grab logs from more than one place:

```
python my_script.py DEV /var/log/apache2/
python my_script.py PROD /var/log/nginx/
```

With command-line arguments, simple changes in argument variables can create a portable and robust automation. Not every script will need to use these types of extra variables, but it's a nice-to-have solution built into the standard Python library and provides some flexibility should you need it.

Aside from these fairly simple and straightforward ways to parse your data and to give your script extra pieces of information, you can use more sophisticated and distributed approaches like cloud data and databasing. We'll look at these next.

Using the Cloud for Data Processing

The cloud is a term used to refer to a shared pool of resources, such as servers. There are many companies that offer cloud services—Amazon Web Services, more commonly referred to as AWS, is one of the best known.

The term *cloud* is often overused. If you are running your code on a cloud-based server, it is better to say "I am running it on a server" rather than "I am running it in the cloud."

When is a good time to use the cloud? The cloud is a good way to process data if the data is too large to process on your own computer or the procedure takes too long. Most tasks you want to automate you'll want to place in the cloud so you don't have to worry about whether the script is running or not when you turn your computer on or off.

If you choose to use AWS, the first time you log in you will see many different service offerings. There are only a few services you will need as a data wrangler (see Table 14-1).

Table 14-1. AWS cloud services

Service	Purpose in data wrangling
Simple Storage Service (S3)	A simple file storage service, used for dumping data files (JSON, XML, etc.).
Elastic Computing (EC2)	A on-demand server. This is where you run your scripts.
Elastic MapReduce (EMR)	Provides distributed data processing through a managed Hadoop framework.

Those are the basic AWS services with which to familiarize yourself. There are also several competitors, including IBM's Bluemix and Watson Developer Cloud (giving you access to several large data platforms, including Watson's logic and natural language processing abilities). You can also use DigitalOcean or Rackspace, which provide cheaper cloud resources.

No matter what you use, you'll need to deploy your code to your cloud server. To do so, we recommend using Git (*https://git-scm.com*).

Using Git to deploy Python

If you'd like to have your automation run somewhere other than your local machine, you'll need to deploy your Python script. We will review a few simple ways to do so, and then some slightly more complex ways.

Version control allows teams to work in parallel on the same repository of code without causing problems for one another. Git allows you to create different *branches*, thus allowing you or others on the team to work on a particular set of ideas or new integrations independently and then merge them back into the main or master branch of the code base easily and without losing any of the core functionality. It also ensures everyone has the most up-to-date code (including servers and remote machines).

The easiest and most intuitive way to deploy Python is to put your repository under version control using Git and use Git deploy hooks to "ship" code to your remote hosts. First, you'll need to install Git (*http://bit.ly/installing_git*).

If you're new to Git, we recommend taking the Code School tutorial on GitHub (*https://try.github.io/levels/1/challenges/1*) or walking through the Git tutorials on Atlassian (*https://www.atlassian.com/git/tutorials/*). It's fairly easy to get started, and you'll get the hang of the most used commands quickly. If you're working on the repository by yourself, you won't have to worry too much about pulling remote changes, but it's always good to set a clear routine.

Once your Git installation is complete, run these commands in your project's code folder:

```
git init .  ❶
git add my_script.py ❷
git commit -a ❸
```

❶   Initializes the current working directory as the root of your Git repository.

❷   Adds *my_script.py* to the repository. Use a filename or folder from your repository—just not your config files!

❸   Commits those changes along with any other running changes (-a) to your repository.

When prompted, you will need to write a commit message giving a brief explanation of the changes you've made, which should be explicit and clear. You might later need to find which commits implemented certain changes in your code. If you always write clear messages, this will help you search for and find those commits. It will also help others on your team or coworkers understand your code and commits.

 Get used to fetching remote changes with `git fetch` or using the `git pull --rebase` command to update your local repository with new commits. Then, work on your code, commit your work, and push your commits to your active branch. When it's time to merge your branch with the master, you can send a pull request (*https://help.github.com/articles/using-pull-requests/*), have others review the merge, and then merge it directly into master branch. Don't forget to delete stale or old branches when they are no longer useful.

It's also essential you set up a *.gitignore* file, where you list all of the file patterns you want Git to ignore when you push/pull changes, as discussed in the sidebar "Git and .gitignore" on page 213. You can have one for each folder or just one in the base folder of the repository. Most Python *.gitignore* files look something like this:

```
*.pyc
*.csv
*.log
config/*
```

This file will prevent compiled Python files, CSV files, log files, and config files from being stored in the repository. You'll probably want to add more patterns, depending on what other types of files you have in your repository folders.

You can host your repository on a number of sites. GitHub (*https://github.com/*) offers free public repositories but no private repositories. If you need your code to be private, Bitbucket (*https://bitbucket.org/*) has free private repositories. If you've already started using Git locally, it's easy to push your existing Git repository to GitHub (*http://bit.ly/set_up_git*) or Bitbucket (*http://bit.ly/create_bitbucket_repo*).

Once you have your repository set up, setting up your remote endpoints (*http://git-scm.com/docs/git-remote*) (server or servers) with Git is simple. Here is one example if you are deploying to a folder you have ssh access to:

```
git remote add deploy ssh://user@342.165.22.33/home/user/my_script
```

Before you can push your code to the server, you'll need to set up the folder on the receiving end with a few commands. You will want to run these commands in the server folder in which you plan to deploy:

```
git init .
git config core.worktree `pwd`
git config receive.denycurrentbranch ignore
```

Here you have initialized an empty repository to send code to from your local machine and defined some simple configurations so Git knows it will be a remote endpoint. You'll also want to set up a post-receive hook. Do so by creating an executable (via permissions) file called *post-receive* in the *.git/hooks* folder in the folder you just initialized. This file will execute when the deploy endpoint receives any Git push. It should contain any tasks you need to run every time you push, such as syncing databases, clearing the cache, or restarting any processes. At a minimum, it will need to update the endpoint.

A simple *.git/hooks/post-receive* file looks like this:

```
#!/bin/sh
git checkout -f
git reset --hard
```

This will reset any local changes (on the remote machine) and update the code.

 You should make all of your changes on your local machine, test them, and then push them to the deploy endpoint. It's a good habit to start from the beginning. That way, all of your code is under version control and you can ensure there are no intermittent bugs or errors introduced by modifying code directly on the server.

Once your endpoint is set up, you can simply run the following command from your local repository to update the code on the server with all the latest commits:

```
git push deploy master
```

Doing so is a great way to manage your repository and server or remote machine; it's really easy to use and set up and makes migration, if necessary, straightforward.

If you're new to deployment and version control, we recommend starting with Git and getting comfortable with it before moving on to more complex deployment options, like using Fabric (*http://www.fabfile.org/*). Later in this chapter, we'll cover some larger-scale automation for deploying and managing code across multiple servers.

Using Parallel Processing

Parallel processing is a wonderful tool for script automation, giving you the ability to run many concurrent processes from one script. If your script needs to have more than one process, Python's built-in `multiprocessing` library will become your *go-to* for automation. If you have a series of tasks you need to run in parallel or tasks you could speed up by running in parallel, multiprocessing is the right tool.

So how can one utilize multiprocessing? Here's a quick example:

```
from multiprocessing import Process, Manager ❶
import requests

ALL_URLS = ['google.com', 'bing.com', 'yahoo.com',
            'twitter.com', 'facebook.com', 'github.com',
            'python.org', 'myreallyneatsiteyoushouldread.com']


def is_up_or_not(url, is_up, lock): ❷
    resp = requests.get('http://www.isup.me/%s' % url) ❸
    if 'is up.' in resp.content: ❹
        is_up.append(url)
    else:
        with lock: ❺
            print 'HOLY CRAP %s is down!!!!!' % url


def get_procs(is_up, lock): ❻
    procs = []
    for url in ALL_URLS:
        procs.append(Process(target=is_up_or_not,
                             args=(url, is_up, lock))) ❼
    return procs


def main():
```

```
        manager = Manager() ❽
        is_up = manager.list() ❾
        lock = manager.Lock() ❿
        for p in get_procs(is_up, lock): ⓫
            p.start()
            p.join()
        print is_up

    if __name__ == '__main__':
        main()
```

❶ Imports the Process and Manager classes from the built-in multiprocessing library to help manage our processes.

❷ Defines our main worker function, is_up_or_not, which requires three arguments: a URL, a shared list, and a shared lock. The list and lock are shared among all of our processes, allowing each of the processes the ability to modify or use them.

❸ Uses requests to ask isup.me whether a given URL is currently online and available.

❹ Tests to see if we can parse the text "is up." on the page. If that text exists, we know the URL is up.

❺ Calls the lock's acquire method through a with block. This acquires the lock, continues executing the indented code, and then releases the lock at the end of the code block. Locks (*http://bit.ly/python_threads_synch*) are blocking and should be used only if you require blocking in your code (for example, if you need to ensure only one process runs a special set of logic, like checking if a shared value has changed or has reached a termination point).

❻ Passes the shared lock and list to use when generating the processes.

❼ Creates a Process object by passing it keyword arguments: the target (i.e., what function should I run?) and the args (i.e., with what variables?). This line appends all of our processes to a list so we have them in one place.

❽ Initializes our Manager object, which helps manage shared items and logging across processes.

❾ Creates a shared list object to keep track of what sites are up. Each of the processes will have the ability to alter this list.

⑩ Creates a shared lock object to stop and announce if we encounter a site that is not up. If these were all sites we managed, we might have an important bit of business logic here for emergencies and therefore a reason to "stop everything."

⑪ Starts each of the processes returned by `get_procs` individually. Once they are started, `join` allows the `Manager` object and therefore all the child processes to communicate until the last one is finished.

When using multiprocessing, you usually have a manager process and child processes. You can pass arguments to your child processes, and you can use shared memory and shared variables. This gives you the power to determine how to utilize and architect your multiprocessing. Depending on the needs of your script, you might want to have the manager run a bunch of the logic of the script and use child processes to run one particular section of high-latency or long-running code.

 A shared lock object (*http://bit.ly/lock_objects*) provides the ability to have multiple processes running simultaneously while protecting certain areas of the internal logic. A nice way to use them is simply by placing your lock logic in a `with` statement (*http://bit.ly/with_statement*).

If you're unsure whether your script is a good candidate for multiprocessing, you can always test out a section of the script or a subtask first, and determine whether you were able to achieve your parallel programming goals or whether it unnecessarily complicates the logic. There are some tasks better completed using large-scale automation and queueing, which we'll discuss later in this chapter.

Using Distributed Processing

In addition to parallel processing or multiprocessing, there is also *distributed processing*, which involves distributing your process over many machines (unlike parallel processing, which occurs on one machine). Parallel processing is faster, when your computer can handle it, but sometimes you need more power.

 Distributed processing touches on more than one type of computing problem. There are tools and libraries working to manage processes distributed across many computers, and others working on managing storage across many computers. Terms related to these problems include distributed computing, MapReduce, Hadoop, HDFS, Spark, Pig, and Hive.

In early 2008, the William J. Clinton Presidential Library and the National Archives released Hillary Clinton's schedule as First Lady from 1993 through 2001. The archive consisted of more than 17,000 pages of PDF images and needed to be optical character recognized, or OCR-ed, in order to be turned into a useful dataset. Because this was during the Democratic presidential primaries, news organizations wanted to publish the data. To accomplish this, *The Washington Post* used distributed processing services to turn the 17,000 images into text. By distributing the work to more than 100 computers, they were able to complete the process in less than 24 hours.

Distributed processing with a framework like Hadoop involves two major steps. The first step is to *map* the data or input. This process acts like a filter of sorts. A mapper is used to say "separate all the words in a text file," or "separate all of the users who have tweeted a certain hashtag in the past hour." The next step is to reduce the mapped data into something usable. This is similar to the aggregate functions we used in Chapter 9. If we were looking at all of the Twitter handles from the Spritzer feed, we might want a count of tweets per handle or an aggregate of handles depending on geography or topic (i.e., all tweets originating from this time zone used these words the most). The reducer portion helps us take this large data and "reduce" it into a readable and actionable report.

As you can probably see, not all datasets will need a map-reduce, and the theories behind MapReduce are already available in many of the Python data libraries. However, if you have a truly large dataset, using a MapReduce tool like Hadoop can save you hours of computing time. For a really great walkthrough, we recommend Michael Noll's tutorial on writing a Hadoop MapReduce program in Python (*http://bit.ly/python_mapreduce*), which uses some word counting to explore Python and Hadoop. There is also great documentation for *mrjob* (*https://pythonhosted.org/mrjob/*), which is written and maintained by developers at Yelp (*http://www.yelp.com*). If you'd like to read more on the topic, check out Kevin Schmidt and Christopher Phillips's *Programming Elastic MapReduce* (O'Reilly).

If your dataset is large but is stored disparately or is real-time (or near-real-time), you may want to take a look at Spark (*http://spark.apache.org/*), another Apache project that has gained popularity for its speed, machine learning uses, and ability to handle streams. If your task handles streaming real-time data (from a service, an API, or even logs), then Spark is likely a more feasible choice than Hadoop and can handle the same MapReduce computing structure. Spark is also great if you need to use machine learning or any analysis requiring you to generate data and "feed" it into your data clusters. PySpark (*http://bit.ly/spark_python_docs*), the Python API for Spark, is maintained by the same developers, giving you the ability to write Python for your Spark processing.

To get started using Spark, we recommend Benjamin Bengfort's detailed blog post (*http://bit.ly/gs_with_spark*) covering how to get it installed, integrated with Jupyter notebooks, and setting up your first project. You can also check out John Ramey's post (*http://bit.ly/ipy_notebook_pyspark*) on PySpark integration with Jupyter notebooks, and further explore the data collection and analysis possibilities in your notebook.

Simple Automation

Simple automation in Python is easy. If your code doesn't need to run on many machines, if you have one server, or if your tasks aren't event-driven (or can be run at the same time daily), simple automation will work. One major tenet of development is to choose the most clear and simple path. Automation is no different! If you can easily use a cron job to automate your tasks, by no means should you waste time overengineering it or making it any more complicated.

As we review simple automation, we'll cover the built-in cron (a Unix-based system task manager) and various web interfaces to give your team easy access to the scripts you've written. These represent simple automation solutions which don't require your direct involvement.

CronJobs

Cron (*http://en.wikipedia.org/wiki/Cron*) is a Unix-based job scheduler for running scripts using your server's logging and management utilities. Cron expects you to determine how often and at what times your task should run.

If you can't easily define a timeline for your scripts, cron might not be a good fit. Alternatively, you could run a regular cron task to test whether the necessary conditions for your task to run exist and then use a database or local file to signal it's time to run. With one more cron task, you would check that file or database and perform the task.

If you've never used a cron file before, they are fairly straightforward. Most can be edited by simply typing:

```
crontab -e
```

Depending on your operating system, if you've never written a cron file before, you may be prompted to choose an editor. Feel free to stick with the default or change it if you have another preference.

You will see a bunch of documentation and comments in the file explaining how a cron file works. Every line of your cron file that doesn't begin with a # symbol is a line to define a cron task. Each of these cron tasks is expected to have the following list of arguments:

```
minute hour day_of_month month day_of_week usercommand
```

If a script should run every hour of the day, but only on weekdays, you'd want to write something like this:

```
0 * * * 1-5 python run_this.py
```

This tells cron to run your script at the top of the hour, every hour, from Monday through Friday. There are quite a lot of good tutorials (*https://help.ubuntu.com/community/CronHowto*) that walk through exactly what options are available to you, but here are a few tips:

- Always set up your `MAIL_TO=`*your@email.com* variable before any lines of code. This way, if one of your scripts fails, cron will email you the exception so you'll know it didn't work. You will need to set up your laptop, computer, or server to send mail. Depending on your operating system and ISP, you may need to do some configuration. There's a good GitHub gist (*http://bit.ly/sendmail_setup*) to get Mac users started, and a handy post by HolaRails (*http://bit.ly/configure_send mail*) for Ubuntu users.

- If you have services running that should be restarted if the computer reboots, use the `@reboot` feature.

- If you have several path environments or other commands that must run to execute your script properly, you should write a *cron.sh* file in your repository. Put all necessary commands in the file and run that file directly, rather than a long list of commands connected with && signs.

- Don't be afraid to search for answers. If you're new to cron and are having an issue, it's quite possible someone has posted a solution that is a simple Google search away.

To test out how to use cron, we'll create a simple Python example. Start by creating a new Python file called *hello_time.py*, and place this code in it:

```
from datetime import datetime

print 'Hello, it is now %s.' % datetime.now().strftime('%d-%m-%Y %H:%M:%S')
```

Next, make a simple *cron.sh* file in the same folder and write the following bash commands in it:

```
export ENV=PROD
cd /home/your_home/folder_name
python hello_time.py
```

We don't need to set the environment variable, since we are not actively using it, and you'll need to update the `cd` line so that it properly changes into the folder the code is in (this is the path to the current file). However, this is a good example of how to use bash commands to set variables, source virtual environments, copy and move files or change into new folders, and *then* call your Python file. You've been using bash since the beginning of the book, so no need to fear even if you are still a beginner.

Finally, let's set up our cron task by editing our file using `crontab -e`. Add these lines below the documentation in your editor:

```
MAIL_TO=youremail@yourdomain.com
*/5 * * * * bash /home/your_home/folder_name/cron.sh > /var/log/my_cron.log 2>&1
```

You should replace the made-up email in this example with your real one and write the proper path to the cron file you just created. Remember, your *hello_time.py* script should be in the same folder. In this example, we have also set up a log file (*/var/log/my_cron.log*) for cron to use. The `2>&1` statement at the end of the line tells cron to put the output and any errors into that log file. Once you have exited your editor and properly saved your cron file, you should see a message confirming your new cron task is now installed. Wait a few minutes and then check the log file. You should see the message from the script in that file. If not, you can check your cron error messages by searching in your system log (usually */var/log/syslog*) or in your cron log (usually */var/log/cron*). To remove this cron task, simply edit your crontab again and delete the line or place a # at the beginning of the line to comment it out.

 Cron can be a very simple way to automate your script and alerting. It's a powerful tool designed by Bell Labs during the initial development of Unix in the mid-1970s, and is still widely used. If it's easy to predict when your automation should run, or it is only a few bash commands away from running, cron is a useful way to automate your code.

If you needed to pass command-line arguments for your cron tasks, the lines in the file might then look like this:

```
*/20 10-22 * * * python my_arg_code.py arg1 arg2 arg3
0,30 10-22 * * * python my_arg_code.py arg4 arg5 arg6
```

Cron is fairly flexible but also very simple. If it fits your needs, great! If not, keep reading to learn some other simple ways to automate your data wrangling.

Web Interfaces

If you need your script, scraper, or reporting task to run on demand, one easy solution is to simply build a web interface where people can log in and push a button to fire it up. Python has many different web frameworks to choose from, so it's up to you which one to use and how much time you'd like to spend working on the web interface.

One easy way to get started is to use Flask-Admin (*https://flask-admin.readthedocs.org/en/v1.0.9/*), which is an administrative site built on top of the

Flask web framework (*http://flask.pocoo.org/*). Flask is a microframework, meaning it doesn't require a lot of code to get started. After getting your site up and running by following the instructions in the quickstart guide (*http://flask.pocoo.org/docs/0.10/quickstart/*), you simply set up a view in your Flask application to execute the task.

 Make sure your task can alert the user or you when it's finished in another way (email, messaging, etc.), as it's unlikely to complete in time to give a proper web response. Also be sure to notify the user when the task starts, so they don't end up requesting the task to run many times in a row.

Another popular and often used microframework in Python is Bottle (*http://bottlepy.org/docs/dev/index.html*). Bottle can be used similarly to Flask, with a view to execute the task if the user clicks a button (or does some other simple action).

A larger Python web framework often used by Python developers is Django (*https://www.djangoproject.com/*). Originally developed to allow newsrooms to easily publish content, it comes with a built-in authentication and database system and uses a settings file to configure most of these features.

No matter what framework you use or how you build your views, you'll want to host your framework somewhere so others can request tasks. You can host your own site fairly easily using DigitalOcean or Amazon Web Services (see Appendix G). You can also use service providers who support Python environments, like Heroku (*https://www.heroku.com/*). If you're interested in that option, Kenneth Reitz has written a great introduction to deploying your Python apps using Heroku (*http://bit.ly/python_heroku*).

 Regardless of what framework or microframework you use, you'll want to think about authentication and security. You can set that up server-side with whatever web server you are using, or explore options the framework gives you (including plug-ins or other support features).

Jupyter Notebooks

We covered how to set up your Jupyter notebooks in Chapter 10, and they are another great way to share code, particularly with folks who may not need to know Python, but who need to view the charts or other outputs of your script. If you teach them how to use simple commands, like running all the cells in the notebook and shutting it down after they've downloaded the new reports, you'll find it can save you hours of time.

Adding in Markdown cells to explain how to use your shared note-books is a great way to ensure everyone is clear on how to use the code and can move forward easily without your help.

If your script is well organized with functions and doesn't need to be modified, simply put the repository in a place where the Jupyter notebooks can import and use the code (it's also a good idea to set your server or notebook's PYTHONPATH (*http://bit.ly/ add_dir_pythonpath*) so the modules you are using are always available). This way, you can import those `main` functions into a notebook and have the script run and generate the report when someone clicks the notebook's "Play All" button.

Large-Scale Automation

If your system is larger than one machine or server can handle or if your reporting is tied into a distributed application or some other event-driven system, it's likely you'll need something more robust than just web interfaces, notebooks, and cron. If you need a true task management system and you'd like to use Python, you're in luck. In this section, we'll cover a robust task management tool called Celery (*http://www.cele ryproject.org*) that handles larger stacks of tasks, automates workers (you'll learn about workers in the next section) and provides monitoring solutions.

We will also cover operations automation, which can be helpful if you manage a series of servers or environments with different needs. Ansible (*http://www.ansible.com*) is a great automation tool to help with tasks as rote as migrating databases all the way up to large-scale integrated deployments.

There are some alternatives to Celery, such as Spotify's Luigi (*https://github.com/ spotify/luigi*), which is useful if you are using Hadoop and you have large-scale task management needs (particularly long-running tasks, which can be a pain point). As far as good alternatives for operations automation, it is a quite crowded space. If you only need to manage a few servers, for Python-only deployment one good option is Fabric (*http://www.fabfile.org/*).

For larger-scale management of servers, a good alternative is SaltStack (*http://salt stack.com/*), or using Vagrant (*https://www.vagrantup.com/*) with any number of deployment and management tools like Chef (*https://www.chef.io/chef/*) or Puppet (*https://puppetlabs.com/*). We've chosen to highlight some of the tools we've used in this section, but they are not the only tools for larger-scale automation using Python. Given the field's popularity and necessity, we recommend following discussions of larger-scale automation on your favorite technology and discussion sites, such as Hacker News (*https://news.ycombinator.com/*).

Celery: Queue-Based Automation

Celery (*http://www.celeryproject.org/*) is a Python library used to create a distributed queue system. With Celery, your tasks are managed using a scheduler or via events and messaging. Celery is the complete solution if you're looking for something scalable, that can handle long-running event-driven tasks. Celery integrates well with a few different queue backends. It uses settings files, user interfaces, and API calls to manage the tasks. And it's fairly easy to get started, so no need to fear if it's your first task management system.

No matter how you set up your Celery project, it will likely contain the following task manager system components:

Message broker (likely RabbitMQ (https://www.rabbitmq.com/))
>   This acts as a queue for tasks waiting to be processed.

Task manager/queue manager (Celery)
>   This service keeps track of the logic controlling how many workers to use, what tasks take priority, when to retry, and so on.

Workers
>   Workers are Python processes controlled by Celery which execute your Python code. They know what tasks you have set them up to do and they attempt to run that Python code to completion.

Monitoring tool (e.g., Flower (http://flower.readthedocs.org/en/latest/))
>   This allows you to take a look at the workers and your queue and is great for answering questions like "What failed last night?"

Celery has a useful getting started guide (*http://bit.ly/first_steps_w_celery*), but we find the biggest problem is not learning how to use Celery, but instead learning what types of tasks are good for queues and what tasks aren't. Table 14-2 reviews a few questions and philosophical ideas around queue-based automation.

Table 14-2. To queue or not to queue?

Queue-based task management requirements.	Requirements for automation without queues.
Tasks do not have a specific deadline.	Tasks can and do have deadlines.
We don't need to know how many tasks we have.	We can easily quantify what tasks need to be done.
We only know the prioritization of tasks in a general sense.	We know exactly which tasks take priority.
Tasks need not always happen in order, or are not usually order-based.	Tasks must happen in order.

Queue-based task management requirements.	Requirements for automation without queues.
Tasks can sometimes take a long time, and other times a short time.	We need to know how long tasks take.
Tasks are called (or queued) based on an event or another task's completion.	Tasks are based on the clock or something predictable.
It's OK if tasks fail; we can retry.	We must be aware of every task failure.
We have a lot of tasks and a strong potential for task growth.	We have only a few tasks a day.

These requirements are generalized, but they indicate some of the philosophical differences between when a task queue is a good idea and when something might be better run on a schedule with alerting, monitoring, and logging.

 It's fine to have different parts of your tasks in different systems, and you'll see that often at larger companies where they have different "buckets" of tasks. It's also OK to test out both queue-based and non-queue-based task management and determine what fits best for you and your projects.

There are other task and queue management systems for Python, including Python RQ (*http://python-rq.org/*) and PyRes (*https://github.com/binarydud/pyres*). Both of them are newer and therefore might not have the same Google-fu in terms of problem solving, but if you'd like to play around with Celery first and then branch out to other alternatives, you have options.

Ansible: Operations Automation

If you are at the scale where you need Celery to manage your tasks, it's quite likely you also need some help managing your other services and operations. If your projects need to be maintained on a distributed system, you should start organizing them so you can easily distribute via automation.

Ansible (*http://www.ansible.com/home*) is an excellent system to automate the operations side of your projects. Ansible gives you access to a series of tools you can use to quickly spin up, deploy, and manage code. You can use Ansible to migrate projects and back up data from your remote machines. You can also use it to update servers with security fixes or new packages as needed.

Ansible has a quickstart video (*http://docs.ansible.com/quickstart.html*) to get to know all of the basics, but we'd also like to highlight a few of the most useful features described in the documentation:

- MySQL database management (*http://docs.ansible.com/mysql_db_module.html*)
- Digital Ocean droplet and key management (*http://bit.ly/ansible_digital_ocean*)
- Guide for rolling upgrades and deployment (*http://docs.ansible.com/guide_roll ing_upgrade.html*)

We also recommend checking out Justin Ellingwood's introduction to Ansible play-books (*http://bit.ly/digital_ocean_ansible*) and the Servers for Hackers extended intro-duction to Ansible (*https://serversforhackers.com/an-ansible-tutorial*).

Ansible is probably too advanced and overcomplicated if you only have one or two servers or you only deploy one or two projects, but it is a great resource if your project grows and you need something to help keep your setup organized. If you have an interest in opera-tions and system administration, it's a great tool to learn and master.

If you'd rather leave your operations to a nice image you've created and can just restart every time, plenty of cloud providers let you do just that! There's no pressing need to become an operations automation expert for your data wrangling needs.

Monitoring Your Automation

It's essential you spend time monitoring your automation. If you have no idea whether a task completed or if your tasks succeeded or failed, you might as well not be running them. For this reason, monitoring your scripts and the machines running them is an important part of the process.

For example, if you have a hidden bug where data is not actually being loaded and every day or week you are running reporting on old data, that would be awful news. With automation, failure is not always obvious, as your script may continue running with old data or other errors and inconsistencies. Monitoring is your view into whether your script is succeeding or failing, even if all signs indicate it is still operat-ing normally.

Monitoring can have a small or large footprint, depending on the scale and needs of your tasks. If you are going to have a large-scale automation running across many servers, you'll probably need to use a larger distributed monitoring system or something that boasts monitoring as a service. If, however, you are running your tasks on a home server, you probably only need to use the built-in Python logging tool.

You'll likely want some alerting and notifications for your script as well. It's easy in Python to upload, download, email, or even SMS the result. In this section, we'll cover various logging options and review ways to set up notifications. After thorough testing and with a strong understanding of all the potential errors from daily monitoring, you can fully automate the task and manage the errors via alerts.

Python Logging

The most basic monitoring your script will need is logging. Lucky for you, Python has a very robust and feature-rich logging environment as part of the standard library. The clients or libraries you interact with usually have loggers integrated with the Python logging ecosystem.

Using the simple basic configuration given in Python's built-in logging module, we can instantiate our logger and get started. You can then use the many different configuration options to meet your script's specific logging needs. Python's logging lets you set particular logging levels (*http://bit.ly/logging_levels*), and log record attributes (*http://bit.ly/logrecord_attributes*) and adjust the formatting. The logger object also has methods and attributes (*http://bit.ly/logger_objects*) that can be useful depending on your needs.

Here's how we set up and use logging in our code:

```
import logging
from datetime import datetime


def start_logger():
    logging.basicConfig(filename='/var/log/my_script/daily_report_%s.log' %
                                datetime.strftime(datetime.now(), '%m%d%Y_%H%M%S'),  ❶
                        level=logging.DEBUG,  ❷
                        format='%(asctime)s %(message)s',  ❸
                        datefmt='%m-%d %H:%M:%S')  ❹


def main():
    start_logger()
    logging.debug("SCRIPT: I'm starting to do things!")  ❺

    try:
        20 / 0
    except Exception:
        logging.exception('SCRIPT: We had a problem!')  ❻
        logging.error('SCRIPT: Issue with division in the main() function')  ❼

    logging.debug('SCRIPT: About to wrap things up!')

if __name__ == '__main__':
    main()
```

❶ Initializes our logging using the logging module's basicConfig method, which requires a log file name. This code logs to our */var/log* folder in a folder, *my_script*. The filename is *daily_report_<DATEINFO>.log*, where *<DATEINFO>* is the time the script began, including the month, date, year, hour, minute, and second. This tells us when the script ran and why, and is good logging practice.

❷ Sets our logging level. Most often, you will want the level set to DEBUG so you can leave debugging messages in the code and track them in the logs. If you'd like even more information, you can use the INFO setting, which will also show more logging from your helper libraries. Some people prefer less verbose logs and set it to WARNING or ERROR instead.

❸ Sets the format of Python logging using the log record attributes. Here we record the message sent to logging and the time it was logged.

❹ Sets a human-readable date format so our logs can easily be parsed or searched using our preferred date format. Here we have month, day, hour, minute, and second logged.

❺ Calls the module's debug method to start logging. This method expects a string. We are prefacing our script log entries with the word *SCRIPT:*. Adding searchable notes like this to your logs will help you later determine which processes and libraries wrote to your log.

❻ Uses the logging module's exception method, which writes a string you send along with a traceback from the Python exception, and can therefore only be used in an exception block. This is tremendously useful for debugging errors and seeing how many exceptions you have in your script.

❼ Logs a longer error message using the error level. The logging module has the ability to log a variety of levels, including debug, error, info, and warning. Be consistent with how you log, and use info or debug for your normal messages and error to log messages specific to errors and exceptions in your script. That way, you always know where to look for problems and how to properly parse your logs for review.

As we've done in the example here, we find it useful to begin log messages with a note to yourself about what module or area of the code is writing the message. This can help determine where the error occurred. It also makes your logs easy to search and parse, as you can clearly see what errors or issues your script encounters. The best way to approach logging is to determine where to put messages to yourself as you are first writing your script, and keep the important messages in the script to determine whether something has broken and at what point.

Every exception should be logged, even if the exception is expected. This will help you keep track of how often those exceptions occur and whether your code should treat them as normal. The `logging` module provides `exception` and `error` methods for your usage, so you can log the exception and Python traceback and also add some extra information with `error` to elaborate on what might have occurred and where in the code it occurred.

You should also log your interactions with databases, APIs, and external systems. This will help you determine when your script has issues interacting with these systems and ensure they are stable, reliable, or able to be worked around. Many of the libraries you interact with also have their own ability to log to your log configuration. For example, the `requests` module will log connection problems and requests directly into your script log.

Even if you don't set up any other monitoring or alerting for your script, you should use logging. It's simple, and it provides good documentation for your future self and others. Logs are not the only solution, but they are a good standard and serve as a foundation for the monitoring of your automation.

In addition to logging, you can set up easy-to-analyze alerting for your scripts. In the following section, we'll cover ways your script can message you about its success or failure.

Adding Automated Messaging

One easy way to send reports, keep track of your scripts, and notify yourself of errors is to use email or other messages sent directly from your scripts. There are many Python libraries to help with this task. It's good to begin by determining exactly what type of messaging you need for your scripts and projects.

Ask yourself if any of the following apply to your script:

- It produces a report which needs to be sent to a particular list of recipients.
- It has a clear success/failure message.
- It is pertinent to other coworkers or collaborators.
- It provides results not easily viewed on a website or through a quick dashboard.

If any of these sound like your project, it's likely a good candidate for some sort of automated messaging.

Email

Emailing with Python is straightforward. We recommend setting up a separate script-only email address through your favorite email provider (we used Gmail). If it doesn't automatically integrate with Python out of the box, it's likely there is a listing of the proper configuration or a useful example configuration online, found via search.

Let's take a look at a script we've used to send mail with attachments to a list of recipients. We modified this code from a gist written by @dbieber (*https://gist.github.com/dbieber/5146518*), which was modified from Rodrigo Coutinho's "Sending emails via Gmail with Python" post (*http://bit.ly/sending_gmail_python*):

```python
#!/usr/bin/python
# Adapted from
# http://kutuma.blogspot.com/2007/08/sending-emails-via-gmail-with-python.html
# Modified again from: https://gist.github.com/dbieber/5146518
# config file(s) should contain section 'email' and parameters
# 'user' and 'password'

import smtplib ❶
from email.MIMEMultipart import MIMEMultipart ❷
from email.MIMEBase import MIMEBase
from email.MIMEText import MIMEText
from email import Encoders
import os
import ConfigParser


def get_config(env): ❸
    config = ConfigParser.ConfigParser()
    if env == "DEV":
        config.read(['config/development.cfg']) ❹
    elif env == "PROD":
        config.read(['config/production.cfg'])
    return config


def mail(to, subject, text, attach=None, config=None): ❺
    if not config:
        config = get_config("DEV") ❻
    msg = MIMEMultipart()
    msg['From'] = config.get('email', 'user') ❼
    msg['To'] = ", ".join(to) ❽
    msg['Subject'] = subject
    msg.attach(MIMEText(text))
    if attach: ❾
        part = MIMEBase('application', 'octet-stream')
        part.set_payload(open(attach, 'rb').read()) ❿
        Encoders.encode_base64(part)
        part.add_header('Content-Disposition',
                        'attachment; filename="%s"' % os.path.basename(attach))
        msg.attach(part)
    mailServer = smtplib.SMTP("smtp.gmail.com", 587) ⓫
    mailServer.ehlo()
    mailServer.starttls()
    mailServer.ehlo()
```

```
        mailServer.login(config.get('email', 'user'),
                          config.get('email', 'password'))
        mailServer.sendmail(config.get('email', 'user'), to, msg.as_string())
        mailServer.close()


def example():
    mail(['listof@mydomain.com', 'emails@mydomain.com'],
         "Automate your life: sending emails",
         "Why'd the elephant sit on the marshmallow?",
         attach="my_file.txt")  ⓬
```

❶ Python's built-in `smtplib` library (*https://docs.python.org/2/library/smtplib.html*)
    gives you a wrapper for SMTP, the standard protocol for sending and receiving
    email.

❷ Python's `email` library (*https://docs.python.org/2/library/email.html*) helps create
    email messages and attachments and keeps them in the proper format.

❸ The `get_config` function loads the configuration from a series of local configu-
    ration files. We pass an environment variable, which is expected to be the string
    `"PROD"` or `"DEV"` to signal whether it's running locally (`"DEV"`) or on our remote
    production environment (`"PROD"`). If you only have one environment, you could
    simply return the only configuration file in your project.

❹ This line uses Python's `ConfigParser` to read in the *.cfg* file and returns `config`
    object.

❺ Our `mail` function takes a list of email addresses as the `to` variable, the subject
    and text of the email, an optional attachment, and an optional `config` argument.
    The attachment is expected to be the name of a local file. The `config` should be a
    Python `ConfigParser` object.

❻ This line sets the default configuration in case it wasn't passed. To be safe, we are
    using the `"DEV"` configuration.

❼ This code uses the `ConfigParser` object to pull the email address out of the con-
    fig file. This keeps the address secure and separate from our repository code.

❽ This code unpacks the list of emails and separates them with commas and a
    space. It expands the list of email addresses to a string, because that's what our
    MIME type expects.

❾ If there is an attachment, this line begins the special handling for MIME multi-
    part standards needed to send attachments.

⑩ This code opens and reads the full file using the filename string passed.

⑪ If you're not using Gmail, set these to match your provider's host and port for SMTP. Those should be easy to identify if there is good documentation. If there isn't, a simple search for "SMTP settings <your provider name>" should give you the details.

⑫ This is some example code to give an idea of what this mail function is expecting. You can see the data types expected (string, list, filename), and the order.

The simple Python built-in libraries `smtplib` and `email` help us quickly create and send email messages using their classes and methods. Abstracting some of the other parts of the script (such as saving your email address and password in your config) is an essential part of keeping your script and your repository secure and reusable. A few default settings ensure the script can always send email.

SMS and voice

If you'd like to integrate telephone messages into your alerting, you can use Python to send text messages or make phone calls. Twilio (*https://www.twilio.com*) is a very cost-efficient way to do so, with support for messages with media and automated phone calls.

 Before you get started with the API, you'll need to sign up to get your authorization codes and keys and install the Twilio Python client (*https://github.com/twilio/twilio-python*). There's a long list of code examples in the Python client's documentation (*https://twilio-python.readthedocs.org/en/latest/*), so if you might need to do something with voice or text, it's likely there is a good feature available.

Take a look at how easy it is to send a quick text:

```
from twilio.rest import TwilioRestClient ❶
import ConfigParser


def send_text(sender, recipient, text_message, config=None): ❷
    if not config:
        config = ConfigParser('config/development.cfg')

    client = TwilioRestClient(config.get('twilio', 'account_sid'),
                              config.get('twilio', 'auth_token')) ❸
    sms = client.sms.messages.create(body=text_message,
                                     to=recipient,
                                     from_=sender) ❹
```

```
def example():
    send_text("+11008675309", "+11088675309", "JENNY!!!!") ❺
```

❶ We'll use the Twilio Python client to interact directly with the Twilio API via Python.

❷ This line defines a function we can use to send a text. We'll need the sender's and recipient's phone numbers (prefaced with country codes) and the simple text message we want to send, and we have the ability to also pass a configuration object. We'll use the configuration to authorize with the Twilio API.

❸ This code sets up a client object, which will authorize using our Twilio account. When you sign up for Twilio, you'll receive an `account_sid` and an `auth_token`. Put them in the configuration file your script uses, in a section named `twilio`.

❹ To send a text, this code navigates to the SMS module in our client and calls the message resource's `create` method. As documented by Twilio (*http://bit.ly/ twilio_message*), we can then send a simple text message with only a few parameters.

❺ Twilio works internationally and expects to see international-based dialing numbers. If you're unsure of the international dialing codes to use, Wikipedia has a good listing (*https://en.wikipedia.org/wiki/List_of_country_calling_codes*).

 If you are interested in having your script "talk" via Python, Python text-to-speech (*https://pyttsx.readthedocs.org/en/latest/*) can "read" your text over the phone.

Chat integration

If you'd like to integrate chat into your alerting, or if your team or collaborators commonly use chat, there are many Python chat toolkits you can use for this purpose. Depending on your chat client and needs, there's likely a Python or API-based solution, and you can use your knowledge of REST clients to go about connecting and messaging the right people.

If you use HipChat, their API (*https://www.hipchat.com/docs/apiv2*) is fairly easy to integrate with your Python application or script. There are several Python libraries (*https://www.hipchat.com/docs/apiv2/libraries*) to make simple messaging to a chatroom or a person straightforward.

To get started using the HipChat API, you'll first need to log in (*https://hipchat.com/ account/api*) and get an API token. You can then use HypChat, (*https://github.com/*

RidersDiscountCom/HypChat) a Python library, to send a quick message to a chat-room.

First, install HypChat using pip:

```
pip install hypchat
```

Now, send a message using Python!

```
from hypchat import HypChat
from utils import get_config


def get_client(config):
    client = HypChat(config.get('hipchat', 'token')) ❶
    return client


def message_room(client, room_name, message):
    try:
        room = client.get_room(room_name) ❷
        room.message(message) ❸
    except Exception as e:
        print e ❹


def main():
    config = get_config('DEV') ❺
    client = get_client(config)
    message_room(client, 'My Favorite Room', "I'M A ROBOT!")
```

❶ We use the HypChat library to talk to our chat client. The library initializes a new client using our HipChat token, which we will keep stored in our config files.

❷ This code uses the `get_room` method, which locates a room matching the string name.

❸ This line sends a message to a room or a user with the `message` method, and passes it a simple string of what to say.

❹ Always use `try...except` blocks with API-based libraries in case of connection errors or API changes. This code prints the error, but you'd likely want it logged to fully automate your script.

❺ The `get_config` function used here is imported from a different script. We follow modular code design by introducing these helper functions and putting them in individual modules for reuse.

If you want to log to chat, you can explore those options with HipLogging (*https://github.com/invernizzi/hiplogging*). Depending on your needs and how your team works, you can set up your chat logging how you'd like; but it's nice to know you can always leave a note for someone where they might see it!

If you'd rather use Google Chat, there are some great examples of how to do so using SleekXMPP (*http://bit.ly/sleekxmpp_send_msg*). You can also use SleekXMPP to send Facebook chat messages (*http://bit.ly/facebook_msg_sleekxmpp*).

For Slack messaging, check out the Slack team's Python client (*https://github.com/slackhq/python-slackclient*).

For other chat clients, we recommend doing a Google search for "Python <your client name>." Chances are someone has attempted to connect their Python code with that client, or there's an API you can use. You know how to use an API from your work in Chapter 13.

With so many options for alerting and messaging about your script's (and automation's) success or failure, it's hard to know which one to use. The important part is to choose a method your or your team regularly use and will see. Prioritizing ease of use and integration with daily life is essential—automation is here to help you *save* time, not to make you spend more time checking services.

Uploading and Other Reporting

If you need to upload your reports or figures to a separate service or file share as part of your automation, there are terrific tools for those tasks. If it's an online form or a site you need to interact with, we recommend using your Selenium scraping skills from Chapter 12. If it's an FTP server, there is a standard FTP library for Python (*https://docs.python.org/2/library/ftplib.html*). If you need to send your reporting to an API or via a web protocol, you can use the `requests` library or the API skills you learned in Chapter 13. If you need to send XML, you can build it using LXML (see Chapter 11).

No matter what service you are looking to speak to, it's likely you have had some exposure to communicating with that service. We hope you feel confident practicing those skills and striking out on your own.

Logging and Monitoring as a Service

If your needs are larger than one script can handle, or you want to incorporate your automation into a larger organizational framework, you might want to investigate logging and monitoring as a service. There are many companies working to make the lives of data analysts and developers easier by creating tools and systems to track logging. These tools often have simple Python libraries to send your logging or monitoring to their platform.

With logging as a service, you can spend more time working on your research and scripts, and less time managing your monitoring and logging. This can offload some of the "Is our script working or not, and if so how well?" issues to the non-developers on your team, as many of the services have nice dashboards and built-in alerting.

Depending on the size and layout of your automation, you may need systems monitoring as well as script and error monitoring. In this section, we'll look at a few services that do both, as well as some more specialized services. Even if you don't have a large enough scale to justify them now, it's always good to know what is possible.

Logging and exceptions

Python-based logging services offer the ability to log to one central service while having your script(s) run on a variety of machines, either local or remote.

One such service with great Python support is Sentry (*https://getsentry.com/welcome/*). For a relatively small amount of money per month, you can have access to a dashboard of errors, get alerts sent based on exception thresholds, and monitor the error and exception types you have on a daily, weekly, and monthly basis. The Python client for Sentry (*https://github.com/getsentry/raven-python*) is easy to install, configure, and use. If you are using tools like Django, Celery, or even simple Python logging (*http://bit.ly/sentry_python*), Sentry has integration points so you don't need to significantly alter your code to get started. On top of that, the code base is constantly updated and the staff is helpful in case you have questions.

Other options include Airbrake (*https://airbrake.io/languages/python_bug_tracker*), which originally started as a Ruby-based exception tracker and now supports Python, and Rollbar (*https://rollbar.com*). It's a popular market, so there will likely be new ones launched before this book goes to print.

There are also services to pull in and parse your logs, such as Loggly (*https://www.loggly.com/*) and Logstash (*https://www.elastic.co/products/logstash*). These allow you to monitor your logs on an aggregate level as well as parse, search, and find issues in your logs. They are really only useful if you have enough logs and enough time to review them, but are great for distributed systems with a lot of logging.

Logging and monitoring

If you have distributed machines or you are integrating your script into your company or university's Python-based server environment, you may want to have robust monitoring of not just Python, but the entire system. There are many services that offer monitoring for system load database traffic, and web applications, as well as automated tasks.

One of the most popular services used for this is New Relic (*http://newrelic.com/*), which can watch your servers and system processes as well as web applications. Using MongoDB and AWS? Or MySQL and Apache? New Relic plug-ins (*http://newrelic.com/plugins*) allow you to easily integrate logging for your services into the same dashboards you are using for monitoring server and application health. In addition, they offer a Python agent (*http://bit.ly/new_relic_python*) so you can easily log your Python application (or script) into the same ecosystem. With all of your monitoring in one place, it's easier to spot issues and set up proper alerting so the right people on your team immediately know about any problems.

Another service for systems and application monitoring is Datadog (*https://www.data doghq.com/*). Datadog allows you to integrate many services (*https://www.data doghq.com/product/integrations/*) into one dashboard. This saves time and effort and allows you to easily spot errors in your projects, apps, and scripts. The Datadog Python client (*https://github.com/DataDog/datadogpy*) enables logging of different events you'd like to monitor, but requires a bit of customization.

No matter what monitoring you use, or whether you decide to build your own or use a service, it's essential to have regular alerting, insight into the services you use, and an understanding of the integrity of your code and automated systems.

 When you depend on your automation to complete other parts of your work and projects, you should make sure your monitoring system is both easy to use and intuitive so you can focus on the bigger parts of your projects without risking missing errors or other issues.

No System Is Foolproof

As we've discussed in this chapter, relying entirely on any system is foolhardy and should be avoided. No matter how bulletproof your script or system appears to be, there's an undeniable chance it will fail at some point. If your script depends on other systems, they could fail at any point. If your script involves data from an API, service, or website, there's a chance the API or site will change or go down for maintenance, or any number of other events could occur causing your automation to fail.

If a task is absolutely mission critical, it should not be automated. You can likely automate parts of it or even most of it, but it will always need supervision and a *person* to ensure it hasn't failed. If it's important but not the most essential piece, the monitoring and alerting for that piece should reflect its level of importance.

As you dive deeper into your own data wrangling and automation, you will spend less time on building higher-quality tasks and scripts, and more time on troubleshooting, critical thinking, and applying your analytical know-how and area knowledge to your work. Automation can help you do this, but it's always good to have a healthy caution regarding what important tasks you automate, and how.

As the programs you've automated mature and progress, you will not only improve the automation you have and make it more resilient, but also increase your knowledge of your code base, Python, and your data and reporting.

Summary

You've learned how to automate much of your data wrangling using small- and large-scale solutions. You can monitor and keep track of your scripts and the tasks and subtasks with logging, monitoring, and cloud-based solutions—meaning you can spend less time keeping track of things and more time actually reporting. You have defined ways automation can succeed and fail and worked to help create a clear set of guidelines around automation (with an understanding that all systems can and will fail eventually). You know how to give other teammates and colleagues access so they can run tasks themselves, and you've learned a bit about how to deploy and set up Python automation.

Table 14-3 summarizes the new concepts and libraries introduced in this chapter.

Table 14-3. New Python and programming concepts and libraries

Concept/Library	Purpose
Running scripts remotely	Having your code run on a server or other machine so you don't have to worry about your own computer use interfering.
Command-line arguments	Using `argv` to parse command-line arguments when running your Python script.
Environment variables	Using environment variables to help with script logic (such as what server your code is running on and what config to use).
Cron usage	Coding a shell script to execute as a cron task on your server or remote machine. A basic form of automation.
Configuration files	Using configuration files to define sensitive or special data for your Python script.
Git deployment	Using Git to easily deploy your code to one or more remote machine(s).

Concept/Library	Purpose
Parallel processing	Python's `multiprocessing` library gives you easy access to run many processes at the same time while still having shared data and locking mechanisms.
MapReduce	With distributed data, you can map data according to a particular feature or by running it through a series of tasks, and then reduce that data to analyze it in aggregate.
Hadoop and Spark	Two tools used in cloud computing to perform MapReduce operations. Hadoop is better for an already defined and stored dataset, and Spark is preferred if you have streaming, extra-large, or dynamically generated data.
Celery (task queue use and management)	Gives you the ability to create a task queue and manage it using Python, allowing you to automate tasks that don't have a clear start and end date.
`logging` module	Built-in logging for your application or script so you can easily track errors, debug messages, and exceptions.
`smtp` and `email` modules	Built-in email alerting from your Python script.
Twilio	A service with a Python API client for use with telephone and text messaging services.
HypChat	A Python API library for use with the HipChat chat client.
Logging as a service	Using a service like Sentry or Logstash to manage your logging, error rates, and exceptions.
Monitoring as a service	Using a service like New Relic or Datadog to monitor your logs as well as service uptimes, database issues, and performance (e.g., to identify hardware problems).

Along with the wealth of knowledge you've taken from previous chapters in this book, you should now be well prepared to spend your time building quality tools and allowing these tools to do the grunt work for you. You can throw out those old spreadsheet formulas and use Python to import data, run analysis, and deliver reports directly to your inbox. You can truly let Python manage the rote tasks, like a robotic assistant, and move on to the more critical and challenging parts of your reporting.

## CHAPTER 15

Conclusion

Congratulations! You've reached the end of the book. When you first began, you likely knew little Python and you hadn't used programming to investigate data.

Your experience now should be quite different. You've gained knowledge and experience finding and cleaning data. You've honed your skills by focusing your questions and determining what you can and cannot answer given a particular dataset. You can write simple regexes and complex web scrapers. You have learned how to store and deploy your code and connect with databases. You can scale your data and processes in the cloud and manage your data wrangling via automation.

The fun doesn't have to end here, however! There is plenty more to learn and do in your career as a data wrangler. You can take the skills and tools you have learned here and continue to push your knowledge, and in turn the boundaries of the field of data wrangling. We encourage you to advance your quest for excellence and keep asking difficult questions of your data, processes, and methods.

Duties of a Data Wrangler

As we've established throughout this book and our investigations, the data out there and the conclusions you can reach as a data wrangler are vast. But along with those opportunities come responsibilities.

There are no data wrangling police; however, you have learned some ethics throughout our book. You've learned to be a conscientious web scraper. You've learned to pick up the phone and ask for more information. You've learned to explain and document your process when you present your findings. You've learned how to ask hard questions about difficult topics, particularly when the data sources may have other motivations.

As you pursue learning and growing as a data wrangler, your ethical sense will grow and help guide and challenge you in your work and processes. In a way, you are now an investigative journalist. The conclusions you reach and the questions you ask can and will make a difference in your field. With that knowledge, you have the burden of duty.

Your duties include:

- Using your knowledge, skills, and ability for just and good causes
- Helping contribute to the knowledge of others around you
- Giving back to the community that helped you
- Challenging opposition to the ethics you have learned so far and continue to develop

We encourage you to step up and meet these challenges through your career as a data wrangler. Do you like working with others and teaching? Become a mentor! Do you enjoy a particular open source package? Become a code or documentation contributor! Have you been researching an important social or health issue? Contribute your findings to the academic or social community! Have you experienced difficulties from a particular community or source? Share your story with the world.

Beyond Data Wrangling

Your skills have developed over the course of this book, but you still have much to learn. Depending on your skillset and interests, there are quite a few areas for further exploration.

Become a Better Data Analyst

This book offered an introduction to statistical and data analysis. If you want to truly hone your statistical and analytical skills, you'll want to spend more time reading about the science behind the methods as well as learning some of the more intensive Python packages, give you more power and flexibility when analyzing your datasets.

To learn more advanced statistics, regression models and the math behind data analysis are essential topics of study. If you haven't taken a statistics course, EdX has a great archived course from the University of California, Berkeley (*http://bit.ly/berkeleyx_stat_2_1x*). If you'd like to explore with a book, *Think Stats* by Allen Downey (O'Reilly) is a great introduction to statistical math concepts and also uses Python. Cathy O'Neill and Rachel Schutt's *Doing Data Science* (also from O'Reilly) provides a deeper analysis of the field of data science.

If you're interested in learning the `scipy` stack and more about how Python can help you perform more advanced math and statistics, you're in luck. One of the main contributors to pandas, Wes McKinney, has written a book that covers pandas in depth (*Python for Data Analysis*; O'Reilly). The pandas documentation (*http://bit.ly/10_min_to_panda*) is also a great place to start learning. You played around a bit in Chapter 7 with numpy. If you are interested in learning some of the numpy internals, check out the SciPy introduction to the basics (*http://bit.ly/numpy_basics*).

Become a Better Developer

If you really want to hone your Python skills, Luciano Ramalho's *Fluent Python* (O'Reilly) discusses some more in-depth design patterns in Python thinking. We also highly recommend taking a look through recent videos of Python events around the world (*http://pyvideo.org/*) and investigating topics that interest you.

If this book is your first introduction to programming, you may want to take an introduction to computer science course. If you want a self-study option, Coursera offers one from Stanford University (*https://www.coursera.org/course/cs101*). If you'd like an online textbook covering some of the theory behind computer science, we recommend *Structure and Interpretation of Computer Programs* (*http://bit.ly/abelson_sussman_sicp*), by Harold Abelson and Gerald Jay Sussman (MIT Press).

If you're interested in learning more development principles through building and working with others, we recommend finding a local meetup group and getting involved. Many such groups host local and remote hackathons, so you can work on code alongside others and learn by doing.

Become a Better Visual Storyteller

If you were particularly interested in the visual storytelling parts of this book, there are many ways to further your knowledge of that field. If you want to continue with the libraries we've used, we highly recommend going through the Bokeh tutorials (*http://bit.ly/bokeh_tutorials*) and experimenting with your Jupyter notebooks.

Learning JavaScript and some of the popular visualization libraries from the JS community will help you become a better visual storyteller. Square offers an introduction to a D3 course (*https://square.github.io/intro-to-d3/*) with a brief introduction to the popular JavaScript library D3 (*http://d3js.org/*).

Finally, if you want to study some of the theories and ideas behind visual storytelling from a data analysis standpoint, we recommend Edward Tufte's *Visual Display of Quantitative Information* (*http://bit.ly/tufte_visual_display*) (Graphics Press).

Become a Better Systems Architect

If learning how to scale, deploy, and manage systems was particularly interesting to you, we have barely scratched the surface in terms of the opportunities within the systems sphere.

If you're interested in learning some more Unix, the University of Surrey has a short introduction covering some good concepts (*http://www.ee.surrey.ac.uk/Teaching/Unix/index.html*). The Linux Documentation Project also has a short introduction to bash programming (*http://tldp.org/HOWTO/Bash-Prog-Intro-HOWTO.html*).

We highly recommend taking time to learn Ansible (*http://docs.ansible.com/ansible/intro_getting_started.html*), a scalable and flexible server and systems management solution. If you're more interested in scaling data solutions, Udacity offers an Intro to Hadoop and MapReduce course (*http://bit.ly/intro_hadoop_mapreduce*). You should also check out Stanford's introduction to Apache Spark (*http://bit.ly/spark_intro*) and the PySpark programming guide (*http://bit.ly/pyspark_api*).

Where Do You Go from Here?

So, where do you go now? You have a litany of new skills, and you have the ability to question both your own assumptions and the data you find. You also have a working knowledge of Python and numerous useful libraries at your fingertips.

If you don't yet have a passion for a particular field or dataset, you'll want to discover ways to continue your progress and advancement as a data wrangler with new fields of study. There are many great data analysts out there writing inspirational stories. Here are a few:

- FiveThirtyEight (*http://fivethirtyeight.com/*), once a blog started by Nate Silver for *The New York Times*, is now a site with numerous writers and analysts investigating a variety of topics. After the Ferguson grand jury decision to not indict Darren Wilson, FiveThirtyEight published an article showing the outcome was an outlier. (*http://bit.ly/ferguson_outlier*) With controversial topics, being able to show a data trend or tendency can help take some of the emotions out of the story and reveal what the data is actually saying.

- A study of income gaps by *The Washington Post* (*http://bit.ly/rich_kids_game_system*) used tax and census data to conclude the "ol' boy network" was still alive in terms of job acquisition and initial salaries, but usually flattened or showed no correlation after those initial jobs were acquired.

- We've studied some of the impacts of groups in Africa who use child labor, including for mining conflict minerals. A recent report by Amnesty International and Global Witness (*http://bit.ly/supply_disclosure*) found most American firms are not adequately checking their supply pipelines to ensure their products do not use conflict minerals.

There are millions of untold stories in the world. If you have a passion or a belief, it's likely your insights and data wrangling skills can help people and communities. If you don't have a passion yet, we encourage you to keep learning by keeping up with data analysis in the news, documentaries, and online.

No matter where your interests lie, there is a wide world of possibilities available to deepen your learning and grasp of the concepts introduced in this book. Whatever sparked your interest the most is a great path for future learning. We hope this book is just a taste of what you'll be doing throughout your career as a data wrangler.

Comparison of Languages Mentioned

Often when you're working with a programming language, others will ask why you use that language. Why not use X or Y? X or Y may vary depending on what the person knows and whether they are an avid developer. It is good to understand why they are asking that question, and to think about your reply—why Python? This appendix compares Python to other useful languages so you can answer these questions and gain some insight into our programming choices.

C, C++, and Java Versus Python

When compared with C, C++, and Java, Python is fairly easy to learn, especially for those without a computer science background. As such, many folks who may have started in your same position have built add-ons and helpful tools to make Python more powerful and useful for the data science and data wrangling realms.

As for the technical differences, Python is a high-level language, while C and C++ are low-level languages. Java is high level, but has some low-level qualities. What does this mean? A high-level language abstracts interactions with the computer architecture—that is, it allows you to type code words (say, a for loop or variable definition), which the language then compiles down to code a computer can execute—while a low-level language deals with them directly. Low-level computer languages can run faster than high-level languages and allow for more direct control over a system to optimize things like memory management. High-level languages are easier to learn because most of those lower-level tasks are already managed for you.

For the purposes of the exercises taught in this book, there is no need to manipulate system control or speed things up by several seconds—so we do not need a low-level language. While Java is a high-level language, it has a higher learning curve than Python, and it would take longer for you to ramp up and get started.

R or MATLAB Versus Python

Python has libraries (supplemental code) with many of the same capabilities as R and MATLAB. Those libraries are called pandas (*http://pandas.pydata.org/*) and numpy (*http://www.numpy.org/*). These libraries handle specific tasks related to big data and statistical analysis. If you would like to learn more about them, you should check out Wes McKinney's book *Python for Data Analysis*. If you have a strong background in R or MATLAB, you can still use those tools for data wrangling. If that is the case, Python is a great supplemental tool. However, having all the pieces of your workflow in the same language makes data processing easier and more maintainable. By learning both R (or MATLAB) and Python, you can pick and choose which language you would like to use based on the needs of a particular project, giving you extra adaptability and convenience.

HTML Versus Python

Explaining why you don't use HTML to wrangle data is like explaining why you don't put water in a gas tank—you just don't. It is not made for that. HTML stands for HyperText Markup Language, and is the language that provides the structure for web pages to be displayed in a browser. Just like we talked about in Chapter 3, when we discussed XML, we can use Python to parse HTML, but not the other way around.

JavaScript Versus Python

JavaScript, which should not be confused with Java, is a language that adds interactivity and functionality to a web page. It runs in the browser. Python is divorced from the browser and runs on the computer system. Python has a rich collection of libraries that add functionality relevant to data analysis. JavaScript has extra functionality relating to browser-specific purposes. You can scrape the web and build charts with JavaScript, but not run statistical aggregation.

Node.js Versus Python

Node.js is a web platform, while Python is a language. There are frameworks written in Python similar to Node.js, like Flask and Django, but Node.js is written in the JavaScript language. While JavaScript is predominantly used on the Node.js allows for you to use JavaScript on the backend. If you use something like Flask or Django, you will probably have to learn JavaScript to use for your frontend needs. However, most of the work in this book is aimed at backend processes and larger data processing. Python is more accessible, easier to learn, and has specific data processing libraries already created for data wrangling use. For that reason, we use Python.

Ruby and Ruby on Rails Versus Python

You may have heard of Ruby on Rails, which is a popular web framework based on the Ruby language. There are many for Python—Flask, Django, Bottle, Pyramid, etc.—and Ruby is also often used without a web framework. We are using Python for its fast processing and data wrangling capabilities—not its web abilities. While we do talk about displaying data, if your goal is to build a website, you are reading the wrong book.

Python Resources for Beginners

This appendix lists groups and resources for new Python developers. This list is by no means comprehensive, but it provides an introduction to many of the sites, forums, chat rooms, and in-person groups you can visit and use in your journey as an aspiring Python developer.

Online Resources

- Stack Overflow (*http://stackoverflow.com*) is a really useful website where you can ask, view, and answer questions regarding coding and Python. The site supports posting code with questions, upvoting answers, and searching through the massive archives of already asked questions. If you are stuck on something, it's likely there is a clue in a Stack Overflow answer waiting for you!

- The Python website (*http://python.org*) is a great tool for researching more about what libraries might be available to help in your development. If you have a question about how something in the Python standard library behaves or what the recommended additional libraries to use are, the Python website is a great place to start.

- Read the Docs (*https://readthedocs.org/*) is a useful website where many Python libraries host their documentation. This is a great place to go if you are looking for more information on how to use a particular library.

In-Person Groups

- PyLadies (*http://pyladies.com*) is a Women in Engineering group started to help promote diversity of all kinds in Python. There are chapters around the globe, an active IRC channel on freenode, and numerous workshops and other helpful tools on the PyLadies website. Most chapters are open to all members, but check out your local chapter's meetup group to ensure the meetups are not gender-specific.

- Boston Python (*http://www.meetup.com/bostonpython/*) is one of the largest Python meetups in the world. Run by a dynamic group of well-known developers and educators, this group helps run workshops, project nights, and many different educational events. If you are ever in the Boston area, check them out!

- PyData (*http://pydata.org/*) is an organization helping to build a community around the Python and data analysis community. They hold worldwide meetups and conferences, and it's likely you can also find a local meetup chapter (or start a new one) in your area.

- Meetup.com (*http://www.meetup.com/*) is a site where many technical educational events are posted. We recommend searching for Python and data meetups in your area. It's easy to sign up and get alerts for new meetup groups that match your interests so you can meet people who have similar interests in data and Python.

- Django Girls (*https://djangogirls.org/*) is a Women in Engineering group aimed at promoting Python development via the major Python web development framework, Django. There are active chapters all over the world with workshops and trainings.

Learning the Command Line

One powerful development tool is the ability to navigate your computer using only the command line. Whatever operating system you use, knowing how to directly interact with your computer will pay off in your data wrangling and coding career. We aren't saying you need to become a systems administrator, but it's good to be somewhat adept at maneuvering via the command line.

One of the greatest feelings as a developer is being able to debug both systems and code problems you encounter. Understanding and working with your computer via the command line will give you some insight into those problems. If you encounter system errors and use the debugging tips you've learned throughout this book, you'll likely learn more about your own computer, the operating system you use, and how to better interact via the command line. Then, when you encounter system errors in your Python code, you'll be one step ahead when debugging and fixing those issues.

In this appendix, we'll cover the basics of bash (used on Macs and many Linux installations) as well as the Windows *cmd* and PowerShell utilities. We will only provide an introduction here, but we encourage you to continue your learning and engagement. We've included suggestions for further reading in each section.

Bash

If you're using a bash-based command line, what you learn as you navigate it will be applicable to any bash-based client, regardless of the operating system you are currently using...cool! Bash is a shell (or command-line) language with a lot of functionality. Let's get started learning bash by covering how to navigate files on your computer.

Navigation

Navigating your computer from the command line will help you understand how to do this with Python, and remaining in your terminal or text editor will keep you focused.

Let's start with the basics. Open up your terminal. It will likely open in ~, which signifies your home directory. If you are using Linux, this is likely */<home/your_computer_name>*. If you are using a Mac, it is likely */Users/<your_name>*. To see what folder you are in, type the following:

```
pwd
```

You should see a response like this:

```
/Users/katharine
```

or:

```
/home/katharine
```

pwd stands for "print working directory." You are asking bash to tell you what folder (or directory) you are in currently. This can be very helpful when first learning to navigate via the command line, especially if you want to double-check you are in the proper folder.

Another useful command is to see what files are in a folder. To see what files are in your current working directory, type:

```
ls
```

You should see a response similar to this:

```
Desktop/
Documents/
Downloads/
my_doc.docx
...
```

Depending on your operating system, the contents will vary, and they may have different colors. ls means "list." You can also call ls with additional arguments, called *flags*. These arguments will change the output. Try this:

```
ls -l
```

The output should be a list of columns, the final one being the same list you saw using only ls. The -l flag shows a detailed (long) view of your directory contents. It shows you the number of files and directories contained therein, as well as the permissions, creator's name, group ownership, size, and last-modified date of each. Here's an example:

```
drwxr-xr-x  2 katharine katharine  4096 Aug 20  2014 Desktop
drwxr-xr-x 22 katharine katharine 12288 Jul 20 18:19 Documents
drwxr-xr-x 26 katharine katharine 24576 Sep 16 11:39 Downloads
```

This level of detail can help you determine any problems you are having with permissions, and it allows you to see file sizes and other information. ls can also list any directory you pass to it. Try checking what's in your downloads folder (type the following):

```
ls -l ~/Downloads
```

You'll see a long output similar to the previous output example but listing all of the files and directories in the *Downloads* folder.

Now that you know how to list files from different folders, let's investigate how to change your current folder. We use the command cd to "change directory." Try this:

```
cd ~/Downloads
```

Now when you test what folder you are in using pwd and check the files in the folder using ls you should notice you are in your downloads folder. What if you wanted to move back to your home folder? We know the home folder is the parent folder. You can navigate to a parent folder using ... Try the following:

```
cd ..
```

Now you are back in your home folder. In bash, .. means "go up/back one directory." You can also chain these together to go back two directories, like so: cd ../...

 When moving around or selecting files in your command line, you should be able to use Tab to autocomplete file and folder names. Simply press Tab after you have typed the first letter or two of the name of the file or folder you want to select, and you should see different matching options (helping you spell and complete it), or, if there are no other files with similar names, the command line will autocomplete it for you. This helps you save time and typing!

You should now feel more comfortable moving around using your command line. Next, we'll learn about how to move and change files using the command line.

Modifying Files

Moving, copying, and creating files with bash is easy. Let's begin by creating a new file. First, navigate to your home directory (cd ~). Then, type the following:

```
touch test_file.txt
```

After that, go ahead and type ls. You should see that there is a new file called *test_file.txt*. touch can be used to create files that don't already exist. The command will look for a file of that name; if that file exists, it will update the last-modified timestamp but make no changes; if it doesn't exist, it will create the file.

Atom Shell Commands

If you are using Atom.io (*https://atom.io*) as your text editor, you can open this file (or any file) easily into Atom using the following command:

```
atom test_file.txt
```

If you get an error, you likely don't have the command-line options installed. To install them, open up the command palette by pressing Shift-Cmd-P and run the command called *Install Shell Commands*.

To see a list of all command-line options for Atom, type `atom --help`.

Now that we have a file to use, let's try copying it into our downloads folder:

```
cp test_file.txt ~/Downloads
```

Here we are saying, "copy *test_file.txt* into *~/Downloads*." Because bash knows *~/Downloads* is a folder, it will automatically copy the file *into* the folder. If we wanted to copy the file and change its name, we could write something like this:

```
cp test_file.txt ~/Downloads/my_test_file.txt
```

What we are doing with this command is telling bash to copy the test file into the downloads folder and call the copy *my_test_file.txt*. Now your downloads folder should have two copies of this test file: one with the original name, and one with this new name.

 If you need to run a command more than once, you can go through your command-line history by simply pressing the up arrow key. If you want to see all recent command-line history, type `history`.

Sometimes you don't want to copy files, but instead want to move them or rename them. Using bash, we can move and rename files using the same command: `mv`. Let's begin by renaming the file we created in our home folder:

```
mv test_file.txt empty_file.txt
```

What we are telling bash to do here is "move the file named *test_file.txt* to a file named *empty_file.txt*." If you use `ls` you should no longer see a *test_file.txt*, but you should now see an *empty_file.txt*. We have renamed our file by simply "moving" it. We can also use `mv` to move files between folders:

```
mv ~/Downloads/test_file.txt .
```

Here we are saying, "move the downloaded folder's *test_file.txt* into *here*". In bash, .
stands for your working directory (just like .. stands for the folder "above" your current directory). Now, if you use `ls` you will notice you have a *test_file.txt* folder in
your home folder again. You can also use `ls ~/Downloads` to see your downloads
folder no longer has the file.

Finally, you might want to delete files using the command line. To do so, you can use
the `rm`, or remove, command. Try the following:

```
rm test_file.txt
```

Now when you `ls` you'll see you have removed the *test_file.txt* from the folder.

Unlike deleting files with your mouse, deleting files with the command line *really* deletes them. There is no "Trash" you can go into
to recover them, so use `rm` with care and set up regular scheduled
backups for your computer and code.

Now that you know how to move, rename, copy, and delete files using bash, we'll
move on to executing files from the command line.

Executing Files

Executing files using bash is fairly straightforward. As you might have already learned
in Chapter 3, to execute a Python file, you simply need to run:

```
python my_file.py
```

Where *my_file.py* is a Python file.

For most languages you use and program, simply typing the name
of the language (`python`, `ruby`, `R`) and then the filename (with the
proper file path, or file location on your computer) will work. If
you are having trouble executing files using a particular language,
we recommend searching the Web for "command-line options"
along with the language name.

There are other execution commands you will come across as a Python developer.
Table C-1 shows some of them, so you can familiarize yourself with commands you
may need to install and run extra libraries.

Table C-1. Bash for execution

Command	Use case	More documentation
sudo	Executing the following command as a *sudo* or (*super*) user. Usually necessary if you are modifying core pieces of the filesystem or installing packages.	*https://en.wikipedia.org/wiki/Sudo*
bash	Executing a bash file or moving back into a bash shell.	*http://ss64.com/bash/*
./configure	Running configuration setup on a package (first step when installing a package from source).	*https://en.wikipedia.org/wiki/GNU_build_system #GNU_Autoconf*
make	Executing a makefile after configuration to compile the code and prepare for installation (second step when installing a package from source).	*http://www.computerhope.com/unix/umake.htm*
make install	Executing the code compiled with make and installing the package on your computer (final step when installing a package from source).	*http://www.codecoffee.com/tipsforlinux/articles/ 27.html*
wget	Executing a call to a URL and downloading the file located at that URL (good for downloading packages or files).	*http://www.gnu.org/software/wget/manual/wge t.html*
chown	Changing ownership of a file or folder. Often used with chgrp to change the group of a file. This can be useful if you need to move files so a different user can execute them.	*http://linux.die.net/man/1/chown*
chmod	Changing the permissions of a file or folder, often to make it executable or available for a different type of user or group.	*http://ss64.com/bash/chmod.html*

As you use your command line, you'll likely come across a variety of other commands and documentation. We recommend you take time to learn, use, and ask questions; bash is another language, and it will take time to learn its quirks and uses. Before we finish our command-line introduction, we'd like to introduce you to using bash to search for files or file contents.

Searching with the Command Line

Searching for files and searching inside files is relatively easy in bash and can be done in numerous ways. We'll show you a few options to get started. First, we will use a command to search for text in a file. Let's start by downloading a file using wget:

```
wget http://corpus.byu.edu/glowbetext/samples/text.zip
```

This should download a text corpus we can use to search. To unzip the text into a new folder, simply type:

```
mkdir text_samples
unzip text.zip text_samples/
```

You should now have a bunch of text corpus files in your new folder, *text_samples*. Change into that directory using cd text_samples. Let's now search inside those files using a tool called grep:

```
grep snake *.txt
```

What you are telling bash to do here is search for the string *snake* in any file in this folder whose name ends with *.txt*. You can learn more about wildcard characters in "RegEx Matching" on page 183; however, * almost always stands for a wildcard and can be used to mean "any matching string."

When you ran that command you should have seen some matching text fly by. grep will return any lines from any matching file containing the search string. This is incredibly useful if you have a large repository and you want to find which files contain the function you need to update or change, for example. grep also has some extra arguments and options you can pass if you want to print surrounding lines.

To see options for any bash command, simply type the command followed by a space and then --help. Type grep --help and read about some of the grep's extra options and features.

Another neat tool is cat. It simply prints out the contents of whatever file you identify. This can be useful especially if you need to "pipe" output somewhere else. In bash, the | character can be used to string together a series of actions you wish to perform with your files or text. For example, let's cat the contents of one of our files and then use grep to search the output:

```
cat w_gh_b.txt | grep network
```

What we did was first return the full text of the file *w_gh_b.txt* and then "pipe" that output to grep, which then searched for the word *network* and returned the lines containing it to our command line.

We can do the same type of pipe using our bash history. Try this:

```
history | grep mv
```

This command lets you find and reuse commands you may have forgotten as you learn bash.

Let's take our search a step further and look for files. First, we are going to use a command called `find`, which looks for matching filenames and can be used to traverse child directories and search for matching files there as well. Let's search for any text files in our current folder or child folders:

```
find . -name "*.txt" -type f
```

What we are saying here is find (starting in this folder and then going through all child folders) files with a filename that matches any string but ends in *.txt* and that are file type *f* (meaning a normal file, rather than a directory, signified by type *d*). You should see a list of matching filenames as output. Now, let's pipe those files so we can grep them:

```
find . -name "*.txt" -type f | xargs grep neat
```

What we are telling bash to do here is, "find those same text files, but this time search those files for the word *neat*." We use `xargs` (*https://en.wikipedia.org/wiki/Xargs*) so we can properly pipe the `find` output to `grep`. `xargs` isn't needed for all piping, but it's useful when using `find` as the `find` command doesn't send output uniformly.

You've learned a few neat tricks for searching and finding, which can be useful, especially as the code and projects you are working with grow larger and more involved. We'll leave you with some more resources and reading on the topic.

More Resources

There are a lot of great bash resources on the Internet (*http://wiki.bash-hackers.org/scripting/tutoriallist*). The Linux Documentation Project (*http://www.tldp.org/LDP/Bash-Beginners-Guide/html/*) has a great guide for beginners which takes you through some more advanced bash programming. O'Reilly also has a great *bash Cookbook* that can jumpstart your learning process.

Windows CMD/Power Shell

The Windows command line (now also supplemented with PowerShell (*https://en.wikipedia.org/wiki/Windows_PowerShell*)), or *cmd*, is a powerful DOS-based utility. You can use the same syntax across Windows versions and server instances, and learning to navigate that syntax can help you be a more powerful programmer for Python and any other languages you choose to learn.

Navigation

Navigating files with *cmd* is very straightforward. Let's begin by opening the *cmd* utility and taking a look at our present directory. Type:

```
echo %cd%
```

What this is telling *cmd* is that you want to echo (or print out) *%cd%*, which is the current directory. You should see a response similar to this:

```
C:\Users\Katharine>
```

To list all of the files in your present directory, type the following:

```
dir
```

You should see output similar to this:

```
13.03.2015  16:07    <DIR>          .ipython
11.09.2015  19:05    <DIR>          Contacts
11.09.2015  19:05    <DIR>          Desktop
11.09.2015  19:05    <DIR>          Documents
11.09.2015  19:05    <DIR>          Downloads
11.09.2015  19:05    <DIR>          Favorites
10.02.2014  15:15    <DIR>          Intel
11.09.2015  19:05    <DIR>          Links
11.09.2015  19:05    <DIR>          Music
11.09.2015  19:05    <DIR>          Pictures
13.03.2015  16:26    <DIR>          pip
11.09.2015  19:05    <DIR>          Saved Games
```

`dir` also has many options you can use (*http://ss64.com/nt/dir.html*) to sort, group, or show more information. Let's take a look at our *Desktop* folder.

```
dir Desktop /Q
```

We are asking *cmd* to show the files in the *Desktop* directory, and to show the owners for those files. You should see the owner of each file as the first part of the filename (e.g., `MY-LAPTOP\Katharine\backupPDF`). This can be tremendously useful in seeing your folders and files. There are also some great options for showing subfolders and sorting by last-modified timestamps.

Let's navigate to our *Desktop* folder. Type the following:

```
chdir Desktop
```

Now when you check your current directory by typing `echo %cd%`, you should see a change. To navigate to a parent folder, simply use `...` For example, if we wanted to navigate to the parent folder of our current directory, we could type:

```
chdir ..
```

You can also string together these "parent folders" symbols (`chdir ..\..` to go into the grandparent folder, etc.). Depending on your file structure, you may receive an error if there is no parent to your current folder (i.e., you are at the root of your file-system).

To get back to your home directory, simply type:

```
chdir %HOMEPATH%
```

You should end up back in the first folder we used. Now that we can navigate using *cmd*, let's move on to creating, copying, and modifying files.

Modifying Files

To start with, let's create a new file we can use to modify:

```
echo "my awesome file" > my_new_file.txt
```

If you use `dir` to take a look at the files in your folder, you should now see *my_new_file.txt*. If you open that file up in your text editor, you can see we wrote "my awesome file" in the file. If you are using Atom, you can launch Atom directly from your *cmd* (see "Atom Shell Commands" on page 434).

Now that we have that file, let's try copying it to a new folder:

```
copy my_new_file.txt Documents
```

Now if we list our documents using:

```
dir Documents
```

we should see *my_new_file.txt* was successfully copied there.

 For easy typing, you can use Tab to autocomplete filenames and paths. Try it out by typing `copy` `my` and then hitting Tab. *cmd* should be able to guess you meant the *my_new_file.txt* file and fill in the file name for you.

We might also want to move or rename files. To move a file using *cmd*, we can use the `move` command. Try the following:

```
move Documents\my_new_file.txt Documents\my_newer_file.txt
```

Now, if you list the files in your *Documents* directory, you should see there is no longer a *my_new_file.txt* and now just a *my_newer_file.txt*. `Move` is useful for renaming files (as we have done here) or moving a file or folder.

Finally, you may want to remove or delete files you don't need anymore. To do so with *cmd*, you can use the `del` command. Try the following:

```
del my_new_file.txt
```

Now, when you check your current files, you should no longer see *my_new_file.txt*. Note that this will *completely* remove the file. You want to make sure you only do this if you absolutely do not need the file. It's also a great idea to make regular hard drive backups in case of any issues.

Now that we can modify files, let's take a look at how to execute files from *cmd*.

Executing Files

To execute files from your Windows *cmd*, you usually need to type the language name and then the path to the file. For example, to execute a Python file, you'll need to type:

```
python my_file.py
```

This will execute the file *my_file.py* as long as it's located in the same folder. You can execute a *.exe* file simply by typing the full filename and path into your *cmd* and hitting Enter.

 As you did when you installed Python, you'll need to make sure installation packages and the file paths for the installed executables are sourced in your Path variable (for details, refer to "Setting Up Python on Your Machine" on page 7). This variable keeps a list of the executable strings for your *cmd*.

For more powerful command-line execution, we recommend learning Windows PowerShell—a powerful scripting language used to write scripts and execute them via a simple command line. Computerworld has a great introduction to PowerShell (*http://bit.ly/powershell_intro*) to get started.

To run installed programs from the command line, you can use the start command. Try the following:

```
start "" "http://google.com"
```

This should open up your default browser and navigate to Google's home page. See the start command documentation (*http://bit.ly/start_command*) for more information.

Now that we know how to execute using the command line, let's investigate how to search for and find files and folders on our machine.

Searching with the Command Line

Let's begin by downloading a corpus we can use. If you have Windows Vista or newer, you should be able to execute PowerShell commands. Try loading PowerShell by typing the following:

```
powershell
```

You should see a new prompt that looks similar to this:

```
Windows PowerShell
...
PS C:\Users\Katharine>
```

Now that we're in PowerShell, let's try downloading a file we want to use for searching (note that this and the following command should be entered on a single line; the commands are wrapped here to fit page constraints):

```
Invoke-WebRequest -OutFile C:\Downloads\text.zip
 http://corpus.byu.edu/glowbetext/samples/text.zip
```

If you don't have the PowerShell version 3.0 or above, the command will throw an error. If you receive an error, try the following command, which will work for older versions of PowerShell:

```
(new-object System.Net.WebClient).DownloadFile(
'http://corpus.byu.edu/glowbetext/samples/text.zip','C:\Downloads\text.zip')
```

These commands use PowerShell to download a word corpus file to your computer. Let's create a new directory to unzip the files:

```
mkdir Downloads\text_examples
```

Now we are going to add a new function to PowerShell to extract our zipped file. Type the following:

```
Add-Type -AssemblyName System.IO.Compression.FileSystem
function Unzip
{
    param([string]$zipfile, [string]$outpath)

        [System.IO.Compression.ZipFile]::ExtractToDirectory($zipfile, $outpath)
}
```

This function is now defined and we can use it to unzip files. Try unzipping the downloaded content into the new folder:

```
Unzip Downloads\text.zip Downloads\text_examples
```

To exit PowerShell, simply type exit. Your prompt should return to the normal *cmd* prompt. If you use dir Downloads\text_examples, you should have a list of text files from the corpus download. Let's use findstr to search within those files:

```
findstr "neat" Downloads\text_examples\*.txt
```

You should see a bunch of text output fly by in your console. Those are the matching lines of the text files that have the word *neat* in them.

Sometimes you want to search for a particular filename, not a string in a file. To do that, you need to use the dir command, but with a filter:

```
dir -r -filter "*.txt"
```

This should find all of your *.txt* files in folders contained within your home folder. If you need to search within those files, you can use piping. A | character "pipes" your output from the first command into the next command. We can use this to, say, find all Python files with a particular function name in them, or find all CSV files containing a particular country name. Let's pipe our findstr output into our find command to try it out:

```
findstr /s "snake" *.txt | find /i "snake" /c
```

This code searches for text files that contain the word *snake* and then uses find to count the number of occurrences of the word *snake* in these files. As you can see, learning more *cmd* commands and usage will help greatly in simplifying tasks like searching for files, executing code, and managing your work as a data wrangler and developer. This appendix has helped introduce you to some of these topics, and is a good stepping stone to learn more.

More Resources

There are some great online resources for looking up *cmd* commands (*http://ss64.com/nt/*) to read through for learning how to use *cmd* for your daily programming and data wrangling needs.

If you'd like to learn more about PowerShell and how to use it to create powerful scripts for your Windows servers and computers, take a look at some tutorials, like Microsoft's *Getting Started with PowerShell 3.0* (*http://bit.ly/gs_with_powershell*). There is also an O'Reilly *Windows Powershell Cookbook* to get you started on writing your first scripts.

Advanced Python Setup

Early in the book, we set up system Python. Why? Because it is quick and easy to use. When you start using more complex libraries and tools, you will likely need a more advanced setup. An advanced Python setup on your machine is helpful when trying to organize projects. An advanced setup also helps if you need to run both Python 2.7 and Python 3+.

 In this appendix, we walk you through setting up your Python environment in *Expert* mode. Because there are a lot of dependencies involved, it is entirely possible some parts of these instructions might not line up with your experience. To resolve issues, we suggest going to the Web to find, or ask, how to continue.

We'll start by installing a couple of core tools, then install Python (2.7, but you could install 3+ at this point). Lastly, we'll install and set up some virtual environments, which isolate projects so you can have different versions of a Python library for each project.

These instructions cover Mac, Windows, and Linux setups. As you read through each step, carefully follow the instructions for your particular operating system.

Step 1: Install GCC

The purpose of GCC (the GNU Compiler Collection) is to take Python libraries with C extensions and turn them into something your machine can understand and execute.

On a Mac, GCC is included in Xcode (*https://developer.apple.com/xcode/*) and Command Line Tools (*https://developer.apple.com/downloads/*). You will need to download either one. In both cases, you will need an Apple ID (*http://bit.ly/create_appleid*) for the download. Also, Xcode can take a while to download depending on your Internet connection (for me it took 20 minutes), so plan to take a break. If you are concerned with time or memory use, opt for Command Line Tools instead. Installing Xcode or Command Line Tools will not take as long. Make sure Xcode or Command Line Tools is installed before moving on to the installation of Homebrew.

If you are using Windows, Jeff Preshing has this helpful tutorial for installing GCC (*http://bit.ly/gcc_install_tutorial*). If you are using Linux, GCC is installed on most Debian-based systems, or you can install it by simply running `sudo apt-get install build-essential`.

Step 2: (Mac Only) Install Homebrew

Homebrew manages packages on your Mac, which means you can type a command and Homebrew will aid in the installation.

 Make sure either Xcode or Command Line Tools is done installing before you install Homebrew. Otherwise, you will have errors in your Homebrew installation.

To install Homebrew, open Terminal, and enter this line (follow any prompts that come up, including the one asking your permission to install Homebrew):

```
$ ruby -e "$(curl -fsSL https://raw.github.com/Homebrew/homebrew/go/install)"
```

Pay attention to the output. Homebrew recommends running `brew doctor` to test and warn you of any issues with the installation. Depending on the state of your system, you might have various items to address. If you have no warnings returned, then continue to the next step.

Step 3: (Mac Only) Tell Your System Where to Find Homebrew

To use Homebrew, you need to tell your system where it's located. To do this, you want to add Homebrew to your *.bashrc* file or other shell you are using (i.e., if you have a custom shell, you'll need to add it there). The *.bashrc* file may not exist yet on your system; if it does exist, it will be hidden in your home directory.

All files that have a . at the beginning of their names do not appear when you type `ls` unless you explicitly request to see all of them. The purpose of this is twofold. First, if the files are not visible you are less likely to delete or edit them inappropriately. Second, these file types are not used regularly, so hiding them gives the system a cleaner appearance.

Let's see what our directory might look like if we show all the files by adding some extra flags to ls. Make sure you're in your home directory, and then enter the following command:

```
$ ls -ag
```

Your output will look something like this:

```
total 56
drwxr-xr-x+ 17 staff     578 Jun 22 00:08 .
drwxr-xr-x   5 admin     170 May 29 09:49 ..
-rw-------   1 staff       3 May 29 09:49 .CFUserTextEncoding
-rw-r--r--@  1 staff   12292 May 29 09:44 .DS_Store
drwx------   8 staff     272 Jun 10 00:45 .Trash
-rw-------   1 staff     389 Jun 22 00:07 .bash_history
drwx------   4 staff     136 Jun 10 00:35 Applications
drwx------+  5 staff     170 Jun 22 00:08 Desktop
drwx------+  3 staff     102 May 29 09:49 Documents
drwx------+ 10 staff     340 Jun 11 23:47 Downloads
drwx------@ 43 staff    1462 Jun 10 00:29 Library
drwx------+  3 staff     102 May 29 09:49 Movies
drwx------+  3 staff     102 May 29 09:49 Music
drwx------+  3 staff     102 May 29 09:49 Pictures
drwxr-xr-x+  5 staff     170 May 29 09:49 Public
```

We do not have a *.bashrc* file, so we will have to create one.

 If you do have a *.bashrc* file, you should back it up in case you have any issues. Making a copy of your *.bashrc* is easiest on your command line. Simply run the following command to copy *.bashrc* to a new file called *.bashrc_bkup*:

```
$ cp .bashrc .bashrc_bkup
```

To create a *.bashrc*, first we need to make sure we have a *.bash_profile* file which is the file that will call the *.bashrc* file. If we add a *.bashrc* file without a *.bash_profile* file, our computer won't know what to do with it.

Before starting, check if you have a *.bash_profile* file. If you do, it will be in the directory list produced by is -ag. If you don't, then you will need to create it.

If you have a *.bash_profile* file, you should back it up so that if you have any issues you can restore to your original settings. Run the following command to copy your *.bash_profile* file to a new file called *.bashrc_bkup*:

```
$ cp ~/.bash_profile ~/.bash_profile_bkup
```

Then run this command to copy it to your desktop and rename it at the same time:

```
$ cp ~/.bash_profile ~/Desktop/bash_profile
```

If you are working with an existing *.bash_profile*, launch your editor and open the version you moved to your desktop. Add the following code to the bottom of the file. The code just says, "if there is a *.bashrc* file, then use it":

```
# Get the aliases and functions
if [ -f ~/.bashrc ]; then
    . ~/.bashrc
fi
```

If you don't already have a *.bash_profile* file, you'll need to create a new file with these contents in your editor. Save the file to your desktop as *bash_profile*, without the dot in front.

Make sure you checked that *.bash_profile* and *.bashrc* didn't already exist in your home directory. If they did, make sure you followed the instructions to create backups of the original files before continuing. If you don't do this, when you execute the following code you could end up overwriting your original files, which could cause problems.

Now go back to Terminal and run the following command to rename the file and move it from the desktop to your home directory:

```
$ mv ~/Desktop/bash_profile .bash_profile
```

Now, if you run `ls -al ~/`, you will see that you have a *.bash_profile* file in your home directory. If you run `more .bash_profile`, you will see the code calling the *.bashrc*, which you put there.

Now that we have a *.bash_profile* file referring to the *.bashrc*, let's edit the *.bashrc* file. Start by opening your current *.bashrc* or a new file in your text editor. Add the following line to the bottom of your *.bashrc* file. This will add the location of Homebrew to your $PATH variable in your settings. The new path will be prioritized over the old $PATH:

```
export PATH=/usr/local/bin:/usr/local/sbin:$PATH
```

Now, save that file to your desktop with the name *bashrc*, without the dot.

Use a Command-Line Shortcut for Your Code Editor

While we are updating settings in our *.bashrc*, let's also create a shortcut to launch our code editor from the command line. This is not required, but it will make your life easier when you are navigating file directories and want to open a file in your code editor. Using your GUI to navigate the file structure will not be as efficient.

If you are using Atom, you already have a shortcut available when you install Atom and the shell commands (*http://bit.ly/cl_open_atom*). Sublime also has commands available for OS X (*http://bit.ly/os_x_cl_sublime*).

If you are using another code editor, you can try typing the program name to see if it launches, or the program name followed by `--help` to see if it has any command-line help. We also recommend searching for "<your_program_name> command-line tools" and see if there are any helpful results.

Back in Terminal, run the following command to rename the file and move it from the desktop to your home directory:

```
$ mv ~/Desktop/bashrc .bashrc
```

At this point, if you run `ls -al ~/`, you will see that you have a *.bashrc* file and a *.bash_profile* in your home directory. Let's confirm it worked by opening a new window in Terminal and checking out our $PATH variable. To check the variable, run the following command:

```
$ echo $PATH
```

You should get an output something like this:

```
/usr/local/bin:/usr/local/sbin:/usr/bin:/bin:/usr/sbin:/sbin:/usr/local/bin
```

Whatever your output is, you will see that the variable information (`/usr/local/bin:/usr/local/sbin`) added to our *.bashrc* now prepends the returned value.

If you do not see the new value in the variable, make sure you opened a new window. Settings changes do not load in your current Terminal window, unless you explicitly source the file into your current terminal (see the bash `source` (*http://ss64.com/bash/source.html*) command for more information).

Step 4: Install Python 2.7

To install Python 2.7 on a Mac, run the following command:

```
$ brew install python
```

If you would like to push forward with Python 3+, you can install that instead. To install Python 3+ on a Mac, run:

```
$ brew install python3
```

For Windows, you will need to follow the instructions in Chapter 1 to properly install from the Windows installer package. For Linux, you likely already have Python installed. It's a good idea to install some extra Python tools in Linux by installing some Python developer packages (*http://bit.ly/install_python_dev_pkg*).

After the process is complete, you will want to test that it worked properly.

Launch your Python interpreter in Terminal:

```
$ python
```

Then, run the following:

```
import sys
import pprint
pprint.pprint(sys.path)
```

Mac output looks similar to this:

```
>>> pprint.pprint(sys.path)
['',
 '/usr/local/lib/python2.7/site-packages/setuptools-4.0.1-py2.7.egg',
 '/usr/local/lib/python2.7/site-packages/pip-1.5.6-py2.7.egg',
 '/usr/local/Cellar/python/2.7.7_1/Frameworks/Python.framework/Versions/
 2.7/lib/python27.zip',
 '/usr/local/Cellar/python/2.7.7_1/Frameworks/Python.framework/Versions/
 2.7/lib/python2.7',
 '/Library/Python/2.7/site-packages',
 '/usr/local/lib/python2.7/site-packages']
```

If you are using a Mac, the output you received should have a bunch of file paths that start with */usr/local/Cellar/*. If you do not see this, you may not have reloaded your settings in your Terminal window. Close your window, and then open a new one and try again. If this did not solve any issues you may have had during this process, return to the beginning of the setup and retrace your steps.

Debugging installation errors is a learning experience. If you have errors not documented in this section, open up your favorite search engine in your browser and search for the error. You are probably not the first one to experience the issue.

If you successfully completed this section, you can move on to the next step.

Step 5: Install virtualenv (Windows, Mac, Linux)

We've set up a second instance of Python, but now we want to set up a way of creating individual Python environments. This is where `virtualenv` helps, by isolating projects and dependencies from one another. If we have multiple projects, we can make sure individual requirements do not conflict.

To get started, we need Setuptools (*http://pythonhosted.org//setuptools/*). When we installed Python, Setuptools came with it. Part of Setuptools is a command-line tool called pip, that we are going to use to install Python packages.

To install *virtualenv* (*http://virtualenv.readthedocs.org/en/latest/*), you will want to run the following command on your command line:

```
$ pip install virtualenv
```

After you run that command, part of the output should be the following: *Successfully installed virtualenv*. If you got that, then everything went well. If not, then you have another issue that you need to account for, so search around online for help.

Step 6: Set Up a New Directory

Before we continue, let's create a directory in which to keep our project-related content. The exact location is a personal preference. Most people create a folder in their user home directory, for easy access and backups. You can put the directory anywhere you like that is both useful and memorable. On a Mac, to make a *Projects* folder in your home directory, run the following command in Terminal:

```
$ mkdir ~/Projects/
```

or for Windows:

```
> mkdir C:\Users\_your_name_\Projects
```

Then we are going to create a folder inside that folder to store the data-wrangling specific-code we will write. On a Mac, you can do that by running this command:

```
$ mkdir ~/Projects/data_wrangling
$ mkdir ~/Projects/data_wrangling/code
```

or for Windows:

```
> mkdir C:\Users\_your_name_\Projects\data_wrangling
> mkdir C:\Users\_your_name_\Projects\data_wrangling\code
```

Lastly, add a hidden folder in your home directory to use for virtualenv environments. Use this command on a Mac:

```
$ mkdir ~/.envs
```

or for Windows:

```
> mkdir C:\Users\_your_name_\Envs
```

If you'd like to hide your folder on Windows, you can do so by editing the attributes via the command line:

```
> attrib +s +h C:\Users\_your_name_\Envs
```

To unhide it, simply remove the attributes:

```
> attrib -s -h C:\Users\_your_name_\Envs
```

At this point, we have our code folder set up in a special file inside our *Projects* folder and our virtual environment folder properly set up in our home directory.

Step 7: Install virtualenvwrapper

`virtualenv` is a great tool, but `virtualenvwrapper` (*http://virtualenvwrapper.readthe docs.org/en/latest/*) makes `virtualenv` easier to access and use. While it has many features (*http://bit.ly/virtualenvwrapper_features*) not mentioned in this appendix, the most powerful feature is one of the simplest.

It takes a command like this:

```
source $PATH_TO_ENVS/example/bin/activate
```

And turns it into this:

```
workon example
```

Installing virtualenvwrapper (Mac and Linux)

To install `virtualenvwrapper` on Mac and Linux, run the following:

```
$ pip install virtualenvwrapper
```

Check the second-to-last line of the output to make sure everything installed correctly. For me that line says, *Successfully installed virtualenvwrapper virtualenv-clone stevedore.*

Updating your .bashrc

You also need to add some settings to your *.bashrc*. We are going to copy the file, edit it, then move it back to where it was.

First, make a backup of your *.bashrc*. If you already have one of these, you can skip this step. If you started with a new file, you will be creating your first backup of your .bashrc. To do so, type this command:

```
$ cp ~/.bashrc ~/.bashrc_bkup
```

I store my settings files (*https://github.com/jackiekazil/dotfiles*) on GitHub, so I always have a backup available. This is so if I make a mistake or my computer dies, I can always recover them. Make sure your home folder doesn't get cluttered with 20 backups as you make adjustments over time to this file. You will rarely edit the *.baschrc* file, but when you do it is the kind of file that you want to back up before editing.

Open your *.bashrc* file using your code editor and add these three lines to the end of the file. If you did not use the same location for your *Projects* folder, then you will want to adjust the file paths accordingly:

```
export WORKON_HOME=$HOME/.envs                    ❶
export PROJECT_HOME=$HOME/Projects/               ❷
source /usr/local/bin/virtualenvwrapper.sh        ❸
```

❶ Defines the WORKON_HOME variable. This is where your Python environments are stored. This should align with the environment folder you created earlier.

❷ Defines the PROJECT_HOME variable. This is where you store your code. This should align with the *Projects* (or for linux projects) folder you created earlier.

❸ Initiates virtualenvwrapper, which makes virtualenv easier to use.

When you're done, save the file and open a new Terminal window where you will load the new settings. Now you will have an easy-to-use set of commands to work with virtual environments.

Installing virtualenvwrapper-win (Windows)

For Windows, there are some extra optional steps to make your life easier. First, you should install the Windows version of virtualenvwrapper (*https://pypi.python.org/pypi/virtualenvwrapper-win*). You can do so by running:

```
>pip install virtualenvwrapper-win
```

You should also add a WORKON_HOME environment variable. By default, virtualenv wrapper will expect you to have a folder named *Envs* in your *User* folder. If you'd rather set up your own folder for your virtual environments, do that and then add the WORKON_HOME environment variable set to the proper file path. If you haven't set up environment variables before and want a quick how-to, there's a nice walkthrough on Stack Overflow (*http://bit.ly/env_variables*).

In order to work with more than one version of Python in Windows, it's also a good idea to install `pywin` (*https://github.com/david marble/pywin*); this allows you to easily switch between Python versions.

Testing Your Virtual Environment (Windows, Mac, Linux)

Before we wrap up this section, let's run a few tests to make sure everything is working. In a new terminal window, create a new virtual environment called *test*:

```
mkvirtualenv test
```

Your output should look something like this:

```
New python executable in test/bin/python2.7
Not overwriting existing python script test/bin/python (you must use
  test/bin/python2.7)
Installing setuptools, pip...done.
```

 If you wanted to create an environment with Python 3+ instead of Python 2.7, then you would define the `python` variable and point it to Python 3. First, identify where your instance of Python 3 is located:

```
which python3
```

Your output should look something like this:

```
/usr/local/bin/python3
```

Now, use that in your `mkvirtualenv` command to define a Python 3+ environment:

```
mkvirtualenv test --python=/usr/local/bin/python3
```

You should see "(test)" prepended to the being of your terminal prompt. That means the environment is currently activated.

 If you got `-bash: mkvirtualenv: command not found` as your output instead, then your terminal is not recognizing `virtualenv wrapper`. First, check to make sure you opened a new Terminal or *cmd* window before running this code, which ensures the new settings are applied. If that's not the issue, then go through the setup and confirm you followed all the steps.

If you were able to successfully create a virtual environment, then you are done with your setup!

Let's deactivate our virtual environment and destroy it, as it was only a test. Run the following commands to remove the *test* environment:

```
deactivate
rmvirtualenv test
```

By this point, you've set up a second Python instance on your machine. You also have an environment where you can create isolated Python environments to protect one project from another. Now we are going to run through some exercises to make you familiar with your shiny new Python environment.

Learning About Our New Environment (Windows, Mac, Linux)

The examples shown here are for a Mac, but the process is the same on Windows and Linux. In this section, we are going to learn a little about how to use our setup and make sure all the components work together.

Let's begin by creating a new environment called *testprojects*. We will activate and use this any time we need a quick environment to exercise a test or something else. To create it, run this command:

```
$ mkvirtualenv testprojects
```

After you create the environment, you should see that your Terminal prompt is now prepended with the name of the environment. For me, that looks like this:

```
(testprojects)Jacquelines-MacBook-Pro:~ jacquelinekazil$
```

Let's install a Python library into our environment. The first library we will install is called ipython. In your active environment, run the following command:

```
(testprojects) $ pip install ipython
```

If this command is successful, then the last couple of lines of your output should look like this:

```
Installing collected packages: ipython, gnureadline
Successfully installed ipython gnureadline
Cleaning up...
```

Now, if you type pip freeze into your Terminal, you will see the libraries in your current environment along with the version number of each installation. The output should look like this:

```
gnureadline==6.3.3
ipython==2.1.0
wsgiref==0.1.2
```

This output tells us that, in the *testprojects* environment, we have three libraries installed: gnureadline, ipython, and wsgiref. ipython is what we just installed. gnureadline was installed when we installed ipython, because it is a dependency library. (This saves you from having to install dependent packages directly. Nice, right?) The third library is `wsgiref`. It was there by default, but isn't a requirement.

So, we've installed a library called `ipython`, but what can we do with it? IPython is an easy-to-use alternative to the default Python interpreter (you can read even more about IPython in Appendix F). To launch IPython, simply type `ipython`.

You should see a prompt similar to this:

```
IPython 3.1.0 -- An enhanced Interactive Python.
?          -> Introduction and overview of IPython's features.
%quickref -> Quick reference.
help       -> Python's own help system.
object?    -> Details about 'object', use 'object??' for extra details.

In [1]:
```

To test it out, type the following:

```
In [1]: import sys

In [2]: import pprint

In [3]: pprint.pprint(sys.path)
```

You should have the same output as earlier when we confirmed that our environment was working. `sys` and `pprint` are what are called *standard library modules*, which come prepackaged with Python.

Let's exit out of IPython. There are two ways to do this. You can either press Ctrl+D, then type y for yes when prompted, or just type `quit()`. This works just like the default Python shell.

Once you have exited, you will be back on the command line. Now we have an environment called *testprojects* with three libraries installed. But what if we want to have another environment, because we are going to work on another project? First, type the following to deactivate the current environment:

```
$ deactivate
```

Then create a new one called *sandbox*:

```
$ mkvirtualenv sandbox
```

After you do this, you'll be in your new environment. If you type `pip freeze`, you will see that you do not have IPython installed in this environment. This is because this is a fresh environment, which is completely separate from the *testprojects* environment. If we install IPython in this environment, it will install a second instance on our computer. This ensures anything we do in one environment doesn't affect the others.

Why is this important? As you work on new projects, you will likely want different libraries and different versions of libraries installed. We recommend setting up one virtual environment for this book, but if you start on a new project, you'll want to start a new virtual environment. As you can see, it's easy to switch between environments as you change projects.

You may sometimes come across a repository with all of the requirements stored in a file called *requirements.txt*. The library's authors used virtual environments and `pip freeze` to save a list so users can install the library and dependencies. To install from a requirements file, you need to run `pip install -r requirements.txt`.

We know how to create an environment and deactivate an environment, but we don't know how to activate one that already exists. To activate our sample environment called *sandbox*, type the following command (if you are already in it, you may have to `deactivate` first to see the difference):

```
$ workon sandbox
```

Lastly, how do you destroy an environment? First, make sure you are not in the environment you want to remove. If you just typed in `workon sandbox` then you should be in the *sandbox* environment. To destroy it, you will want to first deactivate, then remove it:

```
$ deactivate
$ rmvirtualenv sandbox
```

Now, the only environment you should have is *testprojects*.

Advanced Setup Review

Your computer is now set up to run an advanced Python library. You should feel more comfortable interacting with your command line and working with installing packages. If you haven't already, we also recommend you take a look at Appendix C to learn more about working with the command line.

Table D-1 lists the commands you will use most often with virtual environments.

Table D-1. Commands to review

Command	Action
mkvirtualenv	Creates an environment
rmvirtualenv	Destroys an environment
workon	Activates an environment
deactivate	Deactivates the environment that is currently active

Command	Action
`pip install`	Installs in the active environment[a]
`pip uninstall`	Uninstalls in the active environment[b]
`pip freeze`	Returns a list of installed libraries in the active environment

[a] If no environment is active, the library will be installed on the secondary copy of Python on your system, which was installed using Homebrew. Your system Python should not be affected.

[b] See previous footnote.

Python Gotchas

Python, like any other language you learn, has its quirks and idiosyncracies. Some of them are shared among scripting languages, so they may not seem surprising if you have scripting experience. Other quirks are unique to Python. We've assembled a list of some of them, but by no means all of them, so you can familiarize yourself. We hope this appendix serves as an aid for debugging and also gives you a bit of insight on why Python does things the way it does.

Hail the Whitespace

As you have probably already noticed, Python uses whitespace as an integral part of code structure. Whitespace is used to indent functions, methods, and classes; to operate *if-else* statements; and to create continuation lines. In Python, whitespace is a special operator and helps turn Python code into executable code.

There are a few best practices for whitespace in your Python files:

- Don't use tabs. Use spaces.
- Use four spaces for each indentation block.
- Choose a good indentation for hanging indents (it can align with a delimiter, an extra indentation, or a single indentation, but should be chosen based on what is most readable and usable; see PEP-8 (*http://bit.ly/pep-8_indentation*)).

PEP-8 (or Python Enhancement Proposals #8) is a Python style guide outlining good practices for indentation and advice on how to name variables, continue lines, and format your code so it is readable, easy to use, and easy to share.

If your code is improperly indented and Python cannot parse your file, you'll get an `IndentationError`. The error message will show you what line you have improperly indented. It's also fairly easy to get a Python linter set up with whatever text editor is your favorite, to automatically check your code as you are working. For example, a nice PEP-8 linter is available for Atom (*https://atom.io/packages/linter-python-pep8*).

The Dreaded GIL

The Global Interpreter Lock (GIL) is a mechanism used by the Python interpreter to execute code using only one thread at a time. This means that when you are running your Python script, even on a multiprocessing machine, your code will execute linearly. This design decision was made so that Python could run quickly using C code but still be thread-safe.

The constraint the GIL puts on Python means with the standard interpreter, Python is never truly parallelized. This has some disadvantages for high-I/O applications or applications relying heavily on multiprocessing.[1] There are some Python libraries to circumvent these issues by using multiprocessing or asynchronous services,[2] but they don't change the fact that the GIL still exists.

That said, there are plenty of Python core developers aware of the issues presented by the GIL, as well as its benefits. There are often good workarounds available for circumstances where the GIL is a pain point, and depending on your needs, there are alternative interpreters available that are written in languages other than C. If you find the GIL is becoming a problem for your code, it's likely that you can either rearchitect your code or utilize a different code base (e.g., Node.js) to fulfill your needs.

= Versus == Versus is, and When to Just Copy

In Python, there are some serious distinctions between seemingly similar functions. We know some of these already, but let's review with some code and output (using IPython):

```
In [1]: a = 1 ❶

In [2]: 1 == 1 ❷
Out[2]: True

In [3]: 1 is 1 ❸
Out[3]: True
```

---

1 For some further reading on how the GIL performs with some visualization, check out "A Zoomable Interactive Python Thread Visualization" (*http://www.dabeaz.com/GIL/gilvis/*) by David Beazley.

2 For some great reading on what these packages do, check out Jeff Knupp's writeup (*http://bit.ly/python_gil_problem*) on how to go about alleviating GIL issues.

```
In [4]: a is 1 ❹
Out[4]: True

In [5]: b = []

In [6]: [] == []
Out[6]: True

In [7]: [] is []
Out[7]: False

In [8]: b is []
Out[8]: False
```

❶ Sets variable a equal to 1

❷ Tests if 1 is equal to 1

❸ Tests if 1 is the *same* object as 1

❹ Tests if a is the *same* object as 1

If you execute these lines in IPython (so you can see the output, similar to what we've shown here) you will notice some interesting and possibly unexpected results. With an integer, we see that it's easy to determine equivalency in a lot of ways. With the list object, however, we find that is acts differently from the other comparison operators. In Python, memory management operates differently than in some other languages. There's a great writeup with visualizations on Sreejith Kesavan's blog (*http://foobarn baz.com/2012/07/08/understanding-python-variables/*) about how Python manages objects in memory.

To see this from another perspective, let's take a look at where the object's memory is held:

```
In [9]: a = 1

In [10]: id(a)
Out[10]: 14119256

In [11]: b = a ❶

In [12]: id(b) ❷
Out[12]: 14119256

In [13]: a = 2

In [14]: id(a) ❸
Out[14]: 14119232
```

```
In [15]: c = []

In [16]: id(c)
Out[16]: 140491313323544

In [17]: b = c

In [18]: id(b) ❹
Out[18]: 140491313323544

In [19]: c.append(45)

In [20]: id(c) ❺
Out[20]: 140491313323544
```

❶ Sets b equal to a.

❷ When we test the id here, we find that both b and a hold the same place in mem-
    ory—that is, they are the same object in memory.

❸ When we test the id here, we find a has a new place in memory. That place now
    holds the value of 2.

❹ With a list, we can see that we have the same id when we assign the list equal to
    the same object.

❺ When we change the list, we find we *do not* change the place in memory. Python
    lists behave differently than integers and strings in this way.

What we want to take away from this is not a deep understanding of memory alloca-
tion in Python, but that we might not always think we are assigning what we are
assigning. When dealing with lists and dictionaries, we want to know and understand
that if we set them equal to a new variable, that new variable and the old variable are
still the *same object* in memory. If we alter one, we alter the other. If we want to only
alter one or the other, or if we need to create a new object as a copy of an object, we
need to use the copy method.

Let's take a look with one final example to explain copy versus assignment:

```
In [21]: a = {}

In [22]: id(a)
Out[22]: 140491293143120

In [23]: b = a

In [24]: id(b)
Out[24]: 140491293143120
```

```
In [25]: a['test'] = 1

In [26]: b ❶
Out[26]: {'test': 1}

In [27]: c = b.copy() ❷

In [28]: id(c) ❸
Out[28]: 140491293140144

In [29]: c['test_2'] = 2

In [30]: c ❹
Out[30]: {'test': 1, 'test_2': 2}

In [31]: b ❺
Out[31]: {'test': 1}
```

❶ With this line, we see that when we modify a we also modify b, as they are stored in the same place in memory.

❷ Using copy we create a new variable, c, which is a copy of the first dictionary.

❸ With this line, we see that copy created a new object. It has a new id.

❹ After we modify c, we see it now holds two keys and values.

❺ Even after c is modified, we see that b remains the same.

With this last example, it should be obvious that if you actually want a copy of a dictionary or list, you will need to use copy. If you want the same object, then you can use =. Likewise, if you want to test whether two objects "are equal" you can use ==, but if you want to see whether these are the same object, use is.

Default Function Arguments

Sometimes you will want to pass default variables into your Python functions and methods. To do so, you want to fully understand when and how Python calls these default methods. Let's take a look:

```
def add_one(default_list=[]):
    default_list.append(1)
    return default_list
```

Now let's investigate with IPython:

```
In  [2]: add_one()
Out [2]: [1]
```

```
In  [3]: add_one()
Out [3]: [1, 1]
```

You might have expected that each function call would return a new list with only one item, 1. Instead, both calls modified the same list object. What is happening is that the default argument is declared when the script is first interpreted. If you want a new list every time, you can rewrite the function like so:

```
def add_one(default_list=None):
    if default_list is None:
        default_list = []
    default_list.append(1)
    return default_list
```

Now our code behaves as we would expect:

```
In  [6]: add_one()
Out [6]: [1]

In  [7]: add_one()
Out [7]: [1]

In  [8]: add_one(default_list=[3])
Out [8]: [3, 1]
```

Now that you understand a bit about memory management and default variables, you can use your knowledge to determine when to test and set variables in your functions and executable code. With a deeper understanding of how and when Python defines objects, we can ensure these types of "gotchas" don't end up adding bugs into our code.

Python Scope and Built-Ins: The Importance of Variable Names

In Python, scope operates slightly differently than you might expect. If you define a variable in the scope of a function, that variable is not known outside of the function. Let's take a look:

```
In [10]: def foo():
   ....:     x = "test"

In [11]: x
.---------------------------------------------------------------
NameError                                 Traceback (most recent call last)
<ipython-input-94-009520053b00> in <module>()
----> 1 x
NameError: name 'x' is not defined
```

However, if we have previously defined x, we will get our old definition:

```
In [12]: x = 1

In [13]: foo()

In  [14]: x
Out [14]: 1
```

This relates to built-in functions and methods. If you rewrite them by accident, then you can't use them from that point in time onward. So, if you rewrite the special words list or date, the built-in functions with those names will not function normally throughout the rest of your code (or from that point in time forward):

```
In [17]: from datetime import date

In [19]: date(2015, 2, 5)
Out[19]: datetime.date(2015, 2, 5)

In [20]: date = 'my date obj'

In [21]: date(2015, 2, 5)
.-----------------------------------------------------------------------
TypeError                                 Traceback (most recent call last)
<ipython-input-105-7f129d4341d0> in <module>()
----> 1 date(2015, 2, 5)

TypeError: 'str' object is not callable
```

As you can see, using variables that share names (or share names with anything other the standard Python namespace or any other libraries you are using) can be a debugging nightmare. If you use specific names in your code and are aware of the variable or module names, you won't end up debugging namespace issues for hours.

Defining Objects Versus Modifying Objects

Defining a new object operates differently compared to modifying an old object in Python. Let's say you have a function that adds one to an integer:

```
def add_one_int():
    x += 1
    return x
```

If you try to run that function, you should receive an error that reads UnboundLoca lError: local variable 'x' referenced before assignment. However, if you define x in your function, you'll see a different result:

```
def add_one_int():
    x = 0
    x += 1
    return x
```

This code is a bit convoluted (why can't we just return 1?), but the takeaway is we must declare variables *before* we modify them, even when using a modification that *looks* like an assignment (+=). It's especially important to keep this in mind when working with objects like lists and dictionaries (where we know modifying an object can have repercussions on other objects held in the same memory).

The important thing to remember is to always be clear and concise about when you intend to modify an object and when you want to create or return a new object. How you name variables and how you write and implement functions is key to writing scripts that are clear and behave predictably.

Changing Immutable Objects

When you want to modify or change immutable objects, you'll need to create new objects. Python will not allow you to modify immutable objects, like tuples. As you learned when we discussed Python memory management, some objects hold the same space. Immutable objects cannot be modified; they are *always* reassigned. Let's take a look:

```
In [1]: my_tuple = (1,)

In [2]: new_tuple = my_tuple

In [3]: my_tuple
Out[3]: (1,)

In [4]: new_tuple
Out[4]: (1,)

In [5]: my_tuple += (4, 5)

In [6]: new_tuple
Out[6]: (1,)

In [7]: my_tuple
Out[7]: (1, 4, 5)
```

What we can see here is that we tried to modify the original tuple using the += operator, and we were able to successfully do so. What we received, however, was a new object containing the original tuple plus the tuple we appended (4, 5). We did not end up changing the new_tuple variable, as what we did was assign a new place in memory to the new object. If you were to look at the memory ID before and after the += after, you would see it changed.

The main thing to remember about immutable objects is that when modified they do not hold the same place in memory, and if you modify them, you are actually creating completely new objects. This is especially important to remember if you are using methods or attributes of a class with immutable objects, as you want to ensure you understand when you are modifying them and when you are creating new immutable objects.

Type Checking

Python allows for easy type casting, meaning you can change strings to integers or lists to tuples, and so on. But this dynamic typing means issues can arise, especially in large code bases or when you are using new libraries. Some common issues are that a particular function, class, or method expects to see a certain type of object, and you mistakenly pass it the wrong type.

This becomes increasingly problematic as your code becomes more advanced and complex. As your code is more abstracted, you'll be holding all of your objects in variables. If a function or method returns an unexpected type (say, None instead of a list), that object may be passed along to another function—possibly one that doesn't accept None and then throws an error. Maybe that error is even caught, but the code assumes the exception was caused because of another problem and continues. It can very quickly get out of hand and become quite a mess to debug.

The best advice for handling these issues is to write very concise and clear code. You should ensure your functions always return what is expected by actively testing your code (to ensure there are no bugs) and keeping an eye on your scripts and any odd behavior. You should also add logging to help determine what your objects contain. In addition, being very clear about what exceptions you catch and not just catching all exceptions will help make these issues easier to find and fix.

Finally, at some point Python will implement PEP-484 (*https://www.python.org/dev/peps/pep-0484/*), which covers type hints, allowing you to check passed variables and your code to self-police these issues. This will likely not be incorporated until a future Python 3 release, but it's good to know it's in the works and you can expect to see a bit more structure around type checking in the future.

Catching Multiple Exceptions

As your code advances, you might want to catch more than one exception with the same line. For example, you might want to catch a TypeError along with an AttributeError. This might be the case if you believe you are passing a dictionary and you are actually passing a list. It might have some of the same attributes, but not all. If you need to catch more than one type of error on a line, you must write the exceptions in a tuple. Let's take a look:

```
my_dict = {'foo': {}, 'bar': None, 'baz': []}

for k, v in my_dict.items():
    try:
        v.items()
    except (TypeError, AttributeError) as e:
        print "We had an issue!"
        print e
```

You should see the following output (possibly in a different order):

```
We had an issue!
'list' object has no attribute 'items'
We had an issue!
'NoneType' object has no attribute 'items'
```

Our exception successfully caught both errors and executed the exception block. As you can see, being aware of the types of errors you might need to catch and understanding the syntax (to put them in a tuple) is essential to your code. If you were to simply list them (in a list or just separated by commas), your code would not function properly and you would not be catching both exceptions.

The Power of Debugging

As you become a more advanced developer and data wrangler, you will come across many more issues and errors to debug. We wish we could tell you it gets easier, but it's likely your debugging will become a bit more intense and rigorous before it becomes easier. This is because you will be working with more advanced code and libraries, and tackling more difficult problems.

That said, you have many skills and tools at your disposal to help you get unstuck. You can execute code in IPython to get more feedback during development. You can add logging to your scripts to better understand what is happening. You can have your web scrapers take screenshots and save them to files if you are having issues parsing a page. You can share your code with others in an IPython notebook or on many helpful sites to get feedback.

There are also some great tools for debugging with Python, including pdb (*https:// docs.python.org/2/library/pdb.html*), which allows you to step through your code (or other code in the module) and see exactly what each object holds immediately before and after any errors. There's a great, quick introduction to pdb (*http://bit.ly/pdb_intro*) on YouTube, showing some ways to use pdb in your code.

Additionally, you should be reading and writing both documentation and tests. We've covered some basics in this book, but we highly recommend you use this as a starting point and investigate both documentation and testing further. Ned Batchelder's recent PyCon talk on getting started with testing (*http://bit.ly/pycon2014_batchelder*) is a great place to begin. Jacob Kaplan-Moss also gave a great talk on getting started with documentation at PyCon 2011 (*http://bit.ly/writing_great_docs*). By reading and writing documentation and writing and executing tests, you can make sure you haven't introduced errors into your code through misinformation, or missed them by not running tests.

We hope this book is a good first introduction to these concepts, but we encourage you to continue your reading and development by seeking out more Python learning and continuing to excel as a Python developer.

IPython Hints

Although your Python shell is useful, it's lacking quite a lot of magic you can discover by using IPython (*http://ipython.org/*). IPython is an enhanced Python shell that offers you some easy-to-use shortcuts and extra power when working with Python in a shell environment. It was originally developed (*http://bit.ly/ipython_nb_history*) by scientists and students who wanted an easier shell for their Python use. It has since become the de facto standard for learning and interacting with Python via an interpreter.

Why Use IPython?

IPython gives you quite a lot of functionality lacking in the standard Python shell. The benefits of installing and using IPython as your shell are numerous. Its features include:

- Easy-to-read documentation hooks
- Autocompletion and magic commands for library, class, and object exploration
- Inline image and chart generation
- Helpful tools to view history, create files, debug your script, reload your script, and more
- Built-in shell command usage
- Auto-imports on startup

It's also one of the core components of Jupyter (*https://jupyter.org/*), a shared notebook server allowing for rapid-cycle data exploration in a browser. We covered using Jupyter for code sharing and presentation in Chapter 10.

Getting Started with IPython

IPython is easy to install with pip:

```
pip install ipython
```

If you are using more than one virtual environment, you might want to install IPython globally or within each virtual environment. To begin using IPython, simply type ipython in your terminal window. You should see a prompt similar to this:

```
$ ipython
Python 2.7.6 (default, Mar 22 2014, 22:59:56)
Type "copyright", "credits" or "license" for more information.

IPython 1.2.1 -- An enhanced Interactive Python.
?          -> Introduction and overview of IPython's features.
%quickref -> Quick reference.
help       -> Python's own help system.
object?    -> Details about 'object', use 'object??' for extra details.

In [1]:
```

You can now type Python commands as you would in a normal Python shell. For example:

```
In [1]: 1 + 1
Out[1]: 2

In [2]: from datetime import datetime

In [3]: datetime.now()
Out[3]: datetime.datetime(2015, 9, 13, 11, 47, 49, 191842)
```

When you need to exit the shell, you can type quit(), exit(), or Ctrl-D on Windows/Linux or Cmd-D on Mac.

Magic Functions

IPython has numerous so-called *magic* functions to help you as you explore and program. Here are some of the most useful ones, especially for beginning developers.

To easily see everything you have imported and all active objects, you can type %whos or %who. Let's take a look at their usage:

```
In [1]: foo = 1 + 4

In [2]: bar = [1, 2, 4, 6]

In [3]: from datetime import datetime

In [4]: baz = datetime.now()
```

```
In [5]: %who
bar baz datetime    foo

In [6]: %whos
Variable    Type        Data/Info
--------------------------------
bar         list        n=4
baz         datetime    2015-09-13 11:53:29.282405
datetime    type        <type 'datetime.datetime'>
foo         int         5
```

This can be incredibly helpful if you have forgotten a variable name or want to see what you have stored in your variables in one concise list.

Another useful tool is the ability to quickly look up documentation related to libraries, classes, or objects. If you type a ? at the end of the name of the method, class, library, or attribute, IPython will attempt to retrieve any related documentation and display it inline. For example:

```
In [7]: datetime.today?
Type:       builtin_function_or_method
String Form:<built-in method today of type object at 0x7f95674e0a00>
Docstring:  Current date or datetime:
            same as self.__class__.fromtimestamp(time.time()).
```

There are *tons* of IPython extensions and functions similar to these that are tremendously useful for development, particularly as you grow as a developer and encounter more complicated issues. Table F-1 lists some of the most useful ones, but there are also some great presentations and conference talks (*http://ipython.org/presentation.html*) and interactive examples (*http://bit.ly/ipynb_docs*) available online, as well as the library's well-written documentation (*http://ipython.org/documentation.html*).

 All IPython extensions must be loaded using %load_ext *extension_name* at the beginning of your IPython session. If you'd like to install extra extensions, there's a great list of available extension and their uses on GitHub (*http://bit.ly/ipython_extensions*).

Table F-1. Useful IPython extensions and functions

Command	Description	Purpose	Documentation
%autoreload	Extension allowing you to reload all imported scripts with one call	Great for active development, when you are changing a script in your editor and debugging it in your IPython shell	*http://ipython.org/ipython-doc/dev/config/extensions/autoreload.html*

Command	Description	Purpose	Documentation
%store	Extension allowing you to store saved variables for use in a later session	Best for use if you need to save some variables you will always need or if you are interrupted and need to save your current work for later use	http://ipython.org/ipython-doc/dev/config/extensions/storemagic.html
%history	Prints your session history	Shows an output of what you've already run	https://ipython.org/ipython-doc/dev/interactive/magics.html#magic-history
%pdb	Debugging module for interactive debugging with longer calls	Powerful debugging library, especially useful when importing longer scripts or modules	https://ipython.org/ipython-doc/dev/interactive/magics.html#magic-pdb
%pylab	Imports numpy and matplotlib to work interactively in your session	Allows you to use statistics and charting functionality within your IPython shell	https://ipython.org/ipython-doc/dev/interactive/magics.html#magic-pylab
%save	Saves your session history to an output file	An easy way to start writing a script if you've spent a long time debugging	https://ipython.org/ipython-doc/dev/interactive/magics.html#magic-save
%timeit	Times the execution of one or more lines of code	Handy for performance-tuning your Python scripts and functions	https://ipython.org/ipython-doc/dev/interactive/magics.html#magic-timeit

There are many more magic commands available (*http://bit.ly/built-in_magic_cmds*). Their usefulness will depend on what you use IPython for in your development, but employing them as you grow as a developer will likely shed light on other tasks IPython can simplify for you.

Final Thoughts: A Simpler Terminal

Whether you use IPython only in a notebook or in your active terminal development, we believe it will help you write and understand Python and grow as a developer. Much of your early development will be exploring how Python *works* and what errors and exceptions you encounter along the way. IPython is great for these lessons, as you can try again on the next input line. We hope IPython will keep you learning and writing Python for many years to come.

Using Amazon Web Services

If you want to get set up to use Amazon and the Amazon cloud services for your data wrangling needs, you'll first need to get a server set up for your use. We'll review how to get your first server up and running here.

We covered some alternatives to AWS in Chapter 10, including DigitalOcean, Heroku, GitHub Pages, and using a hosting provider. Depending on your level of interest in different deployment and server environments, we encourage you to use several and see what works best for you.

AWS is popular as a first cloud platform, but it can also be quite confusing. We wanted to include a walkthrough to help you navigate the process. We can also highly recommend using DigitalOcean as a start into the cloud; their tutorials (*http://bit.ly/ digital_ocean_gs*) and walkthroughs (*http://bit.ly/digital_ocean_server_setup*) are quite helpful.

Spinning Up an AWS Server

To spin up (or "launch") a server, from the AWS console (*https:// console.aws.amazon.com*), select "EC2" under "Compute" (you'll need to sign in or create an account to access the console). This will take to you the EC2 landing page (*https://console.aws.amazon.com/ec2/v2/home*). There, click the "Launch Instance" button.

At this point, you'll be taken to a walkthrough to set up your instance. Whatever you select here can be edited, so don't worry if you don't know what to choose. This book provides suggestions to get a server up and running cheaply and quickly, but this doesn't mean it will be the solution you need. If you run into an issue such as space, you may need a larger, and therefore more expensive, setting/instance.

That said, in the following sections we'll walk you through our recommendations for this setup.

AWS Step 1: Choose an Amazon Machine Image (AMI)

A machine image is basically an operating system image (or snapshot). The most common operating systems are Windows and OS X. However, Linux-based systems are usually used for servers. We recommend the latest Ubuntu system, which at the time of writing is "Ubuntu Server 14.04 LTS (HVM), SSD Volume Type - ami-d05e75b8."

AWS Step 2: Choose an Instance Type

The instance type is the size of the server you spin up. Select "t2.micro (Free tier eligible)." Do not size up until you know you need to, as you will be wasting money. To learn more about instances, check out the AWS articles on instance types (*https:// aws.amazon.com/ec2/instance-types/*) and pricing (*https://aws.amazon.com/ec2/pricing/*).

Select "Review and Launch," which takes you to Step 7.

AWS Step 7: Review Instance Launch

At the top of the page that appears, you will notice a message that says, "Improve your instances' security. Your security group, launch-wizard-4, is open to the world." For true production instances or instances with sensitive data, doing this is highly recommended, along with taking other security precautions. Check out the AWS article "Tips for Securing Your EC2 Instance" (*http://bit.ly/securing_ec2_instance*).

AWS Extra Question: Select an Existing Key Pair or Create a New One

A key pair is like a set of keys for the server, so the server knows who to let in. Select "Create a new key pair," and name it. We have named ours *data-wrangling-test*, but you can call it any good name you will recognize. When you are done, download the key pair in a place where you will be able to find it later.

Lastly, click "Launch Instances." When the instance launches, you will have an instance ID provided onscreen.

 If you are worried about your server costs, create billing alerts in your AWS preferences (*https://console.aws.amazon.com/billing/home?#/preferences*).

Logging into an AWS Server

To log into the server, you need to navigate to the instance in the AWS console to get more information. From the console, select EC2, then select "1 Running Instances" (if you have more than one, the number will be larger). You'll see a list of your servers. Unless you provided one earlier, your server won't have a name. Give your instance a name by clicking on the blank box in the list. We named ours *data-wrangling-test* for consistency.

To log into our server, we are going to follow the instructions in the AWS article about connecting to a Linux instance (*http://bit.ly/aws_connect_to_linux*).

Get the Public DNS Name of the Instance

The public DNS name is the web address of your instance. If you have a value there that looks like a web address, continue to the next section. If the value is "--", then you need to follow these additional steps (from StackOverflow (*http://bit.ly/ec2_no_public_dns*)):

1. Go to *console.aws.amazon.com*.
2. Go to Services (top nav) → VPC (near the end of the list).
3. Open your VPCs (lefthand column).
4. Select the VPC connected to your EC2.
5. From the "Actions" drop-down, select "Edit DNS Hostnames."
6. Change the setting for "Edit DNS Hostnames" to "Yes."

If you return to the EC2 instance, you should see it now has a public DNS name.

Prepare Your Private Key

Your private key is the *.pem* file you downloaded. It's a good idea to move it to a folder you know and remember. For Unix-based systems, your keys should be in a folder in your home folder called *.ssh*. For Windows, the default is either *C:\Documents and Settings\<username>\.ssh* or *C:\Users\<username>\.ssh*. You should copy your *.pem* file to that folder.

Next, you need to run the chmod command to change the *.pem* permissions to 400. Changing the permissions to 400 means the file is only accessible to the owner. This keeps the file secure in a multiaccount computer environment:

```
chmod 400 .ssh/data-wrangling-test.pem
```

Log into Your Server

At this point, you have all the pieces you need to log into the server. Run the following command, but replace *my-key-pair.pem* with the name of your key pair and *public_dns_name* with your public web address:

```
ssh -i ~/.ssh/my-key-pair.pem_ ubuntu@_public_dns_name
```

For example:

```
ssh -i data-wrangling-test.pem ubuntu@ec2-12-34-56-128.compute-1.amazonaws.com
```

When prompted with *Are you sure you want to continue connecting (yes/no)?* type in yes.

At this point, your prompt will change slightly, showing you are in the console of the server you set up. You can now continue getting your server set up by getting your code onto the server and setting up automation to run on your machine. You can read more about deploying code to your new server in Chapter 14.

To exit your server, type Ctrl-C or Cmd-C.

Summary

Now you have your first AWS server up and running. Use the lessons learned in Chapter 14 to deploy code to your server and run your data wrangling in no time!

Index

using cloud for data processing, 390-394
when not to automate, 416
with cron, 398-400
with web interfaces, 400
AWS (Amazon Web Services), 391, 401,
475-478
Amazon Machine Image, 476
launching a server, 475
logging into a server, 477-478

B

backup strategies, 141
bad data, 169-175
bar chart, 254
bash, 431-438
commands, 439-443
executing files, 435
modifying files, 433-435
navigation from command line, 432
online resources, 438
searching with command line, 437-438
Beautiful Soup, 300-304
beginners, Python resources for, xiii, 5, 429
best practices, 200
bias, 251
binary mode, 47
blocks, indented, 48
blogs, 270
Bokeh, 258-261
Booleans, 19
Boston Python, 430
Bottle, 401
browser-based parsing, 317-335
screen reading with Ghost.py, 329-335
screen reading with Selenium, 318-329
built-in functions/methods, 465
built-in tools, 34-38

C

C++, Python vs., 425
C, Python vs., 425
calling variables, 24
Canada, data sources from, 134
capitalization, 50-52
case sensitivity, 50-52
cat command, 437
cd command, 14, 50, 97, 433
Celery, 403-404
Central Asia, data sources from, 134

charts/charting, 254-261
with Bokeh, 258-261
with matplotlib, 255-258
chat, automated messaging with, 411
chdir command, 439
chmod command, 436, 477
chown command, 436
cloud
data storage, 147
for data processing automation, 390-394
using Git to deploy Python, 391-394
cmd, 438-443
code
length of well-formatted lines, 106
saving to a file, 49
sharing with Jupyter, 273-276
whitespace in, 459
code blocks, indented, 48
code editor, 15
coding best practices, 200
command line
bash-based, 431-438
making a file executable via, 207
navigation via, 431-443
running CSV data files from command line,
50-52
Windows CMD/PowerShell, 438-443
command-line arguments, automation with,
389
command-line shortcuts, 449
commands, 431-443
cat, 437
cd, 14, 50, 97, 433
chdir, 439
chmod, 436, 477
chown, 436
cp, 434
del, 440
dir, 35-36, 439, 442
echo, 440-438
find, 61, 438
history, 434, 438
if and fi, 448
ls, 50, 432-435, 446
make and make install, 436
move, 440
pwd, 14, 50, 432, 435
rm, 435
sudo, 14, 436

IPython, 471-474
   (see also Jupyter)
   installing, 16, 472
   magic functions, 472-474
   reasons for using, 471
is (comparison operator), 461
iterators, 219
itersiblings method, 308

J

Java, Python vs., 425
JavaScript console
   and web page analysis, 293-297
   jQuery and, 295-297
   style basics, 293-295
JavaScript, Python vs., 426
Jekyll, 272
join method, 232
jQuery, 295-297
JSON data, 52-55
Jupyter, 273-276
   (see also IPython)
   shared notebooks, 275
   sharing automation code with, 401
   sharing data presentation code with, 273-276

K

key pair, AWS, 476
keys
   API, 364-366
   in Python dictionary, 27

L

lambda function, 226
latency, 357
legal issues, 280
libraries (packages), 471
   (see also specific libraries, e.g.: xlutils library)
   defined, 46
   for working with Excel files, 73, 75
   math, 22
   statistical, 242
line chart, 254
LinkedIn API, 361
Linux
   installing Python on, 7

learning about new environment, 455-457
virtual environment testing, 454
virtualenv installation, 450
virtualenvwrapper installation, 452
list generators, 154
list indexes, 66
list methods, 32
lists, 25-27
   and addition, 32
   indexing, 66, 83
local files, automation with, 384-386
logging
   and exceptions, 415
   and monitoring, 415
   as a service, 414
   for automation monitoring, 406-408
logging module, 407
Loggly, 415
Logstash, 415
ls command, 50, 432-435, 446
Luigi, 402
LXML
   and XPath, 308-315
   features, 315
   installing, 305
   reading web pages with, 304-315

M

Mac OS X
   Homebrew installation, 446
   installing Python on, 8
   learning about new environment, 455-457
   Python 2.7 installation, 449
   telling system where to find Homebrew, 446-449
   virtual environment testing, 454
   virtualenv installation, 450
   virtualenvwrapper installation, 452
Mac prompt ($), 12
machine-readable data, 43-71
   CSV data, 44-52
   file formats for, 43
   JSON data, 52-55
   XML data, 55-70
magic commands, 152
magic functions, 472-474
main function, 206
make and make install commands, 436
markup patterns, 308-315

version (Python), choosing, 6
Vi, 15
video, 268
Vim, 15
virtual environment
    learning about, 455-457
    testing, 454
virtualenv, 450
virtualenvwrapper
    installation, 452
    updating .bashrc, 452
virtualenvwrapper-win, 453
visualization of data, 254-268
    charts, 254-261
    images, 268
    interactives, 267
    maps, 263-266
    time-related data, 261
    video, 268
    with illustrations, 268
    with words, 267
voice message automation, 411

W

web interfaces, 400
web page analysis, 282-298
    and JavaScript console, 293-297
    in-depth, 297
    inspection of markup structure, 282-290
    Timeline/Network tab analysis, 290-292
web pages
    reading with Beautiful Soup, 300-304
    reading with LXML, 304-315
    requests, 298-300
web scraping
    advanced techniques, 317-358
    and network problems, 355-358
    basics, 279-316
    browser-based parsing, 317-335
    ethical issues, 358
    legal issues, 280, 358
    reading web pages with Beautiful Soup,
        300-304

reading web pages with LXML, 304-315
screen reading with Ghost.py, 329-335
screen reading with Selenium, 318-329
simple text scraping, 280-282
web page analysis, 282-298
web page requests, 298-300
with Scrapy, 336-355
with spiders, 335-355
with XPath, 308-315
wget command, 436
where function, 226
whitespace, 38, 50-52, 459
Windows
    installing Python on, 7, 9-11
    learning about new environment, 455-457
    virtual environment testing, 454
    virtualenv installation, 450
    virtualenvwrapper-win installation, 453
Windows 8, 9-11
Windows command line, 438-443
    executing files from, 441
    modifying files from, 440
    navigation, 439
    online resources, 443
    searching with, 441-443
Windows PowerShell, 441-443
Windows prompt (>), 12
WordPress, 270
wrapper libraries, 145

X

xlrd library, 75-79
xlutils library, 75
xlwt library, 75
XML data, 55-70
XPath, 308-315

Z

Zen of Python, 198
zip function, 105
zip method, for data cleanup, 157-164

About the Authors

Jacqueline Kazil is a data lover. In her career, she has worked in technology focusing in finance, government, and journalism. Most notably, she is a former Presidential Innovation Fellow (*https://www.whitehouse.gov/innovationfellows*) and cofounded a technology organization in government called 18F (*https://18f.gsa.gov/*). Her career has consisted of many data science and wrangling projects including Geoq (*https://geo-q.com/geoq/*), an open source mapping workflow tool; a Congress.gov (*https://www.congress.gov/*) remake; and Top Secret America (*http://projects.washingtonpost.com/top-secret-america/*). She is active in Python and data communities—Python Software Foundation (*https://www.python.org/psf/*), PyLadies (*http://www.pyladies.com/*), Women Data Science DC (*http://www.meetup.com/WomenDataScientistsDC/*), and more. She teaches Python in Washington, D.C. at meetups, conferences, and mini bootcamps. She often pairs programs with her sidekick, Ellie (@ellie_the_brave). You can find her on Twitter @jackiekazil or follow her blog, The coderSnorts (*https://medium.com/coder-snorts*).

Katharine Jarmul is a Python developer who enjoys data analysis and acquisition, web scraping, teaching Python, and all things Unix. She worked at small and large startups before starting her consulting career overseas. Originally from Los Angeles, she learned Python while working at *The Washington Post* in 2008. As one of the founders of PyLadies, Katharine hopes to promote diversity in Python and other open source languages through education and training. She has led numerous workshops and tutorials ranging from beginner to advanced topics in Python. For more information on upcoming trainings, reach out to her on Twitter (@kjam) or her website (*http://kjamistan.com*).

Colophon

The animal on the cover of *Data Wrangling with Python* is a blue-lipped tree lizard (*Plica umbra*). Members of the Plica genus are of moderate size and, though they belong to a family commonly known as neotropical ground lizards, live mainly in trees in South America and the Caribbean. Blue-lipped tree lizards predominantly consume ants and are the only species in their genus not characterized by bunches of spines on the neck.

Many of the animals on O'Reilly covers are endangered; all of them are important to the world. To learn more about how you can help, go to *animals.oreilly.com*.

The cover image is from Lydekker's *Natural History*. The cover fonts are URW Typewriter and Guardian Sans. The text font is Adobe Minion Pro; the heading font is Adobe Myriad Condensed; and the code font is Dalton Maag's Ubuntu Mono.

Learn from experts.
Find the answers you need.

Sign up for a **10-day free trial** to get **unlimited access** to all of the content on Safari, including Learning Paths, interactive tutorials, and curated playlists that draw from thousands of ebooks and training videos on a wide range of topics, including data, design, DevOps, management, business—and much more.

Start your free trial at:

oreilly.com/safari

(No credit card required.)

Milton Keynes UK
Ingram Content Group UK Ltd.
UKHW011009190924
448478UK00007B/117